ACCLAIM FOR THE MESSAGE OF *Strange Fire*

Testimonies from people whose lives were
changed by the truth of God's Word

"I am grateful to the Lord for John MacArthur and the clear way he is exposing the many errors of charismatic teaching."

—CARLA

"I stayed six years in the charismatic church, until John MacArthur helped me reevaluate the teaching by comparing it to Scripture. My heart goes out to those still in the Charismatic Movement that are deceived. The prosperity they are promised eludes them. I saw people giving everything they owned of value, expecting to receive one-hundred-fold back. When the reward they sought did not materialize, they were told their faith was deficient. It is very sad."

—MADALENA

"We lost a child a few years ago, and several members of the church we attended told us that we just didn't have enough faith for her healing. Others told us that we must have had sin in our lives. I praise the Lord for the ministry of John MacArthur. My wife and I have learned so much through his books and teachings, enough to leave the charismatic church environment we were in for over a decade. There are so many misguided charismatics out there that desperately need to hear the truth."

—MICHAEL

"My wife and I served for sixteen years in French-speaking West Africa. Pastors in west Africa are bombarded with false teaching—mostly from American televangelists and charismatic church leaders. John MacArthur's teaching on the Charismatic Movement gave me the tools I needed to confront the errors we faced."

—LARRY

"My husband and I are seniors, but it goes to show that whatever age a person is, the Lord can work mightily. We have been married nearly forty-nine years and for the first thirty-eight years we went to a charismatic church where feelings and experiences took precedence over Scripture. I felt uneasy and didn't know what to do about it. Then John MacArthur helped us take a new look at the Charismatic Movement through the lens of Scripture. He taught us to be Bereans."

—VALRAE

"I have often thought recently that the Word of Faith movement is one of the greatest threats to real Christianity today. The message seems Christian enough to new and young believers. It definitely sounds good in a world obsessed with prosperity. It looks good for people who want to be wealthy, healthy, and happy. I used to attend a Word of Faith church. This church teaches us that God wants us to have total victory—in our finances, relationships and our health! Then why isn't the pastor healthy? Why are people losing their jobs? They aren't prosperous right now in their finances. They're struggling and can't make ends meet. People begin to wonder if God let them down. Why didn't He fulfill His end of the bargain? The Word of Faith doctrine is a dangerous false gospel, and I'm grateful to John MacArthur for pointing us back to Scripture."

—JEREMY

"I am thirty-five years old and live in west Norway. As a new believer I was in a Pentecostal church for about two years. What they taught and practiced were not the things I read about in Scripture—your best life now, positive confession, material prosperity, earthly fame, and so on. I never heard anything about repentance or laying down my life and certainly not anything about being a slave of Christ. I started listening to John MacArthur's teaching on these things about a year ago. It's liberating to learn and embrace the truth that God's Word, the Bible, is my true authority—rather than constantly being enslaved to my own feelings."

—BJORN

"I was raised in a church where I was taught to speak in tongues and listen for God to speak to me personally. The God I was raised to believe in was mysterious, strange, mystical, and confusing. It was total chaos. I was so upset by those things, and by prophecies that never came true, that I turned from anything relating to the Bible. I wandered spiritually and avoided God's Word for about ten years. The whole time, though, I knew I was wrong, and I did believe in God. I just did not understand how to live for Him. About three years ago, I discovered the teaching ministry of John MacArthur online. I went immediately to the sermons on 1 Corinthians to see what he said about speaking in tongues. It was refreshing to hear a sermon that made sense. I downloaded countless sermons. I was relearning the Bible. I joined a Bible-teaching church near me with a pastor who is committed to the Word without compromise. I am so excited about what the Lord is doing in my life."

—JUSTIN

"I came out of a charismatic background, and John MacArthur's teaching has been a real eye-opener. I am grateful to God for delivering my family—and our congregation—out of total heresy."

—CRYSTAL

STRANGE
FIRE

STRANGE FIRE

THE DANGER
OF OFFENDING THE
HOLY SPIRIT WITH COUNTERFEIT
WORSHIP

JOHN MACARTHUR

NELSON
BOOKS

An Imprint of Thomas Nelson

Published in Nashville, Tennessee, by Nelson Books, an imprint of Thomas Nelson. Nelson Books and Thomas Nelson are registered trademarks of HarperCollins Christian Publishing, Inc.

Thomas Nelson, Inc., titles may be purchased in bulk for educational, business, fund-raising, or sales promotional use. For information, please e-mail SpecialMarkets@ThomasNelson.com.

The websites recommended in this book are intended as resources for the reader. These websites are not intended in any way to be or to imply an endorsement on behalf of Thomas Nelson, nor does the publisher vouch for online content for the life of this book.

Unleashing God's Truth, One Verse at a Time® is a trademark of Grace to You. All rights reserved.

Unless otherwise indicated, Scripture quotations are taken from the THE NEW KING JAMES VERSION. © 1982 by Thomas Nelson, Inc. Used by permission. All rights reserved.

Scripture quotations marked NASB are taken from the NEW AMERICAN STANDARD BIBLE®, © The Lockman Foundation 1960, 1962, 1963, 1968, 1971, 1972, 1973, 1975, 1977, 1995. Used by permission.

Scripture quotations marked NIV are taken from the Holy Bible, New International Version®. Copyright © 1973, 1978, 1984, 2011 by Biblica, Inc.™ Used by permission of Zondervan. All rights reserved worldwide. www.zondervan.com.

Scripture quotations marked ESV are taken from THE ENGLISH STANDARD VERSION. © 2001 by Crossway Bibles, a division of Good News Publishers.

Italics added to Scripture quotations are the author's own emphasis.

ISBN: 978-1-4002-0641-4 (IE)

Library of Congress Cataloging-in-Publication Data

MacArthur, John, 1939-
  Strange fire : the danger of offending the Holy Spirit with counterfeit worship / John MacArthur.
    pages cm
  Includes bibliographical references and index.
  ISBN 978-1-4002-0517-2
1. Holy Spirit. 2. Worship. I. Title.
  BT123.M148 2013
  231'.3--dc23

2013015552

Printed in the United States of America

19 20 21 LSC 18 17 16 15 14 13

CONTENTS

Contents

INTRODUCTION

FOR THE SAKE OF HIS NAME

Nadab and Abihu were not shamans or snake-oil salesmen who infiltrated the camp of the Israelites in order to spread the Canaanites' superstitions among the people. They were by all appearances righteous, respectable men and godly spiritual leaders. They were priests of the one true God. And they were no middling Levites. Nadab was heir apparent to the office of the high priest, and Abihu was next in line after him. They were the eldest sons of Aaron. Moses was their uncle. Their names head the list of "nobles of the children of Israel" (Ex. 24:11). Aside from their father, Aaron, they are the only ones singled out by name the first time Scripture mentions Israel's "seventy elders," the group of leaders who shared spiritual oversight in the Hebrew nation (Num. 11:16–24). Scripture does not introduce them to us as sinister figures or notoriously wicked men—quite the opposite.

These two brothers, together with the other seventy elders, were privileged at Sinai to ascend the mountain partway and watch from a distance as God conversed with Moses (Ex. 24:9–10). The people of Israel had been instructed to stand at the foot of the mountain and "not go up to the mountain or touch its base" (Ex. 19:12). While God was up there talking to Moses, if so much as a stray beast wandered onto the skirt of Sinai, that animal was to be stoned or shot (v. 13). From the base of the mountain, all the rank-and-file Israelites could see was smoke and lightning. But Nadab and Abihu were expressly named by the Lord Himself, who invited them to come up and bring the seventy elders. And "they saw God, and they ate and drank" (Ex. 24:11).

In other words, Nadab and Abihu had been closer to God than almost anyone. No other Israelite except Moses himself had ever been given a higher privilege. These men certainly *seemed* to be godly, trustworthy spiritual leaders and faithful servants of God—young men of renown. No doubt virtually everyone in Israel esteemed them highly.

And no doubt everyone in Israel was staggered when God suddenly struck Nadab and Abihu dead with a blast of holy fire. This occurred, apparently, on the first day of their service in the tabernacle. Aaron and his sons were anointed in a seven-day-long ceremony when the building of the tabernacle was complete. On the eighth day (Lev. 9:1), Aaron offered the first sin offering ever made in the tabernacle, and the ceremony was punctuated with a miracle: "Fire came out from before the Lord and consumed the burnt offering and the fat on the altar. When all the people saw it, they shouted and fell on their faces" (Lev. 9:24).

Moses records what happened next:

> Now Nadab and Abihu, the sons of Aaron, took their respective firepans, and after putting fire in them, placed incense on it and offered strange fire before the Lord, which He had not commanded them. And fire came out from the presence of the Lord and consumed them, and they died before the Lord. Then Moses said to Aaron, "It is what the Lord spoke, saying, 'By those who come near Me I will be treated as holy, and before all the people I will be honored.'" (Lev. 10:1–3 NASB)

Most likely Nadab and Abihu had taken fire from some source other than the brazen altar and used it to light their censers of incense. Remember that God Himself set the altar ablaze with fire from heaven. Apparently Nadab and Abihu had filled their censers with fire of their own making, or coals from some fire in the camp of Israel. The actual source from which they obtained their fire is not recorded. Nor is it important. The point is they used something other than the fire God Himself had ignited.

Their offense may seem trifling to someone accustomed to the type of casual, self-indulgent worship our generation is known for. They may have also been drinking, and perhaps they had imbibed enough that their judgment was poor. (Leviticus 10:9 seems to suggest this was the case.) Still, what Scripture expressly condemns is the "strange fire" they offered. The crux of their sin was approaching God in a careless, self-willed, inappropriate manner, without the reverence He deserved. They did not treat Him as holy or exalt His name before the people. The Lord's response was swift and deadly. The "strange fire" of Nadab and Abihu ignited the unquenchable flames of divine judgment against them, and they were incinerated on the spot.

This is a sobering and terrifying account, and it has obvious implications for the church in our time. Clearly, it is a serious crime to dishonor the Lord, to treat Him with contempt, or to approach Him in a way He detests. Those who worship God must do so in the way He requires, treating Him as holy.

The Holy Spirit—the glorious third member of the Trinity—is no less God than the Father or the Son. Thus, to dishonor the Spirit is to dishonor God Himself. To abuse the Spirit's name is to take God's name in vain. To claim He is the one who empowers self-willed, whimsical, and unbiblical worship is to treat God with contempt. To turn the Spirit into a spectacle is to worship God in a way that He deplores. That's why the many irreverent antics and twisted doctrines brought into the church by the contemporary Charismatic Movement are equal to (or even worse than) the strange fire of Nadab and Abihu. They are an affront to the Holy Spirit, and therefore to God Himself—grounds for severe judgment (cf. Heb. 10:31).[1]

When the Pharisees attributed the Spirit's work to Satan (Matt. 12:24), the Lord warned them that such hard-hearted blasphemy was unforgivable. Ananias and Sapphira were instantly struck dead after lying to the Holy Spirit. As a result, "great fear came upon all the church and upon all who heard these things" (Acts 5:11). Simon Magus, when he asked to purchase the Spirit's power with money, received this severe rebuke in response: "May your silver perish with you, because you thought you could obtain the gift of God with money!" (Acts 8:20 NASB). And the author of Hebrews, writing to those in danger of insulting the Spirit of grace, offered his readers this sober admonition: "It is a fearful thing to fall into the hands of the living God" (Heb. 10:31).

The third member of the Trinity is dangerous to anyone who would offer Him strange fire!

REINVENTING THE HOLY SPIRIT

Of course, you wouldn't know that from the way the Holy Spirit is treated by scores of professing Christians today. On the one hand, some mainstream evangelicals are guilty of neglecting the Holy Spirit altogether. For them, He has become the forgotten member of the Trinity—as they attempt to grow the church through their own cleverness rather than His power. For the sake of popular appeal, they deemphasize personal holiness and the Spirit's sanctifying work. They contend that biblical preaching, in which the sword of the Spirit is wielded with care and precision, is now passé. In its place, they offer entertainment, edginess, empty platitudes, or the elevation of uncertainty—thereby exchanging the authority of the Spirit-inspired Scriptures for cheap and impotent substitutes.

On the other hand, the modern Pentecostal and Charismatic Movements[2] have pushed the pendulum to the opposite extreme. They have fostered an unhealthy preoccupation with supposed manifestations of the Holy Spirit's power. Committed charismatics talk incessantly about phenomena, emotions, and the latest wave or sensation. They seem to have comparatively little (sometimes *nothing*) to say about Christ, His atoning work, or the historical facts of the gospel.[3] The charismatic fixation with the Holy Spirit's supposed work is false honor. Jesus said, "When the Helper comes, whom I shall send to you from the Father, the Spirit of truth who proceeds from the Father, *He will testify of Me*" (John 15:26). So when the Holy Spirit becomes the focal point of the church's message, His *true* work is undermined.

The "Holy Spirit" found in the vast majority of charismatic teaching and practice bears no resemblance to the true Spirit of God as revealed in Scripture. The real Holy Spirit is not an electrifying current of ecstatic energy, a mind-numbing babbler of irrational speech, or a cosmic genie who indiscriminately grants self-centered wishes for health and wealth. The true

Spirit of God does not cause His people to bark like dogs or laugh like hyenas; He does not knock them backward to the ground in an unconscious stupor; He does not incite them to worship in chaotic and uncontrollable ways; and He certainly does not accomplish His kingdom work through false prophets, fake healers, and fraudulent televangelists. By inventing a Holy Spirit of idolatrous imaginations, the modern Charismatic Movement offers strange fire that has done incalculable harm to the body of Christ. Claiming to focus on the third member of the Trinity, it has in fact profaned His name and denigrated His true work.

Whenever God is dishonored, those who love the Lord feel both pain and righteous indignation. That is what David experienced in Psalm 69:9 when he exclaimed, "Zeal for Your house has eaten me up, and the reproaches of those who reproach You have fallen on me." The Lord Jesus quoted that verse when He cleansed the temple; clearing out the money changers who had treated God's temple and His people's worship with brazen disrespect. I have long felt a similar burden in response to the appalling ways in which the Holy Spirit is maligned, mistreated, and misrepresented by so many within charismatic circles.

It is a sad twist of irony that those who claim to be most focused on the Holy Spirit are in actuality the ones doing the most to abuse, grieve, insult, misrepresent, quench, and dishonor Him. How do they do it? By attributing to Him words He did not say, deeds He did not do, phenomena He did not produce, and experiences that have nothing to do with Him. They boldly plaster His name on that which is not His work.

In Jesus' day, the religious leaders of Israel blasphemously attributed the work of the Spirit to Satan (Matt. 12:24). The modern Charismatic Movement does the inverse, attributing the work of the devil to the Holy Spirit. Satan's armies of false teachers, marching to the beat of their own illicit desires, gladly propagate his errors. They are spiritual swindlers, con men, crooks, and charlatans. We can see an endless parade of them simply by turning on the television. Jude called them clouds without water, raging waves, and wandering stars "for whom is reserved the blackness of darkness forever" (v. 13). Yet they claim to be angels of light—gaining credibility for their lies by invoking the name of the Holy Spirit, as if there's no penalty to pay for that kind of blasphemy.

The Bible is clear that God demands to be worshipped for who He truly is. No one can honor the Father unless the Son is honored; likewise, it is impossible to honor the Father and the Son while dishonoring the Spirit. Yet every day, millions of charismatics offer praise to a patently false image of the Holy Spirit. They have become like the Israelites of Exodus 32, who compelled Aaron to fashion a golden calf while Moses was away. The idolatrous Israelites claimed to be honoring the Lord (vv. 4–8), but instead they were worshipping a grotesque misrepresentation, dancing around it in dishonorable disarray (v. 25). God's response to their disobedience was swift and severe. Before the day was over, thousands had been put to death.

Here's the point: we can't make God into any form we would like. We cannot mold Him into our own image, according to our own specifications and imaginations. Yet that is what many Pentecostals and charismatics have done. They have created their own golden-calf version of the Holy Spirit. They have thrown their theology into the fires of human experience and worshipped the false spirit that came out—parading themselves before it with bizarre antics and unrestrained behavior. As a movement, they have persistently ignored the truth about the Holy Spirit and with reckless license set up an idol spirit in the house of God, dishonoring the third member of the Trinity in His own name.

A TROJAN HORSE OF SPIRITUAL CORRUPTION

In spite of their gross theological error, charismatics demand acceptance within mainstream evangelicalism. And evangelicals have largely succumbed to those demands, responding with outstretched arms and a welcoming smile. In so doing, mainstream evangelicalism has unwittingly invited an enemy into the camp. The gates have been flung open to a Trojan horse of subjectivism, experientialism, ecumenical compromise, and heresy. Those who compromise in this way are playing with strange fire and placing themselves in grave danger.

When the Pentecostal Movement started in the early 1900s, it was largely considered a cult by theological conservatives.[4] For the most part, it was isolated and contained within its own denominations. But in the 1960s, the movement began to spill over into the mainline denominations—gaining a foothold in Protestant churches that had embraced theological liberalism and were already spiritually dead. The start of the Charismatic Renewal Movement is usually traced to St. Mark's Episcopal Church in Van Nuys, California. Just two weeks before Easter in 1960, their pastor, Dennis Bennett, announced he had received a Pentecostal baptism of the Holy Spirit. (He revealed he and a small group of parishioners had been holding covert meetings for some time, during which they practiced speaking in tongues.)

Liberal Episcopal leaders were less than enthusiastic about Father Bennett's announcement. In fact, Bennett was soon fired from the Van Nuys church. But he remained in the Episcopal denomination and was eventually called to serve as rector in a liberal, dying urban church in Seattle. That church immediately began to grow, and Bennett's neo-Pentecostalism gradually spread and took root in several other spiritually parched congregations. By the end of the decade, desperate and dying mainline churches around the world were embracing charismatic doctrine and seeing numerical growth as a result.[5]

The emotional experientialism of Pentecostalism brought a spark to those otherwise stagnant congregations, and by the 1970s the Charismatic Renewal Movement was beginning to gain real momentum. In the 1980s, two professors at Fuller Theological Seminary—a mainstream evangelical school that had abandoned its commitment to biblical inerrancy in the early 1970s[6]— began to promote charismatic ideas in the classroom. The result has been termed "The Third Wave," as Pentecostal and charismatic theology infiltrated evangelicalism and the Independent Church Movement.

The results of that charismatic takeover have been devastating. In recent history, no other movement has done more to damage the cause of the gospel, to distort the truth, and to smother the articulation of sound doctrine. Charismatic theology has turned the evangelical church into a cesspool of error and a breeding ground for false teachers. It has warped genuine worship through unbridled emotionalism, polluted prayer with private gibberish, contaminated true spirituality with unbiblical mysticism, and corrupted faith by turning it into a creative force for speaking worldly desires into existence. By elevating the authority of experience over the authority of Scripture, the Charismatic Movement has destroyed the church's immune system—uncritically granting free access to every imaginable form of heretical teaching and practice.

Put bluntly, charismatic theology has made no contribution to true biblical theology or interpretation; rather, it represents a deviant mutation of the truth. Like a deadly virus, it gains access into the church by maintaining a superficial connection to certain characteristics of biblical Christianity, but in the end it always corrupts and distorts sound teaching. The resulting degradation, like a doctrinal version of Frankenstein's monster, is a hideous hybrid of heresy, ecstasy, and blasphemy awkwardly dressed in the tattered remnants of evangelical language.[7] It calls itself "Christian," but in reality it is a sham—a counterfeit form of spirituality that continually morphs as it spirals erratically from one error to the next.

In earlier generations, the Pentecostal-Charismatic Movement would have been labeled heresy. Instead, it is now the most dominant, aggressive, and visible strain of so-called Christianity in the world. It claims to represent the purest and most powerful form of the gospel. Yet it primarily proclaims a gospel of health and wealth, a message completely incompatible with the good news of Scripture. It threatens all who oppose its doctrine with charges of grieving, quenching, resisting, and even blaspheming the Holy Spirit. Yet no movement drags His name through the mud with greater frequency or audacity.

The incredible irony is that those who talk the most about the Holy Spirit generally deny His true work. They attribute all kinds of human silliness to Him while ignoring the genuine purpose and power of His ministry: freeing sinners from death, giving them everlasting life, regenerating their hearts, transforming their nature, empowering them for spiritual victory, confirming their place in the family of God, interceding for them according to the will of God, sealing them securely for their eternal glory, and promising to raise them to immortality in the future.

To promulgate a corrupted notion of the Holy Spirit and His work is nothing less than blasphemy, because the Holy Spirit is God. He is to be exalted, honored, and adored. Along with the Father and the Son, He is to be glorified at all times for all He is and all He does. He is to be loved and thanked by those whom He indwells. But for that to occur, He must be worshipped in truth.

How Should We Then Respond?

It is high time for the evangelical church to take a stand and to recover a proper focus on the person and work of the Holy Spirit. The spiritual health of the church is at stake. In recent decades, the Charismatic Movement has infiltrated mainstream evangelicalism and exploded onto the global scene at an alarming rate. It is the fastest-growing religious movement in the world. Charismatics now number more than half a billion worldwide. Yet the gospel that is driving those surging numbers is not the true gospel, and the spirit behind them is not the Holy Spirit. What we are seeing is *in reality* the explosive growth of a false church, as dangerous as any cult or heresy that has ever assaulted Christianity. The Charismatic Movement was a farce and a scam from the outset; it has not changed into something good.

This is the hour for the true church to respond. At a time when there is a revival of the biblical gospel and a renewed interest in the *solas* of the Reformation, it is unacceptable to stand by idly. All who are faithful to the Scriptures must rise up and condemn everything that assaults the glory of God. We are duty-bound to apply the truth in a bold defense of the doctrine of the Holy Spirit. If we claim allegiance to the Reformers, we ought to conduct ourselves with the same level of courage and conviction they displayed as we contend earnestly for the faith. There must be a collective war against the pervasive abuses on the Spirit of God. This book is a call to join the cause for His honor.

I also hope to remind you what the *true* ministry of the Holy Spirit looks like. It's not chaotic, flashy, and flamboyant (like a circus). It's usually concealed and inconspicuous (the way fruit develops). We cannot be reminded too often that the Holy Spirit's primary role is to *exalt Christ*, especially to elicit *praise for Christ* from His people. The Spirit does this in a uniquely personal way, first of all by reproving and convicting us—showing us our own sin, opening our eyes to what true righteousness is, and making us sense deeply our accountability to God, the rightful Judge of all (John 16:8–11). The Holy Spirit indwells believers, empowering us to serve and glorify Christ (Rom. 8:9). He leads us and gives us assurance of our salvation (vv. 14–16). He prays for us with groanings too deep for words (v. 26). He seals us, keeping us secure in Christ (2 Cor. 1:22; Eph. 4:30). The Spirit's daily presence is the source and the secret of our sanctification as He conforms us to the image of Christ.

That is what the Holy Spirit is truly doing in the church even now. There's nothing baffling, bizarre, or irrational about being Spirit-filled or Spirit-led. His work is not to produce a spectacle or to foment chaos. In fact, where you see those things, you can be certain it is *not* His doing, "for God is not the author of confusion but of peace" (1 Cor. 14:33, 40). What the Spirit of God *does* produce is fruit: "love, joy, peace, longsuffering, kindness, goodness, faithfulness, gentleness, self-control. Against such there is no law" (Gal. 5:22–23).

My prayer for you as you read this book is that the Spirit Himself will give you a clear understanding of His true ministry in your own life, that you will embrace a biblical perspective on the Spirit and His gifts, and that you will refuse to be duped by the many spiritual counterfeits, false doctrines, and phony miracles that vie for our attention today.

Soli Deo Gloria.

PART ONE

Confronting a Counterfeit Revival

ONE

MOCKING THE SPIRIT

An editorial column from an African news website recently came across my desk. As I read it, I was struck by its blunt honesty and insightfulness. The piece, though penned by a Pentecostal man, is sharply critical of the chaos that characterizes the Charismatic Movement in that part of the world.

After blasting the "bizarre spirit-possession" and "odd ritual practices" of Pentecostalism in a general way, the author focuses on speaking in tongues. Observing a man supposedly filled with the Holy Spirit, he described the frenetic scene with these words:

> One sees the man's body forcibly shaking in spasms, with the hands trembling, the voice quivering in such staccato mumblings as: Je-Je-Je-Jee-sus . . . Jeee-sus . . . Je-Je-Je-Jee-sus . . . aassh . . . aassh . . . ah . . . aassh Jee-sus.
>
> Then follows some stuttering tongues-speaking: shlababababa—Jah-Jeey-balika—a syndrome which an American psychologist Peter Brent calls "a born-again fixation," and an observer brands as "a Pentecostal anthem." Only recently a reverend minister of an orthodox church queried, "If the possessed voodoo priest says: 'shiri-bo-bo-bo-boh' in a staccato stammer over his

black whisk he holds, and the possessed born-again Christian rattles: 'shla-ba-ba-bah-shlabalika' over his Bible, what can be the difference?"[1]

The rhetorical question is left ringing in the ears of the reader.

The author continues with a stinging exposé of a Pentecostal church service—inviting his readers to "watch some possessed prayerful: some, especially women, begin to hop about on one leg like grasshoppers let loose, and others roll on the floor, overturning benches and chairs. Order and discipline—these have gone to the winds, giving way to rowdy pandemonium, a babble of din." In disbelief, he poses the obvious question: "Can that be the biblical way to serve God?" Again, the rhetorical question remains unanswered.

He then recounts the story of a Pentecostal prayer meeting held just a few weeks earlier, in which a "Spirit-filled" woman fell down in ecstasy and knocked over a boy who was speaking in tongues. After crashing into the pews, the boy got up, nursing a bloody lip, and lamented, "Oh why?" in his own native language.

The incident raises more unanswerable questions. Our author wonders why the "tongue-speaking spirit should, in a split second, leave the bleeding lips and speak in native dialect." But more important, he wants to know, *how could the Holy Spirit be responsible for this kind of mayhem?* As he puts it, "Indeed, this incident raised the eyebrows of onlookers and anxious visitors: how [was it] that the Holy Spirit in someone should knock down the Holy Spirit in another so [as] to hurt him? Is the Holy Spirit now made to be a pugilist, or dancing boxer like old-time Cassius Clay to give a knockout? All were mystif[ied]." Their bewilderment is understandable. Surely the Spirit of God would not injure one of His own. But that realization forces them into an impossible dilemma: If the Holy Spirit is not behind the hype, then who is?

Though that specific account comes out of Africa, the general description it gives could fit Pentecostal and charismatic congregations in any part of the world.[2] The questions raised by the editorial's author are the questions every believer should ask, especially those who are part of charismatic churches. Why does the modern version of speaking in tongues parallel pagan worship practices? How can a God of order be honored by confusion and disarray?

Does the Holy Spirit really cause people to fall down like bowling pins? Why has the Charismatic Movement turned Him into something He is not? And, most important, what happens to people when they realize He's not the one behind the hysteria?

DISHONORING THE SPIRIT

It is deeply ironic that a movement supposedly devoted to honoring and emphasizing the ministry of the Holy Spirit in fact treats Him with such casual contempt and condescension. In practice, charismatics often seem to reduce the Spirit of God to a *force* or a *feeling*. Their bizarre practices and their exaggerated claims make Him look like a *farce* or a *fraud*. The sovereign glory of His holy person is exchanged repeatedly for the hollow shell of human imagination. The result is a movement whose most visible leaders—televangelists, faith healers, self-proclaimed prophets, and prosperity preachers—boldly claim His name while simultaneously dragging it through the mud.

The number of scams and scandals that continually arise out of the charismatic world is staggering. J. Lee Grady, contributing editor to *Charisma* magazine, acknowledged in *Christianity Today* that the charismatic world "has been shaken to its core in recent years by a number of high-profile leaders who have divorced or had moral failures. Many charismatics I know are troubled by this, and they feel it is time for deep introspection, repentance and a rejection of the shallow, celebrity Christianity that has typified much of our movement."[3]

One of the fundamental claims of charismatic teaching is that charismatics are privy to a sanctifying spiritual power not available to every believer. Those who have had a charismatic experience have been baptized with the Spirit, they say—and that supernaturally empowers obedience, fosters holiness, and produces the fruit of the Spirit. If their claims were true, charismatics ought to be producing leaders renowned for Christlikeness rather than flamboyance. Moral failures, financial chicanery, and public scandals would be comparatively rare in their movement.

But charismatics dominate the list of celebrity pastors and televangelists who have brought disgrace on the name of Christ over the past three decades—from Jim Bakker and Jimmy Swaggart to Ted Haggard and Todd Bentley. An entry entitled "List of Scandals Involving Evangelical Christians" on the popular website *Wikipedia* identified fifty well-known, publicly disgraced church leaders. The article indiscriminately labels the group "evangelical," but at least thirty-five of those listed are from Pentecostal and charismatic backgrounds.[4] A *Wikipedia* entry may not be authoritative in its use of doctrinal labels, but it serves as an accurate barometer of public perception. When charismatic leaders fail, whether for moral failure or financial impropriety, it is evangelicalism's reputation that gets besmirched. More important, the name of Christ is tarnished and the Spirit of God dishonored.

Bizarre doctrines and behavior have become so commonplace within the Charismatic Movement that they hardly make headlines anymore. Unbiblical practices—like speaking gibberish, falling backward to the floor, laughing uncontrollably, or writhing on the ground—are seen as necessary evidence that the Spirit is moving. YouTube has a seemingly endless collection of charismatic nonsense that is blatantly blasphemous—whole congregations doing the "Holy Ghost Hokey Pokey," people "tokin' the Ghost" (pretending to inhale the Holy Spirit and get high, as if He were an invisible reefer), and women writhing on the floor, miming the process of childbirth.[5] Old-fashioned snake handlers look tame by comparison.

It is all wild nonsense; yet it is unabashedly attributed to the Holy Spirit of God, as if He were the author of confusion and the architect of disorder. Charismatic authors usually describe His presence with expressions like "a jolt of electricity"[6] and "a remarkable tingling, electrifying sensation [that] started to spread over my feet, up my legs, up to my head, through my arms and down to my fingers."[7] Never mind the fact that such descriptions have no precedent in Scripture—and Scripture itself warns us that Satan can do signs and wonders. What if all the tingling, trances, and tremors are actually evidence of demonic activity? That concern is not at all far-fetched, given the dark, outlandish, and turbulent nature of so many of these phenomena.

Even violent assaults have been committed in the Holy Spirit's name. Kenneth Hagin says he punched a woman in the stomach in an attempt to heal her because God told him to do so. Rodney Howard Browne slapped a deaf man so hard he fell to the ground. Benny Hinn regularly has people fall over violently. Sometimes he does this as if by magic, waving his coat or his hand at them. Other times he pushes them backward with considerable force. The fact that an elderly woman was once fatally injured in the process hasn't stopped him from making this a regular feature of his miracle crusades.[8] Unimaginably absurd acts are credited to the Spirit's influence. For example, charismatic evangelist Todd Bentley justifies his brutal healing techniques with claims like this:

> I said "God, I prayed for like a hundred crippled people. Not one [got healed]?" He said, "That's because I want you to grab that lady's crippled legs and bang them up and down on the platform like a baseball bat." I walked up and I grabbed her legs and I started going BAM! BAM! I started banging them up and down on the platform. She got healed. And I'm thinking, "Why is not the power of God moving?" He said, "Because you haven't kicked that woman in the face." And there was this older lady worshipping right in front of the platform. *And the Holy Spirit spoke to me*; the gift of faith came on me. He said "Kick her in the face—with your biker boot!" I inched closer and I went like this. BAM! And just as my boot made contact with her nose she fell under the power of God.[9]

In spite of such outrageous comments, Bentley was hailed by charismatic leaders like Peter Wagner for his part in the 2008 Lakeland Revival.[10] Though his ministry temporarily stalled due to an illicit relationship with a female staff member, Bentley returned to full-time ministry just a short time later—after getting divorced and remarried.

Benny Hinn made headlines in the early 1990s when he threatened to weaponize the Holy Spirit in an attack on his critics. In a lengthy tirade during a Trinity Broadcasting Network *Praise-a-Thon*, Hinn retorted, "Those who put us down are a bunch of morons. . . . You know, I've looked for one verse in the Bible, I just can't seem to find it. One verse that says, 'If you don't like 'em, kill 'em.' I really wish I could find it. . . . Sometimes I wish God would give me a Holy Ghost machine gun—I'll blow your head off!"[11]

Though not as hostile as her husband, Benny's wife, Suzanne, made a media splash of her own several years later when she referenced the Holy Spirit in a particularly graphic and inappropriate way. As she frantically paced back and forth on the stage, Mrs. Hinn declared: "You know what, my engines are revvin' to go. It's revvin' up. How 'bout yours? And if it's not, you know what? If your engine is not revvin' up, you know what you need? *You need a Holy Ghost enema right up your rear end!* Because God will not tolerate—He will not tolerate anything else."[12] When her antics were later aired on Comedy Central's *The Daily Show*, Hinn's lawyers threatened a defamation lawsuit but to no avail. She had made herself a laughingstock. In reality, the only person whose character was defamed was the Holy Spirit.

THE SPIRIT OF FRAUD

The Charismatic Movement claims to exalt the third member of the Trinity. Truth be told, it has turned Him into a sideshow. It would be bad enough if such blasphemy were confined to the private audience of a local congregation. But the circus of sacrilege is endlessly exported through a global network of print, radio, and television media. As former Pentecostal Kenneth D. Johns explains, "In the past the influence of these hapless leaders has had certain limitations. Their distortion of the Bible message was limited in its dissemination to preaching in the local church, classrooms of a college or a seminary, books, and radio programs. In the last thirty to forty years all of that has changed because of television."[13]

Influenced by TV's most popular preachers, many charismatics treat the sovereign Spirit of God as if He were their slave—a heavenly butler bound to wait on their every command. Their teaching is not substantially different from the New Age poison popularized by the 2006 international best seller *The Secret*, in which author Rhonda Byrne suggests, "You are the Master of the universe, and the Genie is there to serve you."[14] Charismatic televangelists and celebrity pastors typically preach a similar message. It is a false gospel of material prosperity popularly known as Word of Faith doctrine. If you have enough faith, they claim, you can literally have whatever you say.

In the words of Kenneth Copeland, "As a believer, you have a right to make commands in the name of Jesus. Each time you stand on the Word, you are *commanding God* to a certain extent."[15] Fred Price urges his followers not to be timid or restrained in what they demand from God: "If you have to say, 'If it be thy will' or 'Thy will be done'—if you have to say that, then you're calling God a fool, because He's the One that told us to ask. . . . If God's gonna give me what He wants me to have, then it doesn't matter what I ask."[16]

This branch of the Charismatic Movement is by far the largest, most visible, most influential, and fastest-growing category of charismatics. Put simply, Word of Faith teachers represent the current drift of the larger movement. And the doctrine of prosperity they teach has nothing whatsoever to do with the true gospel of Jesus Christ. They are promoting crass superstition blended with false doctrines purloined from assorted Gnostic and metaphysical cults, cloaked in Christian terms and symbols. It is not authentic Christianity.

For the hundreds of millions who embrace Word of Faith theology and the prosperity gospel, "the Holy Spirit is relegated to a quasi-magical power by which success and prosperity are achieved."[17] As one author observed, "The believer is told to use God, whereas the truth of biblical Christianity is just the opposite—God uses the believer. Word of Faith or prosperity theology sees the Holy Spirit as a power to be put to use for whatever the believer wills. The Bible teaches that the Holy Spirit is a Person who enables the believer to do God's will."[18]

Silver-tongued televangelists boldly promise unending health and wealth to all who have enough faith—and more important, to all who send in their money. On program after program, people are urged to "plant a seed" with the promise God will miraculously make them rich in return. It's known as the seed-faith plan, so named by Oral Roberts, the key pioneer in using television to spread charismatic doctrine. Most charismatic televangelists and faith healers use Roberts's seed-faith plan or something similar to manipulate viewers to donate more than they can really afford.[19]

Paul Crouch, founder and chairman of Trinity Broadcasting Network, is one of the doctrine's staunchest defenders. "Plant a significant seed," Crouch wrote in a 2011 TBN fund-raising letter. "Give it fully expecting the glorious return that Jesus promised. One final note: name your seed—'out of debt,' 'job,' 'home,' 'husband,' 'wife'—or whatever you desire from God!"[20] Another letter ended with these words: "I know prices for gas and most everything else is up, but remember Jesus' words: 'Give and it shall be given [unto you].'"[21] The message is anything but subtle. An article in the *Los Angeles Times* summarized Crouch's approach this way:

> Pastor Paul Crouch calls it "God's economy of giving," and here is how it works: People who donate to Crouch's Trinity Broadcasting Network will reap financial blessings from a grateful God. The more they give TBN, the more he will give them. Being broke or in debt is no excuse not to write a check. In fact, it's an ideal opportunity. For God is especially generous to those who give when they can least afford it. "He'll give you thousands, hundreds of thousands," Crouch told his viewers during a telethon last November. "He'll give millions and billions of dollars."[22]

For Crouch and others at the top of this pyramid scheme, prosperity theology works flawlessly. Viewers send in billions of dollars,[23] and when there is no return on investment, God is the one held liable.[24] Or the people who have sent money are blamed for some defect in their faith when the sought-after miracle never materializes.[25] Disappointment, frustration, poverty, sorrow, anger, and ultimately unbelief are the main fruits of this kind of teaching, but the pleas for money only get more urgent and the false promises grow more exaggerated.

Masked in the language of faith and generosity, the entire charade is a deceptive ruse designed to exploit the greedy and swindle the desperate.[26] It has replaced the Spirit of God with a spirit of fraud. Even so, its message of false hope remains extremely popular, and it's easy to see why: *the promise of physical well-being, material riches, and a life of ease appeals to the flesh.* It is pure carnality; there's nothing truly spiritual about it.

More moderate prosperity preachers, like Joel Osteen, salt their sermons with subtlety and a smile. But the underlying message is still the same: God is here to make our dreams come true. Michael Horton puts it succinctly: "Osteen represents a variety of the moralistic, therapeutic deism that in less extreme versions seems to characterize much of popular religion in America today. Basically, God is there for you and your happiness. He has some rules and principles for getting what you want out of life, and if you follow them, you can have what you want. Just *declare it* and prosperity will come to you."[27] From a marketing perspective, it's an effective formula. Blank-check promises of health and wealth, mixed with inane doses of positive thinking and shallow platitudes, may boost ratings and sell books. But it is all a massive swindle, and it has nothing to do with biblical Christianity.

In hawking their gospel of greed, materialism, and self-promotion, Word of Faith teachers have made lucrative careers out of bad theology—backing up their false teachings by twisting the Scriptures or claiming new revelation from God. Some go so far as to assert that believers are *little gods* who can speak their worldly desires into existence.[28] Paul Crouch responded to naysayers on national television with these words: "I am a little god. I have His name. I am one with Him. I'm in covenant relation. I am a little god. Critics be gone!"[29] Kenneth Copeland similarly told his listeners, "You're all god. You don't have a God living in you; you *are* one! You are part and parcel of God."[30] More recently, televangelist Creflo Dollar echoed the teachings of Copeland and Crouch: "I'm going to say something, *we are gods*, in this earth, and it's about time we start operating like gods instead of a bunch of mere powerless humans."[31] Only one adjective fully describes that level of blasphemous arrogance: *satanic* (cf. Gen. 3:5).

While elevating themselves to divine status, Word of Faith teachers simultaneously deny the sovereignty of the true God.[32] As Myles Munroe announced to a TBN audience, "God cannot do anything in the earth without a human's permission!"[33] Andrew Womack, whose television show *The Gospel Truth* airs daily on Trinity Broadcasting Network, insists God lost His authority in this world by delegating it to Adam and the human race. As a result, the Holy Spirit was powerless to bring Jesus into physical existence; He was forced to wait until willing human participants made the incarnation possible by speaking the right faith-words.

In a 2009 broadcast Womack told his viewers, "The reason it took four thousand years for Jesus to come on the scene is because it took four thousand years for God to find enough people who would yield to Him, who would speak, and who would deliver the words that needed to be said—God-inspired words—to create this physical body of the Lord Jesus. . . . The Holy Spirit took these words and impregnated Mary."[34] That is heretical teaching, with no basis whatsoever in Scripture. It comes straight out of the twisted imagination of the speaker. Worse yet, it blatantly demeans the Holy Spirit—as if God needed help from sinful people to send His Son to this world.

Examples like those could be multiplied many times over. Sadly, within the broader Charismatic Movement, such atrocities against the Holy Spirit are not the exception; they have become the rule. Peter Masters accurately describes the trend:

> With unbelievable rapidity charismatics have lurched from one excess to another, so that now we are confronted by a scene of utter confusion. Many in the charismatic fraternity have gone over to ideas and practices which come straight from pagan religions, and large numbers of young and impressionable believers have been spiritually corrupted in the process. Leading healers have arisen who unite the subtle tricks of the theatrical hypnotist with ancient occult techniques in their quest for results, and multitudes follow them.[35]

Significantly, those words were penned more than two decades ago, around the same time I wrote *Charismatic Chaos*.[36] In the years since, the situation has grown dramatically worse.

In Gold We Trust

There is no escaping the fact that all sorts of spiritual deception, theological error, and outright skulduggery find shelter within the broader charismatic world—including the bald materialism and brash self-centeredness of the prosperity gospel. Some might argue, however, that such heretical elements represent only the lunatic fringe of an otherwise orthodox movement.

More moderate charismatics like to portray the prosperity preachers, faith healers, and televangelists as safely isolated on the extreme edge of the charismatic camp.

Unfortunately, that is not the case. Thanks to the global reach and incessant proselytizing of religious television and charismatic mass media, the *extreme* has now become *mainstream*. For most of the watching world, flamboyant false teachers—with heresies as ridiculous as their hairdos—constitute the public face of Christianity. And they propagate their lies in the Holy Spirit's name.

When it comes to religious broadcasting, Satan is indeed the prince of the power of the air(waves). On networks like TBN, almost no false prophecy, erroneous doctrine, rank superstition, or silly claim is too outlandish to receive airtime. Jan Crouch tearfully gives a fanciful account of how her pet chicken was miraculously raised from the dead.[37] Benny Hinn trumps that claim with a bizarre prophecy that if TBN viewers will put the caskets of their dead loved ones in front of a television set and touch the dead person's hand to the screen, people will "be raised from the dead . . . by the thousands."[38] Ironically, one doesn't even need to be an orthodox trinitarian in order to broadcast on the Trinity Broadcasting Network. Bishop T. D. Jakes, well known for his association with Oneness Pentecostalism,[39] is a staple on TBN. And though he later recanted, Benny Hinn infamously told TBN listeners there are nine persons in the Godhead.[40]

As the largest religious television network on the planet, TBN beams its product 24/7 to more than one hundred countries on seventy satellites through more than eighteen thousand TV channels and cable affiliates.[41] Its Internet presence extends that reach even farther. The media organization claims to be empowered by the Holy Spirit to reach "a troubled world with the hope of the gospel."[42] But it is the *false* hope of a *false* gospel. Virtually all the network's main celebrities advocate prosperity theology—telling listeners that God will give them healing, wealth, and other material blessings in return for their money. And TBN is not the only culprit. The network's major competitors (like Daystar and LeSEA) provide similar platforms for Word of Faith teachers.

So is it any wonder the health-and-wealth prosperity gospel has taken our planet by storm?[43] In the Two-Thirds World of Asia, Africa, and Latin America—where the Charismatic Movement is growing at an unprecedented rate—experts estimate well over half of Pentecostal and charismatic adherents hold to the prosperity gospel.[44] As John T. Allen explains:

> Perhaps the most controversial element of the Pentecostal outlook is the so-called "prosperity gospel," meaning the belief that God will reward those with sufficient faith with both material prosperity and physical health. Some analysts distinguish between "neo-Pentecostal," which they see as focused on the prosperity gospel, and classic Pentecostalism, oriented toward the gifts of the Spirit such as healings and tongues. Yet the Pew Forum data suggests that the prosperity gospel is actually a defining feature of all Pentecostalism; majorities of Pentecostals exceeding 90 percent in most countries hold to these beliefs.[45]

In reality, the rapid expansion of charismatic theology is primarily due to the popularity of the prosperity gospel. It is not the convicting work of the Holy Spirit that is drawing converts, but the allure of material possessions[46] and the hope of physical healing.[47]

The fastest-growing and largest charismatic congregations all preach some form of this message,[48] from David Yonggi Cho in South Korea, whose church claims more than eight hundred thousand members, to Bishop Enoch Adeboye of Nigeria, whose monthly prayer meetings regularly draw three hundred thousand in attendance. Pentecostal historian Vinson Synan, clearly thrilled by the surging numbers, wrote, "Generally known as the 'prosperity gospel' or the 'Word of Faith Movement,' this movement is now an international force that is gaining millions of enthusiastic followers around the world. Led by popular teachers and evangelists such as Kenneth Copeland, David Yonggi Cho and Reinhard Bonnke, the teaching has inspired some of the largest churches and evangelistic crusades in the history of the Church."[49] The global success of the Word of Faith Movement has made the Pentecostal-Charismatic Movement the fastest-growing religious movement in the world.[50]

Of course, the prosperity gospel's enthusiastic reception is not limited to churches outside the United States. Even on American soil, it is one of the fastest-growing segments of Christianity.[51] High-profile pastors, leading some of the nation's largest churches, shamelessly promote a gospel of health, wealth, and happiness—from Joel Osteen to Joyce Meyer to T. D. Jakes. Their influence is permanently altering the American religious landscape: "The prosperity gospel is spreading beyond the confines of the charismatic movement, where it has been traditionally strong, and is taking root in the larger evangelical church. A recent survey found that in the United States, 46 percent of self-proclaimed Christians agree with the idea that God will grant material riches to all believers who have enough faith."[52]

Though the church has historically repudiated greed and consumerism, that appears to be changing quickly.[53] Nearly half of American Christians, in any denomination, and roughly two-thirds of American Pentecostals now embrace the basic premise of the prosperity gospel: God wants you to be happy, healthy, and rich.[54]

Recent studies estimate the total number of Pentecostals and charismatics worldwide at just over 500 million—with 80 million in North America, 141 million in Latin America, 135 million in Asia, 126 million in Africa, and 38 million in Europe.[55] Those numbers initially sound impressive, suggesting charismatic Christianity represents one-fourth of global Christendom.[56] The reality is that the vast majority of Pentecostals and charismatics—measuring in the hundreds of millions—embrace some form of the prosperity gospel. In terms of raw numbers alone, health-and-wealth theology has become the larger movement's defining feature.[57] As Ted Olsen observed in *Christianity Today*, most Pentecostals and charismatics "overwhelmingly agree that 'God will grant material prosperity to all believers who have enough faith.'"[58]

The health-and-wealth prosperity gospel may be popular, but it is *not* the true gospel. David Jones and Russell Woodbridge note the stark contrasts:

The message preached in some of the largest churches in the world has changed.
A new gospel is being taught today. This new gospel is perplexing—it omits

Jesus and neglects the cross. Instead of promising Christ, this gospel promises health and wealth, and offers advice such as: declare to yourself that everything that you touch will prosper, for, in the words of a leading prosperity gospel preacher, "There is a miracle in your mouth." According to this new gospel, if believers repeat positive confessions, focus their thoughts, and generate enough faith, God will release blessings upon their lives.[59]

Such a gospel is powerless to save. It is empowered by human desire, not the Holy Spirit. Moreover, it offers temporal relief at the expense of eternal life. And even then, except for those in the highest positions of leadership, it rarely delivers as advertised.

THE HEART OF THE PROBLEM

Without question, the prosperity gospel is a "different gospel," which is really no gospel at all (Gal. 1:6–8). But how has such blatant heresy managed to not only survive but flourish in charismatic circles? The answer points to a critical and systemic defect within charismatic theology—a flaw that accounts for just about every theological aberration or abnormality that makes its home within the Charismatic Movement. It is this: *Pentecostals and charismatics elevate religious experience over biblical truth.* Though many of them pay lip service to the authority of God's Word, in practice they deny it.[60]

If Scripture alone were truly their final authority, charismatic Christians would never tolerate patently unbiblical practices—like mumbling in nonsensical prayer languages, uttering fallible prophecies, worshipping in disorderly ways, or being knocked senseless by the supposed power of the Holy Spirit. They ought to reinterpret their experiences to match the Bible; instead, they reinterpret Scripture in novel and unorthodox ways in order to justify their experiences.[61] As a result, any aberrant teaching or practice can be legitimized, especially when a new "revelation from God" conveniently authenticates it as having His approval. Though written nearly a half century ago, the words of René Pache still ring true:

The excessive preeminence given to the Holy Spirit in their devotions and their preoccupation with gifts, ecstasies, and "prophecies" has tended to neglect of the Scriptures. Why be tied to a Book out of the past when one can communicate every day with the living God? But this is exactly the danger point. Apart from the constant control of the written revelation, we soon find ourselves engulfed in subjectivity; and the believer, even if he has the best intentions, can sink rapidly into deviations, illuminism or exaltation. Let each remind himself of the prohibition of taking anything away from Scripture or adding anything to it (Deut. 4:2; Rev. 22:18–19). Almost every heresy and sect has originated in a supposed revelation or a new experience on the part of its founder, something outside the strictly biblical framework.[62]

By abandoning the final authority of the text, the Charismatic Movement has made itself susceptible to the worst kinds of doctrinal deception and spiritual exploitation.[63]

Other aspects of charismatic theology only exacerbate the problem: the labeling of church leaders as *prophets* and *apostles*, the constant hunt for miracles and supernatural events, the desire to encounter God in mystical ways, and the willingness to bypass the mind in worship. With its lack of biblical controls and its emphasis on experience-driven subjectivism, the Charismatic Movement is custom-made for false teachers and spiritual con men.[64] Even those as blatantly blasphemous as the prosperity preachers feel welcome within its borders.

As troubling as they are, the constant shenanigans that go on within charismatic circles are merely symptoms of this deeper issue. In fact, I believe it is the elevation of experience over the authority of Scripture that grieves and demeans the Holy Spirit most of all. It is the Spirit who inspired the Word of God (2 Peter 1:19–21) and who illuminates its truth in the hearts of His people (1 Cor. 2:10–15). Thus, it is a brazen affront to His authority to claim an experience of His power that goes contrary to His Word. To twist the Scriptures that He inspired, or to ignore them altogether, is to treat Him with disdain and disrespect. Yet that is exactly what happens throughout the charismatic world every single day—from the rankest heresies of the leading televangelists to the private revelations of self-styled prophets in small congregations.[65] It is *all* an insult to the true person and work of the Holy Spirit. Christopher Wright says it well:

> There are the televangelists and purveyors of prosperity "gospel" (an abuse of the term, since it is far from good news), appealing to and exploiting for profit, people's innate material greed in the name of God's blessing. Add to that the inflated claims and grossly insensitive publicity of some of the great "healing miracle merchants." And even at the lowly level of ordinary local churches there are those who abuse the Holy Spirit by claiming his authority for their latest "revelation" or for the latest fashionable theory, style, song, or method.[66]

And that brings us back to where we began this chapter. It is deeply ironic that the movement most concerned with emphasizing the Holy Spirit is, in fact, the one that treats Him with the greatest contempt and condescension.

TWO

A NEW WORK OF THE SPIRIT?

I t was the dawn of the twentieth century, in the early morning hours of New Year's Day 1901. A group of Bible school students had come together hours earlier for a New Year's Eve prayer service. But even though it was long past midnight, they were still there—earnestly seeking to experience the presence and power of the Holy Spirit. All of them desperately hoped for something amazing.

Over the previous weeks, the students had been intently studying portions of the book of Acts. They were particularly interested in what the apostolic record taught about the baptism of the Holy Spirit—an experience that, in keeping with their Wesleyan Holiness background, they believed took place subsequent to conversion. Their study eventually centered on the miraculous phenomenon of speaking in tongues, which the students concluded was the true sign of Spirit baptism.[1] They observed how the apostles had spoken in tongues on the day of Pentecost, as well as Cornelius in Acts 10 and John the Baptist's former disciples in Acts 19. And they wondered: if tongues-speaking was a sign of the Spirit's presence in apostolic times, maybe the same was still true at the outset of the twentieth century.

By the time they gathered for a prayer service on New Year's Eve, they had all arrived at the same two conclusions—namely, speaking in tongues was the sign of Spirit baptism, and the gift of tongues was still available for them to experience. So with heartfelt determination, they pleaded with God to be baptized by His Spirit. Their teacher, a Methodist Holiness minister named Charles Fox Parham, had encouraged them along these lines. And now they were eager to experience the Spirit's power firsthand.

Sometime in those early morning hours, something extraordinary happened. One of the students, a young woman named Agnes Ozman, asked her teacher to lay hands on her and pray that she would receive the Holy Spirit.[2] What happened next would change the course of modern church history. As Charles Parham later recounted, "I laid my hands upon her and prayed. I had scarcely completed three dozen sentences when a glory fell upon her, a halo seemed to surround her head and face, and she began speaking the Chinese language and was unable to speak English for three days. When she tried to write in English to tell us of her experience she wrote the Chinese."[3]

Ozman's experience would soon be shared by both her teacher and her fellow students. During the series of revival meetings that followed, more than twenty different languages were reportedly spoken through the Spirit's supernatural power, including Russian, Japanese, Bulgarian, French, Bohemian, Norwegian, Hungarian, Italian, and Spanish. Charles Parham himself claimed to speak in Swedish as well as other languages.

Such was the beginning of the modern Pentecostal Movement. As Pentecostal historian Vinson Synan explains, "Ozman's experience thus became the prototype experience for all the millions of Pentecostals who were to follow."[4] Within a decade, more than fifty thousand people would experience the same phenomenon as Agnes Ozman. Enthusiasm continued to mushroom, especially on the West Coast, where another of Parham's students—a man named William J. Seymour—similarly promoted speaking in tongues as the sign of Spirit baptism. No one could have imagined how a simple prayer meeting at a small Bible school in Kansas would change the world. Just over a century later, the Pentecostal and neo-Pentecostal Movements would grow to include more than half a billion charismatic adherents.

A New Pentecost?

Pentecostalism's beginnings may sound supernatural and even a bit romantic. Charles Parham named his new movement the "Apostolic Faith Movement," and he claimed his experiences constituted a new Pentecost.[5] He and his students were convinced they had received the Holy Spirit in the same way as the apostles in Acts 2. Their experiences in 1901 were the spark that lit the fires of the modern Charismatic Movement.[6]

Further investigation, however, calls the legitimacy of Parham's claims into serious question on at least three fronts. First, there are conflicting versions of the story, even from the principal participants involved. As noted above, Parham stated that Ozman did not speak in English for three days after her experience, but Ozman reported praying in English after only one day.[7] Parham further claimed that Ozman's experience occurred on New Year's Eve, while Ozman insisted it happened on New Year's Day.[8] While Parham took credit for directing his students to the book of Acts before their historic prayer meeting, Ozman contradicted that claim, asserting "she had no part of any Bible study assignment by Parham prior to her tongues speaking experience. In fact she says she pointed students to Acts 2 in answer to their questions about her glossolalic experience."[9] Discrepancies like those have caused historians like Martin E. Marty to question key aspects of the story:

> Like all such mythically cast stories, these had certain features that remain open to question. In an earlier stratum of testimony Miss Ozman referred to having spoken in tongues three weeks before New Year's Day, a less neat date, but one which others corroborated. She also claimed that she realized the significance of her speaking only later, but it is known that Parham had instructed her in advance to look for precisely that sign.[10]

Furthermore, though Agnes Ozman interpreted her experience through the lens of Acts 2, not all her fellow students were convinced. "*The Topeka Daily Capital* reported that not everyone at the school embraced the new experience. In an interview with the newspaper, S. J. Riggins said of Parham and his fellow students, 'I believe the whole of them are crazy.'"[11]

Second, and more important, Charles Parham, Agnes Ozman, and the other students never actually experienced the supernatural sign they were seeking. They were convinced speaking in tongues entailed the miraculous ability to speak in authentic foreign languages, just as the apostles did on the day of Pentecost in Acts 2.[12] *That* was the gift they so desperately desired. The "gift" they experienced, however, consisted of nothing more than nonsensical gibberish.[13] This reality became painfully obvious when Parham insisted that Pentecostal missionaries could go to foreign lands without first going to language school.[14]

He boasted to the *Topeka State Journal*, "The Lord will give us the power of speech to talk to the people of the various nations without having to study them in schools."[15] Several weeks later, he told the *Kansas City Times*, "A part of our labor will be to teach the church the uselessness of spending years of time preparing missionaries for work in foreign lands when all they have to do is ask God for power."[16] Within weeks, newspapers as far afield as Hawaii were echoing Parham's promise—embellished, it seems, with a number of bald-faced falsehoods:

TOPEKA, May 20.—Rev. Charles F. Parham, of the "College of Bethel," at Topeka, and his followers are preparing to give the people of the churches some new work along the line of missionary endeavor.

His plan is to send among the heathen, persons who have been blessed with the "gift of tongues"—a gift which, he says, no others have ever had conferred upon them since apostolic times. His missionaries, as he points out, will have the great advantages of having the languages of the various peoples among whom they work miraculously conferred upon them and will not be put to the trouble of learning them in the laborious way by which they are acquired by other prospective missionaries.

[Said Parham:] ". . . There is no doubt that at this time they will have conferred on them the 'gift of tongues,' if they are worthy and seek it in faith, believing they will thus be made able to talk to the people whom they choose to work among in their own language, which will, of course, be an inestimable advantage.

"The students of Bethel College do not need to study in the old way to learn the languages. They have them conferred on them miraculously. Different ones have already been able to converse with Spaniards, Italians, Bohemians, Hungarians, Germans, and French in their own language. I have no doubt various dialects of the people of India and even the language of the savages of Africa will be received during our meeting in the same way. I expect this gathering to be the greatest since the days of Pentecost."

———

He claims that he and his disciples have received all the gifts that Christ conferred upon His earliest disciples.[17]

Unfortunately, that same sort of deliberately embroidered, wildly exaggerated testimony is all too common in charismatic circles even today. But naive people still take such reports at face value, mistaking gullibility for faith.

In spite of Parham's confident-sounding guarantees, his missionary strategy backfired, rather badly. Jack Hayford and David Moore, charismatic authors, acknowledge the wholesale failure of Parham's expectations: "Sadly, the idea of xenoglossalalic tongues [i.e. foreign languages] would later prove an embarrassing failure as Pentecostal workers went off to mission fields with their gift of tongues and found their hearers did not understand them."[18] Robert Mapes Anderson adds:

S. C. Todd of the Bible Missionary Society investigated eighteen Pentecostals who went to Japan, China, and India "expecting to preach to the natives in those countries in their own tongue," and found that by their own admission "in no single instance have [they] been able to do so." As these and other missionaries returned in disappointment and failure, Pentecostals were compelled to rethink their original view of speaking in tongues.[19]

In addition to speaking in tongues, Agnes Ozman and other Pentecostals also "wrote in tongues," scribbling down what they believed to be characters of a foreign language. Photographs of these messages were published in newspapers like the *Topeka Daily Capital* and the *Los Angeles Daily Times*.[20] The chicken-scratches resembled no known language and were completely incomprehensible.[21]

Third, the personal character of Charles Parham calls into question whether the Holy Spirit would spark a worldwide revival through Parham's ministry. A short time after his students spoke in tongues, in spite of his predictions that massive growth was about to begin, Parham was forced to close the Bible school in Topeka. He traveled to other parts of Kansas and the Midwest, holding healing and revival meetings and gathering disciples. Soon he was claiming more than five thousand devotees.[22] He referred to his growing network of followers as the Apostolic Faith Movement (echoing the name of his biweekly magazine, *Apostolic Faith*) and gave himself the title "Projector of the Apostolic Faith Movement."[23]

But the movement barely survived a string of severe blows to Parham's reputation. In the fall of 1906, he held a series of meetings in Zion, Illinois, and some months later five of his followers there beat a disabled woman to death in an attempt to drive the demon of rheumatism from her. Although Parham himself was long gone from Zion when the woman was killed, the ensuing murder trial garnered nationwide publicity, and newspapers across the nation identified the killers as "members of the Parham cult."[24] When the chief perpetrators of the crime were found guilty, the national media reported, "Other arrests are expected in the case as the result of evidence given at the inquest, and Parham, leader of the cult to which those now in jail belong, may himself be taken under surveillance."[25] Parham was not charged in that case, but his name became a synonym for deadly religious fanaticism.

When a young girl in Kansas died because her parents refused medical treatment and instead sought healing through Parham's ministry, the Pentecostal evangelist was forced to leave Kansas and go to Texas.[26] It was there that he met William J. Seymour, a thirty-five-year-old African American who—after embracing Parham's teachings on the Holy Spirit and the gift of tongues—subsequently sparked the Azusa Street Revival in Los Angeles in 1906. But their friendship soon soured. When Parham visited Seymour's work in Southern California, he did not approve of the wild behavior that characterized the meetings.[27] He tried to assert his leadership over the revival but was rebuffed.

From there, Parham's story quickly gets worse. On July 19, 1907, he was arrested at a hotel in San Antonio, Texas, on charges of sodomy. He was released from custody four days later. Though he claimed to be innocent, his opponents alleged that he had written a full confession in exchange for his release.[28] In spite of his protests to the contrary, Parham's reputation was permanently besmirched, and his influence began to dwindle. As R. G. Robbins explains, "What actually transpired on that hot summer night may never be known, but Parham's standing suffered irreparable harm, notwithstanding the fact that charges were later dropped. News of the scandal shot through Holiness and Pentecostal circles, delighting Parham's enemies and disheartening his dwindling cadre of friends. Meanwhile, the Apostolic Faith Movement shattered."[29]

In a desperate attempt to salvage his reputation, Parham decided he needed to accomplish something truly remarkable to distract from the allegations. He began a fund-raising campaign for an expedition to the Holy Land, on which he promised to find both Noah's ark and the lost ark of the covenant.[30] But the trip ended before it began. Parham's biographer, James R. Goff, tells what happened: "After parading the plan before the press and raising sufficient funds, Parham journeyed to New York in December 1908 to board a steamer for Jerusalem. [But] his ticket for the Middle East was never purchased. Parham returned home to Kansas in January 1909 on money loaned to him by a friend. Dejectedly, he explained to his followers that he had been mugged shortly after arriving in New York and never even had an opportunity to buy his ticket."[31]

Like the majority of preachers affiliated with the Holiness Movement in that era, Parham was attracted to doctrines that were marginal, novel, extreme, or totally unorthodox. He was an ardent advocate of conditional immortality (the idea that the wicked will be annihilated rather than subjected to eternal torment)—and at times he sounded like a universalist.[32] He had an unorthodox view of human fallenness, and he clearly did not understand the bondage of sin. He seemed to believe sinners could redeem themselves with a combination of their own effort and God's help, and he apparently viewed grace as something God owed to humanity. He taught that sanctification guarantees physical healing and it is therefore an act of unbelief to seek medical treatment for any ailment.[33]

Parham also advocated a form of Anglo-Israelism,[34] teaching that the western European races (particularly Anglo-Saxon people) descended from the ten tribes of Israel after they were dispersed in the Assyrian captivity—and white Europeans are therefore the true "chosen people." That view naturally tends to foster racial bigotry.[35] Indeed, as time passed, Charles Parham grew increasingly outspoken as an advocate for racial segregation. On one occasion, he asserted that the reason God flooded the world was in response to interracial marriage. The sermon, titled "Creation and Formation," was printed in the August 13, 1905, edition of the *Houston Daily Post*. In Parham's own words: "Thus began the woeful intermarriage of races for which cause the flood was sent in punishment, and has ever been followed by plagues and incurable diseases upon the third and fourth generations, the offspring of such marriages. Were time to last and intermarriage continue between the whites, the blacks and the reds of America, consumption and other diseases would soon wipe the mixed bloods off the face of the earth."[36]

After visiting Azusa Street in 1906 and being repulsed by its emotional excesses, Parham railed against it. But his antagonism also betrayed an inherent racism. "Using crude racial slurs, Parham denounced white women who consorted with black men in worship at the Azusa mission, and deplored that white and black men and women knelt together and fell across one another. Such 'foolishness,' he charged, had followed the Azusa work everywhere."[37] By the end of his life, Parham openly endorsed the Ku Klux Klan, publicly praising the organization in 1927. Summarizing Parham's racist views, Frederick Harris notes that Pentecostalism's "theological founder, Charles Parham, sympathized with the Ku Klux Klan, racially segregated students at his Bible school in Topeka, preached against the intermingling of races, and believed that Anglo-Saxons were the master race."[38]

Not surprisingly, scandal and opprobrium dogged Parham's trail, and his reputation suffered. Others within Pentecostal circles soon began to distance themselves from their founder. "Along with concerns over financial management, his eccentric doctrines, and racist attitudes Parham became an embarrassment to the Pentecostal Movement as it grew in the first decades of the twentieth century."[39] But, like it or not, contemporary Pentecostals (and by extension, all charismatics) are stuck with Charles Parham as the theological architect of their movement.[40] As Anthony Thiselton explains, "Charles Parham is widely regarded as the founder of classical Pentecostalism. . . . Parham formulated the classic four marks of Pentecostal theology and experience: salvation, baptism in the Holy Spirit, healing, and expectancy of the 'second coming' of Christ."[41]

All this raises significant questions about the claims of the modern Pentecostal Movement, given the dubious nature of its initial beginnings: from the conflicting testimony of those involved, to the nonsensical nature of the "tongues" that were spoken, to the disreputable character of the movement's first leader. Added to that, Pentecostalism arose out of the defective soteriology of the nineteenth-century Holiness Movement, of which Charles Parham and William J. Seymour were both part.[42] In spite of passages like 1 John 1:8–10, Holiness theology wrongly asserts that believers can experience a "second blessing" sometime after their conversion, at which point they attain to a state of "Christian perfection" in this life.[43] Some nineteenth-century Holiness leaders also taught a "third blessing," which they identified with the "baptism of the Holy Spirit," and which Pentecostalism subsequently linked with speaking in tongues.[44]

But here is the point of all this history: *If the Holy Spirit intended to re-create the day of Pentecost, is this really how He would do it?* Even a basic comparison between what happened in Acts 2 and what took place nineteen centuries later in Topeka, Kansas, highlights striking contrasts between the two events. The original day of Pentecost did not arise from a defective soteriology, nor did it result in contradictory eyewitness accounts. The apostolic gift of tongues was not some form of irrational vocalization. Rather, the apostles miraculously spoke in authentic foreign languages they had never learned (Acts 2:9–12). Moreover, the Spirit's power was not only exhibited in their fervent preaching, but it was also evident in their godly character—as the Spirit continued to sanctify them over the course of their entire lives.

The "new Pentecost" of the Charismatic Movement could not have been more different. It grew out of the deficient soteriology of the Holiness Movement; it was marked by inconsistent eyewitness testimony; it produced counterfeit religious experiences; and it was initiated by a disreputable spiritual leader. Such factors call its legitimacy into serious question.

A "NEW THOUGHT" APPROACH?

Around the same time that Charles Parham was directing his students to seek tongues as the sign of Spirit baptism, another American minister was encouraging his followers to use positive confession to speak their desires into existence.

"What I confess, I possess."[45] That slogan, popularized by later Word of Faith preachers, was first coined by Essek William Kenyon—a Free Will Baptist pastor and educator who lived from 1867 to 1948. Though raised in a Methodist household, Kenyon became a Baptist through the influence of popular evangelist A. J. Gordon. But Kenyon was also exposed to the metaphysical cults of the nineteenth century, and he allowed those errors to taint his theology.

In 1892 he attended Emerson College of Oratory in Boston, which specialized in training lecturers for the metaphysical science cults (in particular, New Thought metaphysics).[46] New Thought originated a generation earlier through the teachings of Phineas P. Quimby, a New England philosopher, hypnotist, and healer who taught that physical realities could be manipulated and controlled through mental and spiritual means. New Thought teachings emphasized that a higher intelligence or divine force was everywhere present, that human beings possessed a divine nature, that they could use their minds to alter physical reality, and that by thinking correctly they could free themselves from sickness and poverty.[47] Quimby's ideas were popularized by his followers, including Mary Baker Eddy, who incorporated New Thought teaching into the cult of Christian Science.

After leaving Emerson College, Kenyon went on to pastor several Baptist churches. In 1898, he started Bethel Bible Institute in Spencer, Massachusetts. He served as the president of the institute until 1923, when he resigned "amid a swirl of controversy that was never made public."[48] Leaving Massachusetts, he came west, settling for several years in Southern California before relocating to Seattle, Washington, in the early 1930s. There he founded New Covenant Baptist Church, established Seattle Bible Institute, and broadcast his teachings via his *Kenyon's Church of the Air* radio program. He was not a Pentecostal, but "in his later years he visited Pentecostal meetings and was invited to speak at Aimee Semple McPherson's famous Angelus Temple in Los Angeles. Although he died just after the end of the Second World War, many of the prominent healing revivalists of the post-war years were clearly influenced by him and quoted his work."[49] Trace the doctrinal pedigree of any Word of Faith teacher, and you will find a line that goes back to E. W. Kenyon.

Kenyon's teaching was seriously aberrant on several levels. In his preaching and teaching, he blended core elements of New Thought philosophy with Christian theology—asserting that people can change their physical circumstances simply by making a "positive confession of the word of God."[50] For example, to be healed, believers merely need to declare they already are healed. As Kenyon explained it, "Confession always goes ahead of healing. Don't watch symptoms, watch the word, and be sure that your confession is bold and vigorous. Don't listen to people. . . . It is God speaking. You are healed. The word says you are. Don't listen to the senses. Give the word its place."[51] Only those who make a *positive* confession can expect positive results. Conversely, those who utter words of pessimism are doomed to failure.

To cite from Kenyon again, "You will seldom rise above your words. If you talk sickness you will go to the level of your conversation. If you talk weakness and failure you will act it. You keep saying, 'I can't get work,' or 'I can't do this,' and your words react to your body. Why is this? It is because you are a spirit being. You are not a physical being. Basically you are a spirit and spirit registers words just as a piece of blotting paper takes ink."[52] By emphasizing the creative power of words and the notion that disease is spiritual, not physical, Kenyon provided the basic premise for later Word of Faith theology.[53]

Kenyon's teachings also laid the foundation for the Word of Faith emphasis regarding material prosperity. For him, the gospel not only offered the hope of future reward in heaven but also promised material blessing on earth, here and now. He wrote, "The value of Christianity is what we get out of it. *We are Christians for what we can get in this life*, and we claim a hope of a world to come. . . . We also *demand* that the God we serve and worship shall hear our petitions, protect us in danger, comfort us in sorrow."[54] According to Kenyon, "God never planned that we should live in poverty, physical, mental or spiritual. He made Israel go to the head of the nations financially. When we go into partnership with Him, and we learn His ways of doing business, we cannot be failures. . . . He will give you the ability to make your life a success."[55] If such statements sound eerily similar to the modern drivel pumped out by prosperity preachers and mainline televangelists, it should. They got their material from Kenyon.

His novel ideas soon infiltrated the Charismatic Movement, where they gave birth to the charismatic Word of Faith Movement. As Dennis Hollinger notes, "Various Pentecostal healing revivalists of the 1940s and 1950s had read Kenyon's works and at times quoted from him."[56] Faith healers like William Branham and Oral Roberts laid a foundation on which the prosperity gospel might be received within charismatic circles.[57] But it was Kenneth Hagin, widely known as the "father of the Word of Faith Movement," who popularized Kenyon's work—even plagiarizing large sections of Kenyon's writings in his own books.[58] Subsequent prosperity preachers—from Kenneth Copeland to Benny Hinn to Creflo Dollar—have all been influenced by Hagin. And as we saw in the previous chapter, the prosperity gospel has become *the dominant force* in modern Pentecostal and charismatic circles.

In the same way that Charles Parham's personal character casts a dark shadow of suspicion over the beginnings of the Pentecostal Movement, E. W. Kenyon's incorporation of New Thought principles betrays the true origins of the Word of Faith Movement and the prosperity gospel. For Parham, who expected to speak in authentic foreign languages, his initial experience was a counterfeit. For Kenyon, who integrated metaphysical philosophy into his sermons, his resulting theology was cultic. The Word of Faith teachers who follow in Kenyon's footsteps owe their ancestry to men like Phineas P.

Quimby—meaning their theology belongs to the same family as Christian Science, Theosophy, Mesmerism, Science of the Mind, Swedenborgianism, and New Thought metaphysics. The resulting prosperity gospel is a mongrel blend of neo-Gnostic dualism, New Age mysticism, and shameless materialism. It is a "destructive heresy" (2 Peter 2:1) that claims health and wealth while leaving its victims morally destitute and spiritually bankrupt.

Why focus on the contributions of Charles Parham and E. W. Kenyon? The answer is simple. These two men are responsible for the theological foundations upon which the entire charismatic system is built. They represent its historic roots. As the founder and theological architect of Pentecostalism, Parham articulated the principles and interpreted the experiences that sparked the modern Charismatic Movement; thus his errors and failures call into question the foundation on which the entire system is built. As the grandfather of the Word of Faith Movement, Kenyon provided later prosperity preachers with a recipe for doctrinal poison. His connection to the metaphysical cults explains the sugarcoated corruption inherent in the popular messages of today's televangelists.

A New Awakening?

In spite of its dubious beginnings, the modern Charismatic Movement has mushroomed into a massive entity. Its unprecedented growth has caused some observers to declare it a "new Reformation." In the words of one scholar, "Christianity is living through a reformation that will prove even more basic and more sweeping than the one that shook Europe during the sixteenth century.... The present reformation is shaking foundations more dramatically than its sixteenth-century predecessor, and its results will be more far-reaching and radical." [59] Another author similarly exclaims, "We are now in the midst of one of the most dramatic shifts in Christianity since the Reformation. Christianity is on the move and is creating a seismic change that is changing the face of the whole Christian movement." [60]

Others have more modestly labeled the modern Charismatic Movement a new Great Awakening. As Vinson Synan explains, "Some historians speak of the Azusa Street Revival of 1906–1909 as the 'Fourth Great Awakening.' More than a million Pentecostal congregations were brought into being around the world as a result of this historic revival. Also proceeding from the Pentecostal Movement was the Charismatic Renewal Movement; it began in 1960 and extended the 'Holy Spirit Renewal' to both Protestant and Catholic mainline churches in all parts of the world."[61] It is not uncommon for charismatics to make connections between their movement and the Great Awakening of the eighteenth century.[62] In part, this is due to the popularity of the New England revival, which took place in the late 1730s and early 1740s under the leadership of notable preachers and theologians like George Whitefield and Jonathan Edwards.

But parallels are also drawn with the emotional outbursts that sometimes characterized the eighteenth-century revival meetings.[63] During the Great Awakening, "people wept in repentance for their sins, some shouted for joy at having been pardoned, and a few were so overwhelmed that they fainted."[64] In some cases, the outbursts were even more extreme. As Douglas Jacobsen explains, "During the Great Awakening that took place in colonial America, people sometimes shook with convulsions, cried out with animal-like grunts and shrieks, or fell into trance-like states. . . . These kinds of physical manifestations of spiritual struggle and release were not invented by pentecostals; spiritual physicality is part of the longer history of revivalism."[65]

Understandably, many of the New England Puritans were skeptical of the revival because of the emotionalism that seemed to accompany it. Among them was a Boston pastor, Charles Chauncy, who complained that "religion, of late, has been more a commotion in the passions, than a change in the temper of the mind."[66] In his 1742 sermon "Enthusiasm Described and Cautioned Against," Chauncy railed against the Great Awakening, arguing that the revival had exchanged true spirituality for unrestrained sensationalism. His later book, *Seasoned Thoughts on the State of Religion in New England*, echoed those same themes, condemning what he considered to be the religious excess that took place in revival meetings.

Jonathan Edwards, an avid supporter of the Great Awakening, was well aware of the concerns raised by Charles Chauncy and other "old light" Puritans. In July 1741, when Edwards preached his most famous sermon, "Sinners in the Hands of an Angry God," the response of the crowd was so intense he couldn't even finish his message. As George Marsden reports, "The tumult became too great as the audience was overcome by screaming, moanings, and crying out: 'What shall I do to be saved? Oh I am going to Hell. Oh what shall I do for Christ?'"[67]

Just a couple of days earlier, Edwards preached at a communion service in Suffield, Connecticut. The response was equally emotional. "A visitor who arrived after the sermon said that from a quarter-mile away he could hear howling, screeching, and groaning 'as of women in the pains of childbirth' as people agonized over the states of their souls. Some fainted or were in trances; others were overcome with extraordinary bodily shaking. Edwards and others prayed with many of the distraught and brought some to 'different degrees of peace and joy, some to rapture, all extolling the Lord Jesus Christ' and urged others to come to the Redeemer."[68]

In defending the Great Awakening from its critics, Edwards recognized he needed to address their concerns about these kinds of emotional outbursts. He did so in the late summer of 1741, dealing directly with the topic in a commencement message he delivered at his alma mater, Yale College.[69] In his message, which was later published as *The Distinguishing Marks of a Work of the Spirit of God*, Edwards explained that the legitimacy of a revival could not be determined on the basis of emotional responses:

> Edwards argued with his usually lucid logic that intense physical phenomena such as "tears, trembling, groans, loud outcries, agonies of body or the failing of bodily strength" did not prove anything one way or the other about the legitimacy of a revival. He did not think that a time of extraordinary gifts of the Holy Spirit had arrived, so he denied (contrary both to some radicals of his day and to later Pentecostals) that ecstatic signs were the best evidence of a true outpouring of the Holy Spirit. At the same time, he insisted, neither were overwhelming emotional outbursts evidences *against* the presence of the Holy Spirit. . . . The real tests or "distinguishing marks" of a genuine

work of the Spirit of God had nothing to do with such dramatic effects or lack thereof. Rather, these tests were found in the changed lives of those who were now living according to the dictates of the gospel and manifested the traits and virtues of true Christians.[70]

Finding his "distinguishing marks" in the first epistle of John, Edwards contended that a true work of the Holy Spirit can only be measured on the basis of biblical criteria. Emotional experiences may be powerful, but they are no proof that God is truly at work.[71] After all, Edwards recognized that "enthusiasm often spread even when evangelists proclaimed false doctrine. And Satan could simulate true awakenings."[72]

As Edwards articulated genuine signs of the Spirit's work, he also delineated "negative signs," or false positives—signs that *might* accompany a true work of God but could also be fabricated by hypocrites.[73] Edwards placed emotional outbursts and physical responses to preaching in that nondeterminative category: by themselves, such phenomena simply do not prove the legitimacy of a revival.[74]

How, then, can one discern a true revival from a false one? Or, more directly, what differentiates a true work of the Spirit from a counterfeit? The answer, Edwards contended, is found by "testing the spirits." Borrowing that phrase from 1 John 4:1, the Puritan theologian extracted five principles from the fourth chapter of John's epistle, and thereby developed a distinctly biblical grid that can be applied to any supposed work of God.[75]

Thus, Edwards evaluated the experiences of his day through the lens of Scripture, bringing biblical principles to bear on the biggest religious controversy of that time period. For that reason, his approach provides a helpful pattern for us to consider. As R. C. Sproul and Archie Parrish explain:

> When signs of revival appear on the landscape of history, one of the first questions that is raised is that of authenticity. Is the revival genuine, or is it a mere outburst of superficial emotion? Do we find empty enthusiasm backed by nothing of substance, or does the enthusiasm itself signal a major work of God? In every recorded revival in church history, the signs that follow it are

mixed. The gold is always mixed with dross. Every revival has its counterfeits; distortions tend to raise questions about the real.

This problem certainly attended the eighteenth-century Great Awakening in New England, in which Jonathan Edwards was a key figure. His *Distinguishing Marks* provides a careful analysis of that revival, noting its substance as well as its excesses. But the Puritan divine's study of the matter has more relevance than its application to that singular awakening. It provides a map to follow for all such periods of revival and for that reason is of abiding value for us today.[76]

In Jonathan Edwards's day, American Christians were trying to determine whether the Great Awakening was a true work of the Holy Spirit. Edwards responded by searching the Scriptures in order to make such an evaluation. He expressed his goal like this: "In the apostolic age there was the greatest outpouring of the Spirit of God that ever was. But as the influences of the true Spirit abounded, counterfeits also abounded. The devil was abundant in mimicking both the ordinary and extraordinary influences of the Spirit of God. This made it very necessary that the church of Christ should be furnished with some certain rules—distinguishing and clear marks—by which she might proceed safely in judging of the true from the false. The giving of such rules is the plain design of 1 John 4, where this matter is more expressly and fully treated than anywhere else in the Bible. In this extraordinary day, when there is so much talk about the work of the Spirit, we must carefully apply these principles."[77]

Similarly, many believers today wonder whether the modern Charismatic Movement represents a true work of the Holy Spirit. As we have seen in this chapter, the historic roots of the movement leave much to be desired. But what about its fruit (cf. Matt. 7:15–20)?

Jonathan Edwards went to the Word of God to make his evaluation. Because the Spirit-inspired Scriptures are timeless, we can use those same biblical truths to evaluate the modern Charismatic Movement. In the following chapters, we will consider the fivefold test Edwards derived from 1 John 4— allowing the principles of God's Word to help us answer the question: *Does the modern Charismatic Movement represent a true work of the Holy Spirit?*

THREE

TESTING THE SPIRITS (PART I)

The New Testament is filled with dire warnings about false teachers and the need for every believer to exercise spiritual discernment. In the Sermon on the Mount, our Lord warned His listeners, "Beware of false prophets, who come to you in sheep's clothing, but inwardly they are ravenous wolves" (Matt. 7:15). The apostle Paul echoed those words in his address to the Ephesian elders: "After my departure savage wolves will come in among you, not sparing the flock. Also from among yourselves men will rise up, speaking perverse things, to draw away the disciples after themselves" (Acts 20:29–30). Similarly, Peter told his readers to be on guard against "false teachers . . . who will secretly bring in destructive heresies" and introduce error into the church (2 Peter 2:1).

False teachers posed a serious threat to the health and unity of the church from the start. We tend to think of the early church as pure and pristine, but heresy began to infest the church in her infancy. The threat of false doctrine was a constant theme in apostolic teaching. Jesus Himself instructed believers to take special care in evaluating any spiritual message or self-appointed messenger who claimed to speak for God. Speaking of fraudulent prophets, Jesus told the crowds in Matthew 7:16, "You will know them by their fruits." The letters of 2 Peter and Jude delineate what those fruits are—including the love of money, sexual sin, arrogance, hypocrisy, and aberrant theology.

In the context of evaluating messages that purport to be prophetic, Paul commanded the Thessalonians to "test all things; hold fast what is good. Abstain from every form of evil" (1 Thess. 5:21–22). Novel doctrines, ostentatious self-promotion, and claims of fresh revelation from God (all quite common characteristics of the Charismatic Movement) are the particular signs of a false teacher. The claim that some new teaching comes from God is absolutely essential for the success of any heretic's agenda. Thus, it is equally essential that believers exercise biblical discernment in recognizing lies. If Christians fail in this regard, they demonstrate the danger of their immaturity—allowing themselves, "like children," to be "tossed to and fro and carried about with every wind of doctrine, by the trickery of men, in the cunning craftiness of deceitful plotting" (Eph. 4:14).

The apostle John penned his first epistle more than half a century after Jesus preached the Sermon on the Mount and several decades after Paul wrote his letters. But nothing had changed. False teachers still posed a major threat to the church. So John encouraged his readers to know and love the truth while simultaneously warning them to guard against the deceptive and destructive doctrines of false prophets.

In 1 John 4:1–8, the apostle outlined a strategy by which believers can become skilled at differentiating between the true work of the Spirit and the counterfeit ministries of false prophets. Though written in the first century, the principles presented in these verses are timeless. They are especially pertinent at a time when so many so-called Christian leaders and religious media outlets are happy to blend truth with errors of all kinds and sell it as God's Word.

The chapter begins with these words: "Beloved, do not believe every spirit, but test the spirits, whether they are of God; because many false prophets have gone out into the world" (1 John 4:1). The Greek word translated *test* was used in ancient times to refer to the metallurgical process of assaying ore to determine its purity and value. Precious metals were tested in a crucible or a furnace (Prov. 17:3), subjected to intense heat that would reveal and burn away dross—worthless matter and impurities that might be mixed with the metal. In a similar way, believers are continually to "test the spirits"—evaluating ministers, their messages, and the animating principles of every teaching to discern between that which is truly valuable and that which is counterfeit.

In verses 2–8, John follows his admonition to *test the spirits* with a fivefold outline for assessing the true nature of any teaching. More than sixteen hundred years after the apostle John died, Jonathan Edwards studied this passage and applied its principles to the Great Awakening. As we have seen, he did not defend the American revival on the basis of its popularity or the emotional enthusiasm it produced. Rather, he allowed the test of Scripture to determine a right response to the spiritual phenomena of his day. Like Edwards, believers today have but one sure standard by which to evaluate contemporary spiritual experiences, including the claims and practices of the modern Charismatic Movement. Only that which holds up to the scrutiny of Scripture can be embraced, while that which falls short must be confronted and rejected. Nothing less is the duty of every pastor and teacher as well as the responsibility of every true believer.

We might frame these tests from 1 John 4:2–8 in the form of five questions: (1) Does the work exalt the true Christ? (2) Does it oppose worldliness? (3) Does it point people to the Scriptures? (4) Does it elevate the truth? (5) Does it produce love for God and others? These are the tests Jonathan Edwards applied to the spiritual revival of the Great Awakening. In this chapter and the next, we will examine the modern Charismatic Movement in light of these same principles.

THE FIRST TEST: DOES IT EXALT THE TRUE CHRIST?

As Jonathan Edwards studied John's first epistle, he identified the initial truth of 1 John 4:2–3, namely that *a true work of the Spirit exalts the true Christ.* In contrast to false prophets, those who are truly empowered by the Holy Spirit place the primary emphasis on the person and work of the Lord Jesus Christ. Thus, a true work of the Spirit shines the spotlight on the Savior, pointing to Him in an accurate, exalting, and preeminent manner. False teachers, by contrast, diminish and distort the truth about Him.

One of the heresies popular in John's day attacked the biblical doctrine of Christ's incarnation by denying Jesus possessed a physical human body. That misguided notion, known as Docetism (from a Greek word meaning *appearance*), taught that the Lord's body was merely an illusion. While that may sound strange to modern ears, it thrived at a time when widespread Greek philosophy asserted that the material universe was evil and only spiritual realities were good. Hence, according to Docetism, Jesus could not have had an actual body or He would have been tainted by evil.

The teachings of Docetism accommodated Greek dualism perfectly. But they were completely at odds with the biblical truth about Christ and His gospel.[1] Recognizing the danger of Docetism, the apostle John exposed it for what it really was—a satanic deception. He wrote, "By this you know the Spirit of God: every spirit that confesses that Jesus Christ has come in the flesh is from God; and every spirit that does not confess Jesus is not from God" (1 John 4:2–3 NASB). The apostle's point was unmistakable: if someone preaches a false version of Jesus (like the one found in Docetism), that person shows himself to be a false prophet whose ministry does not come from God.

From this passage, Jonathan Edwards articulated the broader principle— namely, that a true work of the Spirit always and necessarily points people to the truth about the Lord Jesus Christ. Commenting on those verses, Edwards wrote, "When that spirit that is at work amongst a people is observed to operate after such a manner, as to raise their esteem of that Jesus that was born of the Virgin, and was crucified without the gates of Jerusalem; and seems more to confirm and establish their minds in the truth of what the Gospel declares to us of his being the Son of God, and the Saviour of men; 'tis a sure sign that that spirit is the Spirit of God."[2] By contrast, those ministries that distract people away from Christ, or distort the truth of His nature and gospel, or seek to diminish His glory are certainly *not* empowered by the Holy Spirit.

As Edwards went on to explain:

[T]he person that the Spirit gives testimony to, and to whom he raises their esteem and respect, must be that Jesus that appeared in the flesh, and not another Christ in his stead; not any mystical, fantastical Christ; such as the light within, which the spirit of the Quakers extols, while it diminishes their esteem of, and dependence upon an outward Christ, or Jesus as he came in the flesh, and leads them off from him; but the spirit that gives testimony for that Jesus, and leads to him. . . . The Devil has the most bitter and implacable enmity against that person [of Christ], especially in his character of the Saviour of men; he mortally hates the story and doctrine of his redemption; he never would go about to beget in men more honorable thoughts of him, and so to incline them more to fear him, and lay greater weight on his instructions and commands.[3]

The devil seeks to twist, confound, and suppress the truth about the Lord Jesus; he wants to draw people's attention away from the Savior by any means possible. A true work of the Spirit does exactly the opposite: it points people to the biblical Christ and affirms the truth of His gospel.

A True Work of the Spirit Points People to Christ

The glorious priority of the Holy Spirit is to point people to the Lord Jesus Christ. As Jesus told His disciples, "But the Helper, the Holy Spirit, whom the Father will send in My name, He will teach you all things, and bring to your remembrance all things that I said to you. . . . He will glorify Me, for He will take of what is Mine and declare it to you" (John 14:26; 16:14). The Spirit's work is always centered on the Savior. Any ministry or movement He empowers will share that same priority and clarity.

In contrast to this, an emphasis on the person and work of Christ is not the defining feature of the Charismatic Movement—where an intense fixation on a caricature of the blessing and gifting of the Holy Spirit has instead taken center stage. As charismatic authors Jack Hayford and David Moore affirm, "In the Pentecostal potpourri only one thing is the same for all: *the passion they have to experience the presence and power of the Holy Spirit.* This is the common denominator. This emphasis on the Holy Spirit, the third person of the Trinity, is what defines the 'charismatic century.'"[4] Ironically, they celebrate a misplaced priority. While claiming to honor the Holy Spirit, charismatics generally ignore the very purpose of the Spirit's ministry—which is to draw all attention to the Lord Jesus. As Steve Lawson rightly observes, "The Holy Spirit's desire is that we be focused on Jesus Christ, not Himself. That *is* the Spirit's chief ministry. He is pointing us to Jesus. Bringing Christ more clearly into focus. When the Holy Spirit becomes an end in Himself, then we have misunderstood His ministry."[5]

Within charismatic circles, a proper focus on Christ is obscured by a preoccupation with alleged spiritual gifts and supernatural empowerment.[6] Listen to the typical charismatic and you might think the Holy Spirit's work is to manifest Himself and call attention to His own works. In the words of Kenneth D. Johns, a former Pentecostal, many charismatic churches "are *Spirit-centered* rather than *Christ-centered*."[7] Reflecting on his own experiences in the movement—with phenomena like the Jericho March, speaking in tongues, and being slain in the Spirit—Johns notes:

> In each case they were thrust upon us as the "sovereign moving of the Spirit" and as a way to receive the power of the Holy Spirit. In achieving these experiences we were exhorted to "yield to the Spirit," "release the Spirit's power in us," "feel his presence and anointing moving upon us," "hear his voice anew and afresh." Jesus was pushed into the background as we tried to have an "experience" of the Spirit.
>
> We were being urged to be Holy Spirit–centered instead of Jesus-centered. The result of this skewed message was an over-emphasis on emotional feelings and an exaggeration of expectations, as though we could lead supernatural lives in which miracles would overcome all negative circumstances. We were told that if we could get to a state of "Spirit-fullness" we would have supernatural power.[8]

Another author similarly recalls it was "profoundly easy to become drunk on God's power—to become obsessed with the miraculous, fixated with spiritual gifting—and lose sight of Jesus Christ in the process."[9]

Such testimonies suggest Ronald Baxter is right when he asks, "What kind of union does the charismatic movement produce? It is one which replaces Christ with an emphasis on the Holy Spirit."[10] Even some charismatic authors, in moments of candor, have acknowledged that their movement is out of balance in its fixation on "experiencing" the Spirit.[11] For example, the Pentecostal pioneer and patriarch Donald Gee, at the end of his life, lamented the fact that "after sixty-five years of history (1966), the Pentecostal people, in large part, still exhibited an obsession toward the emotional, the spectacular, and sign-seeking."[12] Half a century later, that obsession is more unbridled than ever.

All this calls into question the foundational premise of the Charismatic Movement: If "the Holy Spirit calls attention to neither Himself nor to man, but focuses all attention on the Lord Jesus Christ and what God has done in and through His Son,"[13] then why isn't the self-proclaimed *movement of the Spirit* defined by that same attribute?[14] Charismatics want to put the spotlight on the Holy Spirit—or at least their impersonation of Him.[15] But the Holy Spirit desires to put the spotlight on the true person and work of Jesus Christ. As the Lord told His disciples in the Upper Room, the Spirit would be sent in *His name*, to remind them of *His teachings*, and to bear testimony to *His work* (John 14:26; 15:26). The Spirit does not speak on His own authority, nor does He draw attention to Himself—rather, He desires to glorify the Son (John 16:13–14). The famed Puritan Matthew Henry summed it up like this: "The Spirit came not to erect a new kingdom, but to glorify Christ."[16] More recently, Kevin DeYoung described the Spirit's role this way:

> Exulting in Christ is evidence of the Spirit's work! The focus of the church is not on the dove but on the cross, and that's the way the Spirit would have it. As J. I. Packer puts it, "The Spirit's message to us is never, 'Look at me; listen to me; come to me; get to know me,' but always, 'Look at *him*, and see *his* glory; listen to *him*, and hear *his* word; go to *him*, and have life; get to know *him*, and taste his gift of joy and peace.'"[17]

The Spirit works in the church so that men might see Jesus as Lord, recognizing His authority and submitting to His will (1 Cor. 12:3; Phil. 2:9–13).[18] Thus, a true work of the Spirit directs people first and foremost to exalt Christ as Lord of all and give their attention and affection to Him. The Spirit is most glorified when we honor the Son.

The Holy Spirit not only directs our attention to the Lord Jesus; He also conforms us to Christ's image. As theologian Bruce Ware explains, "Clearly the Spirit's central focus and unfailing activity is to bring honor and glory to Christ. . . . The Spirit works in believers, then, to accomplish the work of the Father, to make his children more and more like Jesus his Son. What does the Spirit do to cause us to be more like Christ? According to 2 Corinthians 3:18, the Spirit focuses our attention on the beauty of the glory of Christ, and by this we are compelled to become more and more like him."[19] By the Spirit's power, believers are directed to behold the glory of the Lord Jesus, and as a result they are transformed into His image. Nothing that distracts from that Christ-centered focus can be rightly attributed to the Spirit's work. Instead it grieves Him.

Perhaps no one stated that point more clearly than the renowned British preacher of the early twentieth century David Martyn Lloyd-Jones. In an extended section, Lloyd-Jones declared:

> The Spirit does not glorify Himself; He glorifies the Son. . . . This is, to me, one of the most amazing and remarkable things about the biblical doctrine of the Holy Spirit. The Holy Spirit seems to hide Himself and to conceal Himself. He is always, as it were, putting the focus on the Son, and that is why I believe, and I believe profoundly, that the best test of all as to whether we have received the Spirit is to ask ourselves, what do we think of, and what do we know about, the Son. Is the Son real to us? That is the work of the Spirit. He is glorified indirectly; He is always pointing us to the Son.
>
> *And so you see how easily we go astray and become heretical if we concentrate overmuch, and in an unscriptural manner, upon the Spirit Himself.* Yes, we must realize that He dwells within us, but His work in dwelling within us is to glorify the Son, and to bring to us that blessed knowledge of the Son and of His wondrous love to us. It is He who strengthens us with might in the inner man (Eph. 3:16), that we may know this love, this love of Christ.[20]

Sadly, it is at this point so many in the Charismatic Movement *actually have* gone astray. They think they are exalting the Spirit by making His gifts and blessings the focal point. In reality the opposite is true. To truly honor the Spirit, the attention must be on Christ. As theologian James Montgomery Boice explained, "If we are told that the Holy Spirit will not speak of himself but of Jesus, then we may conclude that any emphasis upon the person and work of the Spirit that detracts from the person and work of Jesus Christ is not the Spirit's doing. In fact, it is the work of another spirit, the spirit of antichrist, whose work is to minimize Christ's person (1 John 4:2–3). Important as the Holy Spirit is, he is never to preempt the place of Christ in our thinking."[21]

Pastor Chuck Swindoll is even more explicit in this regard: "Mark it down: *the Spirit glorifies Christ.* I'll go one step further: If the Holy Spirit Himself is being emphasized and magnified, He isn't in it! *Christ* is the One who is glorified when the Spirit is at work. He does His work behind the scenes, never in the limelight."[22] When spiritual gifts, miraculous power, or promises of health and wealth are put front and center, the focus is directed away from Jesus Christ. That kind of diversion is not the Holy Spirit's doing.

Pastor Dan Phillips makes the point succinctly:

Show me a person *obsessed* with the Holy Spirit and His gifts (real or imagined), and I will show you a person *not* filled with the Holy Spirit.

Show me a person focused on the person and work of Jesus Christ—never tiring of learning about Him, thinking about Him, boasting of Him, speaking about and for and to Him, thrilled and entranced with His perfections and beauty, finding ways to serve and exalt Him, tirelessly exploring ways to spend and be spent for Him, growing in character to be more and more like Him—and I will show you a person who *is* filled with the Holy Spirit.

We should learn what the Bible says about the Holy Spirit. We should teach what the Bible says about the Holy Spirit. We should seek to live lives full of the biblically defined ministry of the Holy Spirit.

But we should never lose sight of this: To the degree that we are filled with the Holy Spirit, we will be targeted on, focused on, the person of the Lord Jesus Christ.[23]

To be Spirit-filled is to be Christ-centered (Heb. 12:2). The Holy Spirit draws our attention to the Savior. That is His primary objective. Any movement that deters from that priority betrays the fact that it is not empowered by the third member of the Trinity.

A True Work of the Spirit Affirms the Truth About Christ

When the Holy Spirit draws our attention to the Lord Jesus Christ, He always presents the Savior in a way that is biblically accurate. Because He is the *Spirit of truth* (John 15:26), His testimony concerning the Lord Jesus Christ always accords with the truth of the Word, which the Holy Spirit Himself inspired. It was He who moved the Old Testament prophets to foretell Messiah's coming (2 Peter 1:21). As the apostle Peter explained in 1 Peter 1:10–11, "Of this salvation the prophets have inquired and searched carefully, who prophesied of the grace that would come to you, searching what, or what manner of time, the Spirit of Christ who was in them was indicating when He testified beforehand the sufferings of Christ and the glories that would follow." The Lord Jesus Christ is the theme of all Scripture (John 5:39), and the Holy Spirit uses the Word of God to point us directly to the glory of Jesus Christ.

Any ministry or message that does not present Jesus Christ in a biblically accurate way is not a true work of the Spirit. That was the apostle John's point when he denounced the false "christ" of Docetism. Jonathan Edwards found similar application in 1 John 4:2–3.[24] As noted earlier, Edwards emphatically rejected "mystical, fantastical" versions of Christ, "such as the 'inner light' of the Quakers." Such imaginations are not reflective of the true Savior. Any movement that presents a warped view of Jesus Christ does *not* represent a true work of the Holy Spirit. Instead, it originates from the spirit of antichrist.

Stories about visions of Jesus are commonplace in charismatic circles. Supposedly, He dresses as a fireman,[25] stands over nine hundred feet tall,[26] shows up unexpectedly in the bathroom,[27] dances atop a garbage dump,[28] sits in a wheelchair at a convalescent home,[29] takes long walks on the beach,[30] or appears in any number of overly imaginative ways. But such fanciful experiences cannot be from the Holy Spirit, since they distort the biblical depiction of who the Lord Jesus really is. When the apostle John saw a vision of the risen Christ, he fell to the ground like a dead man (Rev. 1:17). Compare that to modern experiences like the vision recounted by one charismatic author, and the differences are striking: "Shortly after the Holy Spirit revealed Himself, I saw Jesus. Then I asked the Lord to take me to His secret place. I was lying in the grass and asked, 'Jesus, would you lie down next to me?' We were right there, looking into each other's eyes. The Father came, too, and reclined next to Jesus."[31] Charismatic visions like that—which range from sappy emotionalism to bizarre fantasy—may be popular in some churches, but they do not find their source in the Holy Spirit. They neither portray the Lord Jesus with biblical accuracy nor exalt Him as infinitely glorious. By contrast, a true work of the Spirit always does both.

To make matters worse, some charismatic teachers openly espouse gross Christological heresies—including bizarre blasphemies like teaching Jesus did not come to earth as God in human flesh,[32] denying He ever claimed to be God,[33] asserting He took on Satan's sinful nature on the cross,[34] and claiming He died spiritually in hell after He died physically on the cross.[35] Prosperity preacher Kenneth Copeland exhibits the blasphemous and unbiblical way in which Jesus Christ is treated in Word of Faith circles:

> How did Jesus then on the cross say, "My God"? Because God was not His Father any more. He took upon Himself the nature of Satan. And I'm telling you Jesus is in the middle of that pit. He's suffering all that there is to suffer. . . . His emaciated, little wormy spirit is down in the bottom of that thing and the devil thinks he's got him destroyed. But, all of a sudden God started talking.[36]

Creflo Dollar, another Word of Faith advocate, displays similar irreverence by openly questioning the deity of Christ:

> Jesus didn't show up perfect, He grew into his perfection. You know Jesus, in one Scripture in the Bible He went on a journey, and He was tired. You better hope God don't get tired. . . . But Jesus did. If He came as God and He got tired—He says He sat down by the well because He was tired—boy, we're in trouble. And somebody said, 'Well, Jesus came as God.' Well, how

many of you know the Bible says God never sleeps nor slumbers? And yet in the book of Mark we see Jesus asleep in the back of the boat.[37]

Ironically, while casting aspersion on the deity of Christ, Word of Faith teachers simultaneously elevate themselves to the position of being little gods.[38] In the twisted words of Kenneth Copeland, who pretends to speak for Jesus: "Don't be disturbed when people accuse you of thinking you are God. . . . They crucified Me for claiming I was God. I didn't claim that I was God; I just claimed that I walked with Him and that He was in Me. Hallelujah! That's what you're doing."[39] To any true believer, the rank arrogance and gross falsehood inherent in such statements sends shivers down the spine. Only the spirit of antichrist would inspire that kind of blatantly unbiblical teaching. By contrast, a true work of the Holy Spirit points people to the truth about "our great God and Savior Jesus Christ" (Titus 2:13).

Similarly, the Holy Spirit points people to the truth about *the gospel of Jesus Christ*. The Spirit was sent to convict the world of sin and unrighteousness so that sinners might believe in the Lord Jesus (John 16:7–11). The Spirit bears witness to the historical truth of the gospel (Acts 5:30–32) and empowers those who preach its saving message (1 Peter 1:12). Anything that undermines the gospel message is not a true work of the Holy Spirit.

A devaluing of gospel truth is seen in the ecumenical umbrella of the broader charismatic world—which includes Catholic charismatics, Oneness Pentecostals, Word of Faith teachers, and other aberrant groups. The unifying feature that binds the Charismatic Movement together is not the truth of the gospel, but rather ecstatic spiritual experiences and physical phenomena like speaking in tongues. As one author observes, "The fact that [the Charismatic Movement] has flourished within the hierarchical system of the Catholic Church, as well as in extremely informal independent churches, suggests that the experience of the gifts of the Spirit and doctrines such as birth in the Spirit are sufficiently flexible to accommodate many different theological convictions on the spectrum of Christian belief."[40] Because sound doctrine is subjugated to spiritual experience, false forms of the gospel are happily embraced by many within the boundaries of the charismatic world.

The Catholic Charismatic Renewal (or CCR) began in 1967, when a group of students reportedly received the baptism of the Spirit and began speaking in tongues. The movement was soon officially recognized by Pope John Paul II, and expanded quickly with the Catholic Church's blessing. According to Allan Anderson, "By 2000 there were an estimated 120 million Catholic Charismatics, some 11 per cent of all Catholics worldwide and almost twice the number of all the classical Pentecostals combined."[41] Such numbers indicate that more than one-fifth of the global charismatic population consists of Roman Catholics. Though Catholic charismatics hold to Roman Catholic doctrine[42]—including Rome's denial that believers are justified by faith alone, belief in the *ex opere operato* efficacy of the seven Roman sacraments,[43] all the idolatry of the Catholic Mass, and the idolatrous veneration of Mary[44]—they have been openly embraced by many Protestant Pentecostal and charismatic groups.

As T. P. Thigpen explains, "Charismatic Catholics, like others in the pentecostal movement, have come to share a basic experience: an encounter with the Holy Spirit with certain charisms that typically follow. These commonalities have made it possible for Catholics and Protestants to take part in charismatic meetings and even live together in covenant communities from the very beginning of the movement."[45] By way of illustration, consider the following report:

> Ten thousand Charismatics and Pentecostals prayed, sang, danced, clapped and cheered under the common bond of the Holy Spirit during a four-day ecumenical convention last summer. . . . About half the participants at the congress on the Holy Spirit and World Evangelization, held July 26 to 29 in Orlando, Florida, were Catholics. . . . "The Holy Spirit wants to break down walls between Catholics and Protestants," said Vinson Synan, theological dean of Pat Robertson's Regent University, who chaired the congress.[46]

In such cases, sound doctrine has been ignored for the sake of a false unity that is based on shared spiritual experiences rather than biblical truth.[47] But insofar as the Roman Catholic Church teaches a corrupted false gospel (as

Protestants who affirm the authority and sufficiency of Scripture have always emphatically maintained), the spirit behind the Catholic charismatic renewal is not the Holy Spirit.

Equally concerning is Oneness Pentecostalism—a segment of the Charismatic Movement (with some 24 million members worldwide)[48] that denies the doctrine of the Trinity.[49] As William Kay explains, "Among narrowly defined classical Pentecostals in the United States, about 25% are 'Oneness' in their theology. This theology has affinities with modalism in the sense that God is understood to be manifested in three modes (i.e. Father, Son and Spirit) rather than three co-equal and coexistent divine Persons as outlined in the Athanasian creed."[50] In church history, modalism was soundly condemned because it rejected the biblical teaching that the Godhead consists of three distinct persons—the Father, the Son, and the Holy Spirit. Instead, the modalists asserted

> that there is one God who can be designated by three different names— "Father," "Son," and "Holy Spirit"—at different times, but these three are not distinct persons. Instead they are different modes (thus, modalism) of the one God. Thus, God can be called "Father" as the Creator of the world and Lawgiver; he can be called "Son" as God incarnate in Jesus Christ; and he can be called "Holy Spirit" as God in the church age. Accordingly, Jesus Christ is God and the Spirit is God, but they are not distinct persons.[51]

Since the Councils of Nicaea (325) and Constantinople (381), modalism has been universally understood by every major branch of Christianity as heretical—falling outside the boundaries of theological orthodoxy. More important, modalism falls short of the clear teaching of Scripture (cf. Matthew 3:13–17; 28:19; and many other passages).

Another example of charismatic ecumenism is seen in the example set by popular prosperity preacher Joel Osteen. Osteen's doctrine is a shallow, saccharine variety of universalism that stands starkly at odds with everything Scripture says about the supremacy and exclusivity of Christ. When asked if he thought people who refuse to accept Jesus Christ are wrong, Osteen responded with uncertainty and ambiguity: "Well, I don't know if I believe they're wrong. I believe here's what the Bible teaches and from the Christian faith this is what I believe. But I just think that only God will judge a person's heart. I spent a lot of time in India with my father. I don't know all about their religion. But I know they love God. And I don't know. I've seen their sincerity. So I don't know. I know for me, and what the Bible teaches, I want to have a relationship with Jesus."[52] On a different occasion, Osteen was asked if Mormons are true Christians. His answer was equally disappointing: "Well, in my mind they are. Mitt Romney has said that he believes in Christ as his Savior, and that's what I believe, so, you know, I'm not the one to judge the little details of it. So I believe they are."[53]

Osteen's muddled comment about Latter-day Saints introduces an interesting point of discussion—especially since the founders of Mormonism claimed to experience the same supernatural phenomena that Pentecostals and charismatics experience today. At the dedication of the Kirtland Temple in 1836, Joseph Smith reported various types of charismatic phenomena—including tongues, prophecy, and miraculous visions.[54] Other eyewitness accounts of that same event made similar claims: "There were great manifestations of power, such as speaking in tongues, seeing visions, administration of angels";[55] and, "There the Spirit of the Lord, as on the day of Pentecost, was profusely poured out. Hundreds of Elders spoke in tongues."[56] More than half a century before Charles Parham and the Pentecostals spoke in tongues, the Latter-day Saints reported similar outbursts,[57] leading some historians to trace the roots of Pentecostalism back through Mormonism.[58]

Even today, similarities between the two groups have led some to seek for greater unity. In their book *Building Bridges Between Spirit-Filled Christians and Latter-Day Saints*, authors Rob and Kathy Datsko assert, "Although there is an incredible language and culture barrier between LDS [Latter-day Saints] and SFC [Spirit-filled Christians], often these two groups believe many of the same basic doctrines."[59] Though Pentecostalism has traditionally rejected the Latter-day Saints,[60] comments like those made by Joel Osteen suggest that a new wave of ecumenical inclusivism may be on the horizon. It is hardly coincidental that Fuller Theological Seminary, the birthplace of the Third

Wave Movement, is currently leading the campaign for greater unity between Mormons and evangelical Christians.[61]

Another major charismatic distortion of the gospel is found in the health-and-wealth promises of the Word of Faith Movement's prosperity gospel, a deadly error that dominates the Charismatic Movement. As we noted in a previous chapter, prosperity theology is "a defining feature of all Pentecostalism" such that "majorities of Pentecostals exceeding 90 percent in most countries hold to these beliefs."[62] The greedy materialism of the prosperity gospel turns the biblical gospel on its head. The true gospel is an offer of salvation from sin and spiritual death. The prosperity gospel ignores those eternal realities and falsely promises deliverance from temporal problems like financial poverty and physical sickness.

Jesus called His disciples to abandon all, take up their crosses, and follow Him (Luke 9:23). By contrast, the prosperity gospel offers carnal comforts, earthly riches, and worldly success to millions of desperate people who literally buy into it.[63] Whereas the true gospel centers on the glory of God, the prosperity gospel puts man's wants and desires front and center. As one author explains, "The peddlers of this perversion stand guilty of selling, literally, a false gospel—one where they have displaced Christ from the center of the gospel and have exalted the temporary above the eternal."[64]

In the process of trafficking their heretical wares, prosperity preachers have made Christianity a laughingstock in the eyes of the watching world. Perhaps Bruce Bickel and Stan Jantz said it best when they quipped, "The prosperity gospel is Christianity's version of professional wrestling: You know it is fake, but it nonetheless has entertainment value."[65] But unlike professional wrestling, there is nothing truly funny about prosperity theology.[66] It is a deadly and damnable heresy, in which the truth of God's Word is intentionally twisted by spiritual swindlers who will one day be punished for their blasphemous conceit (Jude 13).

If one were to add up the number of people connected to heretical groups like the Catholic Charismatic Renewal, Oneness Pentecostalism, and the Word of Faith Movement (with its gospel of health, wealth, and prosperity), the sum would easily be in the hundreds of millions. Together, these groups represent a vast majority within the modern Charismatic Movement. Although they advocate false forms of the gospel, they are largely accepted within the charismatic world on the basis of shared "spiritual" experiences.

NOT MAKING THE GRADE

As we have seen in this chapter, a true work of the Holy Spirit points people to the truth about Christ. Jonathan Edwards applied that test to the spiritual experiences of his day; and we are wise to do the same in ours. When we evaluate the Charismatic Movement on that basis, we find that it fails this test in at least two important ways.

First, the charismatic obsession with the supposed gifts and power of the Holy Spirit diverts people's attention away from the person and work of Jesus Christ. The Holy Spirit points to Christ, not to Himself. Those who are truly Spirit-filled share that same passion. Second, the movement has allowed false forms of the gospel to thrive openly within its borders—including errors ranging from the works righteousness of Roman Catholicism to the rank materialism of the prosperity gospel. Significantly, these deviations are not relegated to the fringes of the movement. They represent the movement's mainstream.

All this raises a critical question: Can a movement that distracts people's attention away from Christ while simultaneously embracing false forms of the gospel be attributed to the Holy Spirit? Jonathan Edwards would have answered that question with a resounding no.[67] Based on the biblical principle found in 1 John 4:2–3, I would heartily agree with that assessment. The Holy Spirit would never use His gifts to authenticate those who propagate a false gospel or lead people away from the truth about Christ. In the following chapter, we will consider the remaining tests from 1 John 4:2–8, as we continue to investigate the question: *Is the modern Charismatic Movement a true work of the Holy Spirit?*

FOUR

TESTING THE SPIRITS (PART 2)

I t was William Shakespeare, in his famous play *The Merchant of Venice*, who coined the phrase "All that glitters is not gold." Two and a half centuries later, during the California gold rush of the late 1840s, adventurous treasure hunters experienced the truth of that statement firsthand. In their quest for precious metal, gold rushers soon discovered that not everything that sparkled was worth keeping. Rock fissures and streambeds might be teeming with golden flecks yet devoid of anything valuable. The counterfeit shimmer of iron pyrite, a common mineral, quickly earned it the nickname "fool's gold." And any decent prospector had to be able to differentiate the glittery lookalike from the genuine commodity.

Like the rivers and mountains of nineteenth-century California, the contemporary Christian landscape is littered with fool's gold. There is plenty that glitters but is spiritually worthless. In the previous chapter, 1 John 4:1–8 provided five questions Christians can ask when evaluating a spiritual movement: (1) Does the work exalt the true Christ? (2) Does it oppose worldliness? (3) Does it point people to the Scriptures? (4) Does it elevate truth? (5) Does it produce love for God and others? Having already looked at the first of these five, we are now ready to consider the remaining four.

THE SECOND TEST: DOES IT OPPOSE WORLDLINESS?

Ask the average charismatic what the Holy Spirit's influence looks like in his or her life, and you're likely to get one of several answers. The classic Pentecostal will probably emphasize speaking in tongues, being slain in the Spirit, or some other imagined manifestation of miraculous gifts. The mainstream charismatic will likely reflect the teaching of popular televangelists by pointing to a form of faith healing or the hope of a financial windfall. Those in either category might claim to have had an extraordinary encounter with God—such as a revelatory vision, a word of prophecy, or a tingling sensation of supernatural empowerment. Based on such criteria, they identify themselves as Spirit-filled Christians. But what do they mean by that label?

Within a charismatic context, almost any subjective experience is construed as evidence of the Spirit's involvement. Charismatics may *think* they are being filled with the Spirit when they utter nonsensical (and often repetitious) syllables, fall backward in a mindless trance, speak fallible words of so-called prophecy, feel a sensation of emotional electricity, or donate money to their favorite health-and-wealth prosperity gospel preacher. But *none* of those things is any indication of the Holy Spirit's presence. A spirit may be at work in such phenomena, but it is not the Spirit of God.

Despite what is commonly emphasized in charismatic circles, the genuine evidence of the Holy Spirit's influence in a person's life is not material prosperity, mindless emotionalism, or supposed miracles. Rather, it is sanctification: the believer's growth in spiritual maturity, practical holiness, and Christlikeness through the power and leading of the Holy Spirit (as He applies biblical truth to the hearts of His saints). A true work of the Spirit convicts the heart of sin, combats worldly lusts, and cultivates spiritual fruit in the lives of God's people.

In Romans 8:5–11, the apostle Paul divided all people into two fundamental categories: those who walk according to the flesh and those who walk according to the Spirit. People who live according to the flesh pursue the passing pleasures of this world (Rom. 8:5; cf. 1 John 2:16–17). They are characterized by a carnal mind that "cannot please God" (Rom. 8:8). The wickedness of their hearts manifests itself in ungodly behavior—including sexual sin, idolatry, arrogance, and the fruits of the flesh listed in Galatians 5:19–21.

By contrast, those who live by the Spirit set their minds on things above, where Christ is (Col. 3:1–2). Their joy is found in serving the Lord Jesus, and their love for Him is seen in their obedience to Him (cf. John 14:15). They are led by the Spirit and, as a result, the fruit of the Spirit is manifested in their lives (Rom. 8:14; Gal. 5:22–23). Where the Holy Spirit is at work, sinful pursuits, passions, and priorities are rooted out as believers "put to death the deeds of the body" (Rom. 8:13). The Spirit's ministry is utterly opposed to the worldly desires of the flesh. As Paul explains in Galatians 5:16–17, "Walk in the Spirit, and you shall not fulfill the lust of the flesh. For the flesh lusts against the Spirit, and the Spirit against the flesh; and these are contrary to one another."

The apostle John, in the context of testing the spirits, echoed those same biblical truths. Speaking of false prophets, John wrote, "You are from God, little children, and have overcome them; because greater is He who is in you than he who is in the world. They are from the world; therefore they speak as from the world, and the world listens to them" (1 John 4:4–5 NASB). False teachers are characterized by their association with *the world*—a reference to the spiritual system of evil, dominated by Satan, which opposes God and pursues temporal lusts (cf. Eph. 2:1–3; 1 John 5:19). Earlier in his epistle, John denounced *worldliness* with these words: "Do not love the world or the things in the world. If anyone loves the world, the love of the Father is not in him. For all that is in the world—the lust of the flesh, the lust of the eyes, and the pride of life—is not of the Father but is of the world" (1 John 2:15–16; cf. James 4:4).

When a movement is characterized by worldly priorities and fleshly pursuits, it raises serious red flags about the spiritual forces behind it. On the other hand, as Jonathan Edwards observed, "when the spirit that is at work operates against the interests of Satan's kingdom, which lies in encouraging and establishing sin, and cherishing men's worldly lusts; this is a sure sign that it is a true, and not a false spirit."[1] In other words, a true work of the Holy Spirit does not tempt people with empty pursuits or the lusts of the flesh; rather, it promotes personal holiness and resists worldly desires.

Nevertheless, the most visible and obvious appeals of contemporary charismatic theology relentlessly cater to overtly *worldly values*. The main attraction is the fulfillment of carnal desires. From televangelists to faith healers to prosperity preachers, charismatic celebrities brazenly present the lusts of this world as if they were the true end of all religion. Their garish claims and gaudy lifestyles stand in glaring contrast to the biblical standard for church leaders (1 Tim. 3:1–7; Titus 1:5–9).

When compared to Christ and the apostles, the true character of the average charismatic televangelist is immediately exposed. The gaudy, self-indulgent lifestyles of the televangelists is nothing at all like "the Son of Man [who had] nowhere to lay His head" (Luke 9:58). Their obsession with money and the way they fleece their listeners (many of whom live in poverty) contrast starkly with the example of Jesus, who "did not come to be served, but to serve, and to give His life a ransom for many" (Matt. 20:28). The way they market miracles and pander for publicity is the polar opposite of Jesus' style. He frequently instructed those whom He healed to "tell no one what had happened" (Luke 8:56; Matt. 8:4; Mark 7:36). Above all, the tawdry reputations and gross moral failures so common among charismatic charlatans have nothing whatsoever to do with Jesus, "who is holy, harmless, undefiled, separate from sinners, and has become higher than the heavens" (Heb. 7:26).

Within the charismatic paradigm, genuine fruits of the Spirit (such as humility, patience, peace, and a sacrificial commitment to Christ's lordship) are often obscured, replaced by a perverse obsession with physical health, material wealth, and temporal happiness. That emphasis on prosperity theology explains the phenomenal growth of the Charismatic Movement in recent decades—promising unregenerate sinners the things their hearts already desire, and then baptizing those carnal lusts in Christian language as if they represent the good news of Jesus Christ. Although almost nine of every ten Pentecostals live in poverty,[2] the prosperity gospel continues to lure people into the movement. The needier the culture, the easier it is for the prosperity preacher to bilk people:

> Over 90 percent of Pentecostals and Charismatics in Nigeria, South Africa,
> India, and the Philippines believe that "God will grant material prosperity

to all believers who have enough faith." And in every country, significantly more Pentecostals than other Christians believe this. . . . With such a great message, it's no wonder people are flocking to sign up. The prosperity gospel is a divinely guaranteed version of the American dream: a house, a job, and money in the bank. And the global success of the prosperity gospel is the exporting of the American dream.[3]

The prosperity message unashamedly calls people to place their hope in the passing pleasures of this world. Rather than denouncing wrong desires, it glorifies worldly lifestyles, feeds on sinful greed, and makes poppycock promises to desperate people: "Get right with the Lord and he will give you a well-paid job, a nice house and a new car."[4] The prosperity gospel is more morally reprehensible than a Las Vegas casino because it masquerades as religion and comes in the name of Christ. But like the casinos, it attracts its victims with glitzy showmanship and the allure of instant riches. After devouring their last cent, like a spiritual slot machine, it sends them home worse off than when they came.

The subjective and mystical nature of charismatic theology is an ideal incubator for prosperity theology because it allows spiritual swindlers to declare themselves prophets, claim divine anointing, and pretend they speak with God's authority in order to escape biblical scrutiny while fleecing people and peddling aberrant doctrines. As Philip Jenkins explains, "At its worst, the gospel of prosperity permits corrupt clergy to get away with virtually anything. Not only can they coerce the faithful to pay their obligations through a kind of scriptural terrorism, but the belief system allows them to excuse malpractice."[5] Such flagrant corruption has caricatured, stereotyped, and soiled the reputation of evangelical Christianity in general. As a result, the church's witness has been severely hampered, as thinking people reject Christianity not because of the true gospel message but because of the bizarre face it wears in the charismatic media.

Admittedly, financial improprieties and moral failures can surface from time to time even in the soundest of churches. But one would think such scandals ought to occur less frequently, not more so, among those who claim to have reached higher levels of spirituality. Therein lies the heart of the problem. By defining "spirituality" in terms of signs, wonders, and spectacular experiences—and by allowing the gross materialism of the prosperity gospel to thrive within its borders—the Charismatic Movement has neglected the path of true spiritual growth. False standards of spirituality cannot restrain the flesh.

Pentecostalism's founder, Charles Parham (whom we met in chapter 2), was by no means the only prominent charismatic whose moral failures were notorious. The halls of Pentecostal and charismatic history are paved with scandal.

In May 1926, Aimee Semple McPherson—a famous prophetess and founder of the International Church of the Foursquare Gospel—went missing while swimming at a Los Angeles beach. Her sudden disappearance was front-page news in every newspaper in America at the time. Her followers mourned her loss, thinking she had drowned. However, "she reappeared a few weeks later, claiming that she had been abducted and imprisoned in Mexico, had broken free, crossed the desert on foot, and daringly evaded her kidnappers. Investigators knocked holes in the story almost at once, especially when evidence from Carmel, farther up the California coast, showed that she had been enjoying herself in a love nest with an engineer from her own radio station."[6] Though she was never imprisoned, her poorly concocted stories of kidnap and escape, "spiced by the motive of sexual adventure, rendered her a laughing-stock. After a year and more of press scrutiny and legal investigation, Aimee Semple McPherson became that from which no public figure can ever recover momentum—an object of public ridicule."[7]

In the 1970s and '80s, Pentecostal evangelist Lonnie Frisbee became one of the most visible faces of the Jesus Movement. The self-proclaimed prophet—whose life was featured in the Emmy-nominated film *Frisbee: The Life and Death of a Hippie Preacher*—was a pioneer and standout figure in the Jesus Movement of the late 1960s and early 1970s. He was later involved with John Wimber in the Signs and Wonders Movement. He was also instrumental (alongside Chuck Smith and then Wimber) in the early development of both Calvary Chapel and the Vineyard Movement. Frisbee's ministry ended in disgrace when it became widely known that he had been a practicing homosexual for years.

Actually, Frisbee's private lifestyle had been an open secret for many years in the West Coast charismatic community. He would engage in gross promiscuity on Saturday night, and then preach on Sunday morning.[8] When it ultimately became impossible to keep Frisbee's debauchery under wraps, John Wimber "became concerned that it could significantly undermine the Vineyard,"[9] and he removed Frisbee from public ministry in that movement. Frisbee eventually contracted AIDS and died in 1993.[10]

In 1983, Neville Johnson, a prominent Assemblies of God pastor in New Zealand, resigned due to immoral conduct. Taking his charismatic theology to a delusional degree, Johnson claimed he had received special revelation from God indicating his wife would soon die and he would be free to remarry. As a result, Johnson asserted he had been granted special grace allowing him to participate in extramarital affairs.[11]

In 1986, the ministry of faith healer Peter Popoff was debunked on national television. Stage magician and paranormal investigator James Randi discovered that the self-proclaimed prophet was using a nearly invisible wireless earpiece to obtain "revelatory" information about people in the audience. "Popoff's wife mingled throughout the audience and casually talked with various participants. Then, using a portable radio transmitter she would tell her husband (who was wearing a miniature headphone) what to say. Popoff would then announce to thousands of thrilled worshippers the specific name, illness, and address of an actual participant."[12] Randi used a digital scanner to capture Popoff's wife's secret communications with her husband. Then he exposed the fraud on *The Tonight Show Starring Johnny Carson*. Within a year, Popoff had to file for bankruptcy.

But in spite of the biblical requirement for ministers to be above reproach, in the charismatic world gross moral and ethical failure doesn't necessarily mean disqualification from public ministry. In these circles, the reproach of a scandal like that has a shockingly short shelf life. Peter Popoff never even stepped out of public ministry. He weathered the financial crisis. By 1998 the *Washington Post* was reporting he had "repackage[ed] himself for an African American audience" and was "making a robust recovery."[13] Today, more than twenty-five years after being exposed as a fraud on live national television (and despite a string of lesser-known but similar exposés), Peter Popoff Ministries seems to be thriving once more. Its website features testimonials of financial windfalls and miraculous healings.[14] In 2007, the organization brought in $23 million, with Popoff selling packets of "Miracle Spring Water" on his late-night television show.[15]

In 1986 and 1987, Jimmy Swaggart made headlines in the United States when he publicly exposed the adulterous affairs of two fellow televangelists, Marvin Gorman and Jim Bakker. Evidence showed that Jim Bakker, in particular, had paid a church secretary $265,000 to keep her quiet about their illicit tryst. Bakker was subsequently sent to prison when it became clear he had bilked ministry donors out of $158 million. In a bizarre twist of irony, shortly after discrediting Gorman and Bakker, Swaggart himself was caught visiting a prostitute. Swaggart's blubbering confession became one of the iconic moments of '80s television. With a tear-streaked face and quivering chin, he said, "I have sinned against You, my Lord, and I would ask that Your precious blood would wash and cleanse every stain until it is in the seas of God's forgetfulness, never to be remembered against me anymore."[16]

He did not, however, step away from public ministry. In 1991, Swaggart was caught by the California Highway Patrol, driving on the wrong side of the road—again in the company of a prostitute. This time he told his constituents, "The Lord told me it's flat none of your business"—and said God had instructed him not to step down from his pulpit.[17] Today both Swaggart and Bakker are still full-time charismatic televangelists, and they do not lack for enthusiastic followers.

In 1991, Kansas City prophet Bob Jones was publicly disgraced when he allegedly used his "prophetic anointing" to persuade women to disrobe.[18] That same year, ABC News investigated Robert Tilton's ministry, which, at the time, was raking in more than $80 million a year. The investigation found that his ministry threw away the prayer requests it received without reading them, opening the envelopes only long enough to retrieve the money inside.[19]

In 2000, Bishop Clarence McClendon got remarried just seven days after divorcing his wife of sixteen years, amid suspicions he had fathered a child out of wedlock. A Pentecostal megachurch pastor in Los Angeles, McClendon was a prominent member of the International Communion of Charismatic Churches. Despite the scandal, McClendon refused to step down or take any time away from his pulpit. In a statement regarding the divorce, he said, "I have a calling to preach, not to be married. . . . It doesn't affect my ministry."[20]

In early 2002, California-based Pentecostal pastor Roberts Liardon shocked his followers when he admitted to having a homosexual relationship with his church's youth minister, John Carette. Incredibly, Liardon was back in full-time ministry just a short time after the incident.[21] In 2004, Enoch Lonnie Ford, a former employee of Trinity Broadcasting Network, threatened to publish a manuscript detailing his alleged homosexual affair with Paul Crouch, which took place in the 1990s. The *Los Angeles Times* reported Crouch had previously paid $425,000 to Ford to keep him from going public with the story.[22]

In 2005, famous charismatic prophet Paul Cain admitted he had "struggled in two particular areas, homosexuality and alcoholism, for an extended period of time."[23] That same year, a lawsuit was filed against Earl Paulk, founder of the International Charismatic Bible Ministries. A married woman in Paulk's church accused him of inducing her to have a fourteen-year affair with him. According to the woman, Paulk said that those who are spiritually exalted can engage in extramarital sex without committing adultery; he labeled these illicit affairs "kingdom relationships."[24]

In 2006, Ted Haggard—who pastored the charismatic-evangelical New Life Church in Colorado Springs—resigned after it became clear that he had paid a homosexual escort for drugs and sexual favors over a three-year period of time. When interviewed by *GQ* magazine in February 2011, Haggard explained, "I think that probably, if I were 21 in this society, I would identify myself as a bisexual."[25] In 2010, he began a new church plant in Colorado.[26]

In 2008, Pentecostal bishop Thomas Wesley Weeks III admitted to physically assaulting his wife, charismatic "prophetess" Juanita Bynum—who said her husband choked her, pushed her to the ground, and stomped on her in a hotel parking lot. He pleaded guilty and was sentenced to three years of probation.[27] Bynum herself later confessed she struggles with lesbian desires and has engaged in illicit relationships with various women over several years' time.[28]

Also in 2008, faith healer Todd Bentley confessed to an illicit relationship with one of his female staff members. After divorcing his wife, Bentley married the staff member with whom he had been inappropriately involved.[29] That same year, news broke that Australian Pentecostal evangelist Michael Guglielmucci faked claims of battling cancer, in part to cover up symptoms of stress related to a lifelong addiction to pornography. In attempting to convince the world he had cancer, Guglielmucci shaved his head, used an oxygen tank, and created fake e-mails from make-believe medical doctors. He also wrote a hit song entitled "Healer," about how the Lord was helping him cope with his disease.[30]

In 2009, Republican senator Chuck Grassley opened an official probe into the ministry finances of Kenneth Copeland, Creflo Dollar, Benny Hinn, Eddie Long, Joyce Meyer, and Paula White. The investigation was sparked by the lavish lifestyles of these prominent televangelists.[31] But suspected financial impropriety is not the only source of scandal in these ministries. In 2010, multiple lawsuits were filed against Eddie Long on the grounds that he sought homosexual relations with teenage boys in his congregation in exchange for money and other benefits.[32] And in 2011, Creflo Dollar was arrested on charges of choking his fifteen-year-old daughter.[33]

Photographs published in a 2010 issue of the *National Enquirer* showed divorced televangelists Benny Hinn and Paula White holding hands while leaving a hotel in Rome.[34] "The article, which released July 23, claimed the two spent three nights in a five-star hotel Hinn booked under a false name."[35] Rumors quickly circulated that the two were having an affair, though both parties denied the accusations. They insisted, instead, they had come to Rome to make financial donations to the Vatican—as if that might somehow make the scandal seem less raunchy. Two years later, in 2012, Hinn announced that he and his wife, Suzanne, would be getting remarried with Pentecostal patriarch Jack Hayford performing the ceremony. Suzanne had filed for divorce in February 2010, citing irreconcilable differences. Benny later claimed their separation was related to his wife's addiction to prescription drugs.[36]

The examples cited above represent only a handful of the many national and international scandals that continually plague the Charismatic Movement.[37] But they provide sufficient evidence of what *Time* magazine calls "the longtime magnetism between celebrity Pentecostal preachers and scandal."[38] Commenting on similar incidents, J. Lee Grady, an editor for *Charisma* magazine, is forced to admit, "I have no personal vendetta against these people, but I have no problem saying they are the modern counterparts of Nadab and Abihu. They are spiritual hoodlums. They are playing with strange fire. They have no business remaining in ministry, and they will answer to God for the damage they have caused."[39]

Grady is right to be alarmed, but he fails to see these scandals as anything more than a peripheral problem. In reality, they are symptoms of systemic errors. Scandals such as those permeate charismatic history. Trace them to their source and you will discover they are rooted in bad doctrine. Put simply, moral and spiritual failures such as we have chronicled in this chapter are the inevitable consequence of rotten pneumatology—false teaching about the Holy Spirit.

It is impossible to ignore the consistent thread that runs through that long list of scandals: no matter how serious the transgression or how profound the initial public outrage, disqualified pastors within the Charismatic Movement are usually restored as rapidly as possible to their pulpit-thrones—sometimes in just a matter of weeks (and sometimes, even in the worst cases, they are permitted to continue with no interruption at all). This is largely owing to the way in which charismatic congregations are taught to view their leaders as transcendent souls who have elevated connections to God personally and are therefore not subject to or accountable to anyone else on a local level.

As theology professor Chad Brand explains, "Because this person is perceived to have charismatic power or anointing, his or her failure . . . is often easily forgiven and overlooked."[40] After noting the 1975 divorce of John Hagee, the 1979 divorce of Richard Roberts (son of Oral Roberts), and the 2007 divorce of Paula and Randy White, Brand adds, "While these divorces have had ramifications for their ministries, in every case the ministry only flourished afterwards. In most other evangelical traditions, the impact of divorces has been more deeply felt by the ministers in question."[41]

The irony is inescapable: the movement that claims to be most in tune with the Holy Spirit is simultaneously the least concerned about personal holiness and purity at the level where Scripture sets the highest standard—the qualifications for those who preach and teach. Because people rise no higher than their leaders, the assembly is full of the same kinds of sins.

A true work of the Spirit produces holiness in people's lives. When the leadership of a movement is continually stained by scandal and corruption, it calls into question the spiritual forces behind it. The Holy Spirit is actively involved in sanctifying His people—empowering them to combat the flesh while growing in Christlikeness. Unrestrained fleshly desires, on the other hand, are characteristic of false teachers (2 Peter 2:10, 19).

The Third Test: Does It Point People to the Scriptures?

A third distinguishing mark of a true work of the Holy Spirit is that it directs people to the Word of God. As Jonathan Edwards explained, "That spirit that operates in such a manner, as to cause in men a greater regard to the Holy Scriptures, and establishes them more in their truth and divinity, is certainly the Spirit of God."[42] Edwards drew this principle from 1 John 4:6, where the apostle John told his readers, "We are of God. He who knows God hears us; he who is not of God does not hear us. By this we know the spirit of truth and the spirit of error." A true work of the Spirit leads believers to submit to apostolic teaching (i.e., the New Testament) and by extension the entire Bible. He guides them to a greater appreciation and love for the Scriptures. Conversely, false prophets belittle God's Word, adding their own ideas to it and twisting its meaning (cf. 2 Peter 3:16).

The Bible reveals an inseparable connection between the Holy Spirit and the Scriptures that He inspired (2 Peter 1:20–21). The Old Testament prophets were moved by Him to predict the coming of the Lord Jesus Christ (1 Peter 1:10–11; cf. Acts 1:16; 3:18). The apostles were similarly inspired by the Spirit to compose the biblical gospels and to write the epistles of the New Testament (John 14:25–26; 15:26). Speaking of the revelation the Holy Spirit would bring to the apostles, the Lord Jesus explained to them, "I have many more things to say to you, but you cannot bear them now. But when He, the Spirit of truth, comes, He will guide you into all the truth; for He will not speak on His own initiative, but whatever He hears, He will speak; and He will disclose to you what is to come. He will glorify Me, for He will take of Mine and will disclose it to you. All things that the Father has are Mine; therefore I said that He takes of Mine and will disclose it to you" (John 16:12–15 NASB). As the Lord made clear, the Holy Spirit would not speak on His own initiative, but would reveal to them the word of Christ. That promise was fulfilled in the writing of the New Testament.

The Bible is the Holy Spirit's book; He inspired it and He empowers it. It is the primary instrument He uses to convict the world of sin (John 16:8–11; Acts 2:37); to point sinners to the Savior (John 5:39; 1 John 5:6); and to conform believers into the image of their Lord (2 Cor. 3:18; 1 Peter 2:2). Accordingly, the Scriptures are described as "the sword of the Spirit." For believers, that sword is a Spirit-empowered means of defense against temptation (Eph. 6:17); for unbelievers, it is an implement of precision used by the Holy Spirit to pierce hearts of unbelief (Heb. 4:12). A comparison of Ephesians 5:18 with Colossians 3:16 demonstrates that the command to "be filled with the Spirit" is parallel to the command to "let the word of Christ dwell in you richly," since they both produce the same results (cf. Eph. 5:18–6:9; Col. 3:16–4:1).

As one commentator explains, "It is not possible for God's Word to dwell in believers unless they are filled with the Spirit; and conversely, Christians can't be filled with the Spirit without the Word of Christ dwelling in them."[43] Being Spirit-filled starts with being Scripture-saturated; as believers submit themselves to the Word of Christ, they simultaneously come under the sanctifying influence of the Holy Spirit. It is the Spirit who illuminates their hearts so that as they grow in their knowledge of the Lord Jesus, their love for the Savior deepens accordingly (cf. 1 Cor. 2:12–16).

The Holy Spirit would never deter people from reading, studying, and applying the Holy Scriptures—the book that He inspired, empowers, and illuminates for salvation and sanctification. Yet the modern Charismatic Movement drives a wedge between the Bible and its divine Author by endorsing *unbiblical* experiences and espousing *extrabiblical* revelations—as if the

Holy Spirit speaks on His own initiative or operates in the church today in a way contrary to the truth of His Word. Having concocted their own version of the Spirit, charismatics expect Him to speak and act in newfangled ways that are unconnected to Scripture. As a result, biblical revelation is flagrantly demeaned, depreciated, and diminished.

The shocking implication in many charismatic circles is that a serious study of God's Word limits or thwarts the work of the Spirit.[44] But nothing could be further from the truth. Querying the text does not *bypass* the Holy Spirit; it *honors* Him (cf. Acts 17:11). To search the Scriptures so as to discern their accurate meaning is to hear directly from the Holy Spirit, since He is the One who inspired every word.

Rather than instilling a greater appreciation for the Spirit-inspired Scripture, which God exalts as high as His own name (Ps. 138:2), the Charismatic Movement drives people to look for divine revelation in boundless places *outside* of the Bible. The ramifications of that faulty premise are disastrous—destroying the doctrine of Scripture's sufficiency and effectively ignoring the close of the canon. Self-proclaimed apostle and Third Wave architect Peter Wagner provides just one example of those who would brashly question the singular uniqueness of biblical revelation by insisting that divine revelation is still being given today. Wagner writes:

> Some object to the notion that God communicates directly with us, supposing that everything that God wanted to reveal He revealed in the Bible. This cannot be true, however, because there is nothing in the Bible that says it has 66 books. It actually took God a couple of hundred years to reveal to the church which writings should be included in the Bible and which should not. That is extra-biblical revelation. Even so, Catholics and Protestants still disagree on the number. Beyond that, I believe that prayer is two way, we speak to God and expect Him to speak with us. We can hear God's voice. He also reveals new things to prophets as we have seen.[45]

That kind of thinking exposes just how dangerous charismatic thinking can be—when something as fundamental as the closed canon of Scripture is openly questioned, and even implicitly denied. It is no wonder Wagner himself has spent his career as a ubiquitous purveyor of manifold heresies, morphing ever lower as he drifts further and further from the anchor of biblical revelation.[46]

Charismatic author Jack Deere goes so far as to label the sufficiency of Scripture a *demonic* doctrine. In his words,

> In order to fulfill God's highest purpose for our lives we must be able to hear his voice both in the written Word and in the word freshly spoken from heaven. . . . Satan understands the strategic importance of Christians hearing God's voice so he has launched various attacks against us in this area. One of his most successful attacks has been to develop a doctrine that teaches God no longer speaks to us except through the written Word. Ultimately, this doctrine is demonic even [though] Christian theologians have been used to perfect it.[47]

Deere insists Christians *must* seek divine revelation beyond the pages of Scripture. Yet he admits the prophecies of charismatic seers are full of error, and he acknowledges it is well-nigh impossible to interpret extrabiblical messages with any degree of confidence. Deere even concedes, "We may mistake our own thoughts for God's revelation."[48] As we will see in chapter 6, imagined revelations and inaccurate "prophecies" are the stock-in-trade of the Charismatic Movement.

In spite of the severe error and potential damage being done by this supposed new "revelation," some charismatic churches continue to regard modern prophecy as more important than the Bible. As one author notes, "Churches that appeal to new revelations that are often valued over the Bible include the Church of the Living Word, founded by John Robert Stevens, and the United House of Prayer for All People. Stevens teaches that the Bible is outdated and needs to be supplemented by prophecies inspired by the Spirit for our time."[49] Most churches do not go to that extreme, of course. However, such examples represent the logical end of the charismatic insistence that God is giving new revelation to the church today. If the Spirit were still giving divine revelation, why wouldn't we collect and add those words to our Bibles?

The reality is that the modern Charismatic Movement falsely calls itself evangelical because it undermines the authority and sufficiency of Scripture. It is neither orthodox nor truly evangelical to elevate spiritual experiences, including imagined revelations from God, above the Bible. Speaking of his own eyewitness experience at the Transfiguration, the apostle Peter gave this revelation:

> For we did not follow cleverly devised myths when we made known to you the power and coming of our Lord Jesus Christ, but we were eyewitnesses of his majesty. For when he received honor and glory from God the Father, and the voice was borne to him by the Majestic Glory, "This is my beloved Son, with whom I am well pleased," we ourselves heard this very voice borne from heaven, for we were with him on the holy mountain. And we have something more sure, the prophetic word, to which you will do well to pay attention as to a lamp shining in a dark place, until the day dawns and the morning star rises in your hearts. (2 Peter 1:16–19 ESV 2007)

At the Transfiguration, Peter witnessed an unparalleled supernatural spectacle. He had a genuine divine, heavenly experience. Even so, the apostle knew that Scripture ("the prophetic word") is "more sure" than even the most sublime experiences. Peter's point is precisely the issue that many charismatics fail to understand. Human experience is subjective and fallible; only the Word of God is unfailing and inerrant, because its Author is perfect.

Like Peter, the apostle Paul also experienced something incredible. He was taken to heaven, "caught up into Paradise" to encounter that which consisted of "inexpressible words, which it is not lawful for a man to utter" (2 Cor. 12:4). Unlike those today who spin fantastic tales about the afterlife, and even make a career on the lecture circuit talking about what they supposedly saw in heaven, Paul said boasting about his experience was "not profitable" (v. 1) or spiritually beneficial. Why? Because even that true experience could not be verified or repeated. If Paul was going to boast, it would be in the truth of the gospel and in the wonder of his own salvation (Gal. 6:14). In fact, to keep Paul from making too much of real visions and revelations, the Lord gave him a severe "thorn in the flesh, a messenger of Satan to torment [him]—to keep [him] from exalting [himself]" (2 Cor. 12:7 NASB). Rather than boasting about his transcendent experiences, Paul was called to preach the Word of God (2 Tim. 4:2) since the biblical gospel is "the power of God to salvation for everyone who believes" (Rom. 1:16).

Who is the source and power behind biblical revelation? If we look back at Peter's account of the Transfiguration, we see he answers that question just two verses later: "For no prophecy was ever produced by the will of man, but men spoke from God as they were carried along by the Holy Spirit" (2 Peter 1:21 ESV). When we submit to the Word of God as our authority, we are submitting to the Spirit Himself, since He inspired every word it contains. No true work of the Spirit will contradict, devalue, or add new revelation to the Scriptures (cf. Rev. 22:17–19). Instead it will elevate biblical truth in the hearts and minds of believers.

THE FOURTH TEST: DOES IT ELEVATE THE TRUTH?

A fourth and closely related test that ought to be applied to any supposed work of the Holy Spirit is this: Does the work emphasize spiritual truth and doctrinal clarity, or does it create confusion and promote error?

In 1 John 4:6, the apostle John wrote simply, "We know the spirit of truth and the spirit of error." The Holy Spirit, who is defined by truth, stands in stark contrast to the false spirits of delusion who are characterized by error and falsehood. When a spiritual movement is known for defending sound theology, denouncing false teaching, and detesting superficial unity—these are strong indications that it is a genuine work of the Holy Spirit.[50] Conversely, believers should be wary of any religious system that ignores sound doctrine, propagates falsehood, or happily endorses ecumenical compromise.

The sad fact is that biblical truth has never been the hallmark of the Charismatic Movement, where spiritual experience is continually elevated above sound doctrine. As theologian Frederick Dale Bruner explains: "Pentecostalism wishes, in brief, to be understood as experiential Christianity, with its experience culminating in the baptism of the believer in the Holy Spirit evidenced, as at Pentecost, by speaking in other tongues. . . . It is important to notice that it is not the *doctrine*, it is the *experience* of the Holy Spirit which Pentecostals repeatedly assert."[51]

An example of this is seen in the history of Pentecostalism, a movement that made speaking in tongues the centerpiece of its theology (based on an errant view of Spirit baptism). As we saw in chapter 2, when the original Pentecostals studied the text of Scripture, they were convinced that tongues in the Bible were *authentic foreign languages*. But what happened when it became obvious that their modern version of the "gift" did not consist of real languages? If Scripture had been their highest authority, they would have abandoned the practice altogether—recognizing the fact that what they were doing did not match the biblical precedent. Instead, they radically changed their interpretation of the New Testament, manipulating the text in order to justify and preserve a counterfeit. Thus, the clear teaching of Scripture about languages was twisted in order to redefine tongues as *nonsensical gibberish* and thereby fit the modern phenomenon.

At the practical level, Pentecostal churches regularly elevate experience over truth. Unbiblical practices like being slain in the Spirit are promoted, not because they have scriptural warrant, but because it makes people feel good. Women are allowed to be pastors in the church, not because the New Testament permits it (1 Tim. 2:12), but because female leadership has always been a hallmark of the Charismatic Movement. Mindless and out-of-control forms of worship are encouraged, not because the Bible condones them (1 Cor. 14:33), but because emotional fervor is necessary to conjure up ecstasy. Many more examples could be given, all illustrating the fact that within Pentecostalism spiritual experience consistently trumps biblical authority.

As we have already seen, the Charismatic Renewal Movement, which launched itself in the 1960s, is fraught with the same problem—a point that is perhaps most clearly seen in the movement's willingness to gloss over major doctrinal differences for the sake of a superficial unity that is built on nothing but shared experiences.[52] The most egregious example of this experience-driven inclusivism, as previously noted, was the acceptance of Catholic charismatics by the broader Charismatic Movement. As a result, the historic distinctives of Protestant doctrine have been set aside (or deemed insignificant) by many charismatics, simply because their Catholic counterparts have spoken in tongues or embraced other aspects of the charismatic *experience*. Today there are even charismatic Mormons.[53] Regardless of what else they teach, if they have had that experience, they are in.

A casual survey of charismatic television further illustrates the fact that for many charismatics, personal experience trumps propositional truth. I have been waiting for many years to hear a charismatic television host interrupt a guest and say, "That is not true. That is not in the Word of God. We will not accept that. You cannot verify that by Scripture." But that kind of confrontation never happens, no matter what is said. It can be the most bizarre theological assertion, or the most ludicrous misinterpretation of Scripture—where the text is ripped out of its context so that its meaning is hopelessly distorted—yet no one ever stops and says, "Hold it; that's heresy. That is not true."

The absence of doctrinal discernment and theological accountability within charismatic circles has led some observers to voice serious concerns: "The charismatic movement as a whole has yet to integrate the great doctrinal truths of Scripture into the lives of its people. In its great emphasis upon experience with the Holy Spirit, the value of diligent study of theology is often neglected."[54] That is putting it mildly. Doctrinally, the Charismatic Movement reflects the period of the Judges—the time in Israel's history in which "everyone did what was right in his own eyes" (Judg. 21:25). As a result, it is nearly impossible to define the Charismatic Movement doctrinally except by its errors. It resists theological categorization because it has such a wide and growing spectrum of viewpoints—each of which is subject to personal intuition or imagination.

Even charismatic authors acknowledge a common complaint against them is that they "first experience something, then rush to the Scripture after the fact to reach for a rationale for what has happened to them."[55] One such author says it this way: "Do not take control, do not resist, do not analyze; just surrender to His love. You can analyze the experience later; just let it happen."[56] But that is completely backward. We ought to begin with the Word of God, allowing a proper interpretation of the text to govern our experiences. A true work of the Spirit thrives on sound doctrine. It promotes biblical truth; it does not dismiss it or see it as a threat. Once experience is allowed to be the litmus test for truth, subjectivism becomes dominant and neither doctrine nor practice is defined by the divine standard of Scripture.

Charismatics downplay doctrine for the same reason they demean the Bible: they think any concern for timeless, objective truth stifles the work of the Spirit. They envision the Spirit's ministry as something wholly free-flowing, infinitely pliable—so subjective as to defy definition. Creeds, confessions of faith, and systematic theology are seen as narrow, confining, not elastic enough for the Spirit to work within. Acknowledging this tendency within charismatic circles, one author wrote, "A college student once warned me of the 'dangerous doctrine of demons'—his description of systematic theology. 'The Lord has given us the Holy Spirit to interpret Scripture,' he explained. 'Teaching doctrine is Satan's attempt to use our minds to understand the Bible rather than relying on the Holy Spirit.'"[57]

That is a shocking statement. In reality, the only thing good theology stifles is error, which is why sound doctrine is the single greatest antidote to charismatic deviations. Remember, the Holy Spirit is the Spirit of *truth* (John 16:13). Any work of His will elevate biblical truth and sound doctrine in the hearts and minds of His people.

THE FIFTH TEST: DOES IT PRODUCE LOVE FOR GOD AND OTHERS?

Jonathan Edwards articulated a fifth and final test in order to evaluate any spiritual movement: a true work of the Spirit causes people to increase in their love for God and others. Edwards drew this principle from 1 John 4:7–8, where the apostle John wrote, "Beloved, let us love one another, for love is of God; and everyone who loves is born of God and knows God. He who does not love does not know God, for God is love." A primary fruit of the Spirit is *love* (Gal. 5:21), and where true love exists, it is evidence of the Spirit's genuine work.

A true work of the Spirit produces a love for God that expresses itself in sober-minded adoration and praise. *That is the definition of biblical worship.* Worship is an expression of love for God and therefore by its nature engages the soul's passions. Most Christians understand that, at least in a rudimentary way.

But too many seem to think we're not truly worshipping until the human intellect is somehow disengaged. I've heard charismatic preachers urging people to suspend their rational faculties because the Spirit supposedly can't work if we're doing too much thinking. That is a totally unbiblical concept. In authentic worship, thoughts and feelings together—along with *all* our human faculties— are focused on God in pure adoration. That principle is implied in the first and great commandment: "You shall love the Lord your God with all your heart and with all your soul and with all your *mind*" (Matt. 22:37 ESV).

The kind of praise the Father seeks is not a cacophony of mindless pande-monium. Worship is not mere frenzy and feelings. "Those who worship Him must worship in spirit and *truth*" (John 4:24). God "delight[s] in truth in the inward being" (Ps. 51:6 ESV). Therefore true worship (like authentic sanctifi-cation) cannot bypass the mind; it is all about the *renewing* of the mind (Rom. 12:1–2; cf. Eph. 4:23–24). As Jonathan Edwards said, genuine, biblical wor-ship should bring people "to high and exalting thoughts of the divine Being and his glorious perfections [and it] works in them an admiring, delightful sense of the excellency of Jesus Christ."[58] The effect is that we become whole new persons—"renewed in knowledge" (Col. 3:10). Scripture knows nothing of any type of spirituality that bypasses intellect and operates only on feelings.

But charismatic worship services are often characterized by disorder and chaos—the type that does not honor the Lord (1 Cor. 14:33). In the words of a Pentecostal theology professor, "I like to call charismatic worship 'full-body worship,' a worship of heart and mind and soul and strength. We go crazy when we think about all God has done for us and with us. Even crazier than we get for our basketball team!"[59] Tune in to TBN or any charismatic television network, and it won't take long to see examples of irrational and ecstatic phenomena: from speaking gibberish to falling over in a trance to laughing uncontrollably or even barking like dogs.[60]

Far too often, charismatics approach worship and prayer without the use of their minds. They are told things like, "Find a quiet place. Empty your mind. Listen to your breathing, focus on one word, an example would be 'Lord' or another way of focusing is to listen to soft, spiritual music quietly allowing the Holy Spirit to speak to you."[61] They come to associate being filled with the Spirit with mindless possession. In the words of one Pentecostal woman, "I was always embarrassed when the Holy Spirit moved me. I believed people thought I was crazy. It was a very powerful experience. It was as though I totally lost control of my body and something took over my body and I could not do anything to stop it."[62]

One of the most vivid examples of chaotic charismatic worship occurred during the Toronto Blessing of the mid-1990s. Sociology professor Margaret M. Poloma describes her firsthand experience at a worship service held at the Toronto Airport Christian Fellowship in 1995:

> The outbreaks of laughter continued to gather momentum. [Evangelist Byron] Mote proclaimed, "God is throwing one major party." He then opened to the first chapter of Luke, seeming to begin a sermon about Mary, the mother of Jesus. As people continued laughing throughout the auditorium, Mote's speech became slurred. . . . He sat down trying to gain composure, looking like a drunk struggling to keep from falling off the bar stool. Mote soon fell to the floor "drunk in the Spirit," as people laughed and applauded. Jan Mote then sought to fill her husband's place as the speaker for the meeting, by returning to a passage from Song of Solomon: "Let him kiss me with the kisses of his mouth." Although Jan Mote, too, was struggling to retain her composure (having to sit down at one point because her "knees were weak"), she spoke about how laughter was opening people up to receive the love of God. Those in the congregation not spiritually drunk, laying on the floor, or laughing out of control then followed her in singing, "My Jesus I love you."[63]

That sort of bizarre behavior flies in the face of biblical worship. It makes a mockery of that which is holy and treats God with drunken disrespect. Though the Toronto Blessing has faded from prominence since the turn of the millennium, it exemplifies the wild behaviors that can arise when unrestrained emotionalism is encouraged in worship. Similar antics characterized the early Pentecostals of the Azusa Street Revival.[64] Even Charles Parham, Pentecostalism's founder, shrank back in horror at some of the things he observed there: "The wild, weird prayer services in many of these fanatical meetings, where the contact of bodies in motion is as certain and damning as in the dance hall, leads to free-love, affinity-foolism and soul-mating."[65]

Peter Masters, pastor of London's Metropolitan Tabernacle, explains why unrestrained emotionalism and the loss of rational control is a key component of charismatic worship:

> Charismatics claim that by maintaining rational control over our minds and actions we are opposing and quenching the work of the Holy Spirit. They say that believers must be prepared to surrender rational control in order that they may be open to direct divine activity in both worship and Christian service. John Wimber observes with concern that "Fear of losing control is threatening to most Western Christians." He insists that we must overcome our fears, because rational control must be forfeited for tongues-speaking to occur; for soaring ecstatic sensations to be felt in worship; for messages from God to be received directly into the mind, and for miraculous events to happen, such as healings.[66]

But losing control in worship is a serious and tragic error. It is a self-willed, self-serving, and ungodly approach to worship, because it reflects either careless neglect or an outright refusal to worship in spirit and *truth* in the way God has said we should worship (John 4:24).[67]

So how should we evaluate worship practices that encourage a loss of rational control? Here is a compelling answer: "This idea of emptying the mind is foreign to Christian thought. It has much more in common with pagan practices such as transcendental meditation, mystical rituals, hypnosis, and other mind-emptying procedures that often open the door to demonic influences. A person who is eager to have a spiritual experience that bypasses the mind may be opening herself up to spiritual entities she wants no part of. . . . When one looks for a short road to spirituality, bathed in mystical or miraculous experiences, he can become vulnerable to Satanic deception."[68]

The *mysticism* of charismatic worship is only made worse when it joins forces with the *materialism* of prosperity theology. As we have seen already, prominent influences within the Charismatic Movement treat God as if He is a cosmic Santa Claus who cheerily grants their every material desire. Others treat the Holy Spirit as if He is an energetic force—a spark of electricity and spiritual power that produces an ecstatic buzz. In either case, charismatic congregants are trained to approach God for what they can get out of Him. As one author explains, "The prosperity gospel is coldhearted materialism in religious disguise. It chooses Bible verses selectively to fit a name-it-and-claim-it theory, but it does not love God. It wants to use God for selfish, infantile purposes."[69] By contrast, true love for God expresses itself in a life of selfless obedience and sacrificial service to Him (Rom. 12:1).

In addition to producing a greater love for God, a true work of the Spirit also instills within believers a sincere and sacrificial love for one another. Such love "rejoices in the truth" (1 Cor. 13:6), meaning it does not tolerate false teaching for the sake of superficial unity. Moreover, it seeks to edify others within the body of Christ. Such is certainly Paul's point in discussing spiritual gifts in 1 Corinthians 12–14: the gifts were to be used within the church for the building up of other believers. His statement in 1 Corinthians 12:7 makes this point explicit: "The manifestation of the Spirit is given to each one for the profit of all." This is echoed in 1 Corinthians 13:5, where Paul explains that true love "does not seek its own."

But charismatics have turned this on its head, claiming certain gifts (in particular the gift of tongues) are to be used for *self-edification*.[70] That was the very problem Paul was writing to correct: a selfish and prideful use of spiritual gifts by the Corinthians. Today, the Charismatic Movement has made the Corinthian error a distinctive of their movement. But such self-centeredness comes with devastating consequences: "It would be impossible to estimate the irreparable harm caused by thinking that spiritual gifts are given for self-edification and may be used to edify ourselves. This is certainly unbiblical. Gifts are given not for self-edification but for the edification of others."[71]

To make matters worse, this self-centered approach to spiritual gifts is often paired with the self-interested demands of the prosperity gospel. In the same way that prosperity theology replaces true worship with a wish list, it also substitutes a genuine love for others with a selfish desire for material gain.

To be sure, charismatics claim their movement is marked by genuine love for others. But Jonathan Edwards warned there is a counterfeit form of love that is often found in aberrant groups. His words of caution seem particularly applicable to the modern Charismatic Movement:

> Indeed, there is a counterfeit of love that often appears amongst those that are led by a spirit of delusion. There is commonly in the wildest enthusiasts a kind of union and affection that appears in them one towards another, arising from self-love, occasioned by their agreeing one with another in those things wherein they greatly differ from all others, and for which they are the objects of the ridicule of all the rest of mankind; which naturally will cause them so much the more to prize the esteem they observe in each other, of those peculiarities that make them the objects of others' contempt: so the ancient Gnostics, and the wild fanatics that appeared in the beginning of the Reformation, boasted of their great love one to another: one sect of them in particular, calling themselves the Family of Love. But this is quite another thing than that Christian love that I have just described; 'tis only the working of a natural self-love, and no true benevolence, any more than the union and friendship which may be among a company of pirates that are at war with all the rest of the world.[72]

The "wildest enthusiasts" and "wild fanatics" of the contemporary Charismatic Movement would certainly have met with Edwards's disapproval. The fanatical fringe of the Reformation, in particular, shared a number of characteristics in common with modern charismatics: including various ecstatic experiences and an insistence they were receiving new revelation from the Holy Spirit. In opposing them for their unbiblical views, Martin Luther sarcastically referred to these theological radicals as those who had "swallowed the Holy Spirit feathers and all."[73]

Granted, Jonathan Edwards is not the final authority for evaluating the merits of a given ministry or spiritual movement. Scripture alone is the standard against which all things must be measured. But when we remember what Scripture says about the essential place of *truth* in God-honoring worship and compare that standard to the chaotic and unrestrained nature of charismatic worship, or when we place Scripture's definition of love next to the self-seeking emphasis inherent in charismatic theology, serious questions arise. Charismatics may compare their movement to the Great Awakening of Edwards's day.[74] But when the tests of 1 John 4 are applied, the differences become immediately evident.

SPIRITUAL TREASURE OR FOOL'S GOLD?

When Jonathan Edwards applied the tests of 1 John 4:1–8 to the Great Awakening in the first half of the eighteenth century, he concluded that while there were some excesses and carnal expressions, the Spirit of God was genuinely at work in the revival: the true Christ was preached, worldliness and sin were opposed, the Scriptures were exalted, the gospel truth was elevated, and a sincere love for God and for others was demonstrated as a result.

The modern Charismatic Movement demonstrates the opposite. The truth about Christ is distorted—the focus often shifted away from the person and work of the Lord Jesus and put instead on the supposed power and blessing of the Holy Spirit. Worldliness is openly promoted by prosperity preachers (who comprise the most influential and fastest-growing segment of the movement), while leadership scandals have become an all-too-frequent stain on those who claim to be "Spirit-filled." Rather than honoring the Spirit-inspired Scriptures, charismatics treat the Bible as insufficient, seeking new, "personalized" revelation as a supplement. As a result, biblical truth is downplayed, indiscriminate ecumenism applauded, and sound doctrine derided as "dead" and "divisive." Love for God ought to manifest itself in sober-minded worship and sincere obedience; love for others ought to respond in selfless service and a desire to edify others. Yet the Charismatic Movement—both in its pursuit of spiritual gifts and in its incorporation of prosperity theology—approaches God in an inherently self-oriented way.

So what are we to conclude, based on the biblical tests? The answer seems self-evident. In many cases, the Charismatic Movement is dominated by false teachers who are actively advocating a false gospel. This is especially true of the rampant Word of Faith Movement and the prosperity gospel it promotes. The New Testament repeatedly warns against those who would introduce error into the church for the sake of dishonest gain; no modern example fits those verses more exactly than the popular faith healers, prosperity preachers, and televangelists who comprise the face of charismatic media. True believers should avoid such spiritual frauds at all costs. As the apostle John warned in 2 John 7–11:

> For many deceivers have gone out into the world who do not confess Jesus Christ as coming in the flesh. This is a deceiver and an antichrist. Look to yourselves, that we do not lose those things we worked for, but that we may receive a full reward. Whoever transgresses and does not abide in the doctrine of Christ does not have God. He who abides in the doctrine of Christ has both the Father and the Son. If anyone comes to you and does not bring this doctrine, do not receive him into your house nor greet him; for he who greets him shares in his evil deeds.

I do believe there are sincere people within the Charismatic Movement who, in spite of the systemic corruption and confusion, have come to understand the necessary truths of the gospel. They embrace substitutionary atonement, the true nature of Christ, the trinitarian nature of God, biblical repentance, and the unique authority of the Bible. They recognize that salvation is not about health and wealth, and they genuinely desire to be rescued from sin, spiritual death, and everlasting hell. Yet, they remain confused about the ministry of the Holy Spirit and the nature of spiritual giftedness.

As a result, they are playing with strange fire. By continually exposing themselves to the false teaching and counterfeit spirituality of the Charismatic Movement, they have placed themselves (and anyone under their spiritual care) in eternal jeopardy. For true believers, the Charismatic Movement represents a massive stumbling block to true spiritual growth, ministry, and usefulness. Its errant teachings regarding the Holy Spirit and the Spirit-inspired Scriptures perpetuate immaturity, spiritual weakness, and an unending struggle with sin.

A parallel exists between those Christians who are trapped in the modern Charismatic Movement and the true believers who were part of the Corinthian church in the first century. The church at Corinth was characterized by moral compromise, carnal desires, and confusion about spiritual gifts. Yet, as counterintuitive as it may sound, its congregation was composed of many true believers. Obviously, the Holy Spirit was not responsible for the errors that had infiltrated the Corinthian congregation. Likewise, He is not the source of contemporary charismatic confusion within the evangelical church. For the true believers at Corinth, the Holy Spirit continued to work in their lives *in spite* of their egregious errors.[75] The same is still true today, though it doesn't negate the seriousness of the corruption.

The charismatic quest for extrabiblical revelation, ecstatic experiences, subjective guidance, unrestrained emotionalism, and material prosperity represents a massive danger. In the same way a child should avoid matches, believers ought to stay away from the strange fire of unacceptable charismatic worship and practice. At its best, it is representative of the Corinthian confusion that Paul corrected. At its worst, it consists of the damnable heresies of false teachers. Of such charlatans the Scripture says, "For many walk, of whom I often told you, and now tell you even weeping, that they are enemies of the cross of Christ, whose end is destruction, whose god is their appetite, and whose glory is in their shame, who set their minds on earthly things" (Phil. 3:18–19 NASB).

PART TWO

EXPOSING THE
COUNTERFEIT GIFTS

FIVE

APOSTLES AMONG US?

I f 1901 was a big year for the Charismatic Movement, 2001 was potentially even bigger. The first date marks the beginning of the modern
Pentecostal Movement, when Agnes Ozman reportedly spoke in tongues
during a prayer meeting in Topeka, Kansas. But the latter date, coming exactly
a century after the first, represents something even more grand in the minds of
some charismatic leaders who assert that 2001 "marked the beginning of the
Second Apostolic Age."[1] Such is the description used by C. Peter Wagner, missiologist, popular author, and chronicler of recent charismatic developments.
He believes a momentous change in the redemptive plan of God occurred at
the beginning of the twenty-first century.

According to Wagner, "We are now seeing before our very eyes the most
radical change in the way of doing church since the Protestant Reformation.
In fact, I think I could make a reasonable argument that it may actually turn
out to be a *more radical* change."[2] The dawn of the twentieth century may
have signaled a renewed interest in miraculous gifts, but the new millennium purportedly ushered in something even more significant: the return of
apostles.[3] In Wagner's words, there is now "widespread recognition that the
office of apostleship was not just a phenomenon of the first couple of centuries
of church history but that it is also functioning in the Body of Christ today."[4]

Wagner calls this modern influx of apostolic leadership the New Apostolic Reformation. He defines the movement like this:

> The name I have chosen for this movement is the New Apostolic Reformation. I use "Reformation" because, as I have said, I believe it at least matches the Protestant Reformation in its overall impact; "Apostolic" because the most radical of all the changes is the widespread recognition of the gift and office of apostle in today's churches; and "New" to distinguish the movement from a number of denominations that use the word "Apostolic" in their official names yet exhibit patterns common to the more traditional churches rather than to these new ones.[5]

Having decided there are still apostles in the church today—based on a handful of modern "prophecies" and a consensus of panelists at the 1996 National Symposium on the Post-Denominational Church hosted by Fuller Theological Seminary—Wagner has since embarked on a mission to see the apostolic office fully embraced by the contemporary church. Wagner believes that in every generation of church history, there have always been individuals who possessed the gift of apostleship, but he contends it was only recently possible "for a critical mass to develop by 2001, the year I have chosen to use as the beginning of the Second Apostolic Age."[6] According to Wagner, contemporary Christians "can begin to approach the spiritual vitality and power of the first-century church only if we recognize, accept, receive and minister in all the spiritual gifts, including the gift of apostle."[7]

Historically, the name "apostle Peter" has been reserved for only one individual: Simon Peter, the outspoken leader of the twelve disciples whose apostolic ministry is featured in Acts 1–12. But in the New Apostolic Reformation, that name has been co-opted by none other than Peter Wagner himself.[8] Wagner began to recognize his own "apostleship" in 1995, when two prophetesses declared he had received an apostolic anointing. In 1998, his apostolic calling was confirmed by another prophetic word at a conference in Dallas. Wagner recounts the somewhat bizarre circumstances surrounding that event:

I was sitting on the front row . . . when somehow or other I found myself kneeling on the platform with Jim Stevens of Christian International getting ready to prophesy over me in public. How I got there I still don't know! I glanced up and there was Charles Doolittle, one of our recognized intercessors, standing over me. Charles was a six-foot-four muscular African-American police officer on the Glendale, California, police force, with an aggressive look on his face and holding a huge three-foot sword over my head! I quickly decided that I'd better behave myself and listen carefully [to] what Jim Stevens said. . . . I have since considered that time to be my prophetic ordination as an apostle.[9]

A short time later, as proof of his apostolic appointment, Wagner claims to have ended mad cow disease in Europe. In his words:

I knew that God wanted me to take the apostolic authority He had given me and decree once and for all that mad cow disease would come to an end in Europe and the U.K., which I did. . . . That was October 1, 2001. A month later, a friend of mine sent me a newspaper article from England saying that the epidemic had broken and that the last reported case of mad cow disease had been on September 30, 2001, the day before the apostolic decree![10]

Given his enthusiasm, Wagner is apparently unaware of the fact that the disease still exists in Europe, such that sixty-seven positive cases of infected cows were reported in 2009 alone.[11] While it is true that aggressive control efforts on the part of European governments have significantly curbed the mad cow epidemic, the notion that Wagner's apostolic pronouncement ended the disease is patently false.

In 2000, Wagner began to lead the newly formed International Coalition of Apostles as the "Presiding Apostle"—a position he held until 2009, when his title changed to Presiding Apostle Emeritus.[12] According to Pentecostal historian Vinson Synan, when the coalition started, "new apostles could join and pay $69 a month as membership dues."[13] Synan himself was invited by Wagner to join, but later declined. As Synan explains, "I didn't consider myself to be an apostle, and I wrote him that at $69 a month, 'I could not afford to be an apostle.'"[14] Membership rates at the end of 2012 varied slightly, depending on the apostle's nation of residency. The base fee was $350 for "International Apostles." The fee for apostles living in North America began at $450 per year, or $650 for married apostles (meaning, apparently, a husband-and-wife team who both consider themselves apostles). Native Americans ("First Nation Apostles") could join for the same fee as an "International Apostle."[15]

In an attempt to organize the New Apostolic Movement, Wagner delineates two primary categories of "apostle" along with several subcategories. "Vertical Apostles" serve as the leaders of various ministries or ministry networks, whereas "Horizontal Apostles" help to bring together peer-level leaders for various purposes. Wagner suggests Peter and Paul were New Testament examples of "Vertical Apostles" because of the nature of their respective ministries and the church networks that fell under their shepherding care. By contrast, James, the brother of our Lord, was an example of a "Horizontal Apostle" because he successfully brought the other apostles together at the Jerusalem Council.[16]

Apostolic subcategories include: Ecclesiastical, Functional, Apostolic team members; Congregational Apostles; Convening, Ambassadorial, Mobilizing, and Territorial Apostles; Marketplace Apostles; and Calling Apostles.[17] Search the New Testament for any of these labels, and you'll quickly find they aren't there.

Nonetheless, the New Apostolic Reformation is rapidly catching on within mainstream Charismatic and Third Wave churches. As one author explains, "It is a characteristic belief of [these] new churches that the Holy Spirit is restoring today the fivefold ministries of Ephesians 4:11: apostles, prophets, evangelists, pastors, and teachers. But the focus is on the ministries of apostle and prophet, because the Evangelical world was already accustomed to the ministries of evangelist, pastor and teacher."[18] Wagner takes great delight in the fact that his New Apostolic Movement is part of the fastest-growing segment of Christianity, seeing it as a sign of divine affirmation.[19]

Based on this growth, Wagner argues that there is a massive, fundamental shift taking place within the church—one he compares to the transition from the Old Covenant to the New Covenant.[20] He goes so far as to compare the New Apostolic Reformation to the "new wineskins" of the New Covenant, stating, "Today we have entered another new wineskin, which I call the Second Apostolic Age. Radical changes in the way we do church are not around the corner; they are already here with us."[21]

Those who reject the New Apostolic Reformation are, in Wagner's view, like the Pharisees: "instead of acclaiming and blessing God's new wineskin, they resisted it."[22] He further asserts that those who oppose his new movement are under demonic influence: "Satan tries to prevent God's new times and seasons from coming by sending evil demonic spirits to work particularly on our minds. If they are successful, we begin to think wrongly about the new wineskins that God desires to develop."[23] Thus, anyone who takes issue with Wagner's premise—that he and other modern charismatic leaders are "apostles"—is derided as legalistic, demonized, or just too scared to embrace a radical new age in the history of the church.

REFORMATION OR DEFORMATION?

In spite of the ad hominem attacks Wagner aims at his detractors, it is high time for someone to expose the New Apostolic Reformation for what it really is: *a fraud*.

It is difficult to overstate the admixture of blatant arrogance and biblical ignorance that pervades the New Apostolic Reformation. In Wagner's discussion of the movement, there is perhaps only one sentence with which I would agree with him, when he wrote, "I am well aware of the fact that what I have said could be regarded as somewhat of a brash statement."[24] That would be an understatement. To claim apostolic appointment is not only the height of prideful presumption; it is also a complete farce. Vinson Synan, himself an avid proponent of Pentecostalism, is right to be scared of Wagner's new movement: "From the outset, I was concerned about any movement that claims to restore apostolic offices that exercise ultimate and unchecked authority in churches. The potential for abuse is enormous. Throughout church history, attempts to restore apostle as an office in the church have often ended up in heresy or caused incredible pain."[25]

Wagner may have labeled his movement the "New Apostolic Reformation." But the reality is that it is none of those three things. It is not *new*, it is not a *reformation*, and it is certainly not *apostolic*. This is not the first time in church history that power-hungry false teachers have nominated themselves as apostles to gain greater spiritual influence over others. False apostles were prevalent even in New Testament times, and Paul denounced them as "deceitful workers, transforming themselves into apostles of Christ. And no wonder! For Satan himself transforms himself into an angel of light" (2 Cor. 11:13–14). In the Middle Ages, the Roman Catholic papacy developed into an abusive, corrupt, autocratic, totalitarian system by claiming apostolic authority through a supposed line of succession back to Peter. Even in the twentieth century, Wagner acknowledges that earlier segments of the Charismatic Movement have attempted to revive the apostolic office. Peter Hocken surveys a number of those earlier groups:

> At the outset of the Pentecostal movement a few groups had proclaimed the restoration of apostles and prophets, particularly the Apostolic Church formed in Wales in 1916, which then institutionalized these ministries. These ministries, rejected by most Pentecostal churches, reappeared in the Latter Rain movement that originated in North Battleford, Saskatchewan, Canada in 1948. The Latter Rain adherents believed in the restoration of the Ephesians 4:11 ministries . . . [which subsequently] exercised an influence on the emerging charismatic movement.[26]

Wagner has simply borrowed the apostolic emphasis of Latter Rain theology and incorporated it into his Third Wave teachings. Thus it is misnomer to call his contemporary movement "new."

It is equally misleading to refer to it as a "reformation."[27] In fact, the Reformation was primarily a reaction against the self-proclaimed apostolic authority of the pope.[28] Moreover, the fundamental principle of the Reformation was a commitment to Scripture alone—a concept to which Wagner's view is emphatically and diametrically opposed. After defining "the spirit of religion" as demonic, Wagner argues that "it causes religious leaders to concentrate not on what the Spirit is saying (present tense), but on what the Spirit said (past tense) in a former season."[29] In other words, according to Wagner, those who look solely to that which the Spirit *said in a former season* (i.e., the Bible) are under demonic influence!

The leaders of the Reformation would have scoffed at such a notion, and rightly so. They argued that Scripture alone is the authority for everything pertaining to faith and practice (cf. 2 Tim. 3:16–17). Of course, the Reformation doctrine of *sola Scriptura* leaves no room for the imagined prophecies of modern charismatics, so it is little wonder Wagner rejects it. (We already saw, in chapter 4, that Wagner openly questions the close of the biblical canon.)

Finally, and most important, the New Apostolic Reformation is not in any way *apostolic*. This can be demonstrated, simply and convincingly, by considering the biblical requirements for true apostles. When compared to the New Testament criteria, the so-called apostles of the New Apostolic Reformation are immediately exposed as counterfeits and pretenders.

THE BIBLICAL CRITERIA FOR APOSTLESHIP

The Charismatic Movement operates on the premise that *everything* that happened in the early church ought to be expected and experienced in the church today. One of the most well-known Pentecostal leaders of a past generation, David du Plessis, expressed that sentiment with these words: "The New Testament is not a record of what happened in one generation, but it is a blueprint of what should happen in every generation until Jesus comes."[30] That assumption, taken to its logical conclusions, leads Wagner and others to argue that there are still apostles in the church today. After all, they reason, if the early church had apostles, we should too.

But there is a fatal flaw in that approach. The biblical criteria for apostleship make it impossible for any credible claim to be made that there are still apostles in the church. In fact, after the death of John, the last surviving apostle (who died around AD 100), no one in church history could ever legitimately claim to be an apostle—based on the specific conditions delineated in the New Testament. Biblically speaking, there are at least six reasons the gift and office of apostleship was unique to the early church. It is not something that can be experienced in the church today.

The Qualifications Necessary for Apostleship

First, it would be impossible for any contemporary Christian to meet the biblical qualifications required for someone to be considered an apostle. The New Testament articulates at least three necessary criteria: (1) an apostle had to be a physical eyewitness of the resurrected Christ (Acts 1:22; 10:39–41; 1 Cor. 9:1; 15:7–8); (2) an apostle had to be personally appointed by the Lord Jesus Christ (Mark 3:14; Luke 6:13; Acts 1:2, 24; 10:41; Gal. 1:1); and (3) an apostle had to be able to authenticate his apostolic appointment with miraculous signs (Matt. 10:1–2; Acts 1:5–8; 2:43; 4:33; 5:12; 8:14; 2 Cor. 12:12; Heb. 2:3–4).

Those qualifications alone conclusively demonstrate that there are no apostles in the church today. No living person has seen the risen Christ with his or her own eyes; no one is able to perform miraculous signs like those done by the apostles in the book of Acts (cf. Acts 3:3–11; 5:15–16; 9:36–42; 20:6–12; 28:1–6); and—in spite of presumptuous claims to the contrary—no one in the modern church has been personally and directly appointed as an apostle by the Lord Jesus. Of course, there are some charismatics who claim to have seen visions of the resurrected Lord. Not only are such claims highly suspect and impossible to verify; they simply do not meet the apostolic criteria—since an apostle had to see the resurrected Christ in the flesh *with his own eyes*. As Samuel Waldron explains:

> Visions and dreams—even if real and genuine—do not qualify one to be an Apostle of Christ. It is clear that the Bible emphasizes the distinction between the inner eye and the outer eye and counts revelation to the outer eye as a mark of superior dignity. Modern claims to have seen Jesus in a vision or dream do not qualify anyone to claim this indispensable characteristic of an Apostle of Christ.[31]

Wayne Grudem, popular author and professor of theology and biblical studies at Phoenix Seminary, is a committed charismatic himself and perhaps the best theologian and apologist for the movement. But even he acknowledges that "since no one today can meet the qualification of having seen the risen Christ with his own eyes, there are no apostles today."[32]

Peter Wagner is well aware of these qualifications. He can't get around them, so instead he simply ignores them! After articulating a version of "apostleship" that fits his New Apostolic Reformation, Wagner admits he intentionally leaves out the biblical qualifications in defining an apostle. In his words:

> There are three biblical characteristics of apostles which some include in their definition of apostle, but which I have chosen not to include: (1) signs and wonders (2 Cor. 12:12), (2) seeing Jesus personally (1 Cor. 9:1), and (3) planting churches (1 Cor. 3:10). My reason for this is that I do not understand these three qualities to be non-negotiables. . . . [I]f a given individual lacks the anointing for one or more of them, this, in my opinion would not exclude that individual from being a legitimate apostle.[33]

We might quibble over whether or not "planting churches" is one of the biblical criteria for apostleship. However, the other two characteristics certainly are. Yet Wagner dismisses them as being *negotiable*. He treats them as moot, for no evident reason other than that the biblical standard would overturn his own claim of apostolic authority. Having declared himself an apostle, he acts as if he has the authority to ignore the clear teaching of Scripture if "in [*his*] opinion," something the Bible teaches is inconvenient, or if it might exclude Wagner himself from the office he believes he is entitled to. That kind of cavalier, condescending attitude toward Scripture pervades the New Apostolic Reformation. After all, the only way Wagner and his supporters can advocate modern-day apostles is by turning a deaf ear to what the Bible clearly teaches.

Paul Was the Last Apostle

Though Paul met all three of the criteria listed above, his apostolic appointment was clearly not the norm. Paul himself emphasized that point in 1 Corinthians 15:5–9, while delineating the post-resurrection appearances of the Lord Jesus. Unlike the Eleven, Paul had not been one of Jesus' disciples during His earthly ministry. He was not present in the Upper Room when the Lord appeared, nor was he among the five hundred witnesses who saw the resurrected Christ. In fact, the Lord's appearance to Paul was not merely after His resurrection, but after His ascension! And it occurred while Paul (who was then called "Saul") was on the way to persecute the followers of Christ in Damascus (Acts 9:1–8).

But lest anyone think they, too, can have an extraordinary apostleship as Paul did, it is important to note two significant details about Paul's unique calling. First, in 1 Corinthians 15:8, Paul states he was the *last* person to whom the resurrected Christ personally and physically appeared. This would preclude anyone after Paul from having a legitimate claim to apostleship—since seeing the resurrected Lord is a prerequisite for apostleship and Paul declared himself to be the last person to have such an experience.

Second, it is important to note that Paul saw his apostleship as unique and extraordinary. He was as one "untimely born" (v. 8), regarding himself as the "least of the apostles" (v. 9) because of the animosity he had expressed toward the church prior to his conversion. Though he never questioned the authenticity of his apostleship, Paul certainly did not see it as a normative pattern for later generations of Christians to follow.

The Apostles Possessed Unique Authority

The New Testament apostles were recognized as the revelatory agents of God, and as such they possessed an unsurpassed level of authority in church history—an authority they derived from Christ Himself. Being an *apostle* of Jesus Christ meant being His representative. In contemporary legal terms, we might refer to the apostles as the Lord's proxies. They were those on whom He had bestowed His own authority.

While it is true the term *apostle* is sometimes used in the New Testament in a nontechnical, generic sense to refer to "apostles [or messengers] of the churches" (2 Cor. 8:23), those individuals should not be confused with the Twelve or the apostle Paul. To be an *apostle of the Lord Jesus Christ* was a specific calling and a profound privilege—something far different from merely being a messenger sent from a local congregation. To be an apostle of the Lord Jesus was to have been personally appointed by Him. It was the highest possible position of authority in the church, a unique office that encompassed a nontransferable commission from Christ to proclaim revelatory doctrine while laying the foundation of the church.

In the Upper Room Discourse, the Lord personally authorized His apostles to lead the church in His absence, promising them that the Holy Spirit would enable them to reveal God's truth to His people (cf. John 14:26; 15:26–27; 16:12–15). Believers in the early church recognized apostolic instruction as carrying with it the authority of Christ Himself. Apostolic writings were inspired, inerrant revelation—to be received and obeyed as the Word of God (1 Thess. 2:13). An inspired letter written with apostolic authority was as authoritative as the Old Testament Scriptures (cf. 1 Cor. 14:37; Gal. 1:9; 2 Peter 3:16). Jude exemplified that attitude when he wrote to the church, "But you, beloved, ought to remember the words that were spoken beforehand by the apostles of our Lord Jesus Christ" (Jude 17 NASB).

The issue of apostolic authority becomes especially important when we consider the doctrine of canonicity. The apostles were authorized by the Lord Jesus Himself to write inspired Scripture. Their authority was the primary test the early church applied to issues regarding canonicity: if a book or epistle claiming to speak with prophetic authority was written by an apostle or under apostolic oversight, it was recognized as inspired and authoritative. On the other hand, writings that were disconnected from apostolic authority were not considered to be part of the Scriptures, no matter what authority the author claimed for himself.[34] And even in the early church there was no shortage of material that lacked apostolic authority but claimed to be divinely inspired (cf. 2 Thess. 2:2; 2 Cor. 11:13; 2 Peter 2:1–3).

All of that raises major questions for modern charismatics who want to reinstate apostles into the contemporary church. Most of these same self-styled "apostles" claim to be privy to special, direct revelation from God. If they truly have apostolic authority, what is to stop them from adding to the Bible? On the other hand, if modern apostles are unwilling to add to the Scriptures, then what does that say about the legitimacy of their apostleship? As Wayne Grudem rightly observes, "This fact in itself should suggest to us that there was something unique about the office of apostle, and that we would not expect it to continue today, for no one today can add words to the Bible and have them be counted as God's very words or as part of Scripture."[35]

That is a profound admission from a leading charismatic theologian. The essential starting point for charismatic doctrine is the claim that all the miracles and spiritual gifts described in Acts and 1 Corinthians are still available to Christians today, that prophetic gifts and signs and wonders were not unique to the apostolic era, and that there is no reason to believe one or more of these phenomena has ceased. That position is known as *continuationism*. Wayne Grudem has acknowledged, however, that he is a *cessationist* (the opposite of a continuationist) when it comes to matters such as the apostolic office and the canon of Scripture. In effect, he has conceded the fundamental argument against charismatic doctrine. We'll revisit that point later in the book, but for now, note that even the leading apologists for continuationism ultimately are forced to confess that *something significant* changed with the passing of the apostolic era.

The most crucial change that all faithful Christians *must* recognize is that the canon of Scripture is closed. And we know it is closed precisely because the apostolic office did not continue past the first century of church history. What has remained as our sole authority today is the written testimony of the apostles—an inspired record of their authoritative teaching contained in the Bible. Hence, the writings of the New Testament constitute *the only true apostolic authority in the church today.*

The Apostles Formed the Foundation of the Church

When writing his epistle to the Ephesians, Paul explained that his readers were part of God's household, "having been built on the foundation of the apostles and prophets, Jesus Christ Himself being the corner stone" (Eph. 2:19–20 NASB). That passage equates the apostles with the church's foundation. It means nothing if it doesn't decisively limit apostleship to the earliest stages of church history. After all, a foundation is not something that can be rebuilt during every phase of construction. The foundation is unique, and it is always laid first, with the rest of the structure resting firmly above it.

When one considers the writings of the church fathers—those Christian leaders who lived shortly after the apostles—it quickly becomes evident they regarded the foundational age of the church to be in the past.[36] Ignatius (c. AD 35–115), in his *Epistle to the Magnesians*, spoke in the past tense of the foundation-laying work of Peter and Paul. Referring to the book of Acts, Ignatius wrote, "This was first fulfilled in Syria; for 'the disciples were called Christians at Antioch,' *when Paul and Peter were laying the foundations of the Church.*"[37]

Irenaeus (c. 130–202) referred to the twelve apostles as "the twelve-pillared foundation of the church."[38] Tertullian (c. 155–230) similarly explained that "*after* the time of the apostles" the only doctrine true Christians accepted was that which was "proclaimed in the churches *of apostolic foundation.*"[39] Lactantius (c. 240–320) in his *Divine Institutes* likewise referred to the past time in which the apostolic foundations of the church were laid. Commenting on the role of the Twelve, he explained that "the disciples, being dispersed through the provinces, everywhere *laid the foundations of the Church*, themselves also in the name of their divine Master doing many and almost incredible miracles; for at His departure He had endowed them with power and strength, by which the system of their new announcement might be founded and confirmed."[40]

Examples could be multiplied, but the point is clear. Modern charismatics may claim that an *apostolic foundation* is still being laid today. But such a notion runs contrary to both the plain sense of Scripture and the understanding of those Christian leaders who immediately followed the apostles in history: they clearly understood the church's apostolic foundation to have been fully completed in the first century. Any notion of modern apostles would simply obliterate the meaning of Paul's metaphor in Ephesians 2:20. If the apostles constitute the foundation of the church, it is sheer folly to try to relocate them to the rafters.

The Post-Apostolic Church Was Led by Elders and Deacons

When the apostles gave instruction regarding the future of the church and how the church ought to be organized, they did not suggest new apostles

97

should be appointed. Instead, they spoke of pastors, elders, and deacons. Thus, Peter instructed elders to "shepherd the flock of God among you" (1 Peter 5:2 NASB). And Paul told Titus to "appoint elders in every city as I directed you" (Titus 1:5 NASB); he similarly outlined the qualifications for both elders and deacons in the third chapter of 1 Timothy. Nowhere in the Pastoral Epistles does Paul say anything about the perpetuation of apostleship, but he says a lot about the organization of the church under the leadership of qualified elders and deacons. As faithful men filled those offices, the church would thrive. Thus, Paul told Timothy, "The things which you have heard from me in the presence of many witnesses, entrust these to faithful men who will be able to teach others also" (2 Tim. 2:2 NASB).

When we look again at church history—considering the testimony of those church leaders who lived shortly after the New Testament age ended—we find that the earliest church fathers did not view themselves as apostles, but rather as the "disciples of the apostles."[41] They understood the apostles were unique, and that after the apostolic age ended, the church was governed by elders (including pastors or bishops) and deacons. Clement of Rome, writing in the 90s, stated that the apostles "appointed the first-fruits" of their labors "to be bishops and deacons of those who would afterwards believe."[42] Ignatius (c. AD 35–115) similarly clarified in his *Epistle to the Antiochians* that he was not an apostle. He wrote, "I do not issue commands on these points *as if I were an apostle*; but, as your fellow-servant, I put you in mind of them."[43]

Those are not unconventional statements I have cherry-picked to make a point. It was the unanimous perspective of the church fathers that the apostolic age was unique, unrepeated, and limited to the first century of church history. Both Augustine and John Chrysostom spoke of the "times of the apostles" as a past-tense, completed reality.[44] In the fourth century, Eusebius, the church historian, traced the entire flow of church history as a progression from the "times of the apostles" to his own present day.[45] Basil of Caesarea referred to church leaders from earlier generations as those "who lived near the times of the apostles."[46] Tertullian emphasized events that took place "after the times of the apostles."[47]

Again, examples could be multiplied to make the point: the unilateral consensus of the early church was that the apostolic period ended and was not expected to continue. Those who came after the apostles clearly stated they were *not* apostles. Instead, they rightly viewed themselves as pastors, elders, and deacons. To quote Wayne Grudem in defense of cessationism again:

> It is noteworthy that no major leader in the history of the church—not Athanasius or Augustine, not Luther or Calvin, not Wesley or Whitefield—has taken to himself the title of "apostle" or let himself be called an apostle. If any in modern times want to take the title "apostle" to themselves, they immediately raise the suspicion that they may be motivated by inappropriate pride and desires for self-exaltation, along with excessive ambition and a desire for much more authority in the church than any one person should rightfully have.[48]

The Apostles Hold a Unique Position of Honor

Not only did the apostles hold a unique position of authority in church history, but they are also given a unique place of honor in eternity. In describing the New Jerusalem, the apostle John explained that "the wall of the city had twelve foundation stones, and on them were the twelve names of the twelve apostles of the Lamb" (Rev. 21:14 NASB). For all eternity, those stones will commemorate God's relationship with the church, of which the apostles were the foundation. The names of the twelve apostles will be forever sealed in the wall of the New Jerusalem.

Do modern-day apostles really believe they deserve the same place of heavenly honor as the New Testament apostles? Some of their followers apparently do. According to one self-proclaimed prophet, "Right now, Apostles such as Dr. Peter Wagner are laying a foundation from which spiritual warfare in the heavenlies can be fought and won. . . . [T]he Apostles [are] being raised up. God has raised up these men to be very visible. We know a lot about a few Apostles in the New Testament. We will know a lot about a few Apostles in the New Jerusalem. We can get offended, or we can get on board."[49]

That is an astonishing statement because it implies that Wagner and his ilk will be eternally honored in the same way as the Twelve and Paul. All true believers ought to be *extremely offended* by that kind of overt arrogance and presumption. The honor accorded to the apostles in the New Jerusalem is unique. It is limited to those personally appointed by Christ in the New Testament. Only misguided false teachers would claim everlasting apostolic honor for anyone alive today.

WHAT ABOUT EPHESIANS 4:11–13?

Proponents of modern-day apostleship often point to Ephesians 4:11–13 to defend their position. It is important, therefore, that we examine that passage carefully. After describing Christ's ascension, Paul wrote:

> And He gave some as apostles, and some as prophets, and some as evangelists, and some as pastors and teachers, for the equipping of the saints for the work of service, to the building up of the body of Christ; until we all attain to the unity of the faith, and of the knowledge of the Son of God, to a mature man, to the measure of the stature which belongs to the fullness of Christ. (NASB)

Advocates of modern-day apostleship make two incorrect assumptions about this passage. First, they assert that the unity, knowledge, and maturity described in verse 13 refer to the second coming of Christ. Second, they contend that all five of the offices listed in verse 11 (apostles, prophets, evangelists, pastors, and teachers) must continue until the Second Coming. But neither of those assumptions is warranted by the text itself.

Let's look at the second assumption first. Does this passage indicate that the offices listed in verse 11 will last *until* the conditions described in verse 13 are met? That interpretation might be possible if verse 12 were omitted from the text. Grammatically, however, the word "until" in verse 13 points back to the nearest participle in verse 12 ("building up"), and not to the distant verb "gave" in verse 11. Thus, Paul's point is that those offices listed in verse 11 were given by Christ so that, according to verse 12, the saints might be equipped to build up the body of Christ (v. 12).

It is the *building up* of the body of Christ by the saints, then, that continues *until* the conditions in verse 13 are realized. Nothing in the text indicates that *apostles* and *prophets* will be present throughout the entire church age, but only that the work they began (equipping the saints to build up the body of Christ) will continue. This grammatical conclusion is strengthened by the context of Ephesians, since Paul has already explained that *apostles* and *prophets* were limited to the foundation age of the church (Eph. 2:20).

We can now consider the unity and knowledge described in verse 13. Some scholars insist that such an ultimate objective is not attainable this side of glory. Thus, they contend, Paul must be describing the church's heavenly unity and knowledge—attributes that will only be realized in the glory of heaven. But that idea does not fit the flow of Paul's thought; he is describing the results produced as the saints build up the church. His focus is not on God's final work of glorification in heaven, but on the work of faithful believers in the church here on earth. Within the church, it is possible for believers to possess a profound unity based on a shared commitment to biblical truth, an intimate knowledge of the Lord Jesus Christ, and a deep level of spiritual maturity. Paul also adds sound doctrine (v. 14) and growth in Christlikeness (v. 15) as additional benefits that result from the saints being properly equipped to build up the body of Christ (v. 12).

Rightly understood, Ephesians 4:11–13 does not teach that a fivefold pattern of ministry (including apostles and prophets) will continue throughout all church history until the second coming of Christ. Rather, this passage demonstrates that the purpose for which the Lord Jesus gave apostles, prophets, evangelists, pastors, and teachers to the church was to equip the saints. When properly equipped, the saints are enabled to build up one another within the body of Christ. And the result is that the church is strengthened—growing in unity, knowledge, maturity, sound doctrine, and sanctification.

Because Paul had already indicated that the apostles and prophets were for the foundation only, he did not need to reiterate that those offices were temporary. Though those two offices did not last beyond the first century of church history, the apostles and prophets still equip the saints through the Spirit-inspired writings they left for us (i.e., the Bible). The other three offices—evangelist, pastor, and teacher—have continued throughout church history. As such, they continue to equip the saints in every generation for the purpose of building up the church.

THE SIGNIFICANCE OF APOSTOLIC CESSATION

Modern charismatic leaders like Peter Wagner may argue for the *continuation* of the gift and office of apostleship; Roman Catholics may similarly insist on an apostolic *succession* that they apply to the pope. But both assertions are severely misguided. Any honest evaluation of the New Testament evidence reveals that the apostles were a unique group of men, hand-picked and personally commissioned by the Lord Jesus Himself to lay the doctrinal foundation for the church, with Christ as the cornerstone. No one alive today can possibly meet the biblical criteria required for apostleship. And even in the first century, when all agree the miraculous gifts were fully operational, only a very select group of spiritual leaders were regarded as apostles.

In subsequent centuries, no church father claimed to be an apostle; rather, Christian leaders from the second century on saw the apostolic period as unique and unrepeatable. That was the consensus of the faithful—until the twenty-first century, when all of a sudden we are being told that we must once again accept the reemergence of apostles in the church. From a purely biblical perspective (and from any clear historical perspective), such modern assertions are as confused as they are conceited.

The reality is that the gift and office of apostleship ceased after the first century. When the apostle John went to heaven, the apostolate came to an end. Of course, apostolic influence has continued through the inspired Scriptures, which the apostles penned. But we should not think of the apostolic foundation as being perpetually laid throughout church history. It was completed within their lifetimes, never needing to be laid down again.

Look again at what the cessation of apostleship means for continuationist-charismatic doctrine. Clearly, not everything that happened in the New Testament church is still happening today. That is an inconvenient and embarrassing confession for any charismatic to make, because the apostolic office itself was a gift. Ephesians 4:11 plainly says so. If that office has ceased, we cannot insist, as charismatics do, that all the spiritual gifts described in Acts and 1 Corinthians have continued. In Thomas Edgar's words: "The fact that the gift of apostle ceased with the apostolic age is a devastating blow to the basic assumption underlying the entire charismatic perspective, namely, the assumption that all gifts are to be operative throughout the church age. We know that at least one gift ceased; therefore, their foundational assumption is incorrect."[50]

Some charismatics, recognizing that apostleship did not continue beyond the first century, attempt to argue that it was only an *office* and not a *gift*. Thus, they contend that while the apostolic *office* ceased, the miraculous *gifts* have all still continued. This clever attempt to circumvent the inevitable ramifications for the charismatic position ultimately falls flat, since *apostles* are listed in Paul's delineation of the spiritual gifts in 1 Corinthians 12:28–29, right alongside prophets, miracle-workers, and tongues-speakers. In the context, it is clearly one of the gifts Paul has in mind, flowing out of the argument he begins in verses 4–5 and concluding in verse 31 (where Paul uses the term *charisma* to refer to the items he had just listed in verses 28–30). Additionally, Paul's point in Ephesians 4:11 is that *apostles* are given by Christ to His church. While it is true that *apostleship* was also an *office*, that does not preclude it from being a gift. Prophecy, for example, encompassed both an office and a gift, as did the gift of teaching.

In the end, despite the protests of some continuationists, there is no escaping the fact that one of the most significant features described in 1 Corinthians 12 (namely, *apostleship*) is no longer active in the church today. It ceased. To acknowledge that point is to acknowledge the foundational premise on which cessationism is based. If apostleship ceased, it demonstrates that not everything that characterized the New Testament church still characterizes the church today. Moreover, it opens the door to the real possibility that some of the other gifts listed in 1 Corinthians 12–14 have also ceased. We will consider those additional gifts in the following chapters.

The Folly of Fallible Prophets

D ry wells, fruitless trees, raging waves, wandering stars, brute beasts, hideous stains, vomit-eating dogs, mud-loving pigs, and ravenous wolves—that is how the Bible describes false prophets (cf. 2 Peter 2; Jude). The New Testament reserves its harshest words of condemnation for those who would falsely claim to speak revelation from God. And what the Bible condemns we must also condemn—doing so with equal vigor and force. But apply those same epithets to today's false teachers, and you're likely to be labeled as *uncharitable* or even *unchristian*. The ecumenical spirit of the age shrinks back in cowardice from the clear denunciation of error, even when Scripture explicitly warrants it.

The growth of the Charismatic Movement has compounded the problem, encouraging and giving a platform to all kinds of people who make ridiculous extrabiblical (and often grossly *un*biblical) utterances in the name of the Holy Spirit. Faithful Christians desperately need to wake up and speak out against the free flow of false prophecies that has come into the church in the wake of the Charismatic Movement.

The New Testament repeatedly warns that the false prophets who are most dangerous are the wolves who come in sheep's clothing or disguise themselves as angels of light in order to permeate their lies. They would never overtly deny Christ or oppose the Holy Spirit. Rather, they come in Christ's name and claim the Holy Spirit's authority. They infiltrate the church by pretense and subterfuge. This is where they do their real damage.

Speaking of the end of the age, the Lord Jesus explained, "Then many false prophets will rise up and deceive many. . . . For false christs and false prophets will rise and show great signs and wonders to deceive, if possible, even the elect" (Matt. 24:11, 24). The apostle Paul similarly warned the Ephesian elders, "Take heed to yourselves and to all the flock. . . . For I know this, that after my departure savage wolves will come in among you, not sparing the flock. Also from among yourselves men will rise up, speaking perverse things, to draw away the disciples after themselves" (Acts 20:28–30). Peter, too, acknowledged that these counterfeits are embedded in the church, falsely professing to have been redeemed by Christ. As he told his readers, "But there were also false prophets among the people [of Israel], even as there will be false teachers *among you*, who will secretly bring in destructive heresies, even denying the Lord who bought them, and bring on themselves swift destruction" (2 Peter 2:1). Other passages could be added (such as 1 John 4:1 and Jude 4), but the point is clear. False prophets represent a genuine threat to the body of Christ.

Of course, false prophets don't advertise themselves as hypocritical heretics. They come in sheep's clothing, masquerade as angels of light, and promise liberty to others while they themselves are enslaved to sinful lusts. Yet false prophets are not that difficult to spot. The Bible gives three criteria for identifying these spiritual pretenders.

First, any self-proclaimed prophet who leads people into *false doctrine and heresy* is a false prophet. In Deuteronomy 13:1–5, Moses told the Israelites:

If there arises among you a prophet or a dreamer of dreams, and he gives you a sign or a wonder, and the sign or the wonder comes to pass, of which he spoke to you, saying, "Let us go after other gods"—which you have not known—"and let us serve them," you shall not listen to the words of that prophet or that dreamer of dreams, for the LORD your God is testing you to know whether you love the LORD your God with all your heart and with all your soul. You shall walk after the LORD your God and fear Him, and keep

His commandments and obey His voice; you shall serve Him and hold fast to Him. But that prophet or that dreamer of dreams shall be put to death, because he has spoken in order to turn you away from the LORD your God, who brought you out of the land of Egypt and redeemed you from the house of bondage, to entice you from the way in which the LORD your God commanded you to walk. So you shall put away the evil from your midst.

The New Testament is relentless in echoing that same warning. Anyone who claims to speak for God while simultaneously leading people away from the truth of God's Word is clearly shown to be a false prophet and a deceiver. Even if such a person makes accurate predictions or performs supposed wonders, he is to be disregarded—since Satan himself is able to perform counterfeit miracles (cf. 2 Thess. 2:9). History is peppered with examples of the devastating influence false prophets can have. Montanus was a second-century false teacher who gave more attention to the errant prophecies of two women than to Scripture. In the seventh century Muhammad claimed to be a prophet who received supposed revelation from the angel Gabriel. In the nineteenth century Joseph Smith founded Mormonism on fantastic claims about angelic visitations and extrabiblical revelations. Those are just a few historical illustrations of how much damage false prophets can inflict on those who follow them.

Second, any self-proclaimed prophet who lives in *unrestrained lust and unrepentant sin* shows himself to be a false prophet. The Lord Jesus Himself explained that false prophets could be identified by the fruits of their life (Matt. 7:20). The epistles of 2 Peter and Jude expand on that concept, noting that false prophets are enslaved to their lusts—being full of pride, greed, adultery, sensuality, rebellion, and corruption. They are motivated by the love of money, exchanging their eternal souls for the sake of sordid gain. Given enough time, false prophets will inevitably evidence their true nature in how they live. Though they claim to represent the Lord Jesus Christ, in reality they are not even genuine believers.

An occasionally accurate prediction is no proof of the gift of prophecy, or even of genuine conversion, as evidenced by unbelievers in Scripture who prophesied correctly (Num. 22–23; John 11:49–52). In fact, the Lord Jesus warned, "Many will say to Me in that day [at the final judgment], 'Lord, Lord, have we not prophesied in Your name, cast out demons in Your name, and done many wonders in Your name?' And then I will declare to them, 'I never knew you; depart from Me, you who practice lawlessness'" (Matt. 7:22–23). One wonders how many self-appointed modern prophets or televangelists with loose morals and lavish lifestyles will find themselves in that very scenario on the last day.

Third, if someone declaring himself a prophet proclaims any *supposed "revelation from God" that turns out to be inaccurate or untrue*, he must be summarily rejected as a spokesman for God. The Bible could not be clearer in its assertion that the prophet who speaks error in the name of the Lord is a counterfeit. In Deuteronomy 18:20–22, the Lord Himself told the Israelites:

> The prophet who presumes to speak a word in My name, which I have not commanded him to speak, or who speaks in the name of other gods, that prophet shall die. And if you say in your heart, "How shall we know the word which the LORD has not spoken?"—when a prophet speaks in the name of the LORD, if the thing does not happen or come to pass, that is the thing which the LORD has not spoken; the prophet has spoken it presumptuously; you shall not be afraid of him. (Deut. 18:20–22)

Any inaccurate prediction or statement made while claiming to relate revelation from God constituted a serious crime. Not only was an erroneous message proof positive the prophet was a fraud, but it also meant, under Old Testament law, he was worthy of the death penalty. God does not take lightly the offense of those who wrongly *presume* to speak for Him—saying, "Thus says the Lord," when in fact the Lord has not spoken. Those who condone or encourage such practices are culpable of sinful presumption and dereliction of their spiritual duty. We are not to listen to such prophecies with an undiscerning ear (cf. 1 Thess. 5:21).

In spite of Scripture's clear warnings and the consequent dishonor to the Spirit of God, charismatics have made *presumptuous prophecy* a hallmark of their movement. They have created a fertile breeding ground for false prophets—granting a platform of authority to anyone brash enough to stand up and claim to have received direct revelation from God, no matter how ludicrous or blasphemous. In previous chapters, we have already surveyed some of the various heresies that are tolerated and even promoted within charismatic ranks (usually legitimized by a "prophetic word" of some kind). And we have briefly noted the numerous scandals that continually plague the lives of the most visible and recognized charismatic leaders (including those who claim to be modern-day "prophets"). Those two factors alone are enough to demonstrate that the so-called prophecy rampant in the broader charismatic world is, in actuality, nothing more than *false* prophecy.

In this chapter, we will focus on that third identifying mark of a false prophet: inaccurate predictions. What the Bible condemns as a capital offense, the Charismatic Movement cherishes as a spiritual gift! In fact, the fallacies, foibles, and flat-out falsehoods that characterize contemporary prophecies are so blatant and well documented that charismatic theologians don't even try to deny them. Charismatic prophet Bill Hamon directly contradicts Deuteronomy 18 when he asserts, "We must not be quick to call someone a false prophet simply because something he said was inaccurate. . . . Missing it a few times in prophecy does not make a false prophet. No mortal prophet is infallible; all are liable to make mistakes."[1]

Jack Deere agrees, arguing that even if a prophet were to "miss it so badly" that his prophecy "had immediate destructive effects" in people's lives, that still doesn't make him a false prophet.[2] But that is not at all what Scripture teaches. Prophets are judged not by how many details they get right (since even demon-possessed people can sometimes make right predictions—Acts 16:16) but by how many they get wrong. Those who deliver direct, revelatory words from God must do so without error; otherwise they prove themselves to be liars.

Perhaps the most bizarre admission of modern prophetic error came during an extended interchange between self-proclaimed prophets Mike Bickle and Bob Jones—two of the most well-known figures associated with the Kansas City Prophets. While discussing the topic of "visions and revelations," Bickle asked Jones to talk about the numerous times his prophecies have been wrong. Here is a transcript of their conversation:

Mike Bickle: "Tell them about the error in your life; the measure of error that you have and the measure of accuracy, 'cause I want people to understand a little bit about that."

Bob Jones: "Well, I've had a lot of measure of error in my life. I remember once that I got into pride. Every time I get into pride, boy, Papa [God] sure knows how to pop my bubble. And I got into pride and called a church into a three-day fast and told them that certain things was going to happen, and they went into a three-day fast. It was terrible. And after that three-day fast—it was terrible, and the Spirit didn't even show up that night . . . ."

Mike Bickle: "You called people to a fast?"

Bob Jones: "I sure did, and it wasn't of the Lord; it was of my pride. I thought you could force the Lord to do something through fasting—boy, I found out real quick you couldn't. So there's a bunch of old saints that was ready to stone me, and so I was ready to get out of there and I went home like any good prophet, and I resigned. And I bawled and I squalled and I finally went to sleep and when I went to sleep the Lord come and took hold of my hand. And [in my vision] I was about like this little girl right here . . . only I was in a lot worse shape because I had a Pamper [diaper] on and I had really messed it good. It was running down both of my legs. And the Lord had a hold of my hand and I was a bawlin' and a squallin'. . . . And I heard a voice sort of speak, puzzled I can say, 'What happened to Bob?' And my [heavenly] counselor spoke up and said, 'He had an accident.'"

Mike Bickle: "Spoke some wrong words."

Bob Jones: "'Yeah. He had an accident. He messed his Pamper real bad.' And I think, 'Oh boy, here it comes.' And then I really got a surprise. A gentle, tender voice said, 'That boy needs more insurance. Let him know we've got him covered from them accidents. Give him a higher insurance policy.' That wasn't what I was looking for because I just resigned. 'Clean him up—tell him to go back into the body and prophesy twice as much. This time, he'll do what I'll tell him to.' . . . The next thing I knew I was back in bed, and boy, I come awake and man, I mean sweat was rolling down." . . .

Mike Bickle: "So there has been errors; there's been a number of errors."

Bob Jones: "Oh, hundreds of them."[3]

Jones's comments illustrate two of the primary problems with modern prophecy: it is chock-full of errors and inaccuracies, and it abounds with a level of sacrilegious lunacy that certainly does not find its source in God. Jones may have chosen just the right analogy in comparing his prophetic errors to a dirty diaper, but he is wrong about everything else. His claims to be a true prophet are obviously bogus. He does not have true visions of heaven. And God has certainly not given him "insurance" that allows him to get away with *hundreds of errors* as if it's no big deal.

Fewer than three years after that interview, Bob Jones was temporarily removed from public ministry by the Metro Vineyard Fellowship of Kansas City in Olathe, Kansas, whose senior pastor was none other than Mike Bickle. It had come to light that Jones was using false "prophecies" as a means of gaining trust from women whom he then abused sexually. "The sins for which [he was] removed from ministry include[d] using his gifts to manipulate people for his personal desires, sexual misconduct, rebelling against pastoral authority, slandering leaders and the promotion of bitterness within the body of Christ."[4] He nevertheless returned to the charismatic limelight after a short hiatus, and as of this writing, he is still speaking in charismatic churches, presenting himself as an anointed prophet of God, and making prophecies that are demonstrably false and often patently ridiculous.[5] Thousands of gullible charismatics still hang on his every word—as if all the scandal and false prophesying never happened. The fact that Jones's online biography compares his ministry to that of the prophet Daniel only heightens the blasphemous nature of the whole fiasco.[6]

FALLIBLE PROPHECY AND THE INFALLIBLE WORD

Additional illustrations of egregious falsehood and bizarre blasphemies in charismatic prophecies are not difficult to find. Benny Hinn made a series of celebrated prophetic utterances in December 1989, none of which came true. He confidently told his congregation at the Orlando Christian Center that God had revealed to him Fidel Castro would die sometime in the 1990s, the homosexual community in America would be destroyed by fire before 1995, and a major earthquake would cause havoc on the East Coast before the year 2000. He was wrong on all counts, but that did not deter Hinn, who kept making bold new false prophecies.

At the beginning of the new millennium, he announced to his television audience that a prophetess had informed him Jesus would soon appear physically in some of Hinn's healing meetings. Hinn said he was convinced the prophecy was authentic, and on his April 2, 2000, TBN broadcast, he amplified it with a prophecy of his own: "Now hear this: *I am prophesying this!* Jesus Christ, the Son of God, is about to appear physically in some churches, and some meetings, and to many of His people, for one reason: to tell you He is about to show up! To wake up! Jesus is coming, saints!"[7]

Hinn's failed prophecies are no less outlandish but not nearly as memorable as the notorious claims Oral Roberts began making several decades ago. In 1977 Roberts said he saw a vision of a nine-hundred-foot-tall Jesus, who instructed him to build the City of Faith, a sixty-story hospital in south Tulsa. Roberts said God told him He would use the center to unite medical technology with faith healing, which would revolutionize health care and enable doctors to find a cure for cancer.

The building, completed in the early 1980s, was a colossal white elephant from the start. When the City of Faith opened for business, all but two stories of the massive structure were completely vacant. By January 1987 the project was saddled with unmanageable debt, and Roberts announced that the Lord had said unless Roberts raised eight million dollars to pay the debt by March 1, he would die. Apparently not willing to test the death-threat prophecy, donors dutifully gave Roberts the needed funds in time (with the help of $1.3 million donated at the last hour by a Florida dog-track owner). But within two years, Roberts was forced to close the medical center anyway and sell the building in order to eliminate still-mounting debt. More than 80 percent of the building had never been occupied. The promised cure for cancer never materialized either.

Rick Joyner, another of the Kansas City Prophets and founder of Morningstar Ministries, predicted in the 1990s that Southern California would experience an earthquake of such magnitude that much of the state would be swallowed by the Pacific Ocean. Though the prediction failed to come to pass, Joyner continues to insist it will happen eventually. In 2011, after a 9.0 magnitude earthquake hit Japan, Joyner claimed (on the basis of prophetic revelation) that the same demonic forces that had empowered Nazi Germany were using global events sparked by the earthquake in Japan to gain inroads into the United States.[8]

A list of equally farcical and failed charismatic prophecies could fill several volumes. One would think such false prophets would live in mortal fear of divine judgment, but amazingly, they just keep spewing out claims that are more fantastic than ever. Incredibly, their influence only continues to grow—even among mainstream evangelicals. And the idea that God routinely speaks directly to His people has found more widespread acceptance today than at any time in the history of the church.

The Charismatic Movement began barely a hundred years ago, and its influence on evangelicalism can hardly be overstated. From its inception by Charles Fox Parham to its most ubiquitous modern representative in Benny Hinn, the entire movement is nothing more than a sham religion run by counterfeit ministers. True biblical interpretation, sound doctrine, and historical theology owes nothing to the movement—unless an influx of error and falsehood could be considered a contribution. Like any effective false system, charismatic theology incorporates enough of the truth to gain credibility. But in mixing the truth with deadly deceptions, it has concocted a cocktail of corruption and doctrinal poison—a lethal fabrication—with hearts and souls at stake.

Instead of enhancing people's interest in and devotion to Scripture, the Charismatic Movement's chief legacy has been an unprecedented interest in extrabiblical revelation. Millions influenced by charismatic doctrine are convinced God speaks to them directly all the time. Indeed, many seem to believe direct revelation is the *main* means through which God communicates with His people. "The Lord told me . . ." has become a favorite cliché of experience-driven evangelicals.

Not all who believe God speaks to them make prophetic pronouncements as outlandish as those broadcast by charismatic televangelists or the Kansas City Prophets. But they still believe God gives them extrabiblical messages—either through an audible voice, a vision, a voice in their heads, or simply an internal impression. In most cases, their "prophecies" are comparatively trivial. But the difference between them and Benny Hinn's predictions is a difference only of scale, not of substance.

The notion that God is constantly giving extrabiblical messages and fresh revelation to Christians today is practically the sine qua non of charismatic belief. According to the typical charismatic way of thinking, if God is not speaking privately, directly, and regularly to each individual believer, He is not truly immanent. Charismatics will therefore fiercely defend all manner of private prophecies, even though it is an undeniable fact that these supposed revelations from on high are often—one might say *usually*—erroneous, misleading, and even dangerous.

Wayne Grudem, for example, wrote his doctoral thesis at Cambridge University in defense of the idea that God regularly gives Christians prophetic messages by bringing spontaneous thoughts to mind. Strong impressions should be reported as prophecy, he says, though he freely admits that such prophetic words "can frequently contain errors."[9] Grudem goes on, "There is almost uniform testimony from all sections of the charismatic movement *that prophecy is imperfect and impure,* and will contain elements which are not to be obeyed or trusted."[10] In light of such an admission, one wonders, how can Christians differentiate a revelatory word of divine origin from one concocted in their own imaginations? Grudem struggles to find an adequate answer to that question:

> Did the revelation *"seem* like" something from the Holy Spirit; did it *seem* to be similar to other experiences of the Holy Spirit which [the person] had known previously in worship. . . . Beyond this it is difficult to specify much further, except to say that over time a congregation would *probably* become more adept at making evaluations of prophecies, . . . and become more adept at recognizing a genuine revelation from the Holy Spirit and distinguishing it from their own thoughts.[11]

Elsewhere, Grudem compared the evaluation of modern prophecy to a game of baseball: "You call it as you see it. I have to use an American analogy. It's an umpire calling balls and strikes as the pitcher pitches the ball across the plate."[12] In other words, within charismatic circles, there are no *objective criteria* for differentiating prophetic words from imaginary ones.

In spite of the acknowledged inaccuracies and obvious subjectivism, the notion that God is speaking outside of the Bible continues to find increasing acceptance in the evangelical world, even among noncharismatics. Southern Baptists, for example, have eagerly devoured *Experiencing God* by Henry Blackaby and Claude King, which suggests the main way the Holy Spirit leads believers is by speaking to them directly. According to Blackaby, when God gives an individual a message that pertains to the church, it should be shared with the whole body.[13] As a result, extrabiblical "words from the Lord" are now commonplace even in some Southern Baptist circles.

Why do so many modern Christians seek revelation from God through means other than Scripture? Certainly not because it is a reliable way to discover truth. As we have seen, all sides admit that modern prophecies are often completely erroneous. The failure rate is astonishingly high. In *Charismatic Chaos*, I quoted a conversation between the two top leaders in the Kansas City Prophets Movement. They were thrilled because they believed two-thirds of the group's prophecies were accurate. One of them said, "Well, that's better than it's ever been up to now, you know. That's the highest level it's ever been."[14]

Put simply, modern prophecy is no more reliable in discerning truth than a Magic Eight Ball, tarot cards, or a Ouija board. And, it should be added, it is equally superstitious. There is no warrant anywhere in Scripture for Christians to listen for fresh revelation from God beyond what He has already given us in His written Word. Going back to Deuteronomy 18, Scripture unsparingly condemns all who speak even one word falsely or presumptuously in the Lord's name. But such warnings are simply disregarded these days by those who claim to have heard afresh from God.

Not surprisingly, wherever there is a movement preoccupied with "fresh" prophecy, there is invariably a corresponding neglect of the Scriptures. After all, why be concerned with working to accurately interpret an ancient Book if the living God communicates directly with us in the current vernacular on a daily basis? These fresh words of "revelation" naturally seem more relevant and more urgent than the familiar words of the Bible. Sarah Young is the author of *Jesus Calling*, a best-selling book consisting entirely of devotional entries she says she received from Christ. The whole book is written in Christ's voice, as if He is speaking through the human author directly to the reader. Indeed, that is precisely the authority Sarah Young claims for her book. She says Jesus gave her the words, and she is merely a "listener." She acknowledges that her quest for extrabiblical revelation began with a nagging feeling that Scripture is simply not sufficient. "I knew that God communicated with me through the Bible," she writes, "but I yearned for more. Increasingly I wanted to hear what God had to say to me personally on a given day."[15] Is it any wonder such an attitude draws people away from Scripture?

That is precisely why modern evangelicalism's infatuation with extra-biblical revelation is so dangerous. It is a return to medieval superstition and a departure from our fundamental conviction that the Bible is our sole, supreme, and *sufficient* authority for all of life. It represents a wholesale abandonment of the Reformation principle of *sola Scriptura*.

The absolute sufficiency of Scripture is summed up well in this section from the *Westminster Confession of Faith:* "The whole counsel of God, concerning all things necessary for His own glory, man's salvation, faith, and life, is either expressly set down in Scripture, or by good and necessary consequence may be deduced from Scripture: *unto which nothing at any time is to be added, whether by new revelations of the Spirit, or traditions of men.*"[16] Historic Protestantism is grounded in the conviction that the canon is closed. No new revelation is necessary, because Scripture is complete and absolutely sufficient.

Scripture itself is clear that the day of God's speaking directly to people in the church age through various prophetic words and visions is past. The truth God has revealed in the canon of the Old and New Testaments is complete (cf. Heb. 1:1–2; Jude 3; Rev. 22:18–19). Scripture—the written Word of God—is perfectly sufficient, containing all the revelation we need. Notice 2 Timothy 3:15–17, where Paul tells Timothy:

From childhood you have known the Holy Scriptures, which are able to make you wise for salvation through faith which is in Christ Jesus. All Scripture is given by inspiration of God, and is profitable for doctrine, for reproof, for correction, for instruction in righteousness, that the man of God may be complete, thoroughly equipped for every good work.

That passage makes two very important statements that pertain to the issue at hand. First, "all Scripture is given by inspiration of God." Scripture speaks with the authority of God Himself. It is certain; it is reliable; *it is true.* Jesus Himself prayed in John 17:17: "Your word is truth." Psalm 119:160 says, "The entirety of Your word is truth." Those statements set Scripture above every human opinion, every speculation, and every emotional sensation. Scripture alone stands as definitive truth. It speaks with an authority that transcends every other voice.

Second, the passage teaches that Scripture is utterly sufficient, "able to make you wise for salvation," and able to make you "complete, thoroughly equipped for every good work." What clearer affirmation of the absolute sufficiency of Scripture could anyone ask for? Are extrabiblical messages from God necessary to equip us to glorify Him? Obviously not. Those who seek fresh messages from God have in effect abandoned the absolute certainty and total sufficiency of the written Word of God. And they have set in its place their own fallen and fallible imaginations. If the church does not return to the principle of *sola Scriptura*, the only revival we will see is a revival of unchecked superstition and spiritual murkiness.

Does this mean God has stopped speaking? Certainly not, but He speaks today through His all-sufficient Word. Does the Spirit of God move our hearts and impress us with specific duties or callings? Certainly, but He works through the Word of God to do that. Such experiences do not involve *new revelation* but *illumination*, when the Holy Spirit applies the Word to our hearts and opens our spiritual eyes to its truth. We must guard carefully against allowing our experience and our own subjective thoughts and imaginations to eclipse the authority and the certainty of the more sure Word.

The renowned twentieth-century British biblical expositor David Martyn

Lloyd-Jones aptly summarized the proper perspective contemporary believers ought to have regarding prophecy. Commenting on Ephesians 4:11, Lloyd-Jones wrote:

> Once these New Testament documents were written the office of a prophet was no longer necessary. . . . [I]n the history of the Church trouble has arisen because people thought that they were prophets in the New Testament sense, and that they had received special revelations of truth. The answer to that is that in view of the New Testament Scriptures there is no need of further truth. That is an absolute proposition. We have all truth in the New Testament, and we have no need of any further revelations. All has been given, everything that is necessary for us is available. Therefore if a man claims to have received a revelation of some fresh truth we should suspect him immediately. . . .
>
> The answer to all this is that the need for prophets ends once we have the canon of the New Testament. We no longer need direct revelations of truth; the truth is in the Bible. We must never separate the Spirit and the Word. The Spirit speaks to us through the Word; so we should always doubt and query any supposed revelation that is not entirely consistent with the Word of God. Indeed the essence of wisdom is to reject altogether the term "revelation" as far as we are concerned, and speak only of "illumination." The revelation has been given once and for all, and what we need and what by the grace of God we can have, and do have, is illumination by the Spirit to understand the Word.[17]

Two Kinds of Prophets?

In an attempt to circumvent the clear-cut parameters of Scripture (and maintain some form of modern prophecy), charismatics are forced to propose there are actually two kinds of prophets described in Scripture—one that was infallible and authoritative, and a second kind that was not. The first category includes Old Testament prophets, New Testament apostles, and the authors of Scripture. Their prophecies consisted of the perfect transmission of God's words to God's people. As a result, their prophetic proclamations were both error-free and immediately binding on the lives of others.

In addition, charismatics contend there was a second tier of prophets in the New Testament church: congregational prophets who spoke a form of prophecy that was *fallible* and *nonauthoritative*, and that came into existence in New Testament times. The congregational prophets in the early church—so the argument goes—sometimes made mistakes in their report of divine revelation; thus, they were not required to meet the same perfect standard of the Old Testament prophets and biblical authors. Following that line of logic, charismatics insist that modern prophecies don't have to be held to a standard of 100 percent accuracy.

The notion of fallible New Testament prophets—spokesmen for God who reported divine revelation in an erroneous and corrupt way—may fit the contemporary charismatic scene. But it has a fatal flaw: it is not biblical. In fact, the Bible only and always condemns erroneous prophets as dangerous and deceptive. *Fallible* prophets are *false* prophets—or at best, misguided nonprophets who should immediately cease and desist from presumptively pretending to speak for God. As they do with everything else, charismatics have forced their modern experiences upon Scripture (labeling their error-laden utterances as "prophecy"), instead of submitting their experiences to the straightforward standards of the biblical text. When compared to the clear criteria set forth in the Word of God, nothing about modern prophecy measures up.

Charismatics may claim that New Testament prophets were not held to the same standard as their Old Testament counterparts, but such an assertion is entirely without warrant. Biblically speaking, no distinction is made in Scripture between the prophets in either Testament. In fact, the New Testament uses identical terminology to describe both Old and New Testament prophets. In the book of Acts, Old Testament prophets are mentioned in Acts 2:16; 3:24–25; 10:43; 13:27, 40; 15:15; 24:14; 26:22, 27; and 28:23. References to New Testament prophets are interspersed using the same vocabulary without any distinction, comment, or caveat (cf. Acts 2:17–18; 7:37; 11:27–28; 13:1; 15:32; 21:9–11).

Surely, if the New Testament prophetic office were categorically different, as charismatics claim, some distinction would have been made. As Sam Waldron rightly points out, "If New Testament prophecy in distinction from Old Testament prophecy was not infallible in its pronouncements, this would have constituted an absolutely fundamental contrast between the Old Testament institution and the New Testament institution. To suppose that a difference as important as this would be passed over without explicit comment is unthinkable."[18]

Of course, a proper understanding of New Testament prophets rests on more than just an argument from silence. When Peter spoke of the type of prophecy that would characterize the church during the apostolic age (in Acts 2:18), he cited Joel 2:28—a clear reference to *Old Testament–type* prophecy. And when the biblical authors described New Testament prophets (such as John the Baptist, the prophet Agabus, and the apostle John in the book of Revelation), they did so in a way that was deliberately reminiscent of Old Testament prophets.[19] The writers of the New Testament further emphasized that the expectations and function were the same for both.[20] Clearly, the early church regarded prophets as the categorical equivalent of their Old Testament predecessors. After an extensive survey of the first several centuries of church history, New Testament professor David Farnell concludes:

> In summary the early post-apostolic church judged the genuineness of New Testament prophets by Old Testament prophetic standards. Prophets in the New Testament era who were ecstatic, made wrong applications of Scripture, or prophesied falsely were considered false prophets because such actions violated Old Testament stipulations regarding what characterized a genuine prophet of God (Deut. 13:1–5; 18:20–22). . . . The early church affirmed the idea of a direct continuity between Old Testament and New Testament prophets and prophetic standards.[21]

In the same way Old Testament prophets were required to speak truth when they proclaimed revelation from God, so also New Testament prophets were held to that same standard. When they declared, "Thus says the Lord," what came next had to be precisely what God said (cf. Acts 21:11). Since authentic words from God will always reflect His perfect, flawless character, such prophecies will always be infallible and inerrant. Testing was necessary, because false prophets presented a constant threat (1 John 4:1; cf. 2 Peter 2:1–3; 2 John 10–11; 3 John 9–10; Jude 8–23). Just as prophecies were to be examined on the basis of previous revelation in the Old Testament (Deut. 13:1–5), so they were to be tested in the New (1 Thess. 5:20–22; cf. Acts 17:11).

No doubt, someone will object by pointing to Romans 12:6, where Paul wrote, "Having then gifts differing according to the grace that is given to us, let us use them: if prophecy, let us prophesy in proportion to our faith." Charismatics use this verse to argue that the accuracy of prophecy is dependent on the measure of a person's faith. However, that is not even close to Paul's true meaning in that verse. The word translated "our" in the New King James is actually the definite article in Greek. It is most accurately translated simply as "the." Hence, Paul is instructing his readers that those with the gift of prophecy must prophesy in accordance with *the* faith—the body of previously revealed biblical truth (cf. Jude 3–4).

Furthermore, the word *prophecy* in this context does not necessarily refer to future predictions or new revelation. The word simply means "to speak forth," and it applies to any authoritative proclamation of God's Word where the person gifted to declare God's truth "speaks edification and exhortation and comfort to men" (1 Cor. 14:3). So a fitting paraphrase of Romans 12:6 would be: "If your gift is proclaiming God's Word, do it according to the faith." Again, the idea is that whatever is proclaimed must conform perfectly with the true faith, being consistent with previous biblical revelation.

Probably the most common argument for fallible prophecy made by charismatics regards the New Testament prophet Agabus. In Acts 21:10–11, Agabus predicted that when Paul arrived in Jerusalem, he would be bound by the Jews and delivered to the Romans. Charismatics make much of the fact that Luke does not repeat those precise details later in Acts 21, when he records the details of Paul's arrest. The implication, in the mind of continuationists like Wayne Grudem, is that Agabus's "prediction was not far off, but it had inaccuracies in detail that would have called into question the validity of any Old Testament prophet."[22] Elsewhere Grudem goes even further, claiming this constitutes "a prophecy whose two elements—'binding' and 'giving over' by the Jews—are explicitly falsified by the subsequent narrative."[23] Thus, according to Grudem, Agabus provides an illustration of fallible prophecy in the New Testament and a paradigm on which to base the charismatic model.

But are the details of Agabus's prophecy *explicitly falsified* by the subsequent narrative? A close examination of the text actually demonstrates the exact opposite. That the Jews "bound" Paul, as Agabus predicted in Acts 21:11, is implied by the fact that they "seized" him (v. 30), "dragged" him (v. 30), and were "beating" him (v. 32). In Acts 26:21, when testifying before Agrippa, Paul reiterated the fact that the Jews "seized" him and "tried to kill" him. In capturing Paul by force and dragging him out of the temple, the violent antagonists would have needed to restrain their unwilling victim with whatever was immediately available to them—using Paul's own belt to tie him up so he could not escape. Since Agabus had already provided this detail in verse 10, Luke did not deem it necessary to repeat it in verse 30. When the Roman soldiers arrived on the scene (v. 33), they officially arrested Paul—removing him from his temporary restraints and placing him in chains. Everything accords perfectly with what Agabus said would take place.

That the Jews "delivered" Paul to the Roman soldiers is also implied by the account in Acts 21. In verse 32, Paul was being assaulted by the angry mob when the cohort of soldiers arrived. Upon seeing the Roman authorities, the Jews stopped beating Paul and allowed the soldiers to arrest him without further incident (v. 33). Again, the implication of Luke's narrative is that the angry crowd backed away and dispersed, willingly surrendering Paul into the hands of the Roman authorities at that point in time.

This understanding of the text is confirmed by Paul's own testimony. In Acts 28:17, Paul explained what had happened to him to a group of Jews in Rome: "Men and brethren, though I have done nothing against our people or the customs of our fathers, yet *I was delivered as a prisoner from Jerusalem into the hands of the Romans*." Paul had done nothing to violate Jewish law, yet he was falsely accused by Jewish leaders who thought he had. They then *delivered* him *as a prisoner* (i.e., one who is bound) into the hands of the Roman authorities. Significantly, the word Paul used for "delivered" (Acts 28:17) was the same Greek word Agabus used in his prophecy (Acts 21:11). Thus, Paul's own testimony verified that the details of Agabus's prophecy were absolutely correct.

Perhaps most significant of all is the fact that when Agabus prophesied, he quoted the Holy Spirit. In much the same way as an Old Testament prophet would declare, "Thus says the Lord," Agabus began his prediction with these words: "Thus says the Holy Spirit." The words that followed were a direct quote from the Holy Spirit Himself, and Luke records them that way. More important, *the Holy Spirit Himself* inspired Luke to record them that way—without any correction or qualification. Therefore, any claim that Agabus erred in the details of his prophecy is a tacit accusation that the Holy Spirit erred in the content of His prophetic revelation.

Clearly, Agabus is *not* the example of fallible prophecy that charismatics make him out to be.[24] That conclusion presents a major blow to extrabiblical prophecy. As Robert Saucy explains, speaking of Agabus, "The prophecy is thus easily interpreted as without error, leaving no example of an errant prophecy to support the concept of fallible prophecy proposed by the [charismatic] position."[25]

WHAT ABOUT 1 THESSALONIANS 5:20–22?

In 1 Thessalonians 5:20–22, the apostle Paul wrote, "Do not despise prophetic utterances. But examine everything carefully; hold fast to that which is good; abstain from every form of evil" (NASB). How are we to interpret Paul's instruction in those verses with respect to the New Testament gift of prophecy?

A proper understanding of this text begins with the realization that true prophetic utterances consisted of divine revelation. Thus, they must not be despised because to do so would be to scorn the words of God Himself. As I have explained elsewhere:

Respect for the supremacy of the revelation of God is what the apostle Paul had in mind when he cautioned the Thessalonians not to despise prophetic utterances. Despise (*exoutheneō*) carries the strong meaning, "to consider as absolutely nothing," "to treat with contempt," or "to look down on." In the New Testament, prophetic utterances (*prophēteia*) can refer either to spoken words or written words. The verb form (*prophēteuō*) means "to speak or proclaim publicly"; thus the gift of prophecy was the Spirit-endowed skill of publicly proclaiming God's revealed truth. New Testament prophets sometimes delivered a brand-new revelation directly from God (Luke 2:29–32; cf. v. 38; Acts 15:23–29). At other times they merely reiterated a divine proclamation that was already recorded (cf. Luke 3:5–6; Acts 2:17–21, 25–28, 34–35; 4:25–26; 7:2–53).[26]

In either case, because it consisted of the proclamation of divine revelation, genuine prophecy invariably reflected the character of God Himself. That is why it could be tested according to the measure of *the* faith (Rom. 12:6), meaning it had to agree with previously revealed truth (cf. Acts 6:7; Jude 3, 20). A prophetic utterance that came from God was always *true* and *consistent* with Scripture. Conversely, a word of alleged prophecy that was erroneous or contrary to God's written Word showed itself to be false. Thus, Paul instructed the Thessalonians to exercise spiritual discernment whenever they heard any message that claimed to have divine origins, testing it carefully by comparing it to prior written revelation. Paul describes those prophecies that failed the test as "evil" (v. 22)—something believers must avoid.

In spite of this, charismatics often point to 1 Thessalonians 5:20–22 to defend erroneous prophecies, thinking these verses support their claim that New Testament prophecy was fallible and full of errors. After all, they contend, why would Paul command the church to test prophetic utterances if New Testament prophecy was equal to the inerrant and authoritative prophecies of the Old Testament?

In asking that question, charismatics fail to recognize that Old Testament prophecy was in fact subjected to the same kind of testing as New Testament prophecy. Paul was not instructing the Thessalonians to do anything other than what God had always required His people to do. The Lord instructed the Israelites to test all prophecy on the basis of *orthodoxy* (Deut. 13:1–5; Isa.

8:20) and *accuracy* (Deut. 18:20–22). Prophecies that did not meet those qualifications were deemed false. Because false prophets were prevalent in Old Testament Israel (Deut. 13:3; Isa. 30:10; Jer. 5:31; 14:14–16; 23:21–22; Ezek. 13:2–9; 22:28; Mic. 3:11), God's people needed to be able to identify and confront them. That same reality applied to New Testament believers as well, which is why Paul instructed the Thessalonians to test prophetic utterances carefully.

Even as an apostle, Paul encouraged others to test his teaching by those same criteria. In the book of Galatians, he reiterated the principle of Deuteronomy 13:1–5 when he said, "But even if we, or an angel from heaven, preach any other gospel to you than what we have preached to you, let him be accursed" (Gal. 1:8). Several years later, immediately after Paul left Thessalonica but before he wrote his first epistle there, he traveled to Berea. The Bereans did not automatically accept Paul's teaching but tested his words against Old Testament revelation. The book of Acts says this about them: "These were more fair-minded than those in Thessalonica, in that they received the word with all readiness, *and searched the Scriptures daily to find out whether these things were so*" (Acts 17:11). That incident may have well been on Paul's mind as he penned this plea for careful, watchful discernment to the Thessalonians shortly thereafter.

The presence of false prophets in the first-century church is a fact that is clearly attested in the New Testament (Matt. 7:15; 24:11; 2 Tim. 4:3–4; 2 Peter 2:1–3; 1 John 4:1; Jude 4). Commands to test prophecy must be understood against that backdrop. Believers were commanded to discern between those who were true spokesmen for God and those who were dangerous counterfeits. The Thessalonians, in particular, needed to be wary of false prophets. Paul's two epistles to them indicate that some within their congregation had already been misled—both with regard to Paul's personal character (1 Thess. 2:1–12) and the eschatological future of the church (1 Thess. 4:13–5:11). Much of Paul's instruction was in response to the erroneous teaching that was wreaking havoc within the Thessalonian church. Perhaps that is why some of the Thessalonians were tempted to despise all prophetic utterances, including those that were true.

It is also important to remember Paul wrote these words at a time when the revelatory gift of prophecy was still active—during the foundation age of the church (cf. Eph. 2:20). His command, "Do not despise prophetic utterances," specifically applies to a time when that revelatory gift was in full operation. When cessationists discredit the false predictions of modern-day "prophets," they are not violating Paul's injunction. Rather, they are taking divine revelation seriously—applying the biblical standards of accuracy and orthodoxy to messages that claim to come from God. In reality, it is charismatics who despise that which is truly prophetic when they indiscriminately endorse a counterfeit form of the gift.

Although the revelatory gift of prophecy has ceased, the proclamation of the prophetic Word still continues today—as preachers exposit the Scriptures and exhort people to obey (2 Tim. 4:2). As a result, the implications of 1 Thessalonians 5:19–22 still apply to the modern church. Every sermon, every message, every application given by contemporary pastors and teachers ought to be examined carefully through the lens of Scripture. If someone claims to speak for God yet his message does not accord with biblical truth, he shows himself to be a fraud. That is where biblical discernment is necessary.

Putting all this together, we see that 1 Thessalonians 5:20–22 does not support the charismatic case for fallible prophecy. Rather, it leads to the opposite conclusion, because it calls Christians to test any message or messenger that claims to come from God. When we apply the tests of Scripture to the supposed revelations of modern-day charismatics, we quickly see their "prophesying" for what it really is: a dangerous counterfeit.

When all the passages regarding prophecy in the New Testament are considered, the charismatic position is immediately exposed as baseless and unbiblical. The plain teaching of the New Testament is that prophets in the first-century church were to be held to the same standard of accuracy as prophets in the Old Testament. Though it may exist in the minds of those who want to justify their errant practices, the evidence necessary to support any notion of fallible prophets is completely absent from the biblical record.

A DANGEROUS GAME

So what is modern charismatic prophecy if it is not a biblical practice? Former prophet Fred L. Volz provides an insightful answer, reflecting on his own experiences in the Charismatic Movement:

> I noticed that the vast majority of the "prophecies" made by these "prophets" were very similar to each other in that they always vaguely predicted great blessings and future opportunities of fortune and success. So of course when another positive "prophecy" came, it was seen as a confirmation of an earlier one and some day it would come to pass.
>
> Sometimes a prophecy would be accompanied by some information about the person's past or present, such as: "There is someone in your family battling alcohol or drugs" or "You love music" (Wow! What are the odds?). A careful study of Scripture, testing it against the Word of God, combined with questions to the pastor, reveals all of this for what it really is, a counterfeit.[27]

Most charismatic prophets are no different from sideshow psychics and palm readers. But in some cases there may be a darker source. Volz continues by comparing charismatic prophecies to the satanic predictions made by New Age prophets. His sobering words should strike fear into the hearts of any who would play with this form of strange fire:

> I do not believe Satan precisely knows the future. If he did, the false prophets would be much more accurate. For instance, there were people who were obviously false prophets of the "New Age" variety who "prophesied" the September 11, 2001 attack on the World Trade Center several months before it happened. . . . According to military experts, that attack had been years in the making. Satan knew every detail of the plan since its inception. That is why false prophets seem uncanny in their accuracy. He has studied human behavior for [thousands of] years and has legions of angels and demons to act as his eyes and ears in all of our affairs. But even so, with all of his knowledge he cannot precisely see the future. He simply guesses right sometimes.[28]

By contrast, *true* prophecy does not come to mind through psychic intuition or New Age mysticism, and it is not discerned by guesswork. "No prophecy of Scripture is of any private interpretation, for prophecy never came by the will of man, but holy men of God spoke as they were moved by the Holy Spirit" (2 Peter 1:20–21). Those who equate their own personal impressions, imaginations, and intuition with divine revelation err greatly. The problem is magnified by the common charismatic practice of knowingly permitting someone who has prophesied falsely to continue to claim he or she speaks for God. To say it as simply and plainly as possible, this approach to "prophecy" is the grossest kind of *rank heresy*, because it ascribes to God that which did not come from Him.

By claiming fallible prophecies as legitimate, charismatics open the door to satanic attack and deception—putting their movement in the same category as cult groups like the Seventh-day Adventists, Mormons, and Jehovah's Witnesses. Errant prophecy is one of the clearest earmarks of a non-Christian cult or false religion. William Miller and Ellen G. White, the founders of Seventh-day Adventism, falsely prophesied that Jesus would return in 1843. When the prediction failed, they changed the date to 1844. When their calculations again proved inaccurate, they insisted their date was not wrong. Instead, they claimed, the event they associated with the date must have been wrong. So they invented a new doctrine, asserting that Christ entered His heavenly sanctuary in 1844 to begin a second work of atonement (in clear contradiction to Hebrews 9:12 and a host of New Testament passages).

Mormon patriarch Joseph Smith similarly prophesied that Jesus would return before the year 1891. Other false predictions included Smith's prophecy that all nations would be involved in the American Civil War; that a temple would be built in Independence, Missouri (such a temple was never built); and that the Mormon "apostle" David W. Patten would go on a mission in the spring of 1839. (Patten was shot and killed on October 25, 1838, thus nullifying his ability to do anything in 1839.)

Throughout their hundred-year history, the Watchtower Society has incorrectly prophesied the return of Christ many times, starting in 1914 and including subsequent predictions for 1915, 1925, 1935, 1951, 1975, 1986, and

2000. Currently, Jehovah's Witnesses expect the end of the world in 2033, since that will be the 120th year after the original prediction of 1914. In the same way Noah built the ark for 120 years, followers of the Watchtower Society are convinced God's judgment will fall on this earth after twelve decades have elapsed from the outset of World War I.

We might laugh at the lunacy of such predictions; and we should certainly use those blatant inaccuracies as an apologetic against the false teachings of those groups. But we might ask, how are those false predictions any different from the ludicrous errors that pervade charismatic prophecies? From an outsider's perspective, there is no definitive distinction. If false predictions can be used to show the bankruptcy of cult groups, the same must be true of modern charismatic prophecy. Exposing the inaccuracies is not being *unloving*; it is being *biblical*—taking us back to the standard established by Deuteronomy 18.

The true prophetic office demanded 100 percent accuracy. Insofar as they declared new revelation from God to the church, New Testament prophets were held to that standard. To be sure, the *proclamation and exposition* of the prophetic word (2 Peter 1:19) continues today through faithful preaching and teaching. In the same way biblical prophets exhorted and admonished people to listen to divine revelation, so gifted preachers throughout all of church history up to the present day have passionately encouraged their congregations to heed the Word of the Lord. The key difference is that, whereas biblical prophets received *new revelation* directly from the Spirit of God, contemporary preachers are called to proclaim only that which the Spirit of God revealed in His inspired Word (cf. 2 Tim. 4:2). Hence, the only legitimate way anyone can say, "Thus says the Lord . . ." is if the next words that follow come directly from the biblical text. Anything other than that is blasphemous presumption, and certainly *not* prophecy.

At its core, it is the charismatic focus on receiving new revelation that makes their view of prophecy so dangerous. But the Bible is clear: the giving of *new revelation* through living prophets in the New Testament era was intended only for the foundation age of the church. As Paul stated definitively in Ephesians 2:20, the church was "built *on the foundation* of the apostles *and prophets*." That the prophets described by Paul in that verse refer to

New Testament prophets is made clear by the rest of Ephesians, where New Testament prophets are delineated in Ephesians 3:5 and 4:11.

Charismatics fail to seriously consider what brazen dishonor they do to God and His Word when they claim revelation from Him when He has not really spoken—declaring words of prophecy that are full of error and corruption. When God speaks, it is always perfect, true, and infallible. After all, God cannot lie (Titus 1:2)! And those who speak lying words in His name place themselves under His judgment.

Truth is the lifeblood of Christianity. Thus, false prophecy (and the false doctrine that accompanies it) represents the single greatest threat to the purity of the church. The Charismatic Movement provides false prophets and false teachers an unguarded entry point into the church. More than that, the movement puts out a welcome mat for those who proliferate the error of their own imaginations, inviting them inside the camp with open arms and affirming their sin with a hearty amen. But the prophets of the Charismatic Movement are not true prophets. So what does that make them?

The answer to that question brings this chapter full circle. According to 2 Peter and Jude, they are dry wells, fruitless trees, raging waves, wandering stars, brute beasts, hideous stains, vomit-eating dogs, mud-loving pigs, and ravenous wolves.

The renowned preacher Charles Spurgeon had this to say to those who came to him with supposed words of revelation from the Holy Spirit:

Take care never to impute the vain imaginings of your fancy to him [the Holy Spirit]. I have seen the Spirit of God shamefully dishonoured by persons—I hope they were insane—who have said that they have had this and that revealed to them. There has not for some years passed over my head a single week in which I have not been pestered with the revelations of hypocrites or maniacs. Semi-lunatics are very fond of coming with messages from the Lord to me, and it may spare them some trouble if I tell them once for all that I will have none of their stupid messages. . . . Never dream that events are revealed to you by heaven, or you may come to be like those idiots who dare impute their blatant follies to the Holy Ghost. If you feel your tongue itch to talk nonsense, trace it to the devil, not to the Spirit of God. Whatever is to be revealed by the Spirit to any of us is in the word of God already—he adds nothing to the Bible, and never will. Let persons who have revelations of this, that, and the other, *go to bed and wake up in their senses.* I only wish they would follow the advice and no longer insult the Holy Ghost by laying their nonsense at his door.[29]

Spurgeon's words may sound harsh, but they reflect the severity with which Scripture itself condemns all such presumption. Jeremiah 23 contains similar warnings about false prophecy. Believers who are part of charismatic churches would do well to pay attention:

Thus says the LORD of hosts: "Do not listen to the words of the prophets who prophesy to you. They make you worthless; they speak a vision of their own heart, not from the mouth of the LORD. . . . I have not sent these prophets, yet they ran. I have not spoken to them, yet they prophesied. But if they had stood in My counsel, and had caused My people to hear My words, then they would have turned them from their evil way and from the evil of their doings. . . . I have heard what the prophets have said who prophesy lies in My name, saying, 'I have dreamed, I have dreamed!' How long will this be in the heart of the prophets who prophesy lies? Indeed they are prophets of the deceit of their own heart. . . . Behold, I am against the prophets," says the LORD, "who use their tongues and say, 'He [the LORD] says.' Behold, I am against those who prophesy false dreams," says the LORD, "and tell them, and cause My people to err by their lies and by their recklessness. Yet I did not send them or command them; therefore they shall not profit this people at all," says the LORD. (Jer. 23:16–32)

SEVEN

TWISTING TONGUES

Pentecostal televangelist and self-acclaimed prophetess Juanita Bynum made headlines in 2011 when she posted strings of incoherent characters on her Facebook page, including "CHCNCFURRIR UNGIGNGNGNVGGGNCG," "RFSCNGUGHURGVHKTGHDKUN HSTNSVHGN," and "NDHDIUBGUGTRUCGNRTUGTIGRTIGRGB-NRDRGNGGJNRIC." In most cases, a little bit of gibberish on a social media site would probably go unnoticed—explained away as a bit of muddled thinking or perhaps blamed on a sticking keyboard. But for charismatics, Bynum's jumble of letters represented something far loftier. An article in the *Christian Post* captured the significance of her odd status updates with the title "Televangelist Juanita Bynum Raises Brows with 'Tongues' Prayer on Facebook."[1]

Although Pentecostal tongues-speech is by definition verbal, it appeared in this incident in a printed form. Bynum's Facebook gibberish serves as a vivid illustration of the so-called tongues that characterize the contemporary Charismatic Movement. While there is less interest in this esoteric behavior than the tangible prosperity gospel (for obvious reasons), it is still a defining staple in the movement. Sometimes referred to as "heavenly speech," "the tongues of angels," or a "private prayer language," modern "tongues" consist wholly of nonsensical babble, a point even charismatics acknowledge.

Reflecting on the first time he spoke in tongues, *Charisma* magazine editor J. Lee Grady wrote, "The next day when I was in my room praying, I could tell that a heavenly language was bubbling up inside me. I opened my mouth and the words spilled out. *Ilia skiridan tola do skantama.* Or something like that. I had no clue what I was saying. It sounded like gibberish. Yet when I prayed in tongues I felt close to God."[2]

Dennis Bennett, whose personal charismatic experiences helped spark the Charismatic Renewal Movement of the 1960s, explains it this way: "You never know what a tongue is going to sound like. I had an acquaintance who sounded like 'rub-a-dubdub' when he spoke in tongues, but he got a great blessing out of doing it."[3] Joyce Meyer, after defending the modern phenomenon merely because "there are millions of people on the earth today" doing it, concludes, "I doubt that many people are making up languages and spending their time talking in gibberish just for the sake of thinking they are speaking in tongues."[4] Ironically, Meyer's silly defense unwittingly acknowledges modern glossolalia (tongues-speech) for what it really is: *"making up languages and . . . talking in gibberish."*

Linguists who have studied modern glossolalia agree with that description. After years of firsthand research, visiting charismatic groups in various countries, University of Toronto linguistics professor William Samarin wrote this:

> There is no mystery about glossolalia. Tape-recorded samples are easy to obtain and to analyze. They always turn out to be the same thing: *strings of syllables, made up of sounds taken from among all those that the speaker knows, put together more or less haphazardly but which nevertheless emerge as word-like and sentence-like units because of realistic, language-like rhythm and melody.* Glossolalia is indeed like language in some ways, but this is only because the speaker (unconsciously) wants it to be like language. Yet in spite of superficial similarities, glossolalia is fundamentally *not* language. All specimens of glossolalia that have ever been studied have produced no features that would even suggest that they reflect some kind of communicative system. . . .
>
> Glossolalia is not a supernatural phenomenon. . . . In fact, anybody can produce glossolalia if he is uninhibited and if he discovers what the "trick" is.[5]

Elsewhere Samarin says, "When the full apparatus of linguistic science comes to bear on glossolalia, this turns out to be only a façade of language."[6]

The *Encyclopedia of Psychology and Religion* puts it more succinctly: "Glossolalia is not a human language and cannot be interpreted or studied as a human language."[7] The *Cambridge Companion to Science and Religion* agrees, noting that glossolalia is unquestionably "not a language."[8]

In response to the obvious reality, charismatic authors have abandoned making any attempt to correlate the modern gift with any known foreign languages. Rather, readers are told that "600 million Christians have received the Holy Spirit gift *of their own spirit language*."[9] Each person's tongues-speech is unique to him or her. And it often begins with nothing more than a syllable thoughtlessly repeated. As one pastor instructs, "When you ask for the Holy Spirit, you may have a syllable bubbling up, or rolling around in your head. If you will speak it in faith, it will be as if you open a dam, and the language will come forth. I like to see it as a spool of thread in your gut and the tip, or the beginning of the thread, is glimpsed at your tongue, but as you begin to pull (speak), out comes the rest of the thread."[10]

Another charismatic author adds this: "You do not understand what you are saying. . . . But it is a praying with the spirit rather than the mind."[11] None other than the *Skeptic's Dictionary* points out an obvious and troubling irony: "When spoken by schizophrenics, glossolalia is recognized as gibberish. In charismatic Christian communities glossolalia is sacred and referred to as 'speaking in tongues' or having 'the gift of tongues.'"[12]

Because it is supposedly an ecstatic expression of faith, modern tongues-speech is not bound to any of the rules that govern legitimate language. But charismatics have spun that into a positive. In the words of one writer, "In speaking in tongues—a sign of possession by the Holy Spirit—language sheds all the grammatical and semantic constraints in order to do what is impossible for any language to do: communicate the ineffable."[13] This positive spin, however, represents a major shift from the first generation of Pentecostals at the turn of the twentieth century. As we have already seen (in chapter 2), Charles Fox Parham, Agnes Ozman, and the earliest Pentecostals thought they had received the supernatural ability to speak in genuine, foreign languages.

As Kenneth L. Nolan explains, "Early Pentecostals believed that glossolalia was given to the Church for the purpose of world evangelism. Many of them left for foreign mission fields fully expecting the Holy Spirit supernaturally to give them the language of the native peoples. This initial expectation and the resulting experience was a bitter disappointment to aspiring missionaries who did not want to invest years in language study."[14] When it became apparent that their "tongues" did not correspond to any known language, Pentecostals were forced to make a choice. They could foolishly continue insisting that tongues were real languages in spite of overwhelming evidence to the contrary, or reconstruct their definition of tongues to fit their failed experiences. Today, nonlinguistic, irrational gibberish remains the *de facto* explanation for charismatic babble.

DOES THE MODERN VERSION OF TONGUES MATCH THE BIBLICAL GIFT?

Charismatics claim that their tongues experience makes them *feel* closer to God. A typical testimony from a charismatic parishioner proclaims, "For me, it is almost as if I am able to tap into God's heart and what he wants. I don't really know what I am saying, but I know it is what God wants me to say and speak. It is more of an enlightenment—you can feel him all around you, and you can feel him speaking through the words that you are saying."[15]

Another churchgoer explained her involvement this way: "I know some people that get a warm, fuzzy feeling going on inside them. For me, I get goose bumps, actually."[16] Such feelings—up to and including trancelike states of altered consciousness—are seen as proof that something significant, presumably something positive, is happening in the spiritual realm. To anyone who reads and understands Scripture, it should be obvious that the underlying argument—*if it feels good, then you should do it*—is useless as a defense and dangerous as a practice.

In reality, the modern expressions of glossolalia are deceptive and dangerous, offering only a pretense of genuine spirituality. Charismatics may claim it is God speaking through them, but there is absolutely no evidence to confirm the notion that modern glossolalia comes from the Holy Spirit or aids His work of producing holiness. Conversely, there are very good reasons to avoid the practice. It is, in fact, a common practice in numerous cult groups and false religions—from the voodoo doctors of Africa to the mystic monks of Buddhism to the founders of Mormonism.[17]

Historically, irrational and ecstatic speech has been associated only with heretical fringe groups, from the Montanists to the Jansenists and Irvingites. Yet the same spiritually empty experience is essentially identical to modern charismatic practice. Today's evangelicals, largely unaware of the history of the practice, seem to think of glossolalia as a more or less mainstream practice dating back in an uninterrupted line of succession to the apostolic era of the church. Not so. What W. A. Criswell said about tongues years ago is still true:

> In the long story of the Church, after the days of the apostles, wherever the phenomenon of glossolalia has appeared it has been looked upon as heresy. Glossolalia mostly has been confined to the nineteenth and twentieth centuries. But wherever and however its appearance, it has never been accepted by the historical churches of Christendom. It has been universally repudiated by these churches as a doctrinal and emotional aberration.[18]

In short, the *glossolalia* practiced by today's charismatics is a counterfeit that by every measure falls short of the gift of tongues described in the New Testament. Today's tongues-speakers claim to have received the biblical gift, but ultimately they have to acknowledge that the gibberish they are speaking has none of the characteristics of real language. Whereas modern "tongues" is a learned behavior consisting of unintelligible stammering and nonsense syllables, the New Testament gift involved the supernatural ability to speak precisely in a foreign language the speaker had never learned. Though charismatics may hijack biblical terminology to describe their practice, the fact remains that such fabricated behavior has no relation to the biblical gift. As Norm Geisler observes:

Even those who believe in [modern] tongues acknowledge that unsaved people have tongues experiences. There is nothing supernatural about them. But there is something unique about speaking complete and meaningful sentences and discourses in a knowable language to which one has never been exposed. This is what the real New Testament gift of tongues entailed. Anything short of this, as "private tongues" are, should not be considered the biblical gift of tongues.[19]

How do we know the precise nature of the biblical gift of tongues? In particular, does the expression "tongues of men and of angels" in 1 Corinthians 13:1 suggest that the gift of tongues might be the ability to speak some other-worldly, angelic language? That, as we shall see, is the claim most charismatics make. They believe it answers the question of why modern "tongues" bear none of the characteristics of actual language.

But the only detailed description of the true gift of tongues in Scripture is found in Acts 2 on the day of Pentecost—a text that clearly identifies this gift as the supernatural ability to speak genuine, meaningful, translatable languages. Acts 2:4 is explicit, regarding the 120 followers of Jesus Christ who were assembled in the Upper Room: "They were all filled with the Holy Spirit and began to speak with other tongues, as the Spirit gave them utterance." That the disciples spoke authentic languages is not only confirmed by the Greek word *tongues* (*glossa*, a term that refers to human languages[20]), but also by Luke's later use of the word *dialect* (vv. 6–7) and his inclusion of a list of the foreign languages that were spoken (vv. 9–11). Due to the celebration of Pentecost, Jews from all over the world had traveled to Jerusalem for the feast (v. 5)—including many pilgrims who had grown up speaking languages other than Aramaic. That a group of uneducated Galileans could suddenly speak fluently in multiple languages was an undeniable miracle, so the pilgrims who heard them were utterly astonished (vv. 7–8).

There were also native Judeans in the crowd who did not speak those languages and thus could not understand what the disciples were saying. In their confusion searching for an explanation, they responded with skepticism and mockery, accusing the disciples of being intoxicated (v. 13). But drunkenness was not the cause of what happened at Pentecost, a point Peter explained (vv. 14–15). As one of the early church fathers affirmed, "The wonder was great, a language spoken by those who had not learnt it."[21]

In Genesis 11, at the Tower of Babel, the Lord had confused the languages of the world as a judgment on humanity. In contrast, on the day of Pentecost, the curse of Babel was miraculously undone, demonstrating that the wonderful words of God, including the gospel of Jesus Christ, were to be taken throughout the whole world to those in every nation. This is precisely how early Christians, in the centuries after the apostles, understood the miracle of languages. Thus, the famed preacher of ancient times John Chrysostom explained:

> And as in the time of building the tower [of Babel] the one tongue was divided into many; so then [at Pentecost] the many tongues frequently met in one man, and the same person used to discourse both in the Persian, and the Roman, and the Indian, and many other tongues, the Spirit sounding within him: and the gift was called the gift of tongues because he could all at once speak divers languages.[22]

Augustine similarly adds:

> In the first days the Holy Spirit fell upon the believers, and they spoke in tongues that they hadn't learned, as the Spirit gave them to speak. These signs were appropriate for the time. For it was necessary that the Holy Spirit be signified thus in all tongues, because the gospel of God was going to traverse all tongues throughout the earth. That was the sign that was given, and it passed.[23]

It bears repeating that this is so obvious even the otherwise aberrant first Pentecostals, at the dawn of the twentieth century, understood the phenomenon in Acts 2 to be actual languages. They knew from simply reading the Bible that the Holy Spirit had given a miraculous, instantaneous ability to speak in foreign languages; and they were convinced that they, too, had received the same ability to expedite missionary work. Their movement, after all, was named for the day of Pentecost. Only later, when it became clear that modern "tongues" are not true languages, did charismatics begin to concoct novel interpretations of Scripture in order to support their unorthodox invention.

In Luke's account of apostolic church history, speaking in tongues is again mentioned in Acts 10:46 and 19:6. Charismatics—in an effort to find a biblical parallel to their modern practice—sometimes suggest that the gift of languages described later in Acts was different than at Pentecost. But such a conclusion is not permitted by the text. In Acts 2:4, Luke records that those in the Upper Room "spoke" (from the Greek word *laleo*) in "tongues" (*glossa*). Luke uses those exact same terms in Acts 10:46 and 19:6 to describe the experiences of Cornelius and the disciples of John the Baptist. Moreover, any notion that the phenomenon of Acts 10, for example, differs from that of Acts 2 is directly contradicted by Peter's testimony in Acts 11:15–17. There the apostle explicitly states that the Holy Spirit came upon the Gentiles *in the same way* as He had come upon the disciples at Pentecost.

In defending nonsensical speech, most charismatics retreat to the book of 1 Corinthians—contending the gift described in 1 Corinthians 12–14 is categorically different from that of Acts. But once again, this assertion is not permitted by the text. A simple word study effectively makes that point, since both passages use the same terminology to describe the miraculous gift. In Acts, Luke uses *laleo* ("to speak") in combination with *glossa* ("tongues") four different times (Acts 2:4, 11; 10:46; 19:6). In 1 Corinthians 12–14, Paul uses forms of that same combination thirteen times (1 Cor. 12:30; 13:1; 14:2, 4, 5 [2x], 6, 13, 18, 19, 21, 27, 39).

These linguistic parallels carry added significance when we consider that Luke was Paul's traveling companion and close associate, even writing under Paul's apostolic authority. Because he penned the book of Acts around AD 60, roughly five years *after* Paul wrote his first epistle to the Corinthians, Luke would have been well aware of their confusion regarding the gift of languages. Certainly Luke would not have wanted to add to that confusion. Thus, he would not have used the exact same terminology in Acts as Paul did in 1 Corinthians unless what had happened at Pentecost was identical to the authentic gift Paul described in his epistle.

The fact that Paul noted "various kinds of tongues" in 1 Corinthians 12:10 (NASB) does not imply that some are real languages and others are merely gibberish. Rather, the Greek word for *kinds* is *genos*, from which we derive the word *genus*. *Genos* refers to a family, group, race, or nation. Linguists often refer to language "families" or "groups," and that is precisely Paul's point: there are various families of languages in the world, and this gift enabled some believers to speak in a variety of them. In Acts 2, Luke emphasized that same idea in verses 9–11, where he explained that the languages that were spoken came from at least sixteen different regions.

Other parallels between Acts and 1 Corinthians 12–14 can be established. In both places, the Source of the gift is the same—the Holy Spirit (Acts 2:4, 18; 10:44–46; 19:6; 1 Cor. 12:1, 7, 11, et al.). In both places, the reception of the gift is not limited to the apostles, but also involved laypeople in the church (cf. Acts 1:15; 10:46; 19:6; 1 Cor. 12:30; 14:18). In both places, the gift is described as a speaking gift (Acts 2:4, 9–11; 1 Cor. 12:30; 14:2, 5). In both places, the resulting message can be translated and thereby understood, either by those who already know the language (as on the day of Pentecost—Acts 2:9–11) or by someone gifted with the ability to translate (1 Cor. 12:10; 14:5, 13).

In both places, the gift served as a miraculous sign for unbelieving Jews (Acts 2:5, 12, 14, 19; 1 Cor. 14:21–22; cf. Isa. 28:11–12). In both places, the gift of languages was closely associated with the gift of prophecy (Acts 2:16–18; 19:6; 1 Cor. 14). And in both places, unbelievers who did not understand what was being spoken responded with mockery and derision (Acts 2:13; 1 Cor. 14:23). Given so many parallels, it is exegetically impossible and irresponsible to claim that the phenomenon described in 1 Corinthians was any different from that of Acts 2. Since the gift of tongues consisted of authentic foreign languages on the day of Pentecost, then the same was true for the believers in Corinth.

Two additional considerations make this understanding absolutely certain. First, by insisting any language spoken in tongues in the church must be translated by someone with the gift of interpretation (1 Cor. 12:10; 14:27), Paul indicated that the gift consisted of rational languages. The word for *interpretation* is *hermeneuo* (from which we get *hermeneutics*), which refers to a "translation" or an "accurate unfolding of the meaning." Obviously, it would be impossible to translate nonsensical gibberish, since translation requires concrete meanings in one language to be rendered correctly into another.

Unless the gift in 1 Corinthians 12–14 consisted of authentic languages, Paul's repeated insistence on interpretation would be meaningless. As Norm Geisler explains, "The fact that the tongues of which Paul spoke in 1 Corinthians could be 'interpreted' shows that it was a meaningful language. Otherwise it would not be an 'interpretation' but a creation of the meaning. So the gift of 'interpretation' (1 Cor. 12:30; 14:5, 13) supports the fact that tongues were a real language that could be translated for the benefit of all by this special gift of interpretation."[24]

Second, Paul explicitly referenced human languages in 1 Corinthians 14:10–11, where he wrote, "There are, it may be, so many kinds of languages in the world, and none of them is without significance. Therefore, if I do not know the meaning of the language, I shall be a foreigner to him who speaks, and he who speaks will be a foreigner to me." On the day of Pentecost, there was no need for an interpreter because people in the crowd already understood the various languages that were spoken (Acts 2:5–11). But in the Corinthian church, where those languages were not known, a translator was required; otherwise, the congregation would not understand the message and, therefore, would not be edified. The apostle's later reference to Isaiah 28:11–12 (a passage in which the "other tongues and other lips" refers to the Assyrian language) confirms that Paul had human foreign languages in mind (1 Cor. 14:21).

When the biblical evidence is considered, there is no question the true gift of languages described in 1 Corinthians 12–14 was precisely the same miraculous rational speech the disciples spoke in Acts 2—namely, the Spirit-given ability to communicate in a foreign language unknown to the speaker. No other explanation is permitted by the text of Scripture. As Thomas Edgar observes:

> There are verses in 1 Corinthians 14 where foreign language makes sense but where unintelligible ecstatic utterance does not (e.g. v. 22). However, the reverse cannot be said. A foreign language not understood by the hearer is no different from unintelligible speech in his sight. Therefore, in any passage

where such ecstatic speech may be considered possible, it is also possible to substitute a language not familiar to the hearers. In this passage there are no reasons, much less the very strong reasons necessary, to depart from the normal meaning of *glossa* and to flee to a completely unsupported usage.[25]

This conclusion represents a deathblow to the modern charismatic version of glossolalia, which shares nothing in common with the actual New Testament gift, but rather mirrors the frenzied speech of the ancient Greco-Roman mystery religions—pagan practices that Scripture condemns (cf. Matt. 6:7).[26]

ANSWERING COMMON QUESTIONS ABOUT THE GIFT OF LANGUAGES

Armed with a right definition, the student of Scripture is now able to accurately interpret the biblical teaching regarding this miraculous ability. In the remainder of this chapter, we will consider ten common questions about the gift of languages.

What Was the Purpose of the Gift of Languages?

Both a primary purpose within the scope of God's sovereign plan for salvation history, and a secondary purpose within the context of the first-century church were met by this gift. Primarily, it demonstrated that a transition was taking place from the old covenant to the new, and as such, it served as a sign to unbelieving Israel. The apostle Paul made that point explicit in 1 Corinthians 14:21–22; and Luke echoed that same purpose in his description of Pentecost in Acts 2:5–21. The ending of Mark's gospel similarly explains that the disciples of Christ would speak in languages that were new to them (16:17), which would be one of the signs that authenticated them as messengers of the true gospel (v. 20).[27]

But there was also a secondary purpose for the church—namely, the edification of fellow believers. In 1 Corinthians 12:7–10, Paul stated clearly that all spiritual gifts were given by the Holy Spirit for the building up of others within the body of Christ (cf. 1 Peter 4:10–11). When used outside the church, the gift of languages was a sign that authenticated the gospel (as demonstrated on the day of Pentecost). But when used in the church, it was for the edification of other believers (per Paul's instruction to the Corinthian Christians). The gift provided another way, before the New Testament was completed, for God to reveal His truth to His church—like prophecy but with the added impact of a linguistic miracle to authenticate it.

Showing love to one another was always the priority, and all spiritual gifts were intended as a means to that end (1 Cor. 13:1–7; cf. Rom. 12:3–21). Thus, to practice any gift for selfish reasons would be as unedifying as a noisy cymbal or an irritating gong (1 Cor. 13:1). As Paul explained to the Corinthians, love "does not seek its own" (1 Cor. 13:5) and earlier in that same letter: "Let no one seek his own good, but that of his neighbor" (1 Cor. 10:24 NASB).

In 1 Corinthians 14:4, when Paul wrote, "He who speaks in a tongue edifies himself, but he who prophesies edifies the church," he was not validating self-edification as an end in itself. To do so would have undermined everything he had just written in the preceding chapter! Rather, he was demonstrating that prophecy (spoken in a language everyone understood) was inherently superior to speaking in foreign languages (which no one could understand) because the latter required interpretation. Because the only proper use of any gift was for the edification of the entire congregation (1 Cor. 14:12, 26), it was essential that the foreign languages be translated for all to understand (1 Cor. 14:6–11, 27).

The Corinthians were using the gift of languages with impure and selfish motives—to satisfy a carnal desire to seem spiritually superior. In the modern era, the same motives often prevail, with no possible edification to others.

Were All Believers Expected to Speak in Tongues?

Many charismatics, especially those influenced by classic Pentecostalism, have insisted that all Christians should speak in tongues—arguing that it is the initial and universal evidence of baptism by the Holy Spirit. But the Pentecostal paradigm is shattered by Paul's teaching in 1 Corinthians 12. In verse 13, Paul made it clear that all of his readers, as believers, had experienced

Spirit baptism at the moment of salvation (cf. Titus 3:5). Yet in the ensuing verses, he also explained that not every one of them had been given the gift of languages. The implications are unmistakable: if all the believers at Corinth were baptized by the Holy Spirit (v. 13) but not all of them could speak in tongues (vv. 28–30), then that gift must not be the one and only sign of Spirit baptism, as Pentecostals claim. This is consistent with what Paul taught earlier in chapter 12, that the Holy Spirit sovereignly distributes *different* gifts to *different* people:

> But the manifestation of the Spirit is given to each one for the profit of all: for to one is given the word of wisdom through the Spirit, to another the word of knowledge through the same Spirit, to another faith by the same Spirit, to another gifts of healings by the same Spirit, to another the working of miracles, to another prophecy, to another discerning of spirits, to another different kinds of tongues, to another the interpretation of tongues. But one and the same Spirit works all these things, distributing to each one individually as He wills. (vv. 7–11)

Even if the supernatural ability to speak foreign languages were still available today, it would not be given to every Christian. When charismatics contend that every believer should seek the gift of tongues, they miss the entire point of Paul's argument in 1 Corinthians 12:14–31 and end up manufacturing counterfeits.

Charismatics often point to 1 Corinthians 14:5, where Paul stated, "I wish you all spoke with tongues," as a proof-text for their insistence that all Christians ought to practice glossolalia. In so doing, they fail to recognize that the apostle was not stating an actual possibility, but rather using hypothetical hyperbole. In this case, Paul was emphasizing again the superiority of prophecy over the gift of languages, as the rest of verse 5 makes clear: "I wish you all spoke with tongues, *but even more that you prophesied*; for he who prophesies is greater than he who speaks with tongues, unless indeed he interprets, that the church may receive edification." Thus, even if it had been possible for Paul to wish such a reality into existence, his true desire was not that all the

Corinthians spoke in tongues but rather that they prophesied—because words of prophecy did not have to be translated in order to edify other members of the church.

Grammatically, Paul's statement is almost identical to his earlier statement in 1 Corinthians 7:7. Referring to his nonmarried status, the apostle wrote, "For I wish that all men were even as I myself." Obviously, in that verse, Paul was not mandating celibacy for all believers, because he knew that not everyone had been given the gift of singleness. The same holds true in 1 Corinthians 14:5 with regard to the gift of languages.

Did Paul Command the Corinthians to Desire the Gift of Tongues?

First Corinthians 12:31 is often translated as a command: "But earnestly desire the best gifts." Yet that choice of translation raises a serious question. If spiritual gifts are given by the Spirit's independent prerogative (1 Cor. 12:7, 18, 28), and if each gift is necessary to the building up of the body of Christ (vv. 14–27), then why would believers be told to desire gifts they had not received? Any such notion would go against Paul's whole argument in 1 Corinthians 12—where each individual believer is to be thankful for his or her unique giftedness, contentedly employing it in ministry for the edification of the church.

In reality, 1 Corinthians 12:31 is not an imperative. Grammatically, the form of the verb *desire* can also be rendered as a statement of fact (indicative), and the context here supports that translation. After all, there is nothing in the flow of Paul's argument to expect a command, but much to commend the indicative.[28] The New International Version rightly captures the apostle's point in its alternate reading of this verse: "But you are eagerly desiring the greater gifts." The Syriac New Testament similarly states, "Because you are zealous of the best gifts, I will show to you a more excellent way."[29]

Paul was rebuking the Corinthians because they aggressively desired the showy gifts while deriding those they deemed as less impressive. The apostle wished to show them a more excellent way—the way of humble love toward others—which launched his discussion on the superiority of love in 1 Corinthians 13.

Motivated by pride and selfish ambition, the Corinthians sought to acquire and display the most ostentatious, manifestly miraculous spiritual gifts. They coveted the applause of men, desiring to appear spiritual when in fact they were operating in the flesh. (It is quite likely, given the nature of Paul's instruction to them, that some within the Corinthian congregation had even begun to mimic the unintelligible utterances of the Greco-Roman mystery religions, sounding much like those within the contemporary Charismatic Movement.) It was wrong then, and still is, to selfishly seek any spiritual gift when we've been told that spiritual gifts are sovereignly chosen and distributed by the Holy Spirit. It is especially wrong to crave a gift we don't have out of self-serving or prideful motives.

What Are the "Tongues of Angels"?

Charismatics often point to Paul's statement in 1 Corinthians 13:1, where he mentions angelic tongues. Invariably, they want to claim that the gibberish we hear in charismatic glossolalia is an otherworldly tongue—some sort of holy, heavenly language that transcends human conversation and belongs to the discourse of angels.

Beyond being an insult to angels, that interpretation of 1 Corinthians 13:1 falls flat when one considers the context. Notice, first of all, that Paul's theme in 1 Corinthians 13 is love, not spiritual gifts. And he introduces the subject this way: "Though I speak with the tongues of men and of angels, but have not love, I have become sounding brass or a clanging cymbal." Paul is describing a hypothetical scenario. (His subsequent examples in verses 2–3 indicate Paul was using extreme illustrations and hyperbolic language to emphasize the value of love.)[30] He did not lack love; he is asking the Corinthians to imagine if he did. Likewise, he is not claiming he had the ability to speak angelic languages; he is supposing the imaginary case of someone who could do so, but who spoke without love—without concern for the edification of others. His conclusion? The result would be of no more use than mere noise.

Ironically, charismatics often focus so intently on the phrase "tongues of angels" that they miss Paul's real point: any selfish use of this gift violated its true purpose—namely, that it be exercised as an expression of loving edification for other believers. Others are not edified by the mere spectacle of someone speaking in tongues (1 Cor. 14:17), nor are they edified by hearing unintelligible gibberish. The practice violates everything Paul is teaching the Corinthians in this epistle.

Of course, even if someone insists on taking the phrase "tongues of angels" literally, it is helpful to note that every time angels spoke in the Bible, they did so in a real language that was understandable to those to whom they spoke. Nothing about the phrase "tongues of angels" in 1 Corinthians 13:1 justifies the modern practice of irrational babble.

What About Paul's Statement That Tongues Will Cease?

In 1 Corinthians 13:8, Paul explained that "whether there are tongues, they will cease." The Greek verb used in that verse (*pauo*) means "to cease permanently," indicating that the gift of tongues would come to an end once and for all. For classic Pentecostals—who admit the miraculous gifts ceased in church history but argue they returned in 1901—the permanence inherent in the verb *pauo* presents a significant problem. And as already demonstrated, whatever modern charismatics are doing, it is *not* the gift of languages. The supernatural ability to speak fluently in unlearned foreign languages, as the disciples did on the day of Pentecost in Acts 2, has been shown to bear no resemblance to modern glossolalia. The New Testament gift ceased after the apostolic age ended and has never returned.

In 1 Corinthians 13:10, Paul noted that partial knowledge and partial prophecy would be done away with "when that which is perfect has come." But what did Paul mean by the *perfect*? The Greek word (*teleion*) can mean "perfect," "mature," or "complete," and commentators have widely disagreed as to its precise meaning—offering numerous possible interpretations. For example, F. F. Bruce suggests that the *perfect* is love itself; B. B. Warfield contends it is the completed canon of Scripture (cf. James 1:25); Robert Thomas argues it is the mature church (cf. Eph. 4:11–13); Richard Gaffin asserts it is the return of Christ; and Thomas Edgar concludes it is the individual believer's entrance into heavenly glory (cf. 2 Cor. 5:8). Significantly, though these scholars disagree on the identification of the "perfect," they all reach the same conclusion—namely, that the miraculous and revelatory gifts have ceased.[31]

Nonetheless, of the possible interpretations, the believer's entrance into the Lord's presence best fits Paul's use of "perfect" in 1 Corinthians 13:10. This makes sense of Paul's later statement in verse 12 about believers seeing Christ "face to face" and possessing full knowledge—descriptions that cannot be realized this side of glory.

It is important to note that Paul's purpose in this chapter was not to identify how long the spiritual gifts would continue into later centuries of church history, as that would have been essentially meaningless to the original readers of this letter. Rather, he was making a point that specifically pertained to his first-century audience: when you Corinthian believers enter the glorified perfection of eternity in heaven,[32] the spiritual gifts you now prize so highly will no longer be necessary (since the partial revelation they provide will be made complete). But love has eternal value, so pursue love because it is superior to any gift (v. 13). Thomas Edgar summarizes the issue with these words:

> If, as seems apparent in the passage, the *teleion* ["perfect"] refers to the individual's presence with the Lord, this passage does not refer to some prophetic point in history. These factors mean that this passage does not teach when gifts will cease or how long they will last. It serves to remind the Corinthians of the abiding nature of love in contrast to the gifts, which by their inherent nature are only temporal, only for this life.[33]

To determine the point in church history when the miraculous and revelatory gifts would pass away, we must look elsewhere than 1 Corinthians 13:10, to passages like Ephesians 2:20, where Paul indicated that both the apostolic and prophetic offices were only for the foundational age of the church.[34] Nonetheless, Paul's broader principle, that love is superior to spiritual giftedness, still applies to modern believers as we also look forward to our heavenly glorification.

What Did Paul Mean When He Said Tongues-Speakers Speak to God, Not to Men?

Charismatics sometimes cling to this phrase in 1 Corinthians 14:2 as a justification for their unintelligible glossolalia. But once again, the context belies that interpretation. The entirety of verses 1–3 reads as follows: "Pursue love, and desire spiritual gifts, but especially that you may prophesy. For he who speaks in a tongue does not speak to men but to God, for no one understands him; however, in the spirit he speaks mysteries. But he who prophesies speaks edification and exhortation and comfort to men."

In those verses, Paul was not extolling the gift of tongues; rather he was explaining why it was *inferior* to the gift of prophecy. Whereas prophecy was spoken in words that everyone could understand, the gift of foreign languages had to be interpreted in order for others to be edified. Paul defined exactly what he meant by the phrase "does not speak to men but to God" in the very next line, "for no one understands." If the language was not translated, only God would know what was being said.

Clearly, Paul was far from commending such a practice. As he had already established (in chapter 12), the purpose of the gifts was the edification of others within the body of Christ. Foreign languages left untranslated did not fulfill that purpose. That is why the apostle put such an emphasis on the necessity of interpretation (vv. 13, 27).

What About Praying in Tongues?

In 1 Corinthians 14:13–17, Paul mentioned that the gift of tongues was used in public prayer for the purpose of edification. Charismatics, however, have tried to redefine the gift of tongues as a special mode of supernatural expression for their personal devotions and private prayers. But notice how different Paul's description is from that of modern tongues-speakers. First, Paul was not commending any form of gibberish, since he had already established that the real gift consisted of speaking in translatable foreign languages (vv. 10–11).

Second, Paul would never extol prayers that bypass the mind, as many charismatics do. That was—and still is today—a pagan practice. In the Greco-Roman mystery religions, ecstatic utterances were commonly employed as a way to circumvent the mind in order to commune with demonic entities. So it is likely that Paul's words in these verses include a sarcastic tone, as he rebuked the Corinthian Christians for their attempt to imitate the mindless practices of their pagan neighbors. Per Paul's instruction, anyone who prayed in a foreign language was to first ask for the ability to translate and understand the message he was speaking (v. 13). Otherwise, his understanding would be "unfruitful" (v. 14), something Paul clearly deemed as a negative (Col. 1:10; Titus 3:14). The proper use of this gift always involved both the spirit and the mind: "What is the conclusion then? I will pray with the spirit, and I will also pray with the understanding. I will sing with the spirit, and I will also sing with the understanding" (v. 15).

Third, the prayer Paul spoke of here was a *public* prayer, not some form of private devotion. Verse 16 makes it clear that others in the church were listening to what was being said. Thus, Paul was referring to a prayer in the church that needed to be translated so the congregation could affirm the message and be edified by its contents. There is no New Testament warrant for the modern charismatic practice of vainly repeating gibberish, either at home by oneself or *especially* at church during a group session of indecipherable mass mumbling.

Did Paul Practice a Private Form of Tongues?

Charismatics often point to 1 Corinthians 14:18–19 in order to argue that Paul himself employed a private "prayer language." There Paul stated, "I thank my God I speak with tongues more than you all; yet in the church I would rather speak five words with my understanding, that I may teach others also, than ten thousand words in a tongue." Because Paul did not specify when or where he spoke in tongues, the charismatic claim that Paul cultivated a private "prayer language" is an invention built on sheer speculation. In the book of Acts, we see the apostles speaking in other languages as part of their evangelistic ministry to unbelievers (Acts 2:5–11). Based on that precedent, it is best to conclude that Paul used his gift in the same missionary way—as a sign that authenticated his apostolic ministry (cf. Mark 16:20; 2 Cor. 12:12).

In 1 Corinthians 14, Paul was certainly not condoning a private, self-serving use of the gift of tongues. Rather, he was confronting the pride of the Corinthian congregation. They thought they were superior because some of them spoke in dialects they didn't know; but Paul, who had miraculously spoken in foreign languages more than any of them, wanted them to understand

151

that love trumped any gift, no matter how spectacular. When Paul exercised his gifts within the body of Christ, his priority was always on building up others in the church. Any notion of the self-centered use of a gift would have undermined the apostle's entire argument in 1 Corinthians 12–14.

How Were Tongues to Operate in the Early Church?

In discussing the gift of tongues in 1 Corinthians 14, Paul gave specific instructions for its operation in the church. In verses 26–28, the apostle explained, "Whenever you come together, each of you has a psalm, has a teaching, has a tongue, has a revelation, has an interpretation. Let all things be done for edification. If anyone speaks in a tongue, let there be two or at the most three, each in turn, and let one interpret. But if there is no interpreter, let him keep silent in church, and let him speak to himself and to God."

In those verses, Paul provided several stipulations for the use of tongues: (1) no more than three people should speak during the church service; (2) they should speak one at a time; (3) their message must be translated for the edification of the congregation; and (4) if no one was able to interpret, they should remain silent. In verse 34, Paul added a fifth proviso: women were not permitted to speak in the church. Given the nature of typical Pentecostal and charismatic church services, simply following that final stipulation would end most of the modern counterfeit.

In contrast to pagan forms of ecstatic speech, the Holy Spirit does not work through people who are irrational or out of control. "The spirits of the prophets are subject to the prophets. For God is not the author of confusion but of peace, as in all the churches of the saints" (vv. 32–33). As one early Christian theologian explained, reflecting on those verses, "The person who speaks in the Holy Spirit speaks when he chooses to do so and then can be silent, like the prophets. But those who are possessed by an unclean spirit speak even when they do not want to. They say things they do not understand."[35]

Only two or three speakers were permitted to utter their revelations in each church meeting, and they were required to speak in turn. The idea that everyone in the congregation should simultaneously burst into a cacophony of gibberish, as frequently occurs in contemporary charismatic churches, is something Paul would never have permitted or attributed to the Holy Spirit. In fact, one of the strongest indictments against the modern Charismatic Movement is the disorderly, selfish, and chaotic manner in which false glossolalia is practiced.

As stated earlier, the foreign languages that were spoken in the Corinthian congregation had to be interpreted. It was imperative that languages be translated so everyone could understand the meaning. The church would know those who had that gift, and if there was no one present with the ability to interpret, the speaker was instructed to remain silent. Paul's statement that he ought to "speak to himself and to God" paralleled the previous command to "keep silent in church" (v. 28). The apostle was not suggesting a private form of tongues-speaking that would take place at home; rather, he was reiterating his command to the speaker, telling him to stay quiet within the assembly and pray silently to God.

Thus, the gift of languages was to be used in an orderly manner in the church (cf. vv. 39–40). Any disruptive or disorderly use violated the way God intended the gift to be used. Obviously, those requirements were given at a time when the gift was still in operation. Though that gift has now ceased, believers today should still maintain order and decency in the way they use the other gifts and conduct their worship.

Should Believers Be Discouraged from Seeking This False Gift?

The apostle Paul ended his discussion regarding the gift of tongues with these words: "Therefore, brethren, desire earnestly to prophesy, and do not forbid to speak with tongues. Let all things be done decently and in order" (1 Cor. 14:39–40). Because all the gifts were still active when that corporate command was written, the Corinthian believers were not to forbid the legitimate and orderly exercise of the gift of languages. The corporate nature of the command is important; this was not a mandate for every individual within the Corinthian congregation to seek the gift of prophecy. Rather, the church as a whole was to prioritize prophecy over tongues—because it did not require translation in order to edify others.

Charismatics sometimes use verse 39 to insist that anyone who forbids the practice of charismatic glossolalia today is violating Paul's injunction. But the apostle's command has nothing to do with the modern imposture. At a time when the authentic gift of foreign languages was still in operation, of course believers were not to forbid its use. But today, it is incumbent upon churches to stop the practice of the spiritual counterfeit. Because unintelligible speech is not the true gift, to dissuade someone from such a practice is not a violation of Paul's command in 1 Corinthians 14:39. Quite the contrary. The disgraceful jumble and irrational blabber of modern glossolalia is actually a violation of verse 40—and those who are committed to decency and order in the church are duty-bound to suppress it.

BRINGING IT ALL TOGETHER

When we consider the biblical passages that describe the gift of languages—from Mark, Acts, and 1 Corinthians—we see in every way that the modern charismatic version is a hoax.[36] The genuine gift endowed a person with the miraculous ability to speak in unlearned foreign languages for the sake of proclaiming the Word of God and authenticating the gospel message. When used in the church, it had to be translated so other believers could be edified by the message.

By contrast, the modern charismatic version consists of nonmiraculous, nonsensical gibberish that cannot be translated. It is a learned behavior that does not correspond to any form of authentic human language. Rather than being a tool to edify the church, contemporary charismatics use the fabrication as a private "prayer language" for the purpose of self-gratification. Though they justify their practice because it makes them feel closer to God, there is no biblical warrant for such unintelligible babble. It is a false spiritual high with no sanctifying value. The fact that modern glossolalia parallels pagan religious rites should serve as a dire warning of the spiritual dangers that can be introduced by this unbiblical practice.

EIGHT

FAKE HEALINGS AND FALSE HOPES

W hen famed televangelist Oral Roberts entered eternity on December 15, 2009, many in the religious world gushed with flowery obituaries praising the "pioneering preacher of the 'prosperity gospel'"[1] for his pervasive contributions to American Christianity. Though it wasn't popular, my opinion of the life and legacy of Oral Roberts could not have been more opposite. In an article published just a few days after his death, I stated it as clearly as I could: "Oral Roberts's influence is not something Bible-believing Christians should celebrate. Virtually every aberrant idea the Pentecostal and charismatic movements spawned after 1950 can be traced in one way or another to Oral Roberts's influence."[2]

That may sound harsh. But it is not nearly as strong as the New Testament, where those who pervert the truth are denounced with the most severe language imaginable. Oral Roberts not only embraced the false gospel of health-and-wealth, but he promoted it into the mainstream—using television to broadcast his doctrinal poison to the masses. In a very real sense, he was the first of the fraudulent healers to capture TV, paving the way for the parade of spiritual swindlers who have come after him.[3]

In *Oral Roberts: An American Life*, biographer David Edwin Harrell Jr. describes how Roberts discovered the prosperity gospel and how it became the centerpiece of his message. One day he opened his Bible randomly and spotted 3 John 2: "Beloved, I pray that you may prosper in all things and be in health, just as your soul prospers." He showed it to his wife, Evelyn, and—utterly divorcing that one verse from its proper context—the couple "talked excitedly about the verse's implications. Did it mean they could have a 'new car,' a 'new house,' a 'brand-new ministry?' In later years, Evelyn looked back on that morning as the point of embarkation: 'I really believe that that very morning was the beginning of this worldwide ministry that he has had, because it opened up his thinking.'"[4] Roberts testified that a shiny new Buick, acquired by unexpected means shortly after that experience, "became a symbol to me of what a man could do if he would believe God."[5]

After he concocted his prosperity doctrine, Oral Roberts subsequently invented his best-known and most far-reaching brainchild: the seed-faith message. Roberts taught that seed-faith giving was the means to prosperity. Money and material things donated to his organization were like kernels planted that would produce a crop of material blessings from the Lord. God, Roberts declared, would multiply in miraculous ways whatever was given to Roberts's ministry—and give many times more back to the donor. It was a simple, quasi-spiritual, get-rich-quick scheme that appealed mainly to poor, disadvantaged, and desperate people. It generated millions for Roberts's media empire.

When the results became apparent, the scheme was quickly adopted by a host of similarly oriented Pentecostal and charismatic media ministries. The seed-faith principle is the main cash cow that built and has supported vast networks of preachers and televangelists who barter for their viewers' money with fervent promises of "miracles"—and the most-sought-after miracles are invariably those that involve health and wealth.

Tragically, the seed-faith message usurped and utterly replaced whatever gospel content there may have been in Oral Roberts's preaching. In all the many times I saw him on television, I never once heard him preach the gospel. His message—every time—was about seed-faith. The reason for that is obvious: the message of the cross—an atoning sacrifice for sins, wrought through Jesus' sufferings—doesn't mesh with the notion that God guarantees health, wealth, and prosperity to people who send money to television preachers. Our fellowship in Jesus' sufferings (Phil. 3:10), and our duty to follow in His steps (1 Peter 2:20–23), are likewise antithetical to the core principles of prosperity doctrine. As previously discussed in chapter 2, the prosperity message is a different gospel (cf. Gal. 1:8–9).

One of the primary emphases of Roberts's ministry was his concentration on alleged healing miracles, a gimmick that was necessary to get people to loosen their wallets. As Pentecostal historian Vinson Synan stated shortly after Roberts's death, "More than any other person, he should be credited with starting the charismatic movement in mainline religion. He brought [divine] healing into the American consciousness."[6] Though he eschewed the label, Roberts made his main reputation on television in the 1950s as a faith healer, and he even claimed to have raised multiple people from the dead. Were those "miracles" real and verifiable? Of course not. Nonetheless, he paved the way for all the charismatic preachers, televangelists, faith healers, con men, and charlatans who dominate religious media today.

In fact, Roberts did more than anyone in the early Pentecostal Movement to influence mainstream evangelicalism into accepting these deceptive ideas. He parlayed his television ministry into a vast empire that has left a deep mark on the church worldwide. In many places today, including some of the world's most illiterate and poverty-stricken regions, Oral Roberts's seed-faith concept is actually better known than the doctrine of justification by faith. The message of health-and-wealth is now the message multitudes think of when they hear the word *gospel*. Countless people worldwide think of the gospel as a message about material riches and physical healing rather than the infinitely greater blessings of forgiveness from sin and the eternal blessing of the believer's spiritual union with Christ. All of those are reasons to lament rather than celebrate Oral Roberts's fame and influence.

Oral Roberts was not the first healing evangelist; he was preceded by Pentecostal ministers like John G. Lake, Smith Wigglesworth, Aimee Semple McPherson, and A. A. Allen. Nor was Roberts the only faith healer of the mid-twentieth century. His friends Kenneth Hagin and Kathryn Kuhlman were well-known contemporaries. Nonetheless, Roberts did more than anyone else to make modern healing mainstream—a feat he accomplished through the medium of television. He went from crude black-and-white broadcasts in dusty tent meetings during the 1950s to slick, sophisticated, high-quality color studio programming in the 1970s and beyond.

Roberts's remarkable success on television spawned a number of spinoffs and copies. A flock of faith healers and charismatic fund-raisers situated their headquarters in Roberts's hometown of Tulsa, Oklahoma. Kenneth Hagin and T. L. Osborne built large ministries there. Tulsa's Oral Roberts University, founded in 1963, became a breeding ground for a new generation of televangelists and faith healers. Joel Osteen, Creflo Dollar, Ted Haggard, Kenneth Copeland, Carlton Pearson, and Billy Joe Daugherty are all alumni of ORU.

In the end, perhaps the best way to measure the true legacy of Oral Roberts is by examining the continued influence of those who have followed in his wake. On the pages that follow, we will consider one such individual—a man who has essentially taken Roberts's place as the most visible and successful of the modern faith healers.

ENTER BENNY HINN

Of all the sordid successors to Oral Roberts, none is more ubiquitous than Toufik Benedictus (Benny) Hinn. Roberts may be gone, but his influence can still be seen through the ministries of Hinn and Hinn-wannabes.[7] Benny Hinn considers himself a protégé of Roberts. In a eulogy published shortly after Oral Roberts's death, Benny Hinn acknowledged his debt to Roberts and underscored his admiration for the late televangelist: "He was a giant in so many ways, and I was privileged to have him as a dear, dear friend for many years. . . . Through the years I have often thought of the standard he has set for so many ministers and believers to follow. . . . I have been ever thankful for the trail he blazed."[8]

Roberts and Hinn were not just friends but ministry allies. On numerous occasions, the duo appeared together in televised broadcasts. When *NBC Dateline* ran a devastating exposé on Hinn's ministry in 2002, Oral Roberts publicly defended him;[9] and Hinn, for his part, served for years as a regent for Oral Roberts University.[10] Perhaps it is appropriate that Benny Hinn has taken Oral Roberts's place as the most well-known face of faith healers everywhere.

In fact, Benny Hinn might credibly argue that his fame has superseded that of Roberts, based on the number of television broadcasts he makes and the enormous viewing audience he draws. Hinn's television show *This Is Your Day* is one of the most popular Christian television programs in the world—reaching more than twenty million people in the United States and two hundred countries around the world.[11] The cover copy on Hinn's books touts him as "one of the great healing evangelists of our time,"[12] and his website boasts that his "crusades have included audiences up to 7.3 million (in three services) in India, the largest healing service in recorded history."[13] According to Hinn, "healings of all kinds occur, and God makes Himself powerfully known"[14] at Hinn's monthly miracle crusades, which explains their appeal to desperate and dying people.

Almost every night on the various charismatic networks (and on many independently owned secular stations), Benny Hinn can be seen working massive crowds into a frenzy, "slaying" people "in the spirit," and claiming healings for all kinds of invisible ailments. Millions of viewers believe Oral Roberts's mantle has fallen on Benny Hinn, and they are utterly convinced he has extraordinary healing and miracle-working power just like his late mentor—perhaps even greater.

A careful look at the reality behind the glitzy television productions reveals a completely different picture.

HEALERS OR HERETICS?

As Rafael Martinez left the church in North Cleveland on a crisp October evening, he couldn't help but notice a young married couple wheeling their sick toddler out of the sanctuary. The boy's "limp body was plugged into hoses and respirators and beeping, blinking life-support packs [were] hanging off his walker." The boy's parents had brought him to the church for a healing service, hoping and praying for a miracle. None other than famed healing evangelist Benny Hinn had led the meeting that night. The atmosphere had been electrifying; emotions were high and expectations even higher. But several hours later everything was over, and their son had not been healed. Now it was time for them to go back home, taking their shattered hopes with them.

The heart-wrenching moment flooded Martinez's mind with haunting questions. Reflecting on that moment, he wrote:

> I wondered if they asked why their child was leaving the same way he came. Did his parents agonize over whether they had a deficient and incomplete faith? What sin might they be asking themselves were they guilty of? What generational curse had to be seed-faith broken? When Hinn told them to believe God for miracles, why didn't God sweep into that place and take that beautiful little boy up in His great nail scarred hands and quicken his body and spare him the uncertain future he faces ahead? I couldn't tear my eyes away and I have not forgotten the poignancy and puzzle of this moment.[15]

The desperate parents of that little boy were not the only casualty of false hope that evening. Martinez observed others—an elderly man with a leg brace who was turned away from the stage rather than being healed; a sick woman from Atlanta who had traveled to Cleveland with no way back home, only to leave unchanged. As he looked around at the end of the service, Martinez saw that "there were scores of these people still scattered all across [the] sanctuary sitting quietly in their wheelchairs or leaning on their canes, crutches and supports." He articulated the obvious question, "How can anyone with a Christian pastoral heart not ache at just what kind of spiritual turmoil, pain, disorientation and confusion these hurting folk have just been plunged into?"[16]

Of course, similar stories could be told from every Benny Hinn healing event. As Los Angeles Times religion reporter William Lobdell reported after covering one of Hinn's crusades in Anaheim, California: "The real drama happened after the pastor left the stage and the music stopped. Terminally ill people remained, just as sick as before. There were folks with Parkinson's disease whose limbs were still twisted and shaking. There were quadriplegics who couldn't move any muscle below their neck. These people—and there were hundreds, maybe thousands of them at each crusade—sat in their chairs, bewildered and crushed that God hadn't healed them."[17] Based on what he observed, Lobdell astutely deduced "the simple logic of Hinn's operations: raise false hope, and extract money."[18]

As a self-proclaimed faith healer, Hinn claims to be following the example of Christ and the apostles. For instance, he defends his approach to public healing by noting times when Jesus merely spoke to heal people rather than laying His hands on individual persons.[19] And, concerning the apostles, he says, "I knew the Lord had told me to pray for the sick as part of preaching the gospel, *just as He told the disciples*, in Mark 16:18: 'They will lay hands on the sick, and they will recover.'"[20] Insisting that "healing is not only for the past, but it is also for the present,"[21] Hinn claims to be "the channel [the Holy Spirit] anoints and uses to bring God's healing power and presence to the hurting and spiritually hungry."[22]

But such claims are nothing more than hot air, fanned by flames of rank arrogance and outright deception. Hinn may wield "gifts" of showmanship, histrionics, crowd manipulation, con artistry, and possibly even mass hypnosis. But one thing he certainly does not possess is the New Testament gift of healing. At best, Hinn's supposed healings are the result of a euphoric placebo effect—in which the body temporarily responds to a trick played on the mind and the emotions. At worst, Hinn's healings consist of outright lies and demonically empowered counterfeits. In either case, a simple comparison between the biblical gift and Benny Hinn's elaborate stage production exposes the latter for what it really is: a scam.

BENNY HINN VERSUS THE BIBLE

Perhaps no place in Scripture indicts the modern charismatic search for signs and wonders more than our Lord's rebuke of the Pharisees in Matthew 16:4: "A wicked and adulterous generation seeks after a sign." Though the multitudes crowded Jesus, desiring to see a miracle or experience a healing, the

Lord "did not commit Himself to them, because He knew all men" (John 2:24). Jesus knew there is a false kind of faith—that which is little more than a superficial curiosity about the supernatural, not a genuine love for the Savior.

The modern Charismatic Movement is characterized by that same kind of superficial faith. Yet it is far worse. In the days of Jesus and the apostles, true miracles were being performed. In our day, though charismatic leaders claim to have that same supernatural power, nothing truly miraculous is being done through them. The so-called ministries of today's faith healers and televangelists are nothing more than a facade. Healers like Benny Hinn are obvious con artists who are getting rich on the backs of gullible and desperate people.

So why devote an entire chapter to Benny Hinn, if he has been publicly and repeatedly discredited? The answer is twofold. First, in spite of his many guffaws, blunders, and scandals, Hinn remains a popular charismatic televangelist and the most well-known face of faith healing. His "ministry" continues to impact hundreds of millions of people around the globe while simultaneously raking in hundreds of millions of dollars. Second, Hinn's insistence on the continuation of miraculous healing for today aptly illustrates the devastating extremes to which the charismatic position on healing logically leads. Faith healers like Hinn claim to be able to replicate the healings of the apostolic age. In reality, their shenanigans have none of the characteristics of the actual New Testament gift of healing. In the rest of this chapter we will consider six stark contrasts between the healings recorded in Scripture and the modern counterfeit.

New Testament Healings Did Not Depend on the Faith of the Recipient

Charismatic healers like Benny Hinn readily blame their countless failures on a lack of faith—not their own faith, of course, but the faith of those who don't get healed. As a result, "many people believe, as Hinn preaches, that God fails to heal them because their faith isn't strong enough. Maybe they didn't give enough money to Hinn's ministry. Or maybe they just didn't *believe* enough."[23] Thus, while Hinn gets all the credit for supposed successes, he takes none of the blame for his countless failures.

Blaming sick people for failed healings might provide the "healer" with a convenient excuse, but it does not hold up biblically. A quick survey of the healing ministries of Christ and the apostles aptly makes the point. Time after time, people were healed without any expression of personal faith. Consider just a few examples.

In Luke 17:11–19, only one of the ten lepers expressed faith, yet all were made clean. The demoniacs of Matthew 8:28–29 and Mark 1:23–26 did not express faith before being set free, the crippled man beside the pool of Bethesda did not even know who Jesus was until after he had been healed (John 5:13), and the blind man in John 9 was similarly healed without knowing Jesus' identity (John 9:36). On several occasions, Jesus raised people from the dead, such as Jairus's daughter and Lazarus; obviously, dead people are not able to make any kind of "positive confession," much less respond with any show of faith. Our Lord also healed multitudes of people in spite of the fact that not all of them believed (cf. Matt. 9:35; 11:2–5; 12:15–21; 14:13–14, 34–36; 15:29–31; 19:2).

The healing ministries of the apostles, likewise, did not require belief from the sick in order to be effective. Peter healed a lame man without requiring faith from him (Acts 3:6–8). Later, he revived a woman named Tabitha after she had died (Acts 9:36–43). Paul likewise delivered an unbelieving slave girl from demon possession (Acts 16:18) and later raised Eutychus after he fell to his death (Acts 20:7–12). A profession of faith was not a prerequisite for any of those healing miracles.

Such is not the case for Hinn and his brood, who put the onus on the faith of the person seeking help. According to Hinn, "Faith is vital to your miracle. Healing is received by faith, and healing is kept by faith."[24] Again, "it takes aggressive faith . . . to bring salvation from that sickness."[25] And again, "You cannot receive healing unless your heart is right with God. . . . Healing is easily attained when your walk with God is right."[26] Elsewhere, he wrote:

> Often in our crusades, I'll tell people to touch the part of their body that they want God to heal. I'll encourage them to begin moving their afflicted arms or bending their hurting legs. These actions do nothing in themselves, but they *do* demonstrate that the person has faith in God's healing power. And in the Scriptures you see again and again that when the Lord Jesus healed the sick He asked them to *do* something *before* the miracle took place.[27]

This idea that people themselves are to blame when they don't get healed is a corollary to Hinn's teaching that it is *always* God's will to heal. In his view, any prayer for healing that includes the phrase "if it be Your will" is an expression of insufficient faith. As Hinn states it, "Never, ever, ever go to the Lord and say, 'If it be thy will.' Don't allow such faith-destroying words to be spoken from your mouth. When you pray 'if it be your will, Lord,' faith will be destroyed."[28]

The implication is obvious, and devastating: if it is always God's will to heal, then the sick and infirm are to blame for their own afflictions. They must not have sufficient faith. When pressed directly on this issue, Hinn himself invariably tries to back away from (or deny) the merciless implications of his own teaching. But as Justin Peters rightly observes:

> If Hinn's logic is followed, as it is with untold millions, if one is sick then that person's healing is contingent upon his or her own faith. If healing does not come, the person is left with the unavoidable conclusion that it is his fault. His walk with God is not pure enough, his faith is not strong enough. Though Hinn says that he is "not going to make harsh statements that put guilt on people and leave them thinking that they are to blame if they are not healed," that is exactly what he is doing.[29]

Though Jesus often responded to people's faith during His ministry, the success of His healing power was certainly not dependent on their level of belief. The phrase "Your faith has made you well" (cf. Matt. 9:22; Mark 5:34; 10:52; Luke 7:50; 8:48; 18:42) is better translated "Your faith has saved you." The Lord's concern about faith was related to the salvation of souls, not the mere repair of physical bodies. But this emphasis on the true gospel is lost on fraudulent healers like Benny Hinn. As Rafael Martinez reported from his firsthand experience at Hinn's healing meeting:

> While there was no altar call given for salvation, there certainly was one of sorts for the offering. . . . In the exhortation, Hinn inexplicably mentioned that he had just signed a 23 million dollar contract to buy and run a private

jet to get him around. . . . This he said was part of the great things God intended as part of an end time "Wealth Transfer" to help finance the "harvest," and that we should be ready to prove ourselves by our giving so God could give us the wealth of the world to preach the Gospel.[30]

Hinn may talk about reaching the world, but he is clearly not interested in preaching the true gospel. The "gospel" he proclaims is grounded in the materialistic mantra of the prosperity gospel—a health-and-wealth message he inherited from Oral Roberts and others like him. It has no basis in Scripture, but it has brought Hinn substantial wealth, which brings us to our second point of contrast.

New Testament Healings Were Not Performed for Money or Fame

The Lord Jesus never healed anyone for material gain. Neither did the apostles. In fact, the one time Peter was offered money in exchange for healing power, he rebuked Simon Magus with a severe denunciation: "Your money perish with you, because you thought that the gift of God could be purchased with money!" (Acts 8:20).

Christ and the apostles focused their healing ministries on the poorest and most destitute members of society—people who had no means of compensation. Blind beggars (Matt. 9:27–31; 20:29–34; 21:14; Mark 8:22–26), leprous outcasts (Matt. 8:2–3; Luke 17:11–21), and impoverished cripples (Matt. 9:1–8; 21:14; John 5:1–9; Acts 3:1–10; 14:8–18) were among the lowest members of a society that associated sickness with sin (cf. John 9:2–3). Yet they were the ones to whom Jesus and His disciples showed compassion. And they never asked for money in return. The New Testament compulsion behind miracles of healing was clearly not financial. Just the opposite was true. Any so-called ministers who were motivated by the love of money were denounced as false teachers (1 Tim. 6:5, 9–10). Jesus said, "You cannot serve God and wealth" (Matt. 6:24 NASB).

Our Lord also avoided the superficial publicity and curiosity-seeking that resulted from His miracle-working. He often commanded those whom He healed to tell no one what had happened (cf. Matt. 8:4; 9:30; Mark 5:43).

When the crowds wanted to make Him king—not because they truly believed in Him but because they desired more miracles—Jesus slipped away to the other side of the Sea of Galilee (John 6:15). In Luke 10:20, He instructed His disciples to rejoice in their eternal salvation, and not in the ability to perform miracles. Though crowds flocked to Jesus throughout His ministry, our Lord was never interested in being popular. Ultimately, despite the miracles He performed, a crowd would cry out for His crucifixion.

Benny Hinn's healing ministry, by contrast, has brought him a great deal of popularity and personal prosperity. As he stated in his autobiography, "How can I criticize the press when they have attracted hundreds of thousands of people to our crusades to hear the Word?"[31]

"To hear the Word"? That claim is a typical bit of make-believe by Benny Hinn. The crowds at his events clearly do not come to hear the Word, and he does not faithfully preach the unadulterated Word of God. As Hinn himself acknowledges, "most people know what those around them have come expecting—they are expecting miracles."[32] Elsewhere, he adds, "People don't just come to hear you preach; they want to see something."[33]

Armed with the same seed-faith message as Oral Roberts, Hinn is more than happy just to convert miracle seekers into ministry donors. As he told a TBN *Praise-a-Thon* audience in 2000, "I believe that God is healing people while they're making a pledge tonight. There are people getting healed making a pledge."[34] Hinn's message at another *Praise-a-Thon* was equally forward: "Make a pledge; make a gift. Because that's the only way you're going to get your miracle. . . . As you give, the miracle will begin."[35] Such appeals are grounded in the materialistic give-to-get absurdity of seed-faith theology, as Hinn explained to one of his television audiences:

> In your prayer requests be specific and then send a gift. Here's why: the Word of God says "give." . . . The Word says sow and then you shall reap. You can't expect a harvest until you sow a seed [of money]. . . . So send that seed today. Whatever amount, and really it depends on your need. . . . Someone came to me in church recently and said, "Well pastor, how much should I give to God?" I said, "Well, what kind of harvest are you looking for?"[36]

The advertising scheme is anything but subtle. If you want to be healed, send in your money; and if you don't get healed, you didn't send enough. Like the wicked religious leaders condemned in Luke 20, Benny Hinn devours "widows' houses" as he hawks false hope in exchange for money; and like the destitute widow of Luke 21, many respond by sending him their last two mites.

While Benny Hinn denies his motives are monetary,[37] his lifestyle betrays the true extent of his avarice and greed. He found himself at the vortex of a scandal a few years ago when it came to light that he took a large cadre of staff and bodyguards to Europe with him on the Concorde—all at donors' expense. The first-class tickets on the Concorde cost $8,850 each, and during that European junket Hinn and his party stayed in five-star hotels at a cost of more than $2,000 per night per room. CNN featured that story, complete with videotape of Hinn and his entourage boarding the Concorde.[38] A brief scandal ensued, temporarily turning the spotlight of public criticism on Hinn's gross extravagance.

Not much has changed since then. "Hinn reportedly earns more than $1 million a year, lives in an oceanfront mansion, drives the latest luxury cars and travels by private jet, the Concorde no longer being an option"[39]—all while sporting gaudy accessories like a "diamond Rolex, diamond rings, gold bracelets and custom suits for all to see."[40] Such ostentatious living may fit the prosperity-gospel paradigm, in which material riches are arrogantly flaunted as a supposed sign of God's blessing. But the contrast with New Testament–style ministry could not be starker. Hinn's healing scams bring in an estimated $100 million annually,[41] as he empties the pockets of desperate people willing to give anything for a miracle.

New Testament Healings Were Completely Successful

The healing miracles of Jesus never failed. Neither did those done by the apostles in the book of Acts. In Matthew 14:36 all who touched the hem of Christ's garment "were made perfectly well." When lepers were healed, their recovery was total, such that they could pass a thorough inspection by the priest (cf. Lev. 14:3, 4, 10). The blind were given 20/20 vision, the lame could run and jump, the deaf could hear a pin drop, and the dead were restored to full health. No New Testament miracle was ever attempted that was not ultimately a complete success.

Some might counter by pointing to the disciples' inability to cast out a demon in Matthew 17:20, or the Lord's decision to heal a blind man in two stages in Mark 8:22–26. But those exceptions only prove the rule—since in both cases full healing was ultimately accomplished. In the case of the disciples, it is significant to note that the failure was caused by a lack of faith on their part (not on the part of the sick child). If modern healers want to find a parallel with that incident, they would have to recognize it is *their own lack of faith* that is the problem.

In the case of the blind man, Jesus healed him in two stages to make a spiritual point—accentuating the spiritual shortsightedness of the disciples (cf. Mark 8:21). Ultimately, the Lord fully restored the man's sight. Thus in every instance, both in the Gospels and in Acts, Christ and the apostles had a success rate of 100 percent. As Thomas Edgar rightly notes, "There were no failures. Every attempt to heal was successful."[42]

Obviously, no modern healing ministry comes anywhere close to this biblical standard. Benny Hinn's spotty track record provides a case in point. As *ABC Nightline* reported in 2009, "Hinn admits he doesn't have medical verification of any of the healings. In fact, some of his supposed healings have turned out not to have been real."[43] The *Nightline* report continues, "At a 2001 Hinn crusade, William Vandenkolk, a 9-year-old with damaged vision, claimed that his eyesight had been restored. Vandenkolk is now 17—and he's still legally blind."[44]

Confronted with the facts, Hinn is forced to admit, "I don't know why every person isn't touched and healed."[45] He tells of times that he has laid hands on people "and nothing happened,"[46] and news reports tell of four seriously ill patients who were released from a Kenyan hospital to attend one of Hinn's miracle crusades in hopes of being healed. Instead of being cured, all four died at the crusade.[47] Such realities contradict Hinn's written claims.

In his book *Rise and Be Healed*, Hinn said of God, "He promises to heal all—every one, any, any whatsoever, everything—all our diseases! That means not even a headache, sinus problem, not even a toothache—nothing! No sickness should come your way. God heals all your diseases."[48] But not even Hinn truly believes that. An article in the *Los Angeles Times* made this poignant observation about Hinn's own failure to come to grips with the reasons healing is often elusive:

> Though he seldom mentions it onstage, the next day at the Four Seasons Hinn says that he does wonder why God doesn't heal some people. It's a question that the pastor has had to wrestle with personally. He says he has a heart condition that God hasn't cured, and his parents have suffered serious medical problems. "That is a very difficult thing for me because I told my daddy to believe," Hinn says. "But he died. Now I don't know why."
>
> The concession that some people don't get healed is relatively new to him. "There was a time in my life I would have never said those things," Hinn admits. "But you have to, I mean, goodness. My mom has diabetes, my daddy died with cancer. That's life."[49]

Though he now reluctantly acknowledges some of his healings have failed, Hinn *still* insists he's not a con man looking for cash: "If I was fake I would absolutely give them back their money."[50] Really? So the proof he is not a liar and a charlatan is that he continues to bilk needy and gullible people while unapologetically living a prodigal lifestyle with the money he has taken from them? Such is the logic of Benny Hinn.

In 2002, he similarly told a television audience, "Now, look in my eyes right here. Give me a close shot, will you, and look at these eyes. I have never lied to you. Never. I never will. I'd rather die than lie to God's people. That's the truth."[51] In reality that was anything but truth. Hinn's vigorous attempts to defend his motives evaporate upon closer examination. After conducting an interview with Hinn, William Lobdell of the *Los Angeles Times* concluded:

> If not for the divine calling, Hinn said he would walk away from the job in an instant. I couldn't look into Hinn's soul, but from where I sat, I saw a gifted actor who parlayed his theatrical skills and feel for the human condition into

the material life of a movie star. I didn't think for a moment he believed a word of what he preached—or that he was bothered that people who didn't get their miracle cure had died. I imagined him behind the doors of his cliff-top Dana Point mansion, giggling to himself at his good fortune as he looked out of the floor-to-ceiling windows at the 180-degree view of the Pacific with surfers bobbing in the waves, dolphins swimming just outside the surf line and sailboats dotting the horizon. He had hit the lottery, his actions pro-tected from the law by the First Amendment.[52]

New Testament Healings Were Undeniable

Unlike Benny Hinn's alleged healings, for which there is no authoritative verification, the miraculous healings performed by Christ and the apostles could not be discounted—even by those openly antagonistic to the gospel. When Jesus cast out demons, the Pharisees could not deny His super-natural power. So instead they attempted to discredit Him by claiming He was empowered by Satan (cf. Matt. 12:24). Later, when the Lord raised Lazarus from the dead, the religious leaders of Israel were again unable to deny what had happened (John 11:47–48). But rather than believe, they resolved to put Him to death. In the book of Acts, those same leaders could not refute the fact that Peter had healed a lame man (Acts 4:16–17). Nor could the pagan owners of a demon-possessed slave girl discount Paul's authority to cast out the demon that plagued her (Acts 16:19).

In addition to the testimony of unbelievers, the writers of the Gospels and Acts took special care to record their histories accurately (cf. Luke 1:1–4). The fact that Luke was a physician (Col. 4:14) adds a layer of credibility to the medical merit of the New Testament miracle reports. Of course, all the Gospel writers were inspired by the Holy Spirit (2 Tim. 3:16–17), who enabled them to remember with precision the details they included in their various accounts (cf. John 14:26). As a result, we can trust the biblical record with absolute certainty.

Benny Hinn's healing crusades are a completely different matter. Although Hinn insists "hundreds of verified healings and thousands of conversions have occurred," it is clear that this is a lie. Though he regularly boasts about "people rising from wheelchairs and leaving crutches . . . blind eyes and deaf ears [that] have been opened and verified,"[53] evidence to support those claims simply does not exist. Mike Thomas investigated Hinn's miracle crusades. He wrote:

> Despite all the thousands of miracles claimed by Hinn, the church seems hard pressed to come up with any that would convince a serious skeptic. If God cures through Hinn, he does not cure ailments such as permanent paralysis, brain damage, retardation, physical deformities, missing eyes or other obvious ailments.[54]

Though he has held hundreds of crusades over the years, Hinn's supposed healings still lack verification. When Hinn provided Christian Research Institute with his three best-documented cases, the results were utterly un-impressive. "All three cases are poorly documented and confused," wrote Hank Hanegraaff of CRI. "If evidence like this is the best Hinn can muster after years of 'miracle rallies'—with a staff working at each rally to document cases of healing—then there is no credible evidence that he has ever been involved in a bona fide healing."[55]

While the list of fantastic claims and incredible healing stories continues to grow at a frantic pace, any real evidence of genuine miracles is conspicuously absent. A 2001 HBO documentary entitled *A Question of Miracles* followed the lives of seven people for a year, after they had supposedly been healed at a Benny Hinn crusade. At the end of that time period, Anthony Thomas, the film's director, concluded that no one had actually been healed.[56]

In an interview with the *New York Times*, Thomas gave this raw assessment: "If I had seen miracles [at Hinn's crusades], I would have been happy to trumpet it . . . but in retrospect, I think they do more damage to Christianity than the most committed atheist."[57]

New Testament Healings Were Immediate and Spontaneous

When Jesus or His disciples healed someone, the sick were made well immediately. No recovery period was necessary—no physical therapy needed, no recuperation time required. Lepers were instantly cleansed (Mark 1:42), blind men were immediately granted sight (Mark 10:52), and people who had been paralyzed one moment could leap for joy the next (Acts 3:8). Some might argue that delayed healings did occur in Mark 8:22–26 (where a blind man was healed in two stages), Luke 17:11–19 (where ten lepers were cleansed while on their way to see the priest), and John 9:1–7 (where a blind man was healed after washing in the Pool of Siloam). But those incidents involved delays of only a few minutes, not weeks or days—and the delays were a purposeful part of the way in which Jesus intended to accomplish the healing miracle. They are, again, the exceptions that prove the rule: the miraculous healings recorded in the New Testament happened right away.

Benny Hinn, by contrast, extols "a lady who went to Katherine Kuhlman's meetings eleven times before she was healed. Eleven times!"[58] All this fits with Hinn's Word of Faith theology. As D. R. McConnell explains:

> In the Faith movement, the believer is instructed that healing is an accomplished "faith fact," but that it is not instantaneously manifested as a physical fact in the believer's body. During the interlude between the confession of healing and its manifestation, the believer might encounter "symptoms" of a disease. These symptoms are not the disease itself [but rather] spiritual decoys with which Satan is attempting to trick the believer into making a negative confession, thereby forfeiting his healing.[59]

So, even if it seems like you are still sick, you have actually been healed. You just need to wait for your body to catch up to that reality. That's why Hinn can tell his followers, "After you have received your miracle, turn away from those who oppose miracles. . . . Continue to see yourself well and whole, healed in Jesus' name."[60] Such a ridiculous statement would never have been said about biblical healings. The immediate results were always evident for all to see.

Moreover, the healings recorded in the New Testament were spontaneous. They were not prearranged but were performed during the normal course of life. In Matthew 8:14–15, the Lord simply arrived at Peter's house, and finding Peter's mother-in-law ill, Jesus healed her. Matthew 9:20 records the healing of a woman who secretly touched the hem of Jesus' garment while He was walking by. Peter and John were merely on their way to the temple when they were interrupted by a crippled beggar (Acts 3:6–7). Numerous other examples could be cited to make the same point: New Testament healings were not carefully orchestrated prescheduled events that occurred in stadiums and meeting halls. Jesus' healings were never "staged," or done with the hope of creating a spectacle so that an appeal could be made to donors.

By contrast, Benny Hinn has made prearranged miracle meetings the bread and butter of his ministry. The services follow a preset schedule and are carefully choreographed. As Richard Fischer explains, "Not only is what the television audience sees edited, what the live audience sees is carefully staged. Those who are terribly deformed, children with Down's syndrome, amputees and the like are kept from the stage and out of sight of TV cameras."[61] A 2004 investigative documentary aired by the Canadian Broadcasting Channel used hidden cameras to demonstrate that those with serious medical conditions—such as quadriplegics, the mentally handicapped, and those with obvious physical ailments—are not allowed to come onstage but are sent back to their seats by a team of vigilant screeners.[62] That kind of careful selectivity would not be necessary if Hinn genuinely had the gift of healing.

Of course, if Benny Hinn could really do what he claims, he could empty hospitals and curb disease in Third World countries. Like Jesus, he would be able to banish sickness and suffering in whatever regions he visited. But because he does not possess the true gift, Hinn requires people come to him—to the place where he can manipulate the audience and control all the details. That obviously flies in the face of the New Testament paradigm. As Robert Bowman rightly points out, "Scheduling the Holy Spirit to come to one's church at 7:00 p.m. on Thursday nights to perform healings is alien to the Bible."[63]

New Testament Healings Authenticated a True Message

A final characteristic of New Testament healings is that they served as a sign to authenticate the gospel message preached by Christ and the apostles. As Peter explained on the day of Pentecost, the Lord Jesus was "a Man attested by God to you by miracles, wonders, and signs" (Acts 2:22). Christ Himself told the skeptical Pharisees, "Though you do not believe Me, believe the works, that you may know and believe that the Father is in Me, and I in Him" (John 10:38). And the apostle John explained the purpose of his gospel with these words: "Truly Jesus did many other signs in the presence of His disciples, which are not written in this book; but these are written that you may believe that Jesus is the Christ, the Son of God, and that believing you may have life in His name" (John 20:30–31).

The apostles, as Christ's ambassadors, were similarly authenticated by the miraculous signs they performed (cf. Rom. 15:18–19; 2 Cor. 12:12). Speaking of that apostolic witness, the author of Hebrews explained, "How shall we escape if we neglect so great a salvation, which at the first began to be spoken by the Lord, and was confirmed to us by those who heard Him, God also bearing witness both with signs and wonders, with various miracles, and gifts of the Holy Spirit, according to His own will?" (Heb. 2:3–4). Those signs validated the fact that the apostles were truly who they claimed to be—authorized representatives of God who preached the true gospel.

Those who would preach any gospel other than that established by Christ and proclaimed by the apostles show themselves to be "false apostles" and "deceitful workers" (2 Cor. 11:13). Paul cursed such people—twice in quick succession, to make the point as emphatic as possible: "But even if we, or an angel from heaven, preach any other gospel to you than what we have preached to you, let him be accursed. As we have said before, so now I say again, if anyone preaches any other gospel to you than what you have received, let him be accursed" (Gal. 1:8–9). The God of truth only validates the true gospel. He would not authenticate bad theology or give supernatural power to people who teach bad theology. Thus, self-proclaimed miracle workers who teach a false gospel either cannot perform miracles or do so by a power that does not come from God (cf. 2 Thess. 2:9).

Though Benny Hinn claims he desires "to somehow reach every home in every country with the gospel,"[64] his "gospel" is not the message of salvation articulated by the New Testament. Instead, it is the false gospel of health, wealth, and prosperity—a grotesque deformation that is, in reality, a damning lie. Tickling ears for the sake of monetary gain not only summarizes Hinn's career, but it is also the mark of a false teacher (2 Tim. 4:3; Titus 1:11). Bizarre doctrinal inventions, proclaimed by Hinn under the alleged influence of the Holy Spirit, only confirm his true nature. What should we conclude about someone who has claimed that the Trinity consists of nine persons;[65] that God the Father "walks in a spirit body" complete with hands, mouth, hair, and eyes;[66] that the Lord Jesus assumed a satanic nature on the cross;[67] and that believers should think of themselves as little Messiahs?[68] It is ludicrous to think Holy God would authenticate such egregious error by giving a false teacher like Benny Hinn miracle power. Such would make God a participant in Hinn's deception. But that is obviously not the case.

Though Hinn has subsequently distanced himself from some of those views, one inescapable fact remains: a hasty *retraction* made to avoid public embarrassment is not the same as true *repentance* demonstrated by a changed life. To date, Hinn has given no evidence of genuine repentance. He remains the fraudulent face of a false ministry, heading for eternal ruin and taking multitudes of desperate people with him.

AN ACCURATE VIEW OF HEALING

The miracle-working ministries of Christ and the apostles were unique. As we have seen in this chapter, the healings they performed were supernaturally powerful, entirely successful, undeniable, immediate, spontaneous, and purposeful—serving as signs that authenticated the message of the gospel. They were not predicated on the faith of the recipient, they were not performed for the sake of money or popularity, and they were not preplanned or choreographed in any way. They were true miracles that resulted in *real* diseases being instantly cured: the blind saw, the lame walked, the deaf heard, and even the dead were raised to life.

Such biblical-quality healing miracles are not being performed today. Benny Hinn may claim to have an apostolic healing ministry, but he obviously does not. Healing miracles of the kind recorded in the Gospels and Acts were unique to the first-century church. After the time of the apostles, healings such as those ceased and have never since been part of church history.

While the Lord still answers prayer and works in providential ways to heal people according to His will, there is no evidence that miraculous healings are occurring today as they did during the apostolic age.[69] Quadriplegics, paralytics, amputees, and people with other significant physical handicaps are not being instantly restored to full health today as in New Testament times. Clearly, there has been no parallel in history to the unique healing miracles that occurred at the time of Christ and the apostles. Today is no exception. The apostolic gift of healing has ceased.

While the New Testament does instruct believers to pray for those who are sick and suffering, trusting the Great Physician to do that which is according to His sovereign purposes (cf. James 5:14–15), that is *not* equivalent to the supernatural gift of healing described in Scripture. Anyone who claims otherwise is fooling himself. Benny Hinn and others like him, who claim to be specially anointed with a healing gift, aptly illustrate the point. They simply *cannot* do apostolic-quality miracles, and when they try to pass parlor tricks, chicanery, showmanship, frauds, and scams off as if they were true signs and wonders, they forfeit their own credibility with most, undermine the authority of Scripture in the minds of many, mislead multitudes who are gullible, and condemn themselves as false prophets and liars before God Himself. In sum, everything about the practice is spiritually destructive.

PART THREE

REDISCOVERING THE SPIRIT'S TRUE WORK

NINE

THE HOLY SPIRIT AND SALVATION

From the invention of Greek coins around 600 BC to the introduction of paper money in thirteenth-century China, counterfeiting has always been regarded as a serious crime. Historically, it was often punishable by death. In colonial America, for example, Benjamin Franklin printed paper currency that included the ominous warning, "To counterfeit is death." The annals of English history relate the executions of numerous counterfeiters, most of whom were hanged, and some of whom were burned at the stake. That level of retribution may sound harsh to our modern ears, but the crime of counterfeiting was severely punished for two main reasons.

First, the law regarded it as a threat to the economic stability of the state and the general well-being of all who lived there. And second, in countries like England, the issuing of currency was considered a prerogative that belonged only to the king. Thus, counterfeiting was not merely a petty theft against the person duped into taking the fake currency; it was regarded as something much more serious—a danger to society at large and a seditious treason against royal authority.

But what about those who counterfeit God's work? The crime of forging money pales in comparison to the treacherous act of counterfeiting the ministry of the Holy Spirit. If the printing of fake currency poses a threat to society, the promotion of fraudulent religious experiences represents a far greater danger. And if the production of bogus coins constitutes an act of treason against a human government, the preaching of a false gospel is an infinitely worse offense against the King of kings. Moreover, the Word of God is not silent as to the consequences of such crimes. Insofar as financial forgers and frauds have been treated harshly throughout history, the perpetuators of counterfeit religion await a much more severe judgment.

Given the seriousness of such crimes, believers must be equipped to identify and warn of that which is false. But being ready to refute error requires knowing what is true. The only way to be certain about all counterfeits is to be intimately familiar with the real thing. In chapters 3 and 4, we surveyed five marks of the Spirit's true work, in contrast to counterfeit revivals and spiritual imitations. In this section, we will revisit a number of those same themes—looking more deeply at the authentic ministry of the Holy Spirit. As we do, the glorious magnificence of the genuine artifact will be exalted, while the false pretenses of contemporary imitations crumble by comparison.

REDISCOVERING THE HOLY SPIRIT

If the previous chapters have demonstrated anything, it is that the church today desperately needs to rediscover the true person and work of the Holy Spirit. The third member of the Trinity has been grossly misrepresented, insulted, and grieved by a counterfeit movement that is being propagated in His name. Operating under false pretenses and propelled by false prophecies, the charismatic flood has rapidly drenched the broader Christian landscape, and it has left a swath of doctrinal error and spiritual ruin in its wake. It is high time for those who love the Holy Spirit to take a bold stand and confront any error that blatantly and blasphemously dishonors the Spirit of God.

Since a true view of the triune God is essential to true worship, an accurate understanding of the Holy Spirit is absolutely vital. As A. W. Tozer observed in his classic work *The Knowledge of the Holy*:

What comes into our minds when we think about God is the most important thing about us. . . . Worship is pure or base as the worshiper entertains high or low thoughts of God. For this reason the gravest question before the Church is always God Himself, and the most portentous fact about any man is not what he at a given time may say or do, but what he in his deep heart conceives God to be like. We tend by a secret law of the soul to move toward our mental image of God. This is true not only of the individual Christian, but of the company of Christians that composes the Church. Always the most revealing thing about the Church is her idea of God.[1]

Tozer's words are both potent and precise. Our view of God is the foundational reality in our thinking, and it encompasses all that we believe about the Holy Spirit. Thinking rightly about Him and His work is essential to our worship, doctrine, and the proper application of theology in everyday conduct.

We have already noted that the Holy Spirit's primary work is to point people to Jesus Christ (John 15:26; 16:14)—bringing sinners to a true knowledge of the Savior through the gospel and conforming them through the Scripture to the glorious image of the Son of God (2 Cor. 3:17–18). Thus, the focus of His ministry is the Lord Jesus, and those who are Spirit-led and Spirit-filled will likewise be Christ-centered. But that does not mean we should ignore what Scripture teaches us about the Spirit or stand idly by while His holy name is stained by spiritual swindlers. To misrepresent Him is to slander God.

The Holy Spirit is equal in essence, majesty, and power to both the Father and the Son. But the mainstream Charismatic Movement mocks His true nature, as if there were no consequences for such blatant blasphemy. Sadly, many within evangelicalism have silently watched the desecration take place. If God the Father or God the Son were mocked in this way, evangelicals would surely protest. Why should we be any less passionate for the glory and honor of the Spirit?

Much of the problem, it seems, is that the modern church has lost sight of the Holy Spirit's divine majesty. While charismatics treat Him like an impersonal force of ecstatic energy, evangelicals have generally reduced Him to the caricature of a peaceful dove, often portrayed on Bible covers and bumper stickers—as if the Spirit of the Almighty were a harmless white bird fluttering quietly in the breeze. Anyone who thinks that way needs to repent and reread the Bible.

Although He descended on Jesus at His baptism in the way a dove would fly down and alight on someone, the Holy Spirit is *not* a dove. He is the omnipotent, eternal, holy, and glorious Spirit of the living God. His power is infinite, His presence inescapable, and His purity a consuming fire. Those who test Him face severe judgment, as those in the days of Noah experienced in the Flood (Gen. 6:3). And those who lie to Him face the real possibility of imminent death, as Ananias and Sapphira learned the hard way (Acts 5:3–5).

In Judges 15:14–15, it was the Spirit of the Lord who came upon Samson when he killed a thousand Philistines with the jawbone of a donkey. And in Isaiah 63:10, the prophet explains the severe consequences of grieving the Holy Spirit. Speaking of the Israelites Isaiah wrote, "But they rebelled and grieved His Holy Spirit; so He turned Himself against them as an enemy, and He fought against them." It could not be clearer than that: to treat the Holy Spirit irreverently is to make God your enemy! Do people really think they can belittle the Holy Spirit and get away with it?

The Holy Spirit is the power of God in a divine person acting from creation to consummation and everything in between (cf. Gen. 1:2; Rev. 22:17). He is wholly God, possessing all the attributes of God in the fullness that belongs to God. There is no sense in which He is God diminished. He participates fully in all of God's works. He is as holy and powerful as the Father and as gracious and loving as the Son. He is divine perfection in its fullness. Thus, He is worthy of our worship as fully as the Father and as fully as the Son. Charles Spurgeon, expressing his own passion for the Spirit's honor, charged his congregation with these words:

> To the believer: Dear brother, honour the Spirit of God as you would honour Jesus Christ if he were present. If Jesus Christ were dwelling in your house you would not ignore him, you would not go about your business as if he were not there. Do not ignore the presence of the Holy Spirit in your soul. I beseech you, do not live as if you had not heard whether there were any

Holy Spirit. To him pay your constant adorations. Reverence the august guest who has been pleased to make your body his sacred abode. Love him, obey him, worship him.[2]

If we are to honor our divine Guest, treating Him with the reverence and respect that is His royal due, we must rightly discern His true ministry—aligning our hearts, minds, and wills with His wondrous work.

What is the Holy Spirit truly doing in the world today? He who was once actively involved in the creation of the material universe (Gen. 1:2) is now focused on spiritual creation (cf. 2 Cor. 4:6). He creates spiritual life—regenerating sinners through the gospel of Jesus Christ and transforming them into children of God. He sanctifies them, equips them for service, produces fruit in their lives, and empowers them to please their Savior. He secures them for eternal glory and fits them for life in heaven. The same Source of explosive power that brought the world into existence out of nothing is today at work in the hearts and lives of the redeemed. And just as creation was an astonishing miracle, so is every new creation—as the Spirit supernaturally brings salvation to those who would have otherwise been condemned to eternal ruin. People who want to see miracles today should stop following fake healers and start engaging in biblical evangelism. To see a spiritually dead sinner made alive in Christ Jesus by the power of the Spirit is to witness an *actual* miracle of God.

In this chapter, we will consider that wondrous reality. As we do, we will discover six aspects of the Spirit's work in salvation—from His convicting work in calling sinners to salvation to His sealing work in securing believers for eternal glory.[3]

THE HOLY SPIRIT CONVICTS UNBELIEVERS OF SIN

In the Upper Room, on the eve of His crucifixion, the Lord Jesus comforted His disciples by promising them that after His ascension He would send the Holy Spirit to minister in and through them. As He told His grieving followers, "Nevertheless I tell you the truth. It is to your advantage that I go away; for if I do not go away, the Helper will not come to you; but if I depart, I will send Him to you" (John 16:7). The disciples must have wondered, "How could anything be better than having the incarnate Son of God physically present in our midst?" Yet Jesus insisted that it would be to their advantage for Him to ascend to heaven and for the Holy Spirit to come.

The Lord continued by explaining the vital work the Holy Spirit would do—empowering the gospel proclamation of the apostles as they went out to preach the truth of salvation to a hostile world. The Spirit would go before them, propelling their preaching into the hearts of those who heard and believed their message. The Lord explained it this way: "And when He has come, He will convict the world of sin, and of righteousness, and of judgment: of sin, because they do not believe in Me; of righteousness, because I go to My Father and you see Me no more; of judgment, because the ruler of this world is judged" (John 16:8–11).

As the general, external call of the gospel goes forth, through the preaching of the message of salvation, unbelievers in the world are confronted with the reality of their sin and the consequences of their unbelief. For those who reject the gospel, the Holy Spirit's work of conviction might be likened to that of a prosecuting attorney. He convicts them in the sense that they are rendered guilty before God and are, therefore, eternally condemned (John 3:18). The Spirit's convicting work is not about making unrepentant sinners feel bad, but about delivering a legal verdict against them. It includes a full indictment of their hardhearted crimes, complete with irrefutable evidence and a death sentence.

Yet for those whom the Spirit draws to the Savior, His convicting work is one of convincing, as He pricks their consciences and cuts them to the quick. Thus, for the elect, this work of conviction is the beginning of God's saving, effectual call.

Our Lord's words indicate that the Holy Spirit's ministry of conviction encompasses three areas. First, He convicts the unredeemed of their sin, exposing them to the reality of their wretched condition before God. In particular, He convicts sinners of their unbelief in the gospel—since, as Jesus explained, "they do not believe in Me" (John 16:9). It is the natural response of fallen men and women to reject the person and work of the Lord Jesus Christ. But the Spirit confronts the world's hardhearted unbelief.

Second, the Holy Spirit convicts unbelievers of righteousness—confronting them with the truth of God's *holy standard* and Jesus Christ's *perfect righteousness*. In the words of one commentator, "The world masquerades as righteous and suppresses any evidence to the contrary, and such behavior requires the Spirit to expose its guilt."[4] By ripping back the facade of self-righteousness, the Spirit exposes the true condition of those who have fallen short of God's perfect requirements. Then He turns their eyes to consider the unfailing righteousness of Jesus Christ—the spotless Lamb of God.

Third, the Holy Spirit convicts sinners that the consequences of divine judgment are just and necessary—namely, that sinners will one day be judged just as "the ruler of this world is judged" (v. 11). Just as Satan is doomed to eternal ruin, having been defeated at the cross, so also all those who are part of Satan's domain are under God's judgment—and their judgment is not only morally justifiable, but it is the only recourse of a righteous deity. As the author of Hebrews explained, those who "trample underfoot the blood of Jesus" by disregarding the gracious offer of the gospel "insult the Spirit of grace" and store up for themselves severe punishment (cf. Heb. 10:29). Thus, "it is a fearful thing to fall into the hands of the living God" (v. 31). Warning unbelievers of the reality of future judgment is both a fearful and a gracious work of the Spirit, alerting them to the dire consequences that await all who do not repent.

As Jesus' words demonstrate, it was essential for the disciples to understand this ministry of the Holy Spirit. Why? As those commissioned to reach sinners with a message the world would violently reject (John 15:18–25), the apostles needed to know that the Holy Spirit would accompany their preaching with His power. As they confronted sinners' unbelief, exalted Christ's righteousness, and warned of God's judgment, the Holy Spirit would convict the hearts of those who heard and convert the elect.

This ministry was vividly illustrated on the day of Pentecost, after Peter preached his powerful gospel message. Luke records the crowd's response: "Now when they heard this, they were cut to the heart, and said to Peter and the rest of the apostles, 'Men and brethren, what shall we do?'" (Acts 2:37).

Their hearts were pierced by the truth; and for three thousand people in that crowd, the Spirit's work of conviction was part of His work of regeneration in their hearts (v. 31).

Two millennia later, our message to the lost world ought to mirror those same themes—with an emphasis on spiritual death, true righteousness, and divine judgment. Admittedly, preaching about human depravity, God's holiness, and eternal punishment is not popular, especially in a postmodern society that celebrates tolerance. But it is the only ministry empowered by the Holy Spirit. He is the power behind the preaching of the gospel (1 Peter 1:12), using His Word to draw sinners to the Savior and regenerate them.

Arthur W. Pink said it this way: "None will ever be *drawn to Christ*: savingly, by mere preaching; . . . there must first be the supernatural operations of the Spirit to open the sinner's heart *to receive* the message!"[5] As we proclaim the truth of Scripture, the Spirit of God uses it to pierce hearts among the unredeemed, convicting them of the truth and converting them from children of wrath into children of God (Heb. 4:12; 1 John 5:6).

THE HOLY SPIRIT REGENERATES SINFUL HEARTS

The effectual call of the elect begins with the Spirit's convicting work, as He awakens their consciences to the reality of sin, righteousness, and judgment. But He does not stop there. The unbelieving heart must be made alive—transformed, cleansed, and renewed (Eph. 2:4). And it is the Holy Spirit who regenerates sinners, such that those who were formerly miserable wretches are reborn as new creations in Christ (2 Cor. 5:17).

As Paul explained in Titus 3:4–7: "But when the kindness and the love of God our Savior toward man appeared, not by works of righteousness which we have done, but according to His mercy He saved us, through the washing of regeneration and renewing of the Holy Spirit, whom He poured out on us abundantly through Jesus Christ our Savior, that having been justified by His grace we should become heirs according to the hope of eternal life."

In John 3, the Lord Jesus explained this aspect of the Spirit's ministry by telling Nicodemus that, in order to be saved, the sinner must be born again. Bewildered by the implications of that truth, Nicodemus asked, "How can a man be born when he is old? Can he enter a second time into his mother's womb and be born?" (v. 4). Jesus responded with these words: "Most assuredly, I say to you, unless one is born of water and the Spirit, he cannot enter the kingdom of God. That which is born of the flesh is flesh, and that which is born of the Spirit is spirit. Do not marvel that I said to you, 'You must be born again.' The wind blows where it wishes, and you hear the sound of it, but cannot tell where it comes from and where it goes. So is everyone who is born of the Spirit" (vv. 5–8).

As the Lord's words make clear, the work of regeneration is the Spirit's sovereign prerogative. In the physical realm, babies don't conceive themselves. Likewise in the spiritual realm, sinners don't initiate or accomplish their own rebirth—regeneration is entirely the Spirit's work.

The phrase "born again" can also be translated "born from above," and both renderings express the truth of Jesus' point. In order to be saved, sinners must experience a completely new beginning of heavenly origination, in which they are radically transformed by the Spirit of God. After all, it is God "who according to His great mercy has caused us to be born again to a living hope through the resurrection of Jesus Christ from the dead" (1 Peter 1:3 NASB).

As Jesus explained to Nicodemus, the kingdom of salvation cannot be earned through human effort or self-righteousness. Only those who are born from above can be saved. Even someone as highly respected and externally religious as Nicodemus—one of the most well-known Bible scholars in Israel—could not contribute anything to his salvation. From God's perspective, the sinner's best efforts are like filthy rags (Isa. 64:6).

All the sinner can do is cry out to God for mercy, like the tax collector of Luke 18:13–14. He cannot save himself, so he must rest completely in the grace and compassion of the Savior. The promise of Scripture is that all who come to Christ in genuine faith—turning from sin and turning to Him—will be saved (Rom. 10:9–10). As the Lord Himself promised in John 6:37, "All that the Father gives Me will come to Me, and the one who comes to Me I will by no means cast out."

The Spirit's work of regeneration gives the sinner a new heart (Ezek. 36:26–27), one in which he is capable of genuine love for God and heartfelt obedience to Christ (cf. John 14:15). The fruit of that transformation will be evidenced in a changed life, manifest in fruits of repentance (Matt. 3:8) and the fruit of the Spirit: "love, joy, peace, longsuffering, kindness, goodness, faithfulness, gentleness, self-control" (Gal. 5:22–23). To accomplish this miraculous work, the Spirit uses His Word. Thus, James 1:17–18 says of God, "Of His own will He brought us forth by the word of truth, that we might be a kind of firstfruits of His creatures." At the moment of salvation, God used His Word to convict our hearts and bring us to life, such that we are now new creatures in Christ.

Regeneration is a transformation of a person's nature, as the believer is given new life, cleansed, and permanently set apart from sin (cf. 2 Thess. 2:13). Those who formerly operated in the flesh now operate in the Spirit (Rom. 8:5–11). Though they were dead, they have been made alive, indwelt by the very Spirit who raised Christ Jesus from the dead (v. 10; cf. 6:11). The Spirit of life has come upon them, empowering them to resist temptation and live in righteousness. This is what it means to be "born of the Spirit" (John 3:8).

THE HOLY SPIRIT BRINGS SINNERS TO REPENTANCE

There can be no repentance or faith until the heart has been re-created. But in the moment of regeneration, the Holy Spirit imparts the gift of repentant faith to sinners—bringing them to saving faith in Christ and enabling them to turn away from sin. The result is a dramatic conversion.

A vivid illustration of this is found in Acts 11:15–18, where Peter reported the conversion of Cornelius to the other apostles in Jerusalem:

> "As I began to speak, the Holy Spirit fell upon them, as upon us at the beginning. Then I remembered the word of the Lord, how He said, 'John indeed baptized with water, but you shall be baptized with the Holy Spirit.' If therefore God gave them the same gift as He gave us when we believed

on the Lord Jesus Christ, who was I that I could withstand God?" When they heard these things they became silent; and they glorified God, saying, "Then God has also granted to the Gentiles repentance to life."

As Peter and the others realized, the undeniable proof Cornelius and his household had truly repented was that they had received the Holy Spirit. They had been convicted of their sin; their hearts were regenerated; their eyes were opened to the truth of Peter's preaching; and they were given the gift of repentant faith (cf. Eph. 2:8; 2 Tim. 2:25)—all of which was the Holy Spirit's work.

Romans 8 stands as one of the richest biblical revelations on the ministry of the Holy Spirit in the life of the believer. This powerful chapter begins with profound words of salvation truth: "There is therefore now no condemnation to those who are in Christ Jesus, who do not walk according to the flesh, but according to the Spirit. For the law of the Spirit of life in Christ Jesus has made me free from the law of sin and death." Most believers have committed those verses to memory; but how many have recognized the Holy Spirit's role in the divine rescue operation? It is the Spirit of life who liberates the redeemed from the principle of sin and death, transforming those who were slaves of sin into lovers of righteousness.

In Romans 8:3–4, Paul explains that the Holy Spirit not only frees believers from the power of sin but also enables them to live in a way that pleases God. As a result, they are able to exhibit fruits of repentance (Matt. 3:8) and the fruit of the Spirit (Gal. 5:21–22). We will discuss the Holy Spirit's role in our sanctification in the next chapter. But it is important to emphasize, in the context of salvation, that the Holy Spirit converts sinners by convicting their hearts—giving them life, which enables them to repent and believe the gospel.

THE HOLY SPIRIT ENABLES FELLOWSHIP WITH GOD

In John 17:3, the Lord Jesus defines eternal life with these words: "This is eternal life, that they may know You, the only true God, and Jesus Christ whom You have sent." Fellowship with God through Christ is the heart of salvation; and it is the Holy Spirit who enables believers to enjoy that intimate communion.

In Colossians 1:13–14, Paul explains that God the Father "has delivered us from the power of darkness and conveyed us into the kingdom of the Son of His love, in whom we have redemption through His blood, the forgiveness of sins." We are given further insight into the nature of that transfer in Romans 8:14–17, where Paul uses the metaphor of a family rather than a kingdom. He wrote, "For as many as are led by the Spirit of God, these are sons of God. For you did not receive the spirit of bondage again to fear, but you received the Spirit of adoption by whom we cry out, 'Abba, Father.' The Spirit Himself bears witness with our spirit that we are children of God, and if children, then heirs—heirs of God and joint heirs with Christ, if indeed we suffer with Him, that we may also be glorified together."

Thus, we are not only citizens of a new kingdom (Phil. 3:20) but members of a new family! Through the Spirit of adoption, we have received the immense privilege of becoming part of the family of God. We can even address the omnipotent Creator of the universe with a term of tender familial endearment, "Abba" or "Papa." The Spirit frees us from the fear and dread that a sinner would naturally have when approaching holy God. Like little children, we can eagerly run into the presence of the Almighty and speak to our Father intimately.

The Spirit produces an attitude of profound love for God in the hearts of those who have been born again. They feel drawn to God, not fearful of Him. They long to commune with Him—to meditate on His Word and to fellowship with Him in prayer. They cast their cares freely on Him, and openly confess their sins without trepidation, knowing that all has been covered by His grace through the sacrifice of Christ. Thus, the Spirit makes it possible for believers to enjoy fellowship with God, no longer fearful of His judgment or wrath (1 John 4:18). As a result, Christians can sing hymns about God's holiness and glory without cowering in terror—knowing they have been securely adopted into the family of their heavenly Father.

The Holy Spirit also enables believers to enjoy fellowship with all other believers. Every child of God is immediately baptized by the Spirit into the body of Christ at the moment of salvation (1 Cor. 12:13). And it is in that church body that the Spirit sovereignly gifts every believer with all the enabling necessary to minister to others (v. 7). While the extraordinary gifts (such as prophecy, languages, and healing) were limited to the apostolic age of church history, the Spirit still bestows His people with teaching and serving gifts for the building up of the church (cf. Rom. 12:3–8; 1 Cor. 12–14). The rich interpersonal fellowship believers enjoy in the church is only possible because of the profound fellowship they share in the Lord Jesus Christ. The Holy Spirit enables both—allowing those who enjoy communion with God to enjoy "the unity of the Spirit" with one another (Eph. 4:3).

THE HOLY SPIRIT INDWELLS THE BELIEVER

At salvation, the Holy Spirit not only regenerates the sinner and imparts saving faith, but He permanently resides in the life of that new believer. The apostle Paul explained it this way in Romans 8:9: "But you are not in the flesh but in the Spirit, *if indeed the Spirit of God dwells in you.* Now if anyone does not have the Spirit of Christ, he is not His." In a marvelous and incomprehensible way, the Spirit of God makes His home in the life of every person who trusts in Jesus Christ.

Life in Jesus Christ is different because the Spirit of God is now within. He is there to empower, equip for ministry, and minister through the gifts He has given us. The Holy Spirit is our Comforter and Helper. He protects, empowers, and encourages us. In fact, the decisive proof of true salvation is the indwelling presence of the Spirit of God—the fruit of that residence being seen in the fact that believers do not walk according to the flesh, but according to the Spirit (cf. Gal. 5:19–22).

In 1 Corinthians 3:16, Paul asked the believers in Corinth, "Do you not know that you are the temple of God and that the Spirit of God dwells in you?" A few chapters later, while admonishing them to avoid sexual immorality, he again reminded them, "Do you not know that your body is the temple of the Holy Spirit who is in you, whom you have from God, and you are not your own? For you were bought at a price; therefore glorify God in your body and in your spirit, which are God's" (1 Cor. 6:19–20). The reality of the Spirit's indwelling presence had life-changing implications for the way in which they lived (cf. 1 Cor. 12:13).

It is important to emphasize that there is no such thing as a genuine believer who does not possess the Holy Spirit. It is a terrible error—one tragically promoted by many within Pentecostalism—to assert that a person could somehow be saved and yet not receive the Holy Spirit. Apart from the Spirit's work, no one could be anything other than a wretched sinner. To reiterate Paul's statement from Romans 8:9, "If anyone does not have the Spirit of Christ, he is not His." Put simply, those who do not possess the Holy Spirit do not belong to Christ. Genuine believers—people in whom the Holy Spirit has taken up residence—think, talk, and act differently. They are no longer characterized by a love for the world; instead, they love the things of God. That transformation is evidence of the Spirit's power at work in the lives of those whom He indwells.

THE HOLY SPIRIT SEALS SALVATION FOREVER

The Bible is clear that sinners who are redeemed can never lose their salvation. The unbreakable chain of Romans 8:30 indicates that all whom God justifies He will glorify. As the Lord Jesus Himself said, "My sheep hear My voice, and I know them, and they follow Me. And I give them eternal life, and they shall never perish; neither shall anyone snatch them out of My hand. My Father, who has given them to Me, is greater than all; and no one is able to snatch them out of My Father's hand" (John 10:27–29).

The apostle Paul echoed that great reality at the end of Romans 8, where he wrote, "For I am persuaded that neither death nor life, nor angels nor principalities nor powers, nor things present nor things to come, nor height nor depth, nor any other created thing, shall be able to separate us from the love of God which is in Christ Jesus our Lord" (vv. 38–39). No person or force can ever sever the bond of fellowship between God and those who belong to Him.

The Holy Spirit Himself personally guarantees that fact. As Paul told the Ephesians, "In Him you also trusted, after you heard the word of truth, the gospel of your salvation; in whom also, having believed, you were sealed with the Holy Spirit of promise, who is the guarantee of our inheritance until the redemption of the purchased possession, to the praise of His glory" (Eph. 1:13–14). Believers are sealed by the Holy Spirit until the day of redemption. He secures them unto eternal glory.

The sealing to which Paul alludes involved an official mark of identification placed on a letter, contract, or other official document. The seal was usually made by placing hot wax on the document and then impressing it with a signet ring. As a result, the seal officially represented the authority of the person to whom the signet belonged.

A Roman seal conveyed authenticity, security, ownership, and authority. And the Spirit of God represents those same realities in the lives of His children. Those who have received the Holy Spirit can rest assured that they are truly saved (authenticity) and that their salvation can never be lost or stolen from them (security). Moreover, the Spirit's presence in their lives demonstrates that God is their Lord and Master (ownership). As they are led by the Spirit, they will manifest a life of submissive obedience to Christ (authority). All this is part of the Spirit's sealing work.

Not only does the Spirit testify that believers are God's children (Rom. 8:16), but He guarantees that they will never be removed from the family. Moreover, He ensures their future resurrection unto life. As Romans 8:11 explains, "If the Spirit of Him who raised Jesus from the dead dwells in you, He who raised Christ from the dead will also give life to your mortal bodies through His Spirit who dwells in you."

Sadly, many charismatic groups completely miss this true ministry of the Holy Spirit. Rather than resting in the security of the Spirit, they teach that believers can lose their salvation. As a result, their people live with the constant fear of an uncertain future and deny honor to the Holy Spirit who keeps believers secure.

What freedom and joy there is in discovering the Spirit's true ministry of sealing those who belong to Him! After all, the reality of life in a fallen world is that we will all die one day. But the day of our death will be better than the day of our birth, because the first time we were born into sin. But when we die, we will awaken into the glorious presence of Christ (cf. 2 Cor. 5:8). And in the day of resurrection, the Holy Spirit will raise believers from the dead, giving them new, glorified bodies that will dwell forever on the New Earth (2 Peter 3:13; Rev. 21:1, 22–27).

REJOICING IN THE SPIRIT'S SAVING WORK

The Holy Spirit is involved in every aspect of salvation—from justification (1 Cor. 6:11) to sanctification (Gal. 5:18–23) to glorification (Rom. 8:11). Yet, in specific and unique ways, the Bible highlights His work of convicting, regenerating, converting, adopting, indwelling, and securing.[6]

As those who have been redeemed, our response to the miracle of salvation should be one of awestruck worship—praising each member of the Godhead for His part in the glorious outworking of redemption. It is right to worship the Father for His electing love, predestining us to salvation from before the foundation of the world. It is right to worship the Son for His perfect sacrifice, providing the means through which fallen men and women can be reconciled to God. And it is equally demanded that we worship the Holy Spirit for His active role in the salvation of sinners, imparting life to dead hearts and sight to spiritually blind eyes.

As the Puritan Thomas Goodwin so eloquently stated:

A man's communion and converse is . . . sometimes with the Father, then with the Son, and then with the Holy Ghost; sometimes his heart is drawn out to consider the Father's love in choosing, and then the love of Christ in redeeming, and so the love of the Holy Ghost, that searcheth the deep things of God, and revealeth them to us, and taketh all the pains with us; and so a man goes from one witness to another distinctly. [Assurance] is not a knowledge by way of argument or deduction, whereby we infer that if one loveth me then the other loveth me, but it is intuitively, as I may so express it, and we should never be satisfied till all three persons lie level in us, and all make their abode with us, and we sit as it were in the midst of them, while they all manifest their love unto us.[7]

Though he lived in the seventeenth century, Goodwin's perspective is still critical for the church today. Believers need to understand the work of each member of the Trinity in order to worship God most fully. To borrow Goodwin's words, "We should never be satisfied till all three persons lie level in us." What a beautiful way to express that lofty truth—that we ought to "sit as it were in the midst of them" and meditate with wonder on the unfathomable love shown to us by the Father, the Son, and the Holy Spirit. Such glorious reflections are the substance of true worship.

Needless to say, such reflections far surpass any sort of irrational ecstasy or mindless charismatic experience. Both may invoke an emotional response, but only one is grounded in truth. Authentic worship requires both spirit and truth (John 4:23). Anything short of that is a blasphemous counterfeit.

TEN

THE SPIRIT AND SANCTIFICATION

W hat does it mean to be filled with the Spirit? And what are the manifest realities that mark the Spirit-filled Christian life? In this chapter we will seek to answer those questions from the Word of God. But first, let's examine the charismatic approach.

As those who claim to have the primary, if not exclusive, right to the title "Spirit-filled Christians," charismatics invariably define being filled with the Spirit in terms of ecstatic experiences. A common explanation, especially from classic Pentecostals, would center on modern tongues-speaking. In the words of one Pentecostal author, "When we are filled with the Spirit, the outward manifestation of this gift is speaking in tongues."[1] Yet, as we saw in chapter 7, the contemporary "gift" of tongues is a nonsensical counterfeit; it has nothing to do with the ancient gift of languages described in the New Testament. Charismatics err when they associate being Spirit-filled with speaking gibberish.

Of course, tongues-speaking is not the only supposed sign of Spirit filling within the charismatic paradigm, nor is it the most dramatic. Even more stunning is "resting in the Spirit" or "falling under the Spirit's power," a phenomenon more commonly referred to as "being slain in the Spirit." Those who are *slain* exhibit trancelike behavior, usually falling backward to the floor like a dead person. At other times, those "overcome by the Spirit" respond with uncontrollable laughter, mongrel barking, erratic twitching, and bizarre symptoms of intoxication.[2] No behavior is regarded as too outlandish to preclude its being credited to the Holy Spirit's "slaying" power.

Convinced it is the result of being Spirit-filled, charismatics enthusiastically endorse the practice of being "slain in the Spirit." Charismatic literature abounds with examples of the phenomenon, all presented in a positive light. Here is a typical example:

> We asked the Holy Spirit to come and fill him up again. Suddenly, it happened. James fell back down to the floor, rolling and crying and clasping his hands over his face. The Holy Spirit had come in a mighty deluge of power, rushing into the wounded places, and filling him with His glory. James laughed. He cried. . . . His face flushed with glory and his body shook under the power of God. And when he finally got off the floor, like on the day of Pentecost, he was drunk with the Holy Spirit.[3]

Other accounts are equally colorful. A Pentecostal layman enthusiastically reports that—under the Spirit's supposed influence—he ended up flat on his back, uttering ecstatic speech and sliding himself under the pews of the church until he finally reached the foyer.[4] A Catholic charismatic faith healer claims that, at one of his meetings, a blind woman was slain in the Spirit along with her German shepherd seeing-eye dog![5] A charismatic prophetess remembers lying on the floor of a church meeting, embarrassed by the fact that she was laughing uncontrollably, after she was "blasted" by a wave of Holy Spirit power.[6] And a Third Wave pastor relates a worship service where more than a hundred people were unexpectedly knocked over. He wrote, "When people arrived for the second service, they couldn't believe their eyes. Bodies, overcome by God, were strewn about on the floor. Some people were laughing; some were shaking."[7]

Benny Hinn, who incorporates "slaying" into his healing meetings, offers similar tales. Reflecting on a three-day miracle crusade in South America, Hinn wrote, "In the middle of my message I felt the power of the Holy Spirit move over the service. I felt His presence, stopped preaching, and told the people, 'He's here!' Ministers on the platform and people in the audience felt the same thing—it was like a gust of wind that entered and swirled inside that place. People stood to their feet in a spontaneous outburst of praise. But they didn't stand for long. All over, people began to collapse and fall to the floor under the power of the Holy Ghost."[8] At another meeting, Hinn reports, "Hundreds of people were packed into the center that evening. After a short message, the Spirit led me to call people forward. The first to respond were six big, strapping Dutchmen; they towered over me. I prayed and, *boom*, down they went—all of them!"[9]

Falling backward to the floor, laughing uncontrollably, babbling non-sense, and acting drunk—is that what it looks like to be a Spirit-filled Christian? What about reports of people who have stood frozen like statues for days, or those who have reportedly levitated in church, under the Spirit's supposed power?[10] Though charismatics associate that kind of hypnotic behavior with the Holy Spirit, the truth is it has nothing to do with Him. Scripture is full of warnings about fraudulent signs and wonders.

Jesus said, "False christs and false prophets will rise and show great signs and wonders to deceive, if possible, even the elect. See, I have told you before-hand" (Matt. 24:24; cf. 7:22; Mark 13:22; 2 Thess. 2:7–9; Rev. 13:13–14). Jesus obviously expected us to take those warnings seriously and guard against the kind of gullibility Benny Hinn and other charismatic miracle workers deliberately foster.

As we have seen, modern charismatic versions of prophecy, tongues, and healing are all counterfeit forms of true biblical gifts. But being "slain in the Spirit" is a modern charismatic invention. The practice is mentioned nowhere in the Bible; it is completely without scriptural warrant. The mod-ern phenomenon has become such a common and popular spectacle that the average charismatic today takes it for granted, assuming it must have some kind of clear biblical or historical pedigree. But not only is this phenomenon completely absent from the biblical record of the early church; it has nothing whatsoever to do with the Holy Spirit.

Charismatics sometimes attempt to defend the practice by pointing to places in Scripture where people fell down before the Lord (like the mob who came to arrest Jesus in John 18, or Paul on the road to Damascus in Acts 9:4, or John when he encountered the risen Christ in Revelation 1:17). But those examples have nothing to do with the modern phenomenon of being "slain in the Spirit."[11] Even the pro-charismatic *Dictionary of Pentecostal and Charismatic Movements* acknowledges that fact: "An entire battalion of Scripture proof texts is enlisted to support the legitimacy of the phenomenon, although Scripture plainly offers no support for the phenomenon as something to be expected in the normal Christian life."[12]

An examination of the supposed proof-texts—passages in which a person or group of people fell down in the presence of God's glory—evidences at least three significant differences between the biblical incidents and the modern phenomenon. First, when people in the Bible fell down in the presence of God's glory, there were no middlemen involved as there are in contemporary charismatic services. It was God (Gen. 17:3; 1 Kings 8:10–11), the Lord Jesus Christ (Matt. 17:6; Acts 26:14), or occasionally an angel (Dan. 8:17; 10:8–11) who directly interacted with men, overwhelming them with heavenly glory such that they fell to the ground.[13]

Second, such encounters occurred very rarely. In the New Testament, apart from a few of the apostles (who fell forward on their faces in reverent worship—cf. Matt. 17:6; Rev. 1:17), only unbelievers were knocked over after being confronted by the glory of Christ (John 18:1–11; cf. Acts 9:4). Such knockouts are never presented in Scripture as the normal experience of believers. Nor do those accounts provide a parallel to being "slain" as modern charismatics display.

Third, and perhaps most important, the New Testament presents Spirit-empowered behavior as being that which exhibits self-control (Gal. 5:22–23; 1 Cor. 14:32), maintains sober-minded alertness (1 Peter 1:13; 5:8), and promotes orderliness in the church (1 Cor. 14:40). Obviously, having bodies lying all over the floor in varying stages of catalepsy does not yield any of those God-honoring qualities, but rather the polar opposite.

The modern phenomenon is embraced by a movement that defines spirituality in terms of behaviors that bypass or transcend rationality—such that seizures, hypnosis, and hysteria are all promoted as the Spirit's true work. But this is not God's doing. No biblical precedent exists for the modern notion of being "slain in the Spirit"—unless, of course, an exception is allowed for Ananias and Sapphira, who were literally struck dead by Him for their premeditated deception (Acts 5:5, 10).

In reality, the stupor that characterizes the modern charismatic phenomenon mirrors pagan practices more than anything Christian.[14] Parallels to the practice can easily be found in false religions and cult groups. As Hank Hanegraaff explains:

> The "slain in the spirit" phenomenon has more in common with occultism than with a biblical worldview. As popular "slain in the spirit" practitioner Francis MacNutt candidly confesses in his book *Overcome by the Spirit*, the phenomenon is externally similar to "manifestations of voodoo and other magic rites" and is "found today among different sects in the Orient as well as among primitive tribes of Africa and Latin America."[15]

Speaking of demon possession in tribal Africa, missiologist Richard J. Gehman reports, "When someone is possessed, he or she displays unusual powers, the personality changes, and the person comes under the total control of the spirit or spirits. These methods also remind us of the same phenomena that occur among charismatic Christians who are 'slain in the Spirit.' Through hypnotic powers they fall into a trance and experience inexpressible feelings of joy."[16]

Parallels also exist in cult groups like Mormonism. None other than Mormon founder Joseph Smith personally experienced the phenomenon. As authors Rob and Kathy Datsko explain: "Being 'slain in the Spirit' is the experience Joseph Smith had and described in JS-H [Joseph Smith History] 1:20: 'When I came to myself again, I found myself lying on my back, looking up into heaven. When the light had departed, I had no strength; but soon recovering in some degree, I went home.'"[17] The authors go on to explain, "In the Book of Mormon, a multitude of people were slain in the Spirit. . . . The experience of being slain in the Spirit is therefore not exclusive to [charismatic Christianity], but is also recorded in both LDS scripture and history."[18] Non-Christian parallels like these reveal the serious spiritual danger inherent in charismatic versions of this experience.

All this raises the pertinent question: If the Holy Spirit is not the force behind modern "slayings," then what is? In many cases, the phenomenon is likely the result of psychological manipulation—produced by emotional expectations, peer pressure, group dynamics, and manipulative techniques used by faith healers and charismatic leaders. But there may also be a more sinister explanation for the phenomenon. As Christian apologist Ron Rhodes rightly warns: "The powers of darkness may also be involved in this experience (2 Thessalonians 2:9). Some people affiliated with Eastern religions claim to be able to make people unconscious merely by touching them."[19]

Even among some thinking charismatics, the practice of being "slain in the Spirit" has received criticism. Speaking of its use by faith healers, Michael Brown raises serious concerns: "Something is wrong. *Most of the people are sick when they fall . . . and sick when they get up.* Although the suffering people collapse and shake, the life of God doesn't seem to take. The anointing—or at least what we call the anointing—was strong enough to knock them over, but not strong enough to make them recover. They got their thrill, but they weren't made well. Is *this* the power of God?"[20] The answer to his rhetorical question is obvious.

The critique by *Charisma* magazine editor J. Lee Grady is even more devastating. In an extended section, he wrote:

This phenomenon can be and often is faked. And we should deplore the counterfeit. . . . We must never use the anointing to manipulate a crowd. We must never fake God's power in order to make others feel we are anointed. If we do that, we take something holy and make it common and trivial. And as a result, holy fire becomes something else—a "strange fire" that does not have the power to sanctify.

This very kind of strange fire is spreading today. In some charismatic churches, people take the stage and throw imaginary "fireballs of anointing" at each other, and then fall down, pretending to be slain by the globs of divine power. One young traveling preacher encourages people to inject themselves with pretend needles when they come to the altar, so they can "get high on Jesus." He actually compares being filled with the Spirit to taking cocaine; he also puts a plastic figurine from a manger scene in his mouth and encourages people to "smoke baby Jesus" so they can experience "Jehovah-juana," a reference to marijuana. This is more serious than trivializing the things of God. This is taking the Lord's name in vain.

I have been in other meetings where women were lying on the floor with their legs spread apart. They were making loud moaning noises and claiming that they were praying and "birthing in the Spirit," as if God would lead them to do something so obscene in a public place.

God help us! We have turned the holy fire of God into a circus sideshow—and naive Christians are buying this without realizing that such shenanigans are actually blasphemous.[21]

Since these kinds of bizarre antics make a mockery of the true power and filling of the Holy Spirit, what does it *really* mean to be filled with the Spirit? In the following pages, we will consider the answer to that question, as we look at the Spirit's work in sanctifying His saints by conforming them to the image of the Savior.

BEING FILLED WITH THE SPIRIT

The definitive New Testament passage on being filled with the Spirit is Ephesians 5:18, where Paul wrote: "Do not be drunk with wine, in which is dissipation; but be filled with the Spirit." In contrast to drunkenness, which manifests itself in irrational and out-of-control behavior, those who are Spirit-filled consciously submit themselves to His holy influence.

Significantly, the command to "be filled" is in the present tense, indicating this is to be an ongoing experience in the life of every Christian. As we have already seen, all believers are baptized (1 Cor. 12:13; Gal. 3:27), indwelt (Rom. 8:9), and sealed (Eph. 1:13) by the Holy Spirit at the moment of salvation.[22]

Those realities occur only once. But if believers are to grow in Christlikeness, they must be continually filled with the Spirit—allowing His power to permeate their lives so that all they think, say, and do reflects His divine presence.

The book of Acts provides several illustrations of the fact that being Spirit-filled is a repeated experience.[23] Though he was initially filled on the day of Pentecost, Peter was again filled with the Spirit in Acts 4:8 as he preached courageously before the Sanhedrin. Many of the same people who were filled with the Spirit in Acts 2 were filled again in Acts 4:31, at which point "they spoke the word of God with boldness." In Acts 6:5, Stephen is described as a man "full of faith and the Holy Spirit." Acts 7:55 reiterates the fact that he was "full of the Holy Spirit" as he delivered his passionate defense before the angry religious leaders.

The apostle Paul was filled with the Spirit in Acts 9:17 shortly after his conversion, and again in Acts 13:9, when he boldly confronted the false prophet Elymas. As they were filled with the Holy Spirit, the apostles and their colleagues were empowered to build up fellow believers in the church (cf. Acts 11:22–24) and to fearlessly proclaim the gospel, even in the face of severe persecution from the world (cf. Acts 13:52).

When we consider the New Testament epistles, where believers are given prescriptive instruction for church life, we find that being filled with the Spirit is demonstrated not through ecstatic experiences but through the manifestation of spiritual fruit. In other words, Spirit-filled Christians exhibit the fruit of the Spirit, which Paul identifies as "love, joy, peace, longsuffering, kindness, goodness, faithfulness, gentleness, self-control" (Gal. 5:22–23). They are "led by the Spirit" (Rom. 8:14), meaning their behavior is directed not by their fleshly desires, but by the sanctifying power of the Holy Spirit. As Paul explained in Romans 8:5–9:

For those who live according to the flesh set their minds on the things of the flesh, but those who live according to the Spirit, the things of the Spirit. For to be carnally minded is death, but to be spiritually minded is life and peace. Because the carnal mind is enmity against God; for it is not subject to the law of God, nor indeed can be. So then, those who are in the flesh cannot please God. But you are not in the flesh but in the Spirit, if indeed the Spirit of God dwells in you. Now if anyone does not have the Spirit of Christ, he is not His.

The apostle's point is that those who are Spirit-filled seek to please God by pursuing practical holiness (cf. 2 Cor. 3:18; 2 Peter 3:18).

The tragic irony is that the movement labeling itself as "Spirit-filled" is notorious for sexual immorality, financial impropriety, and ostentatious worldliness in the lives of its most visible leaders. As we saw in chapter 4, the Charismatic Movement is regularly stained by scandal. No matter how many times people are "slain in the Spirit" or "speak in tongues," it is the fruit of their lives that reveals the true nature of their hearts. Those whose behavior is characterized by the works of the flesh (Gal. 5:19–21) are not filled with the Spirit—no matter how many ecstatic episodes they claim to have experienced.

After commanding believers to be filled with the Spirit in Ephesians 5:18, Paul continues in the subsequent verses by giving specific examples of what that looks like. Those who are Spirit-filled are characterized by joyful singing in worship (5:19), hearts full of thanksgiving (5:20), and selflessness toward others (5:21). If they are married, their marriage honors God (5:22–33); if they have children, their parenting patiently unfolds the gospel (6:1–4); if they work for an earthly master, they work hard for the Lord's honor (6:5–8); and if they have people working for them, they treat their subordinates with benevolence and fairness (6:9). *That* is what it looks like to be a Spirit-filled Christian. His influence in our lives makes us rightly related to God and to others.

In Colossians 3:16–4:1, a parallel passage to Ephesians 5:18–6:9, Paul explains that if believers "let the word of Christ dwell in [them] richly," they will likewise respond by singing psalms, hymns, and spiritual songs. They will do everything in the name of the Lord Jesus, "giving thanks to God the Father through Him." Wives will be submissive to their husbands; and husbands, in turn, will love their wives. Children will obey their parents, and parents will not exasperate their children. Servants will work diligently for their masters, and masters will respond by treating their workers with fairness.

A comparison of Colossians 3:16 with Ephesians 5:18 demonstrates the inseparable relationship between the two passages—since the fruit produced in each case is the same. Thus, we can see that obeying the command to be filled with the Spirit does not involve emotional hype or mystical encounters. It comes from reading, meditating on, and submitting to the Word of Christ, allowing the Scriptures to permeate our hearts and minds. Said another way, we are filled with the Holy Spirit when we are filled with the Word, which He inspired and empowers. As we align our thinking with biblical teaching, applying its truth to our daily lives, we come increasingly under the Spirit's control.

To be filled with the Spirit, then, is to yield our hearts to the authority of Christ, allowing His Word to dominate our attitudes and actions. His thoughts become the object of our mediation, His standards become our highest pursuit, and His will becomes our greatest desire. As we submit to God's truth, the Spirit leads us to live in a way that honors the Lord.

Moreover, as the Holy Spirit sanctifies individual saints through the power of the Word, He energizes them to show love to one another within the corporate body of Christ (1 Peter 1:22–23). In fact, it is in the context of edifying fellow believers within the church that the New Testament epistles discuss the gifts of the Spirit (cf. 1 Peter 4:10–11). Significantly, spiritual gifts are not the sign of being Spirit-filled. Sanctification is. As believers are sanctified—coming under the Spirit's control—they are equipped to use their spiritual gifts effectively for the purpose of serving others.

Whenever the New Testament epistles discuss spiritual gifts, the emphasis is on showing love to one another—never on self-gratification or self-promotion (Rom. 12; 1 Cor. 13). As Paul expressly told the Corinthians, "The manifestation of the Spirit is given to each one *for the profit of all*" (1 Cor. 12:7). Though the spectacular sign gifts did not continue past the foundational age of the church (a point we established in chapters 5–8), believers today are still gifted by the Holy Spirit for the purpose of building up the body of Christ—through gifts of teaching, leadership, administration, and so on. As they minister to others, using their giftedness to edify the church through the power of the Spirit, believers become a sanctifying influence in the lives of their fellow Christians (Eph. 4:11–13; Heb. 10:24–25).

WALKING IN THE SPIRIT

The New Testament describes the Spirit-filled life using the analogy of walking in the Spirit. Paul stated it this way in Galatians 5:25: "If we live in the Spirit, let us also walk in the Spirit." Just as walking requires taking one step at a time, being filled with the Spirit involves living under the Spirit's control in a thought-by-thought, decision-by-decision manner. Those who are truly Spirit-filled yield every step to Him.

A survey of the New Testament reveals that, as believers, we are commanded to walk in newness of life, purity, contentment, faith, good works, a manner worthy of the gospel, love, light, wisdom, a Christlike manner, and truth.[24] But for those qualities to characterize the way we walk, we must first walk in the Spirit. He is the one who produces the fruit of righteousness in and through us.

As Paul explained, "Walk in the Spirit, and you shall not fulfill the lust of the flesh. For the flesh lusts against the Spirit, and the Spirit against the flesh; and these are contrary to one another, so that you do not do the things that you wish" (Gal. 5:16–17). The concept of *walking* refers to a person's regular manner of life. Those whose lives are characterized by *walking in the flesh* demonstrate they are yet unsaved. By contrast, those who *walk in the Spirit* give evidence of the fact they belong to Christ.

In Romans 8:2–4, the apostle Paul elaborated on that same theme: "For the law of the Spirit of life in Christ Jesus has made me free from the law of sin and death. For what the law could not do in that it was weak through the flesh, God did by sending His own Son in the likeness of sinful flesh, on account of sin: He condemned sin in the flesh, that the righteous requirement of the law might be fulfilled in us who do not walk according to the flesh but according to the Spirit."

Because the power of sin has been broken for believers, they have the ability to fulfill God's law through the power of the Holy Spirit. As those who walk according to the Spirit, they are able to do those things that please God. The unredeemed, by contrast, are hostile toward God and dominated by fleshly pursuits (cf. vv. 5–9).

The Lord delights in the moral and spiritual excellence of those who belong to Him (cf. Titus 2:14). As Paul told the Ephesians, "For we are His workmanship, created in Christ Jesus for good works, which God prepared beforehand that we should walk in them" (Eph. 2:10). Peter reiterated that truth with these words: "As He who called you is holy, you also be holy in all your conduct, because it is written, 'Be holy, for I am holy'" (1 Peter 1:15–16; cf. Heb. 12:14). Having been regenerated by grace apart from works, believers eagerly desire to follow Christ (1 Thess. 1:6), and the Holy Spirit enables them to do just that. Thus, it is their profound joy, through the power of the Spirit, "to deny ungodliness and worldly desires and to live sensibly, righteously and godly in the present age" (Titus 2:12 NASB).

Of course, that does not mean Christians no longer struggle against sin and temptation. Though we have been made new creations in Christ (2 Cor. 5:17), all believers still battle against the sinful flesh—the as-yet-unredeemed part of our fallen humanness that tempts us to sin. The flesh is the enemy within, the remnant of the old man that wars against godly desires and righteous living (Rom. 7:23). To fall prey to the flesh is to grieve the Holy Spirit (Eph. 4:28–31).

Conversely, if believers are to gain victory over the lusts of their flesh, and grow in holiness, we must function in the Spirit's power. It is imperative that we "put on the whole armor of God" (Eph. 6:11), including "the sword of the Spirit, which is the word of God" (v. 17), in order to fend off the fiery attacks of the evil one and mortify the flesh. As Paul explained in Romans 8:13–14, "If by the Spirit you put to death the deeds of the body, you will live. For as many as are led by the Spirit of God, these are sons of God."

The believer's sole defense against sin's constant assault is the protection provided by the Holy Spirit, who arms His saints with the truth of Scripture. On the other hand, the believer's single power for spiritual growth is the Spirit's sanctifying work—as He grows and strengthens His people through the pure milk of the Word (1 Peter 2:1–3; cf. Eph. 3:16). Though the Christian life requires personal spiritual discipline (1 Tim. 4:7), it is vital to remember that we cannot sanctify ourselves through our own efforts (Gal. 3:3; Phil. 2:12–13). It was the Holy Spirit who set us apart from sin at the moment of salvation (2 Thess. 2:13). And as we submit to His influence each day, He empowers our victory over the flesh.

Thus, to walk in the Spirit through the indwelling influence of the Word is to fulfill the ultimate potential and capacity of our life on this earth as children of God.

BEING CONFORMED TO THE IMAGE OF CHRIST

If we want to know what a Spirit-filled life looks like, we need look no further than the Lord Jesus Christ. He stands alone as the foremost example of One who operated fully and perfectly under the Spirit's control.[25] Throughout Jesus' earthly ministry, the Spirit was His inseparable companion. In His incarnation, the Son of God voluntarily emptied Himself by laying aside the independent use of His divine attributes (Phil. 2:7–8). He took on human flesh and completely submitted Himself to the will of His Father and to the power of the Holy Spirit (cf. John 4:34). As He told the religious leaders in Matthew 12:28, "I cast out demons by the Spirit of God." But they denied the true source of His power, insisting that it was actually Satan who was working through Him. In response, the Lord warned them that such blasphemy came with eternal consequences: "Therefore I say to you, every sin and blasphemy will be forgiven men, but the blasphemy against the Spirit will not be forgiven men" (v. 31). The Holy Spirit so clearly empowered every aspect of Jesus' ministry that to deny Him as the source of Christ's power was to commit an unpardonable sin of hardhearted, unrepentant unbelief.

The Holy Spirit was active in the virgin birth, as the angel Gabriel explained to Mary: "The Holy Spirit will come upon you, and the power of the Highest will overshadow you; therefore, also, that Holy One who is to be born will be called the Son of God" (Luke 1:35). The Spirit was active at Jesus' temptation, leading Him into the wilderness (Mark 1:12) and equipping Him to use the sword of the Spirit to fend off the devil's attacks (Matt. 4:4, 7, 10). The Spirit was active at the launch of Jesus' public ministry (Luke 4:14), empowering Him to cast out demons and perform miracles of healing (Acts 10:38). At the end of

Jesus' ministry, the Holy Spirit was still at work, empowering the perfect Lamb of God to endure the cross (Heb. 9:14). Even after Christ's death, the Spirit was intimately involved in our Lord's resurrection (Rom. 8:11).

At every point, the life of our Lord was under the power of the Holy Spirit. Jesus Christ was perfectly filled with the Holy Spirit, always operating under the Spirit's full control. His life of absolute obedience and perfect compliance to the will of the Father is a testament to the fact that there was never a time when He was not walking in the Spirit. Thus, our Lord Jesus is the perfect prototype of what it looks like to live a Spirit-filled life—in full obedience and complete compliance to the will of God.[26]

Is it any wonder, then, that the Holy Spirit actively works in the hearts of His saints to conform them into the image of Jesus Christ? It is the Spirit's great delight to bear witness to the Son of God (John 15:26). He glorifies Christ by pointing people to Him (John 16:14), and by compelling them to joyfully submit to His lordship (1 Cor. 12:3). That is what interests the Holy Spirit— not knocking people over, flopping them on the floor, making them rattle off nonsense, and giving them an emotional buzz. The charismatic circus of confusion does not conform anyone to the image of Christ—who Himself perfectly reflected the image of His Father (Col. 1:15). Thus, it is a totally false paradigm for sanctification.

Paul expanded on this Christ-centered aspect of the Spirit's ministry in 2 Corinthians 3:18. There he wrote, "But we all, with unveiled face, beholding as in a mirror the glory of the Lord, are being transformed into the same image from glory to glory, just as by the Spirit of the Lord." As believers are exposed to the glory of Christ as revealed in His Word—reflecting on His perfect life of obedience and resting in His perfect sacrifice for sin—the Spirit increasingly transforms them into the image of their Savior.

Sanctification, then, is the work of the Spirit by which He shows us Christ, in His Word, and then progressively molds us into that same image. Thus, through the Spirit's power, as we gaze at the glory of the Savior, we become more and more like Him. The Holy Spirit not only introduces believers to the Lord Jesus Christ at the moment of their salvation, energizing their faith in the gospel, but also continues to disclose to them the glory of Christ by illuminating His Word in their hearts. In that way, He progressively grows them in Christlikeness over the course of their entire lives.

In Romans 8:28–29, in the midst of Paul's profound discourse on the Spirit's ministry, the apostle wrote, "And we know that all things work together for good to those who love God, to those who are the called according to His purpose. For whom He foreknew, He also predestined to be conformed to the image of His Son, that He might be the firstborn [or, preeminent One] among many brethren." Those familiar verses underscore the great purpose of our salvation—which is to conform us into the image of Jesus Christ so that He might be eternally glorified as the preeminent One among many who have been made like Him.

The previous verses in Romans 8 underscore the fact that the Holy Spirit liberates believers from the power of the law (vv. 2–3), indwells them (v. 9), sanctifies them (vv. 12–13), adopts them into the family of God (vv. 14–16), helps them with their weaknesses (v. 26), and intercedes on their behalf (v. 27). The purpose of all this is to conform us to the image of Jesus Christ. That conformity will only be fully realized in the life to come (Phil. 3:21; 1 John 3:2). But even on this side of heaven, the Spirit enables us to grow in Christlikeness, becoming more and more like the Lord whom we love (cf. Gal. 4:19). Thus, for those who wonder if they are truly being filled with the Holy Spirit, the proper question is not, "Have I had an ecstatic experience?" Rather, it is, "Am I becoming more and more like Jesus?"

In all of this, God's purpose is to make believers like His Son in order to create a great multitude of redeemed and glorified humanity over whom the Lord Jesus Christ will reign in eternal preeminence. Forever, the redeemed will glorify the Savior in whose likeness they have been made. Forever, they will join with the angels in heaven, exclaiming:

> "Worthy is the Lamb who was slain to receive power and riches and wisdom, and strength and honor and glory and blessing!" And every creature which is in heaven and on the earth and under the earth and such as are in the sea, and all that are in them, I heard saying: "Blessing and honor and glory and power be to Him who sits on the throne, and to the Lamb, forever and ever!" (Rev. 5:12–13)

THE SPIRIT'S SANCTIFYING WORK

As the New Testament makes clear, being a "Spirit-filled" Christian has nothing to do with uttering mindless gibberish, crashing to the carpet in a hypnotic trance, or any other mystical encounter of supposed ecstatic power. Rather, it has everything to do with submitting our hearts and minds to the Word of Christ, walking in the Spirit and not the flesh, and daily growing in love and affection for the Lord Jesus unto the service of His whole body, the church.

Truly, the Christian life in all of its fullness is a desired life lived in the power of the Holy Spirit. He is to be the dominating influence in our hearts and lives. He alone enables us to live victoriously over sin, to produce the fruit of the Spirit, and to be pleasing to our heavenly Father. It is the Holy Spirit who brings us into greater intimacy with God. He illuminates the Scripture, glorifies Christ in us and to us, guides us into God's will, strengthens us, and also ministers to us through other believers. The Spirit intercedes for us constantly and incessantly before the Father, always in accordance with the perfect will of God. And He does all this to conform us into the image of our Lord and Savior, guaranteeing we will one day be totally perfected when we see Christ face-to-face.

Rather than being hopelessly distracted by charismatic counterfeits, believers need to rediscover the real ministry of the Holy Spirit, which is to activate His power in us through His Word, so that we can truly conquer sin for the glory of Christ, the blessing of His church, and the benefit of the lost.

ELEVEN

THE SPIRIT AND THE SCRIPTURES

The Protestant Reformation is rightly regarded as the greatest revival in the last thousand years of church history—a movement so massive it radically altered the course of Western civilization. Names like Martin Luther, John Calvin, and John Knox are still well-known today, five centuries after they lived. Through their writings and sermons, these courageous Reformers—and others like them—left an enduring legacy for the generations of believers who have followed them.

But the true power behind the Reformation did not flow from any one man or group of men. To be sure, the Reformers took bold stands and offered themselves as sacrifices for the cause of the gospel; but even so, the sweeping triumph of sixteenth-century revival cannot ultimately be credited to either their incredible acts of valor or their brilliant works of scholarship. No, the Reformation can only be explained by something far more profound: a force infinitely more potent than anything mere mortals could produce on their own.

Like any true revival, the Reformation was the inevitable and explosive consequence of the Word of God crashing like a massive tidal wave against the thin barricades of man-made tradition and hypocritical religion. As the common people of Europe gained access to the Scriptures in their own language, the Spirit of God used that timeless truth to convict their hearts and convert their souls. The result was utterly transformative, not only for the lives of individual sinners, but for the entire continent on which they resided.

The principle of *sola Scriptura* (Scripture alone) was the Reformers' way of acknowledging that the unstoppable power behind the explosive advance of religious reform was the Spirit-empowered Word of God. Speaking of the Reformation, one historian observes:

> The story of such change is told through the lives of those who [participated in] it, *and at the center was the Bible.* A plaque in St. Peter's Cathedral in Geneva describes the reformer John Calvin simply as a "Servant of the Word of God." [Martin] Luther said, "All I have done is put forth, preach and write the Word of God, and apart from this I have done nothing. . . . It is the Word that has done great things. . . . I have done nothing; the Word has done and achieved everything."[1]

For the Reformers, *sola Scriptura* meant the Bible was the only divinely revealed word and therefore the believer's true authority for sound doctrine and righteous living. They understood the Word of God to be powerful, life altering, and wholly sufficient "for doctrine, for reproof, for correction, for instruction in righteousness, that the man of God may be complete, thoroughly equipped for every good work" (2 Tim. 3:16–17). Like the church fathers who had come before them, they rightly viewed God's Word as the authoritative foundation for their Christian faith.[2] They embraced the inerrancy, infallibility, and historical accuracy of Scripture without question, gladly submitting to its divine truth.

Though they were part of a major social upheaval, the Reformers understood the real battle was not over politics, money, or land. It was a fight for biblical truth. And as the truth of the gospel shone forth, empowered by the Holy Spirit, it ignited the flames of revival.

FROM REFORMATION TO RUIN

Like a torch blazing at midnight, the light of Reformation truth burned brightly against the pitch darkness of Roman Catholic corruption. But as the centuries passed, the fires of religious reform slowly began to cool in Europe, so much so that the birthplace of history's greatest revival eventually gave rise to the false gospel of theological liberalism. Two hundred twenty-two years after Martin Luther died, another influential German theologian was born named Friedrich Schleiermacher. But unlike Luther, Schleiermacher allowed doubt to overwhelm his soul, and as a result he rejected the gospel truth he had been taught by his Lutheran parents. Schleiermacher's crisis of faith plunged him into sinister depths of disbelief; and as he sank, he dragged others down with him—creating a riptide of unbelief that would soon challenge the foundations of biblical Christianity. Indeed, it would eventually engulf the whole world of theological education and drown denominations in lies about the Bible.

While a student at the University of Halle, Schleiermacher was exposed to the antibiblical attacks of Enlightenment thinkers—unbelieving skeptics who denied the historical accuracy of the Bible and secular philosophers who exalted human reason above divine revelation. Their assault proved too much to withstand for the impressionable young Schleiermacher. His doubt soon gave way to outright denial. His biographer recounts the tragic tale:

In a letter to his father, Schleiermacher drops the mild hint that his teachers fail to deal with those widespread doubts that trouble so many young people of the present day. His father misses the hint. He has himself read some of the skeptical literature, he says, and can assure Schleiermacher that it is not worth wasting time on. For six whole months there is no further word from his son. Then comes the bombshell. In a moving letter of 21 January 1787, Schleiermacher admits that the doubts alluded to are his own. His father has said that faith is the "regalia of the Godhead," that is, God's royal due.

Schleiermacher confessed: "Faith is the regalia of the Godhead, you say.

Alas! dearest father, if you believe that without this faith no one can attain to salvation in the next world, nor to tranquility in this—and such, I know, is your belief—oh! then pray to God to grant it to me, for to me it is now lost. I cannot believe that he who called himself the Son of Man was the true, eternal God; I cannot believe that his death was a vicarious atonement."[3]

Schleiermacher's words resound with grief. But it would prove to be merely the sorrow of rejection, not repentance. Like an eighteenth-century Judas Iscariot, Schleiermacher betrayed the faith of his heritage; he abandoned the truth claims of Scripture and rejected the gospel—denying both the deity of Christ and His substitutionary work on the cross.

Surprisingly, though he turned his back on the biblical gospel, Schleiermacher did not wish to abandon religion altogether. Instead, he looked for a new authority on which to base his "Christianity." If the Scriptures were no longer his foundation, Schleiermacher would have to find a new one. He did so in Romanticism.

Romanticism—which emphasized beauty, emotion, and experience—was a philosophical response to the Enlightenment's rationalistic focus on empirical science and human reason. It was Enlightenment Rationalism (and its inherent antisupernaturalism) that had caused Schleiermacher to doubt his Christian faith in the first place. Now, in an effort to restore some semblance of that Christianity, he turned to the philosophical tenets of Romanticism. His primary work, *On Religion: Speeches to Its Cultured Despisers*, was first published in 1799. It formed the basis for his later treatise *The Christian Faith*, which was published in 1821–22 and then revised and republished in 1830–31.

In these works, Schleiermacher tried to defend religion from Enlightenment critics by arguing that the basis for belief in God is not found in the objective truth claims of Scripture (a primary point of rationalist attack), but rather in personal feelings of religious consciousness (a point beyond the reach of Rationalism).[4] Ironically, in trying to defend his faith through emotional confirmation, he destroyed the very thing he was claiming to protect.

Schleiermacher foolishly sought to replace the foundation on which Christianity rests by exchanging the objective truths of Scripture for subjective spiritual experiences. That kind of theological tampering inevitably leads to disastrous consequences (Ps. 11:3). In Schleiermacher's case, the planting of his poisonous ideas led to the deadly crop of theological liberalism—a form of religion that called itself "Christian" while simultaneously denying the accuracy, authority, and supernatural character of the Bible.

Since Schleiermacher's time, there have been several iterations of his pioneering idea: attempts to find an authoritative basis for Christianity in something other than the revealed Word of God. Later a German named Albrecht Ritschl, for example, argued that Christianity ought to be defined in terms of *ethical conduct in society.* Ritschl's ideas gave birth to the social gospel, which replaced the biblical gospel in many mainline Protestant churches, both in Europe and America. Rather than emphasizing personal sin and salvation from eternal judgment, the social gospel stripped the Bible of its true message and focused instead on an impotent moralism intent on saving society from its cultural ills.

The social gospel saved no one from the wrath of God. But it became the predominant form of liberal Christianity in the twentieth century—as most of the mainline denominations shipwrecked on the sharp rocks of unbelief. Popular authors and prominent pastors spewed Ritchl's ideas to the masses. But the heart of liberalism went all the way back to Schleiermacher and his wrongheaded claim that Christianity could be built on a foundation other than biblical truth.

Like any form of false religion, theological liberalism began as an abandonment of the authority of God's Word. Centuries earlier, the medieval Roman Catholic Church had experienced a similar, though more gradual, departure—exchanging the authority of Scripture for the authority of ecclesiastical tradition and papal decree. That is why the Reformation was necessary. By departing from the sole authority of Scripture, both Roman Catholicism and theological liberalism became enemies of true Christianity, fraudulent versions of the very thing they claimed to represent.

The modern charismatic counterfeit is following down that same perilous path—basing its belief system on something other than the sole authority of Scripture and poisoning the church with a twisted notion of faith. Like the medieval Catholic Church, it muddles the clear teaching of Scripture and obscures the true gospel; and like Schleiermacher, it elevates subjective feelings and personal experiences to the place of highest importance. The extent to which both of those corrupt systems destroyed the lives of millions is matched by the doctrinal devastation spreading from charismatic error and confusion.

Though many charismatics give lip service to the primacy of Scripture, in practice they deny both its authority and sufficiency. Preoccupied with mystical encounters and emotional ecstasies, charismatics seek ongoing revelation from heaven—meaning that, for them, the Bible alone is simply not enough. Within a charismatic paradigm, biblical revelation must be supplemented with personal "words from God," supposed impressions from the Holy Spirit, and other subjective religious experiences. That kind of thinking is an outright rejection of the authority and sufficiency of Scripture (2 Tim. 3:16–17). It is a recipe for far-reaching theological disaster.

Honoring the Author of the Word

Any movement that does not honor God's Word cannot rightfully claim to honor Him. If we are to reverence the omnipotent Sovereign of the universe, we must wholly submit to the things He has spoken (Heb. 1:1–2). Anything less is to treat Him with contempt and rebel against His lordship. Nothing is more offensive to the Author of Scripture than to disregard, deny, or distort the truth He has revealed (Rev. 22:18–19). To mishandle the Word of God is to misrepresent the One who wrote it. To reject its claims is to call Him a liar. To ignore its message is to snub that which the Holy Spirit inspired.

As God's perfect revelation, the Bible reflects the glorious character of its Author. Because He is the God of truth, His Word is infallible. Because He cannot lie, His Word is inerrant. Because He is the King of kings, His Word is absolute and supreme. Those who wish to please Him must obey His Word. Conversely, those who fail to honor the Scriptures above every other truth-claim dishonor God Himself.

Occasionally, someone will suggest that such a high view of Scripture makes the Bible itself an object of worship. Point out that Scripture is vastly superior to (and infinitely more authoritative than) the dreams and visions of contemporary charismatics, and you are practically guaranteed to be labeled a *bibliolator*.

Such an accusation utterly misconstrues what it means to honor God's Word. It's not the physical book that we revere, but God, who has revealed Himself infallibly therein. Furthermore, Scripture is pictured in 2 Timothy 3:16 as the very breath of God—meaning it speaks with *His* authority. There can be no more reliable source of truth. To entertain any lower view of Scripture (or to suggest that belief in the absolute trustworthiness of the Bible is a kind of idolatry) is a serious affront to God. He Himself has exalted His Word to the highest place. David made that point explicit in Psalm 138:2. Speaking to God, he exclaimed, "You have magnified Your word above all Your name."[5]

Because they recognized Jesus Christ alone as the Head of the church, the Reformers gladly submitted to His Word as the sole authority within the church. Thus, they acknowledged what all true believers throughout history have affirmed—that the Word of God alone is our supreme rule for life and doctrine. Consequently, they also confronted any false authority that might attempt to usurp Scripture's rightful place; and in so doing, they exposed the corruption of the entire Roman Catholic system.

Believers today are likewise called to defend the truth against all who would seek to undermine the authority of Scripture. As Paul wrote, "We destroy arguments and every lofty opinion raised against the knowledge of God, and take every thought captive to obey Christ" (2 Cor. 10:4–5 ESV). Jude similarly instructed his readers to "contend earnestly for the faith which was once for all delivered to the saints" (v. 3). In referring to "the faith," Jude was not pointing to an indefinable body of religious doctrines; rather, he was speaking of the objective truths of Scripture that comprise the Christian faith (cf. Acts 2:42; 2 Tim. 1:13–14). As the rest of the verse makes clear:

> Jude defines *the faith* in succinct, specific terms as that *which was once for all handed down to the saints*. The phrase "once for all" refers to something that is accomplished or completed one time, with lasting results and no need of repetition. Through the Holy Spirit, God revealed the Christian faith

(cf. Romans 16:26; 2 Timothy 3:16) to the apostles and their associates in the first century. Their teachings, in conjunction with the Old Testament Scriptures, make up the "true knowledge" of Jesus Christ, and are all that believers need for life and godliness (2 Peter 1:3; cf. 2 Timothy 3:16–17).

The authors of the New Testament did not discover the truths of the Christian faith through mystical religious experiences. Rather God, with finality and certainty, delivered His complete body of revelation in Scripture. Any system that claims new revelation or new doctrine must be disregarded as false (Revelation 22:18–19). God's Word is all-sufficient; it is all that believers need as they contend for the faith and oppose apostasy within the church.[6]

From the very beginning, the battle between good and evil has been a battle for the truth. The serpent, in the garden of Eden, began his temptation by questioning the truthfulness of God's previous instruction: "Now the serpent was more cunning than any beast of the field which the LORD God had made. And he said to the woman, 'Has God indeed said, "You shall not eat of every tree of the garden"?' . . . Then the serpent said to the woman, 'You will not surely die. For God knows that in the day you eat of it your eyes will be opened, and you will be like God, knowing good and evil'" (Gen. 3:1, 4–5). Casting doubt on the straightforward revelation of God has been Satan's tactic ever since (cf. John 8:44; 2 Cor. 11:44).

With eternity at stake, it is no wonder Scripture reserves its harshest words of condemnation for those who would put lies in the mouth of God, usurping His Word with dangerous experience that is paltry in comparison. The serpent was cursed in the garden of Eden (Gen. 3:14), and Satan told of his inevitable demise (v. 15). In Old Testament Israel, false prophecy was a capital offense (Deut. 13:5, 10), a point vividly illustrated by Elijah's slaughter of the 450 prophets of Baal following the showdown on Mount Carmel (1 Kings 18:19, 40). But the Israelites often failed to expel false prophets; and by welcoming error into their midst, they also invited God's judgment (Jer. 5:29–31). Consider the Lord's attitude toward those who would exchange His true Word for a counterfeit:

This is a rebellious people, lying children, children who will not hear the law of the LORD; who say to the seers, "Do not see," and to the prophets, "Do not prophesy to us right things; speak to us smooth things, prophesy deceits." . . . Therefore thus says the Holy One of Israel: "Because you despise this word, and trust in oppression and perversity, and rely on them, therefore this iniquity shall be to you like a breach ready to fall, a bulge in a high wall, whose breaking comes suddenly, in an instant." (Isa. 30:9–13)

"Shall I not punish them for these things?" says the LORD. "Shall I not avenge Myself on such a nation as this? An astonishing and horrible thing has been committed in the land: The prophets prophesy falsely, and the priests rule by their own power; and My people love to have it so." (Jer. 5:29–31)

And the LORD said to me, "The prophets prophesy lies in My name. I have not sent them, commanded them, nor spoken to them; they prophesy to you a false vision, divination, a worthless thing, and the deceit of their heart. Therefore thus says the LORD concerning the prophets who prophesy in My name, whom I did not send, and who say, 'Sword and famine shall not be in this land'—By sword and famine those prophets shall be consumed!" (Jer. 14:14–16)

Thus says the LORD God: "Woe to the foolish prophets, who follow their own spirit and have seen nothing! . . . They have envisioned futility and false divination, saying, 'Thus says the LORD!' But the LORD has not sent them; yet they hope that the word may be confirmed. Have you not seen a futile vision, and have you not spoken false divination? You say, 'The LORD says,' but I have not spoken."

Therefore thus says the LORD God: "Because you have spoken nonsense and envisioned lies, therefore I am indeed against you," says the Lord GOD. "My hand will be against the prophets who envision futility and who divine lies; they shall not be in the assembly of My people, nor be written in the record of the house of Israel, nor shall they enter into the land of Israel. Then you shall know that I am the Lord GOD." (Ezek. 13:3–9)

The point of those passages is unmistakable: God hates those who misrepresent His Word or speak lies in His name. The New Testament responds to false prophets with equal severity (cf. 1 Tim. 6:3–5; 2 Tim. 3:1–9; 1 John 4:1–3; 2 John 7–11). God does not tolerate those who falsify or fake divine revelation. It is an offense He takes personally, and His retribution is swift and deadly. To sabotage biblical truth in any way—by adding to it, subtracting from it, or mixing it with error—is to invite divine wrath (Gal. 1:9; 2 John 9–11). Any distortion of the Word is an affront against the Trinity, and especially against the Spirit of God because of His intimate relationship to the Scriptures.

Martin Luther put it this way: "Whenever you hear anyone boast that he has something by inspiration of the Holy Spirit and it has no basis in God's Word, no matter what it may be, tell him that this is the work of the devil."[7] And elsewhere, "Whatever does not have its origin in the Scriptures is surely from the devil himself."[8]

In the remainder of this chapter, as we consider the true ministry of the Holy Spirit, we will consider three facets of His work in and through the Scriptures: inspiration, illumination, and empowerment.

THE HOLY SPIRIT INSPIRED THE SCRIPTURES

Within the Trinity, the Holy Spirit functions as the divine agent of transmission and communication. He is the divine Author of Scripture; the One through whom God revealed His truth (1 Cor. 2:10). Although the Spirit worked through many human authors, the resulting message is entirely His. It is the perfect and pure Word of God.

The process by which the Holy Spirit transmitted divine truth through human agents is called *inspiration*. The apostle Peter gives us a glimpse into that process in 2 Peter 1:20–21. There he wrote, "No prophecy of Scripture is of any private interpretation, for prophecy never came by the will of man, but holy men of God spoke as they were moved by the Holy Spirit." Peter's point is that the Bible is not a fallible collection of human insights; rather, it consists of the perfect revelation of God Himself, as the Holy Spirit worked through godly men to convey divine truth. The word *interpretation* translates the Greek word *epilusis*, which speaks of something that is released or sent forth.[9] Peter's point, then, is that no prophecy of Scripture came forth or originated from the private musings of men—it was not the product of human initiative or will, but the result of the Spirit's supernatural working through holy men of God.

As those godly men were carried along by the Holy Spirit, He superintended their words and used them to produce the Scriptures. As a sailing ship is carried along by the wind to reach its final destination, so the human authors of Scripture were moved by the Spirit of God to communicate exactly what He desired. In that process, the Spirit filled their minds, souls, and hearts with divine truth—mingling it sovereignly and supernaturally with their unique styles, vocabularies, and experiences, and guiding them to produce a perfect, inerrant result.

In Hebrews 1:1–2 we are given further insight into the way God revealed His truth in both the Old and New Testaments. The author of Hebrews wrote, "God, who at various times and in various ways spoke in time past to the fathers by the prophets, has in these last days spoken to us by His Son, whom He has appointed heir of all things, through whom also He made the worlds."

As verse 1 indicates, Old Testament revelation was delivered through the prophets as they spoke the things God commanded them to speak. Similarly, verse 2 explains that New Testament revelation came through the Lord Jesus Christ (cf. John 1:1, 18)—and by extension through His apostles whom He authorized to communicate divine truth to the church (cf. John 14–16). In both the Old and New Testaments, the Scriptures consist of God's infallible self-disclosure—His perfect revelation given through His chosen spokesmen and written down in exactly the way He wanted.

In all of this, the Spirit of God was intimately involved. According to 1 Peter 1:11, it was specifically the Holy Spirit who worked through the Old Testament prophets (cf. 1 Sam. 19:20; 2 Sam. 23:2; Isa. 59:21; Ezek. 11:5, 24; Mark 12:36). Moreover, it was the Spirit who superintended the Old Testament authors to write what they did (cf. Acts 1:16; 2 Peter 1:21). In the Upper Room, the Lord Jesus assured His disciples that He would send the Holy Spirit to remind them of the things He had said to them (John 14:17, 26)—a promise that was fulfilled in the writing of the Gospels. He also promised that the Spirit would give them additional revelation (John 16:13–15; cf. 15:26). That revelation, given to the apostles by the Holy Spirit, makes up the epistles of the New Testament. Thus, every part of Scripture—from the Old Testament to the New—constitutes the Spirit-inspired Word of God.

In 2 Timothy 3:16–17, Paul wrote, "All Scripture is given by inspiration of God, and is profitable for doctrine, for reproof, for correction, for instruction in righteousness, that the man of God may be complete, thoroughly equipped for every good work." The phrase "inspiration of God" literally means "breathed out by God" and undoubtedly includes an implicit reference to the Holy Spirit—the omnipotent breath of the Almighty (Job 33:4; cf. John 3:8; 20:22). Of course, Paul's emphasis in that passage is on the all-sufficient benefits that believers enjoy through the God-breathed Scriptures. All that we need for life and godliness is revealed to us in the Word, such that believers may be complete and thoroughly equipped to honor the Lord in all things.

The Bible is a supernatural book that provides supernatural benefits! It has been given to us as a gift from the Holy Spirit, the One who revealed its truths to godly men, inspiring them to speak and write the Word of God without any errors or inconsistencies. But the Spirit has done more than just give us the Bible; He also promises to help us understand and apply its truths—a point that brings us to a second way in which the Spirit works through the Scripture.

THE HOLY SPIRIT ILLUMINATES THE SCRIPTURES

Divine revelation would be useless to us if we were not able to comprehend it. That is why the Holy Spirit enlightens the minds of believers, so they are able to understand the truths of Scripture and submit to its teachings. The apostle Paul explained the Spirit's ministry of illumination in 1 Corinthians 2:14–16. There he wrote, "The natural man does not receive the things of the Spirit of God, for they are foolishness to him; nor can he know them, because they are spiritually discerned. But he who is spiritual judges all things, yet he himself is rightly judged by no one. For 'who has known the mind of the LORD that he may instruct Him?' But we have the mind of Christ." Through the illumination of the Word, the Holy Spirit enables believers to discern divine truth (cf. Ps. 119:18)—spiritual realities that the unconverted are unable to truly comprehend.

The sobering reality is that it is possible to be familiar with the Bible and still fail to understand it. The religious leaders of Jesus' day were Old Testament scholars, yet they completely missed the point of the Scriptures (John 5:37–39). As Christ asked Nicodemus, exposing the latter's ignorance about the basic tenets of the gospel, "Are you the teacher of Israel, and do not know these things?" (John 3:10). Devoid of the Holy Spirit, unbelievers operate only in the realm of the natural man. To them, the wisdom of God seems foolish. Even after Jesus was raised from the dead, the Pharisees and Sadducees still refused to believe (Matt. 28:12–15). Stephen confronted them with these words: "You stiff-necked and uncircumcised in heart and ears! You always resist the Holy Spirit; as your fathers did, so do you" (Acts 7:51; cf. Heb. 10:29).

The truth is that no sinner can believe and embrace the Scriptures without the Holy Spirit's divine enabling. As Martin Luther observed, "In spiritual and divine things, which pertain to the salvation of the soul, man is like a pillar of salt, like Lot's wife, yea, like a log and a stone, like a lifeless statue, which uses neither eyes nor mouth, neither sense nor heart. . . . All teaching and preaching is lost upon him, until he is enlightened, converted, and regenerated by the Holy Ghost."[10]

Until the Holy Spirit intervenes in the unbeliever's heart, the sinner will continue to reject the truth of the gospel. Anyone can memorize facts, listen to sermons, and gain some level of intellectual understanding about the basic points of biblical doctrine. But devoid of the Spirit's power, God's Word will never penetrate the sinful soul.[11]

Believers, on the other hand, have been made alive by the Spirit of God, who now indwells them. Thus Christians have a resident Truth Teacher who enlightens their understanding of the Word—enabling them to know and submit to the truth of Scripture (cf. 1 John 2:27). Though the Spirit's work of inspiration applied only to the human authors of Scripture, His ministry of illumination is given to all believers. Inspiration has given us the message inscribed on the pages of Scripture. Illumination inscribes that message on our hearts, enabling us to understand what it means, as we rely on the Spirit of God to shine the light of truth brightly in our minds (cf. 2 Cor. 4:6).

As Charles Spurgeon explained, "If you do not understand a book by a departed writer you are unable to ask him his meaning, but the Spirit, who inspired Holy Scripture, lives forever, and He delights to open the Word to those who seek His instruction."[12] It is a glorious ministry of the Holy Spirit that He opens the minds of His saints to understand the Scriptures (cf. Luke 24:45) so that we can know and obey His Word.

Of course, the doctrine of illumination does not mean that believers can unlock every theological secret (Deut. 29:29), or that we do not need godly teachers (Eph. 4:11–12). It also does not preclude us from disciplining ourselves for the purpose of godliness (1 Tim. 4:8) or from doing the hard work of careful Bible study (2 Tim. 2:15).[13] Yet we can approach our study of God's Word with joy and eagerness—knowing that as we investigate the Scriptures with prayerfulness and diligence, the Holy Spirit will illuminate our hearts to comprehend, embrace, and apply the truths we are studying.

Through His ministry of inspiration, the Holy Spirit has given us the Word of God. And through His ministry of illumination, He has opened our eyes to understand and submit to biblical truth. Yet, He does not stop there.

THE SPIRIT EMPOWERS THE SCRIPTURES

In perfect concert with His ministry of illumination, the Holy Spirit empowers His Word so that as it goes forth, it convicts the hearts of unbelievers and sanctifies the hearts of the redeemed. In the previous two chapters, we considered the Spirit's work in salvation and sanctification. It bears repeating here that His Word is the instrument He uses to powerfully accomplish both of those ministries.

In evangelism, the Holy Spirit energizes the proclamation of the biblical gospel (1 Peter 1:12), using the preaching of His Word to pierce the heart and convict the sinner (cf. Rom. 10:14). As Paul told the Thessalonians, "For our gospel did not come to you in word only, but also in power, and in the Holy Spirit and in much assurance" (1 Thess. 1:5). Elsewhere, he explained to the believers at Corinth, "And my speech and my preaching were not with persuasive words of human wisdom, but in demonstration of the Spirit and of power, that your faith should not be in the wisdom of men but in the power of God" (1 Cor. 2:4–5). If the Spirit did not empower the proclamation of His Word, no one would ever respond in saving faith. Charles Spurgeon vividly illustrated that point with these words:

> Unless the Holy Ghost blesses the Word, we who preach the gospel are of all men most miserable, for we have attempted a task that is impossible. We have entered on a sphere where nothing but the supernatural will ever avail. If the Holy Spirit does not renew the hearts of our hearers, we cannot do it. If the Holy Ghost does not regenerate them, we cannot. If he does not send the truth home into their souls, we might as well speak into the ear of a corpse.[14]

The Holy Spirit is the omnipotent force behind the Lord's promise in Isaiah 55:11—"So shall My word be that goes forth from My mouth; it shall not return to Me void, but it shall accomplish what I please, and it shall prosper in the thing for which I sent it." Without His divine empowerment, preaching the gospel would be nothing more than dead letters falling upon dead hearts. But through the Spirit's power, the Word of God is "living and powerful, and sharper than any two-edged sword, piercing even to the division of soul and spirit, and of joints and marrow, and is a discerner of the thoughts and intents of the heart" (Heb. 4:12).

Apart from the Holy Spirit, the most eloquent sermon is nothing but hot air, empty noise, and lifeless oratory; but when accompanied by the almighty Spirit of God, even the simplest message slices through calloused hearts of unbelief and transforms lives.

The apostle Paul similarly described the Word of God as "the sword of the Spirit" in Ephesians 6:17. In that context, Scripture is depicted as a Spirit-empowered weapon that believers ought to use in their battle against sin and temptation (cf. Matt. 4:4, 7, 10). The Word of God is not only the divinely energized means by which sinners are regenerated (cf. Eph. 5:26; Titus 3:5; James 1:18), but it is also the means by which believers resist sin and grow in holiness. As Jesus prayed in John 17:17, speaking to His Father about those who would believe in Him, "Sanctify them by Your truth. Your Word is truth."

We already saw the sanctifying effects of God's inspired Word in 2 Timothy 3:16–17, where Paul explained that the inspired Scriptures are sufficient to fully equip believers for spiritual maturity.

In 1 Peter 2:1–3, Peter made a similar point: "Therefore, laying aside all malice, all deceit, hypocrisy, envy, and all evil speaking, as newborn babes, desire the pure milk of the word, that you may grow thereby, if indeed you have tasted that the Lord is gracious." Those who have tasted of God's grace in redemption continue to grow in sanctification through the internalization of His Word. True believers are marked by a hunger for the Scriptures, delighting in God's Word with the intensity with which a baby craves milk (cf. Job 23:12; Ps. 119). In all of this, we are being conformed into the image of Christ—a ministry that the Spirit accomplishes by exposing our hearts to biblical revelation about the Savior (2 Cor. 3:18). He makes it possible for "the Word of Christ [to] dwell in you richly" (Col. 3:16), a phrase that parallels Paul's command to "be filled with the Spirit" (Eph. 5:18), so that the fruit of a transformed life is seen in the way we express our love to God and to others (cf. Eph. 5:19–6:9; Col. 3:17–4:1).

Where the Holy Spirit's power is manifest, it does not produce mindless flops on the ground, gushing incoherent babble, ecstatic buzz, or hot flashes of emotion. All those behaviors have nothing to do with His authentic ministry. In reality, they are a mockery of His genuine work. When the Holy Spirit is moving, sinful people are sanctified through the power of His Word, having been transformed into new creations in Christ. They become excited about holiness, energized for worship, empowered for service, and eager to learn the Scriptures. Because they love the Spirit's true work, they love the Book He has given to the church. Thus, their lives are characterized by a reverent, profound, and faithful love for both the Word of God and the God of the Word.

HONORING THE SPIRIT BY HONORING THE SCRIPTURES

Although charismatics claim to represent the Holy Spirit, their movement has shown a persistent tendency to pit Him against the Scriptures—as if a commitment to biblical truth somehow might quench, grieve, or otherwise inhibit the Spirit's ministry.[15] But nothing could be further from the truth. The Bible is the Holy Spirit's book! It is the instrument He uses to convict unbelievers of sin, righteousness, and judgment. It is the sword by which He energizes the proclamation of the gospel, piercing the hearts of the spiritually dead and raising them to spiritual life. It is the means by which He unleashes His sanctifying power in the lives of those who believe, growing them in grace through the pure milk of biblical instruction.

Thus, to reject the Scriptures is to rebuff the Spirit. To ignore, disdain, twist, or disobey the Word of God is to dishonor the One who inspired, illuminates, and empowers it. But to wholeheartedly embrace and submit to biblical truth is to enjoy the fullness of the Spirit's ministry—being filled by His sanctifying power, being led by Him in righteousness, and being equipped with His armor in the battle against sin and error. Charles Spurgeon explained it this way to his congregation:

> We have a more sure word of testimony, a rock of truth upon which we rest, for our infallible standard lies in, "It is written . . ." The Bible, the whole Bible, and nothing but the Bible, is our religion. . . . It is said that it is hard to understand, but it is not so to those who seek the guidance of the Spirit of God. . . . A babe in grace taught by the Spirit of God may know the mind of the Lord concerning salvation, and find its way to heaven by the guidance of the Word alone. But be it profound or simple; that is not the question; it is the Word of God, and is pure, unerring truth. Here is infallibility, and nowhere else. . . . This grand, infallible book . . . is our sole court of appeal. . . . [It is] the sword of the Spirit in the spiritual conflicts which await. . . . The Holy Spirit is in the Word, and it is, therefore, living truth. O Christians, be ye sure of this, and because of it make you the Word your chosen weapon of war.[16]

The Bible is a living book because the living Spirit of God energizes and empowers it. The Word convicts us, instructs us, equips us, strengthens us, protects us, and enables us to grow. Or more accurately, the Holy Spirit does all those things as He activates the truth of Scripture in our hearts.

As believers, we honor the Spirit when we honor the Scriptures—studying them diligently, applying them carefully, arming our minds with their precepts, and embracing their teaching with all our hearts. The Spirit has given us the Word. He has opened our eyes to understand its vast riches. And He empowers its truth in our lives as He conforms us into the image of our Savior.

It is difficult to imagine why anyone would ever disdain or neglect the words of this Book, especially in light of the divinely promised blessings that come from cherishing it. As the psalmist declared:

Blessed is the man who walks not in the counsel of the ungodly, nor stands in the path of sinners, nor sits in the seat of the scornful; but his delight is in the law of the Lord, and in His law he meditates day and night. He shall be like a tree planted by the rivers of water, that brings forth its fruit in its season, whose leaf also shall not wither; and whatever he does shall prosper. (Ps. 1:1–3)

TWELVE

AN OPEN LETTER TO MY CONTINUATIONIST FRIENDS

This final chapter is a personal appeal to fellow leaders in the conservative evangelical movement who proclaim the true gospel yet insist on remaining open to the continuation of the revelatory and miraculous gifts in the modern age.

I titled this chapter "An Open Letter to My Continuationist *Friends*" because I want to emphasize, from the outset, that I regard as brothers in Christ and friends in the ministry all who are faithful fellow workmen in the Word and the gospel, even if they give a place of legitimacy to the charismatic experience. I have good friends among them who label themselves as "reformed charismatics" or "evangelical continuationists."

The Charismatic Movement is teeming with false teachers and spiritual charlatans of the worst kind, as can be aptly illustrated by turning the channel to TBN (or any of several smaller charismatic television networks). Certainly I do not view my continuationist friends in the same light as those spiritual mountebanks and blatant frauds. In this chapter, I'm writing to Christian leaders who have proven their commitment to Christ and His Word over the years. Their allegiance to the authority of Scripture and the fundamentals of the gospel has been consistent and influential—and it is on that basis that we share rich fellowship in the truth.

I am thankful for the extensive contributions they have made to the truth and life of the church. I have personally benefited, along with my congregation, from books written by continuationist authors—including systematic theologies, biblical commentaries, historical biographies, devotional works, and treatises defending fundamental doctrines such as substitutionary atonement, biblical inerrancy, and the God-given roles for men and women.

Regarding the charismatic issue, many evangelical continuationists have courageously condemned certain aspects of that movement they recognize to be in direct contradiction to the Word of God, including the outrageous claims of the prosperity gospel. Moreover, the bizarre excesses that characterize the movement as a whole are not tolerated. Even the term *continuationist* is an implicit protest against the pervasive corruption that characterizes mainstream charismatic teaching. As one continuationist author explained, "The term *charismatic* has sometimes been associated with doctrinal error, unsubstantiated claims of healing, financial impropriety, outlandish and unfulfilled predictions, an overemphasis on the speech gifts, and some regrettable hairstyles. . . . That's why I've started to identify myself more often as a continuationist rather than a charismatic."[1]

That kind of distancing is critical because it puts a necessary wall of distinction between mainstream charismatics and conservative evangelicals who believe in the continuation of the gifts. Still, I do not believe it goes far enough. I am grateful that the doctrines we agree on outweigh the things on which we disagree. But that does not mean those latter issues can rest easily.

Thus, while I am thankful we are together for the gospel, I am equally convinced that the unity we share in the core of the gospel must not preclude us from addressing other extended gospel issues; rather, it should motivate us to sharpen one another for the sake of biblical accuracy. Love for the truth, without any lack of personal charity, is what motivates me to write a book like this. It is also what compels me to state plainly that I believe the continuationist position exposes the evangelical church to continuous danger from the charismatic mutation.

Closet Cessationists

Before discussing the dangerous consequences of holding a conservative charismatic position (e.g., continuationism), it's important to state one of the great ironies of that position—namely, that continuationists actually hold to an incipient form of cessationism. Let me explain what I mean.

The continuationist position asserts that modern prophecy is fallible and nonauthoritative, it acknowledges that the prevalent practice of modern tongues-speaking does not consist of authentic foreign languages, and it generally denies that healing miracles like those recorded in the Gospels and Acts are being repeated today. Moreover, continuationists concede that the unique office of apostleship ceased after the first century of church history. Thus, continuationists agree that there have been no apostles in the past nineteen hundred years, and that any inerrant prophetic gift of New Testament times has ceased (with inerrant revelation continuing only in the Bible).

Continuationists largely admit that the miraculous ability to speak fluently in authentic foreign languages, as described in Acts 2, did not survive past the apostolic age. And they generally recognize that instantaneous, undeniable, public, and complete healings like those performed by Christ and His apostles have not been replicated since the first century. As a well-known continuationist pastor stated in a recent interview, "It seems to me, both biblically and experientially, that there was an extraordinary outcropping of supernatural blessing surrounding the incarnation, which has not been duplicated at any point in history. Nobody has ever healed like Jesus healed. He never failed, he did it perfectly, he raised people from the dead, he touched and all sores went away, and he never blew it."[2]

That observation is absolutely correct: the miracles of Christ and, by extension, His apostles were unique and unrepeatable. To acknowledge that plain fact is to concede the fundamental premise of cessationism.

Those willing to make a fair and candid comparison between the charismatic phenomena of today and the miracles of Christ and His apostles quickly discover it is impossible to be an unqualified continuationist. It is all too obvious that the modern charismatic versions of apostleship, prophecy, tongues, and healing do not match the biblical precedents. Anyone with a modicum of integrity will have to admit that. But in conceding that much, they corroborate the heart of the cessationist argument—no matter what protests are made to the contrary.

Nevertheless, continuationists insist on using biblical terminology to describe contemporary charismatic practices that *do not* match the biblical reality. Thus, any personal impression or fleeting fancy might be labeled "the gift of prophecy," speaking in gibberish is called "the gift of tongues," every remarkable providence is labeled a "miracle," and every positive answer to prayers for healing is seen as proof that someone has the *gift* of healing. All of that poses a major problem, because it is *not* how the New Testament describes those gifts. For any evangelical pastor or church leader to apply biblical terminology to that which does not match the biblical practice is not merely confusing; it is potentially dangerous teaching for which that person is culpable.

THE DANGEROUS RAMIFICATIONS OF THE CONTINUATIONIST POSITION

Some conservative continuationists might consider this issue to be a relatively minor, secondary issue—one that has only small ramifications for the church at large. Others seem comfortably indifferent to the issue, giving it almost no thought at all. In reality, the implications are massive and the consequences potentially disastrous. Here are eight reasons why.

1. The continuationist position gives an illusion of legitimacy to the broader Charismatic Movement.

Although theologically respectable conservative continuationists represent a very small minority within the Charismatic Movement, they provide the entire movement with an aura of theological credibility and respect.

When I wrote *Charismatic Chaos* more than twenty years ago, people accused me of only addressing the wacky fringe of the Charismatic Movement. I'm sure some will say the same thing about this book. In reality, however, this book deals with the *mainstream* Charismatic Movement. Reformed continuationists are the ones who are actually on the fringe because they do not exemplify the vast majority of charismatics. However, when notable continuationist scholars give credence to charismatic interpretations or fail to directly condemn charismatic practices, they provide theological cover for a movement that ought to be exposed for its dangers rather than defended.

One of the most respected New Testament scholars in the evangelical world provides an example of this very thing. As a careful exegete who seeks to be faithful to the New Testament text, this man correctly identifies the gift of tongues with authentic languages. However, his continuationist presuppositions inhibit him from concluding that the gift of languages has ceased. As a result, he is forced to devise a baffling hypothesis in which he asserts that modern babbling may seem like gibberish, but can constitute a rational language at the same time. In an extended discussion on this point, he provides the following example to illustrate his view:

Suppose the message is:

Praise the Lord, for his mercy endures forever.

Remove the vowels to achieve:

PRS TH LRD FR HS MRC NDRS FRVR.

This may seem a bit strange; but when we remember that modern Hebrew is written without most vowels, we can imagine that with practice this could be read quite smoothly. Now remove the spaces and, beginning with the first letter, rewrite the sequence using every third letter, repeatedly going through the sequence until all the letters are used up. The result is:

PTRRMNSVRHDHRDFRSLFSCRR.

Now add an "a" sound after each consonant, and break up the unit into arbitrary bits:

PATARA RAMA NA SAVARAHA DAHARA

DAFARASALA FASA CARARA.

I think that is indistinguishable from transcriptions of certain modern tongues. Certainly it is very similar to some I have heard. But the important point is that it conveys information *provided you know the code*. Anyone who knows the steps I have taken could reverse them in order to retrieve the original message. . . .

It appears, then, that tongues may bear cognitive information even though they are not known human languages—just as a computer program is a "language" that conveys a great deal of information, even though it is not a "language" that anyone actually speaks.[3]

While such a suggestion is innovative, it has no exegetical basis and adds layers of unnecessary complexity that are not warranted by the New Testament description of the gift of languages. Unique explanations like this, though well intentioned, attempt to do the impossible. All efforts to reconcile the biblical miracle of speaking foreign languages and the modern practice of nonsensical jabber fail.

If that interpretation did not come from one of the most respected academic authors of our day, it would probably gain no traction in any serious forum. But because of that particular writer's reputation as a distinguished evangelical scholar, many charismatics cling to his idea as if it were a credible defense of their position. It's not. It is a transparently desperate attempt to defend the indefensible. Implausible theories like that from respected sources only serve to legitimize a movement that, in reality, is built on untenable arguments and exegetical fallacies.

In an online interview, another continuationist pastor insists the modern version of ecstatic speech is a legitimate expression of the gift, even though he admits it is often faked in charismatic circles. Speaking of his own desire to speak in tongues, he says:

Just this morning I was pacing in my living room . . . [and] I thought of tongues. I said, "I haven't asked for tongues for a long time." And so, I just paused. . . . And I said, "Lord, I'm still eager to speak in tongues. Would you give me that gift?"

Now at that point, you can try to say "banana" backwards if you want to. I used to sit in the car outside church singing in tongues, but I knew I wasn't. I was just making it up. And I said this isn't it. I know this isn't it.

But this is what they try to get you to do if you're in that certain group. And I just, I did everything to try to open myself to this, and the Lord has always said to me without words, "No." "No." . . .

But I don't assume this is His last word. And so every now and then, I'm just gonna go back to Him like a child and say, "A lot of my brothers and sisters have this toy, have this gift. Can I have it too?"[4]

This testimony illustrates the angst that is caused by a wrong understanding of the gifts: desiring God to give something He removed from the church long ago. On the one hand, I am thankful that this pastor is honest enough to acknowledge he has never experienced the contemporary phenomenon—especially since the modern version constitutes a counterfeit experience. On the other hand, this respected pastor's belief that unintelligible ecstasy can be a genuine expression of spiritual giftedness grants legitimacy to all those who associate mindless babble with the Spirit of God. Though this pastor is a well-known defender of sound doctrine in many vital ways, his position on tongues provides a platform of plausibility for millions of charismatics who are far less responsible than he is.

2. The continuationist position degrades the miraculous nature of the true gifts that God bestowed upon the first-century church.

The Gospel narratives, along with the book of Acts, record the most extensive and dramatic miracles that ever occurred in all human history. God was giving new revelation to the church, through His apostles and prophets, so the New Testament could be written. The Holy Spirit enabled those with the gift of languages to speak foreign words they had never learned. And He bestowed the gift of healing on select individuals—enabling them to heal people who were blind, crippled, deaf, and leprous—to validate their message. The purpose of those miracles, and their relationship to the initial unveiling of gospel truth, is made clear in Hebrews 2:3–4: "[The gospel] at the first began to be spoken by the Lord, and was confirmed to us by those who heard Him, God also bearing witness both with signs and wonders, with various miracles, and gifts of the Holy Spirit, according to His own will." That text is rendered meaningless by the charismatic notion that signs, wonders, miracles, and gifts of tongues, prophecy, and healing belong to the everyday experience of all Christians.

Furthermore, when continuationists use the terminology of the New Testament gifts, but then define those terms to fit charismatic practice, they depreciate the remarkable nature of the *real thing*. As a result, they diminish the glorious way the Holy Spirit worked in the foundational stages of church history. If the gifts practiced in charismatic churches today are equivalent to the gifts described in the New Testament, then those original gifts were not miraculous at all. Saying things that are full of error is not consistent with the biblical gift of prophecy. Speaking gibberish is not the real gift of tongues. And praying for healing, while knowing that those prayers might not be answered, is not the apostolic gift of healing.

As evangelical Christians, we desire to see the triune God honored and His Word exalted. When charismatics hijack New Testament terminology and redefine the biblical gifts, they degrade what God was miraculously doing in the first century. Conservative continuationists aid in this misrepresentation.

3. The continuationist position severely limits the ability of its advocates to confront others who fall into charismatic confusion.

By granting credence to the basic premises of a degraded movement, continuationists end up surrendering the ability to confront other evangelical leaders who practice bizarre charismatic behavior or make outlandish claims based on supposed revelations from God.

A vivid illustration of this came to light several years ago, when a popular but provocative young pastor started claiming that God was showing him graphic visions of specific people engaging in sex acts—including rape, fornication, and child molestation.[5] With an air of brash bravado, the pastor described his supposed visions to his audience with salacious detail, such that the X-rated result constituted a clear violation of Ephesians 5:12, 1 Timothy 4:12, and a host of other biblical passages. Those messages were then made publicly available via his ministry's website.

Obviously visions of that sort are not from God, originating instead from an imagination that has been overly exposed to worldly influences. While cessationists were quick to point out the pastor's pornographic presumption, some continuationist leaders found themselves in a quandary. On the one hand, they could not be comfortable with the lewd images this young man claimed had come to him from God. On the other, they could not definitively deny his claim that the Holy Spirit was giving him new revelation, no matter how lurid or garish. In the end, they remained awkwardly silent, and their silence was interpreted as acceptance.

Other examples could also be listed, demonstrating that while reformed charismatics want to distance themselves from the mainstream Charismatic Movement, they have placed themselves in a position that makes it nearly impossible for them to critique it effectively. An influential evangelical pastor recently reiterated the fact that he had been openly intrigued by the Third Wave Movement in the early 1990s, seeing John Wimber's Vineyard Movement as a genuine revival.[6] A well-known systematic theologian implies that being slain in the Spirit can be a good thing as long as it produces positive results in people's lives.[7] Another widely read evangelical author resigned his pastorate in 1993 to become something of a theological mentor to the Kansas City Prophets.[8] When that group fragmented, their erstwhile mentor left Kansas City and founded a ministry of his own that takes a much more low-key approach to the charismatic gifts. But he still insists that fallible prophecy is authentic.[9]

Rather than confronting charismatic errors head-on, continuationist leaders repeatedly find themselves flirting with aspects of a movement that is full of serious error and corrupt leadership. Because they have allowed the modern Charismatic Movement to redefine the gifts for them, they have severely weakened their ability to counter that error authoritatively. But giving up that exegetical high ground is utterly unnecessary.

4. By insisting that God is still giving new revelation to Christians today, the Continuationist Movement opens the gates to confusion and error.

The acceptance of fallible prophecy within continuationist circles has exposed the entire Evangelical Movement to the fallible doctrines that accompany those prophecies.

The countless false prophecies of Jack Deere, Paul Cain, Bob Jones, and the Kansas City Prophets are sufficient to illustrate this point. When I met privately in my office with former Dallas Theological Seminary professor Jack Deere and self-proclaimed prophet Paul Cain in 1992, Deere attempted to convince me that he represented a doctrinally sound segment of the Charismatic Movement. He brought Cain along to prove to me and two of my fellow elders that the gift of prophecy was still operating in the church. During our meeting, Cain was almost completely incoherent, acting like a drunk man. Though Deere apologized for Cain's bizarre behavior, he wanted us to believe it was the result of the Spirit's anointing.

As our conversation progressed, both men acknowledged that their prophecies were frequently wrong. Of course, we pointed out that Scripture definitively condemns all false prophecy. Biblical prophets were held to a standard of 100 percent accuracy. Deere's defense was to point to the work of a noted evangelical who argued for the continuation of the prophetic gift.[10] By purporting the possibility of fallible prophecy, this respected evangelical theologian provided Deere and Cain with a veneer of legitimacy—despite the fact that they were clearly violating the biblical requirements for prophecy found in Deuteronomy 13 and 18. The popular continuationist premise that the New Testament gift of prophecy is frequently erroneous openly invites false prophets into the church (cf. Matt. 7:15), while simultaneously promoting a form of congregational gullibility—in which even sincere Christians can be led to believe that God is speaking (when in fact He is not).

Some years later, Paul Cain's ministry was discredited when he admitted to both long-term drunkenness and homosexuality. Ironically, none of the other so-called prophets in that movement foresaw his demise. In fact, they had hailed him as the superior prophet with the greatest gift. So much for prophetic discernment! If such charismatic prophets don't know the truth about their associates, the people whom they influence have no hope of knowing it either.

In spite of Paul Cain's exposure, some continuationist leaders still insist that he *really did* prophesy, even if he was subsequently exposed as an immoral charlatan. In the words of one evangelical leader:

Paul Cain was a prophet in those days, and he's been utterly discredited. And I went to an event of Paul Cain, and he prophesied over me. And he missed it. I watched him preach twice, and the way he used the Bible was to use it as a pump primer to get to the real thing, and the real thing was, "The man at the back with the red T-shirt, he's going to Australia in three weeks, and he's nervous, and I want to assure him that his visa will come through." Now, that happened, and I believe it really happened. I have a place in my theology that the Holy Spirit can do that, and Paul Cain can be a charlatan. He was a charlatan, I think. But he really prophesied.[11]

While it is true that false prophets can sometimes make accurate predictions (e.g., Balaam [Num. 23:6–12]; Caiaphas [John 11:49–51]), that anecdote illustrates the confusion inherent in the continuationist position. Why would anyone not label the immoral Paul Cain a false prophet when he gives false prophecies? Crediting the Holy Spirit for words that could be from demons through the mouth of a false prophet is a serious misjudgment that highlights the dangerous game continuationists are forced to play.

The continuationist position invites any Christian to interpret any personal impression or subjective feeling as a potential revelation from God. Moreover, it removes any authoritative, objective standard for questioning the legitimacy of someone's supposed revelation from God. Within the continuationist paradigm, it's normal for a person not to know for sure if an impression came from God or from some other source. But that is a direct by-product of corrupt charismatic theology that degrades and discounts discernment and diverts people from the truth.

That point was vividly illustrated in the experience of a well-known continuationist pastor whose life was rocked by a woman in his congregation who approached him with a supposed word from God. He tells the story this way:

A woman came to me, while my wife is pregnant with my fourth child. And she says, "I have a very hard prophecy for you." I said, "OK." She says—in fact she wrote it down and gave it to me—"Your wife is going to die in childbirth and you're going to have a daughter." I went back to my study—I

thanked her, I said, "I appreciate that." I forget what I said but it wasn't—,
I didn't want to hear that. I went back to my study, I got down and I just
wept. . . . And when we delivered our fourth *boy*, not *girl*, I gave a "whoop,"
which I always do, but this whoop was a little extra; because I knew as soon
as the boy was born this was not a true prophecy.[12]

If counterfeit prophecy can have that kind of effect in the life of this evangelical leader, imagine the devastating effects it has on laypeople who do not
have his level of biblical discernment.

Within the broader Charismatic Movement, this problem is far worse than
with theologically conservative continuationists—since it is not restrained by
the sound doctrine of reformed theology. The fact that the charismatic world
is filled with false teachers and spiritual scam artists is certainly no coinci-
dence. The elevation of imagined experiences and subjective impressions has
opened the door to all sorts of deception. The notion that Christians should
regularly expect to receive extrabiblical revelation from God through mystical
experiences, combined with the outrageous idea that even erroneous revelations are authentic expressions of the prophetic gift, has created the theological
train wreck that is the Charismatic Movement. Sadly, some conservative continuationist scholars are in no position to stop the carnage.

5. By insisting that God is still giving new revelation to Christians today, the Continuationist Movement tacitly denies the doctrine of *sola Scriptura*.

Here the whole movement is most concisely defined. At its core, it is a
deviation away from the sole authority of Scripture.

Obviously, no conservative continuationist would deny the closed canon
outright. Nor would he deny the authority or sufficiency of Scripture. In fact,
my continuationist friends are among some of the most outspoken defenders
of biblical inerrancy, and I am grateful for their commitment to the primacy
of Scripture and their unwavering affirmation of the fact that Scripture alone
is our authoritative guide for life and doctrine.

Yet, in reality, the continuationist view actually defaults on the sole sufficiency of Scripture at the most practical levels—because it teaches believers

to look for additional revelation from God outside of the Bible. As a result, people are conditioned to expect impressions and words from God beyond what is recorded on the pages of Scripture. By using terms like *prophecy*, *revelation*, or *a word from the Lord*, the continuationist position has the real potential to harm people by binding their consciences to an erroneous message or manipulating them to make unwise decisions (because they think God is directing them to do so). Though continuationists insist that congregational prophecy is not authoritative (at least, not at the corporate level), it is not difficult to imagine countless ways it might be abused by unscrupulous church leaders.

On the one hand, continuationists insist modern prophecy is revelation from God. On the other hand, they acknowledge it is often full of errors and mistakes, which is why they warn people never to base any future decisions on a word of prophecy. That kind of double-speak only amplifies the theological confusion inherent in the continuationist position.

In essence, the continuationist view allows people to say, "Thus says the Lord" (or "I have a word from the Lord") and then to give a message which is full of errors and therefore, in fact, is something the Lord did not say. As a result, it allows people to ascribe to the Spirit of truth messages that are not true. That borders on blasphemous presumption, and it puts its advocates in a spiritually precarious position. Obviously, that kind of error cannot be supported by Scripture. Hence, proponents of modern prophecy are ultimately forced to defend their view by appealing to anecdotes. They make their own experience the authority, rather than the clear teaching of Scripture—and that again undermines the Reformation principle of *sola Scriptura*.

6. By allowing for an irrational form of tongues-speaking (usually as a private prayer language), the Continuationist Movement opens the door to the mindless ecstasy of charismatic worship.

Continuationists generally define the gift of tongues as a devotional prayer language that is available to every believer. Unlike the apostolic gift (described in Acts 2), tongues does not primarily consist of authentic human foreign languages. Rather, it is characterized by the vocalization of incoherent strings of syllables that are subsequently labeled "the tongues of angels" or a "heavenly language." While continuationists are more careful than mainstream charismatics about controlling the practice of glossolalia in church services, tongues are still encouraged for use in private prayer.

Any affirmation of modern glossolalia—even if it is relegated only to the prayer closet—encourages believers to seek deeper spiritual intimacy with God through *mystical*, *muddled*, and even *mindless* experiences. This is a dangerous practice for believers, who are called to *renew* their minds, not *bypass* their intellectual faculties or subjugate reason to raw emotion. Any emphasis on tongues can also foster spiritual pride in the church (even as it did for the Corinthians). Those who have experienced the "gift" can easily view themselves as somehow superior to those who haven't. Moreover, the continuationist view of tongues affirms a selfish use of the gifts. First Corinthians 12 is clear that all the gifts were given for the edification of others within the body of Christ, and not for any self-aggrandizing purpose, including the manipulation of one's own passions.

Endorsing babble opens the door into broader Pentecostalism, since "speaking in tongues" is the hallmark of the Pentecostal Movement. From there, it paves a pathway to ecumenism, since this phenomenon is experienced within many doctrinally diverse groups (including Roman Catholics and even non-Christian religions). Again, the continuationist finds himself in a doctrinal dilemma: If modern tongues is a gift from the Holy Spirit, then why do Roman Catholics and other non-Christian groups, who are devoid of the Spirit, do it?

Jesus stated that true prayer should not be characterized by vain repetition, and the apostle Paul emphasized that the true God is not a God of disorder. Yet the jumbled disorder and mindless repetition of sounds without meaning stands in direct contradiction to those biblical injunctions. The continuationist view (that tongues can be something other than authentic human languages) is foreign not only to the clear description of Scripture but also to the universal testimony of church history. No one in church history equated the "gift of languages" with gibberish until the modern Charismatic Movement. The only possible exceptions come from heretics, cult groups, and false religions—all sources from which conservative evangelicals would rightly wish to distance themselves.

7. By asserting that the gift of healing has continued to the present, the continuationist position affirms the same basic premise that undergirds the fraudulent ministries of charismatic faith healers.

Continuationists define the gift of healing as the occasional ability to heal (as God so directs) primarily through the means of prayer. Such healings are not always effective, visible, or immediate in their intended results; however, those with the gift of healing, or with the gift of faith, may see their prayers for the sick answered more frequently or more quickly.

Continuationists are quick to differentiate this modern gift from the healing ministries of Christ and the apostles (as recorded in the book of Acts). Whereas those healings were clearly miraculous, immediate, public, and undeniable, the continuationist understanding of healing essentially reduces the gift of healing to a prayer for someone to get well that *might* be answered over an extended period of time. I wholeheartedly believe in the power of prayer. All cessationists do. But special acts of divine providence in answer to prayer are *not* equivalent to the miraculous gift of healing described in the New Testament. To reduce the gift in that way is to belittle what was happening in the first century of church history.

Though they attempt to distance themselves from the faith healers of the mainstream Charismatic Movement, continuationists give faith-healing swindlers unnecessary legitimacy by affirming some continuation of the biblical gift of healing. It is an outright cruelty to give any credence to fraudulent healers who prey on desperate people by selling false hope. To be fair, when evangelical continuationists take up the subject of the health-and-wealth prosperity gospel, they generally excel in their denunciation of that error. I am thankful for their condemnation of such a false gospel, and I only wish they would speak out even more on the subject. But why advocate a modern "gift of healing" at all? Doing so provides a platform for quacks and con artists. Let the gift of healing stand for what it really was: the miraculous, God-given ability to immediately heal people in the same way as Christ and His apostles.

No one today possesses such a gift. (There is a reason why no supposed healer today heals in hospitals or among the war-wounded.)

As they do with the gift of prophecy (where the accuracy of the prophecy is seen as being dependent on the faith of the prophet), continuationists tend to view the success of healings as being dependent on the faith of the healer. While this is better than placing the onus on the faith of the person being healed (as Benny Hinn and most other charismatic faith healers do), it nonetheless serves as a convenient excuse when the sick are not healed. But any kind of "healing" that leaves *most* people sick and infirm rather than healed and healthy hardly matches the biblical gift. Why not acknowledge that?

8. The continuationist position ultimately dishonors the Holy Spirit by distracting people from His true ministry while enticing them with counterfeits.

All true believers love God the Father, the Lord Jesus Christ, and the Holy Spirit. They are profoundly thankful for the Spirit's work of regeneration, indwelling, assurance, illumination, conviction, comfort, filling, and sanctifying enablement. They would never want to do anything to detract from the honor due His name, nor would they ever desire to distract others away from His true work. Albeit unintentionally, the continuationist position does that very thing.

The primary tool the Holy Spirit uses to sanctify believers is His inspired Word. By insisting that God speaks directly through intuitive revelation, mystical experiences, and counterfeit gifts, continuationists actually diminish God's true means of sanctification. As a result, believers are tempted to turn from the Word and thereby forfeit genuine spirituality, choosing instead the barrenness of subjective feelings, emotional experiences, and imaginative encounters. But truly being filled with the Spirit comes from being indwelled by the Word of God (Eph. 5:18; Col. 3:16–17). Walking in the Spirit is seen by the fruit of a changed life (cf. Gal. 5:22–23). Evidence of the Spirit's work is measured in terms of growth in holiness and Christlikeness, not emotional outbursts or ecstatic experiences.

In actuality, the continuationist position sets stumbling blocks in the path to sanctification and spiritual growth, because it endorses a paradigm with practices that do not lead toward greater holiness or Christlikeness. In that way it detracts from and interferes with the true work of the Spirit in believers' lives.

A Final Call to Action

I am convinced that the dangers inherent in the continuationist position are such that a clear warning needs to be issued. There is too much at stake for my reformed charismatic and evangelical continuationist friends to ignore the implications of their view. As leaders in the evangelical world, they wield a great deal of influence; the trajectory they set will determine the course for the next generation of young ministers and the future of evangelicalism. That is why a line in the sand needs to be drawn, and those who are willing to stand up and defend the Spirit's true work must do so.

The New Testament calls us to guard carefully that which has been entrusted to us (2 Tim. 1:14). We must stand firm on the truth of the gospel—the faith once for all delivered to the saints (Jude 3). Whoever compromises with the error and subjectivism of charismatic theology allows the enemy into the camp. I am convinced that the broader Charismatic Movement opened the door to more theological error than perhaps any other doctrinal aberration in the twentieth century (including liberalism, psychology, and ecumenism). That's a bold statement, I know. But the proof is all around us. Once experientialism is allowed to gain a foothold, there is no brand of heresy or wickedness that will not ride it into the church.

Charismatic theology is the strange fire of our generation, and evangelical Christians have no business flirting with it at any level. I cannot understand why anyone would want to legitimize a practice that has no biblical precedent—especially when the modern practice has shown itself to be a gateway to all sorts of theological error. Continuationists seem blissfully unaware of this and unconcerned by it. Their failure to notice how their teaching undermines the authority, sufficiency, and uniqueness of Scripture amounts to negligent malfeasance.

As I stated in the introduction to this book, this is the hour for the true church to respond. At a time when there is a revival of the biblical gospel and a renewed interest in the *solas* of the Reformation, it is unacceptable to stand by idly. All who are faithful to the Scriptures must rise up and condemn everything that assaults the glory of God. We are duty-bound to apply the truth in a bold defense of the sacred name of the Holy Spirit. If we claim allegiance to the Reformers, we ought to conduct ourselves with their level of courage and conviction as we contend earnestly for the faith. There must be a collective war against the pervasive abuses on the Spirit of God. This book is a call to join the cause for His honor.

My prayer is that my continuationist friends (and all who are willing to join this cause) would see the dangers in charismatic theology, that they would boldly reject that which the Bible condemns as error, and that together we would apply the mandate of Jude 23, rescuing souls from the strange fire of false spirituality.

ACKNOWLEDGMENTS

The work of Nathan Busenitz, professor of theology and church history at The Master's Seminary, was crucial in the planning, compilation, and polishing of this work. His grasp of the doctrinal and historical roots of Pentecostalism, together with his literary and theological skills, added immeasurably to the project. Without his partnership and unflagging diligence from start to finish, it would have been impossible to meet publisher's deadlines and readers' expectations. I'm profoundly grateful to Nathan, and privileged to have him as a fellow-laborer. Thanks also to Phil Johnson, who applied his deft editorial hand to the final draft. And particular thanks to Bryan Norman and the editorial staff at Thomas Nelson for editorial guidance, encouragement, and helpful suggestions along the way.

APPENDIX

VOICES FROM CHURCH HISTORY

Traditionally, charismatics have acknowledged that the miraculous gifts of the first-century church ceased sometime in early church history. Rather than arguing that the gifts have continued throughout the centuries, they contend instead that the gifts returned in 1901 when Agnes Ozman purportedly spoke in tongues. Those who hold to this view often appeal to "the former rain and the latter rain" of Joel 2:23, insisting that the former rain was the Spirit's coming at Pentecost and the latter rain was a second outpouring of the Spirit in the twentieth century. What they fail to realize is that, in the context of Joel 2, verse 23 is a promise regarding literal rainfall during the millennial kingdom. The former rain refers to autumn rain, and the latter rain to spring showers. In context, Joel was explaining that on the millennial earth both of those rains will fall "in the first month." His point was that, due to God's blessing during that future age, crops will flourish and vegetation will grow in abundance. The following verses (vv. 24–26) make that point abundantly clear. Thus, the "former and latter rain" has nothing to do with either the day of Pentecost or the modern Pentecostal Movement. To base a whole movement on an intentional misrepresentation of a passage is onerous.

Recognizing the deception of that traditional position, other charismatics have attempted to trace a line of miraculous gifts that continued throughout the entirety of church history. To do this, they either have to redefine the gifts to make them fit historical accounts (much as they redefine the gifts to fit modern experiences), or they are forced to align themselves with fringe groups like the Montanists, the extreme radicals of the Reformation, the Quakers, the Shakers, the Jansenists, the Irvingites, or even cult groups like the Mormons. Nonetheless, some continuationists insist that the charismatic position has been normative throughout church history—and that it is the cessationists who represent a new approach to the Christian life. Some have even gone so far as to claim that cessationism itself is a product of the naturalistic rationalism of the Enlightenment.

This appendix, then, is intended to help set the record straight. Not only does it prove that cessationism was not a product of the Enlightenment, but it also demonstrates the way prominent church leaders throughout history have understood the biblical teaching on this important topic. What were their conclusions regarding the perpetuation of the revelatory and miraculous gifts of the apostolic age? You be the judge.

John Chrysostom (c. 344–407)

[Commenting on 1 Corinthians 12:] "This whole place is very obscure: but the obscurity is produced by our ignorance of the facts referred to and by their cessation, being such as then used to occur but now no longer take place."[1]

Augustine (354–430)

"In the earliest times, the Holy Spirit fell upon them that believe and they spoke with tongues, which they had not learned, as the Spirit gave them utterance. These were signs adapted to the time. For there was this betokening of the Holy Spirit in all tongues to show that the gospel of God was to run through all tongues over the whole earth. That thing was done for a sign, and it passed away."[2]

"For who expects in these days that those on whom hands are laid that they may receive the Holy Spirit should forthwith begin to speak with tongues? But it is understood that invisibly and imperceptibly, on account of the bond of peace, divine love is breathed into their hearts, so that they may be able to say, 'Because the love of God is shed abroad in our hearts by the Holy Ghost which is given unto us.'"[3]

THEODORET OF CYRUS (C. 393–C. 466)

"In former times those who accepted the divine preaching and who were baptized for their salvation were given visible signs of the grace of the Holy Spirit at work in them. Some spoke in tongues which they did not know and which nobody had taught them, while others performed miracles or prophesied. The Corinthians also did these things, but they did not use the gifts as they should have done. They were more interested in showing off than in using them for the edification of the church. . . . Even in our time grace is given to those who are deemed worthy of holy baptism, but it may not take the same form as it did in those days."[4]

MARTIN LUTHER (1483–1546)

"In the early Church the Holy Spirit was sent forth in visible form. He descended upon Christ in the form of a dove (Matt. 3:16), and in the likeness of fire upon the apostles and other believers. (Acts 2:3.) This visible outpouring of the Holy Spirit was necessary to the establishment of the early Church, as were also the miracles that accompanied the gift of the Holy Ghost. Paul explained the purpose of these miraculous gifts of the Spirit in 1 Corinthians 14:22, 'Tongues are for a sign, not to them that believe, but to them that believe not.' Once the Church had been established and properly advertised by these miracles, the visible appearance of the Holy Ghost ceased."[5]

———

"Whenever you hear anyone boast that he has something by inspiration of the Holy Spirit and it has no basis in God's Word, no matter what it may be, tell him that this is the work of the devil."[6]

———

"Whatever does not have its origin in the Scriptures is surely from the devil himself."[7]

JOHN CALVIN (1509–1564)

"Though Christ does not say exactly whether He wished [miracle-working] to be an occasional gift, or one to abide in His Church for ever, yet it is more likely that miracles were only promised for the time, to add light to the new and as yet unknown Gospel. . . . We certainly see that their use ceased not long after [the apostolic age], or at least, instances of them were so rare that we may gather they were not equally common to all ages. It was the result of absurd greed and self-seeking among those who followed on [in later church history], that they made up empty fabrications in order that they should not altogether lack miracles. This threw the door wide open to Satan's lies, not only with delusions taking the place of faith, but with simple men being pulled off the right road by the pretext of signs."[8]

———

"That gift of healing, like the rest of the miracles, which the Lord willed to be brought forth for a time, has vanished away in order to make the new preaching of the gospel marvelous forever."[9]

JOHN OWEN (1616–1683)

"Gifts which in their own nature exceed the whole power of all our faculties, that dispensation of the Spirit is long since ceased and where it is now pretended unto by any, it may justly be suspected as an enthusiastic delusion."[10]

THOMAS WATSON (1620–1686)

"Sure, there is as much need of ordination now as in Christ's time and in the time of the apostles, there being then extraordinary gifts in the church which are now ceased."[11]

MATTHEW HENRY (1662–1714)

"What these gifts were is at large told us in the body of the chapter [1 Corinthians 12]; namely, extraordinary offices and powers, bestowed on ministers and Christians in the first ages, for conviction of unbelievers, and propagation of the gospel."[12]

"The gift of tongues was one new product of the Spirit of prophecy and given for a particular reason, that, the Jewish pale being taken down, all nations might be brought into the church. These and other gifts of prophecy, being a sign, have long since ceased and laid aside, and we have no encouragement to expect the revival of them; but, on the contrary, are directed to call the

Scriptures the more sure word of prophecy, more sure than voices from heaven; and to them we are directed to take heed, to search them, and to hold them fast, 2 Peter i.19."[13]

JOHN GILL (1697–1771)

"In those early times, when the gift of doing miracles was bestowed, it was not given to all, only to some; and now there are none that are possessed of it."[14]

JONATHAN EDWARDS (1703–1758)

"In the days of his [Jesus'] flesh, his disciples had a measure of the miraculous gifts of the Spirit, being enabled thus to teach and to work miracles. But after the resurrection and ascension, was the most full and remarkable effusion of the Spirit in his miraculous gifts that ever took place, beginning with the day of Pentecost, after Christ had risen and ascended to heaven. And in consequence of this, not only here and there an extraordinary person was endowed with these extraordinary gifts, but they were common in the church, and so continued during the lifetime of the apostles, or till the death of the last of them, even the apostle John, which took place about a hundred years from the birth of Christ; so that the first hundred years of the Christian era, or the first century, was the era of miracles.

"But soon after that, the canon of Scripture being completed when the apostle John had written the book of Revelation, which he wrote not long before his death, these miraculous gifts were no longer continued in the church. For there was now completed an established written revelation of the mind and will of God, wherein God had fully recorded a standing and all-sufficient rule for his church in all ages. And the Jewish church and nation being overthrown, and the Christian church and the last dispensation of the church of God being established, the miraculous gifts of the Spirit were no longer needed, and therefore they ceased; for though they had been continued in the church for so many ages, yet then they failed, and

God caused them to fail because there was no further occasion for them. And so was fulfilled the saying of the text, 'Whether there be prophecies, they shall fail; whether there be tongues, they shall cease; whether there be knowledge, it shall vanish away.' And now there seems to be an end to all such fruits of the Spirit as these, and we have no reason to expect them anymore."[15]

"The extraordinary gifts of the Spirit, such as the gift of tongues, or miracles, or prophecy, &c., are called extraordinary, because they are such as are not given in the ordinary course of God's providence. They are not bestowed in the way of God's ordinary providential dealing with his children, but only on extraordinary occasions, as they were bestowed on the Prophets and Apostles to enable them to reveal the mind and will of God before the canon of Scripture was complete, and so on the primitive church, in order to the founding and establishing of it in the world. But since the canon of the Scripture has been completed, and the Christian church fully founded and established, these extraordinary gifts have ceased."[16]

James Buchanan (1804–1870)

"The miraculous gifts of the Spirit have long since been withdrawn. They were used for a temporary purpose. They were the scaffolding which God employed for the erection of a spiritual temple. When it was no longer needed the scaffolding was taken down, but the temple still stands, and is occupied by his indwelling Spirit; for, 'Know ye not that ye are the temple of God, and that the Spirit of God dwelleth in you?' (1 Cor. iii. 16)."[17]

Robert L. Dabney (1820–1898)

"After the early church had been established, the same necessity for supernatural signs now no longer existed, and God, Who is never wasteful in His expedients, withdrew them. . . . Miracles, if they became ordinary, would cease to be miracles, and would be referred by men to customary law."[18]

CHARLES SPURGEON (1834–1892)

"Dear brother, honour the Spirit of God as you would honour Jesus Christ if he were present. If Jesus Christ were dwelling in your house you would not ignore him, you would not go about your business as if he were not there. Do not ignore the presence of the Holy Ghost in your soul. I beseech you, do not live as if you had not heard whether there were any Holy Spirit. To him pay your constant adorations. Reverence the august guest who has been pleased to make your body his sacred abode. Love him, obey him, worship him!

"Take care never to impute the vain imaginings of your fancy to Him. I have seen the Spirit of God shamefully dishonoured by persons—I hope they were insane—who have said that they have had this and that revealed to them. There has not for some years passed over my head a single week in which I have not been pestered with the revelations of hypocrites or maniacs. Semi-lunatics are very fond of coming with messages from the Lord to me, and it may spare them some trouble if I tell them once for all that I will have none of their stupid messages. . . . Never dream that events are revealed to you by heaven, or you may come to be like those idiots who dare impute their blatant follies to the Holy Ghost. If you feel your tongue itch to talk nonsense, trace it to the devil, not to the Spirit of God. Whatever is to be revealed by the Spirit to any of us is in the word of God already—he adds nothing to the Bible, and never will. Let persons who have revelations of this, that, and the other, go to bed and wake up in their senses. I only wish they would follow the advice, and no longer insult the Holy Ghost by laying their nonsense at his door."[19]

———

"They had attained the summit of piety. They had received 'the powers of the world to come.' Not miraculous gifts, which are denied us in these days, but all those powers with which the Holy Ghost endows a Christian."[20]

———

"The works of the Holy Spirit which are at this time vouchsafed to the Church of God are every way as valuable as those earlier miraculous gifts which have departed from us. The work of the Holy Spirit, by which men are quickened from their death in sin, is not inferior to the power which made men speak with tongues."[21]

———

"As a result of the ascension of Christ into heaven the church received apostles, men who were selected as witnesses because they had personally seen the Saviour—an office which necessarily dies out, and properly so, because the miraculous power also is withdrawn. They were needed temporarily, and they were given by the ascended Lord as a choice legacy. Prophets, too, were in the early church."[22]

———

"We must have the heathen converted; God has myriads of His elect among them, we must go and search for them somehow or other. Many difficulties are now removed, all lands are open to us, and distance is almost annihilated. True, we have not the Pentecostal tongues; but languages are now readily acquired, while the art of printing is a full equivalent for the lost gift."[23]

GEORGE SMEATON (1814–1889)

"The supernatural or extraordinary gifts were temporary, and intended to disappear when the Church should be founded and the inspired canon of Scripture closed; for they were an external proof of an internal inspiration."[24]

ABRAHAM KUYPER (1837–1920)

"The charismata must therefore be considered in an economical sense. The Church is a large household with many wants; an institution to be made efficient by the means of many things. They are to the Church what light and fuel are to the household; not existing for themselves, but for the family, and to be laid aside when the days are long and warm. This applies directly to the charismata, many of which, given to the apostolic Church, are not of service to the Church of the present day.[25]

WILLIAM G. T. SHEDD (1820–1894)

"The supernatural gifts of inspiration and miracles which the apostles possessed were not continued to their ministerial successors, because they were no longer necessary. All the doctrines of Christianity had been revealed to the apostles, and had been delivered to the church in a written form. There was no further need of an infallible inspiration. And the credentials and authority given to the first preachers of Christianity in miraculous acts, did not need continual repetition from age to age. One age of miracles well authenticated is sufficient to establish the divine origin of the gospel. In a human court, an indefinite series of witnesses is not required. 'By the mouth of two or three witnesses,' the facts are established. The case once decided is not reopened."[26]

BENJAMIN B. WARFIELD (1887–1921)

"These gifts . . . were part of the credentials of the Apostles as the authoritative agents of God in founding the church. Their function thus confined them to distinctively the Apostolic Church and they necessarily passed away with it."[27]

ARTHUR W. PINK (1886–1952)

"As there were offices extraordinary (apostles and prophets) at the beginning of our dispensation, so there were gifts extraordinary; and as successors were not appointed for the former, so a continuance was never intended for the latter.

The gifts were dependent upon the officers: see Acts 8:14–21; 10:44–46; 19:6; Rom. 1:11; Gal. 3:5; 2 Tim. 1:6. We no longer have the apostles with us and therefore the supernatural gifts (the communication of which was an essential part of 'the signs of an apostle:' 2 Cor. 12:12) are absent."[28]

D. Martyn Lloyd-Jones (1899–1981)

"Once these New Testament documents were written the office of a prophet was no longer necessary. Hence in the Pastoral Epistles which apply to a later stage in the history of the Church, when things had become more settled and fixed, there is no mention of the prophets. It is clear that even by then the office of the prophet was no longer necessary, and the call was for teachers and pastors and others to expound the Scriptures and to convey the knowledge of the truth.

"Again, we must note that often in the history of the Church trouble has arisen because people thought that they were prophets in the New Testament sense, and that they had received special revelations of truth. The answer to that is that in view of the New Testament Scriptures there is no need of further truth. That is an absolute proposition. We have all truth in the New Testament, and we have no need of any further revelations. All has been given, everything that is necessary for us is available. Therefore if a man claims to have received a revelation of some fresh truth we should suspect him immediately. . . .

"The answer to all this is that the need for prophets ends once we have the canon of the New Testament. We no longer need direct revelations of truth; the truth is in the Bible. We must never separate the Spirit and the Word. The Spirit speaks to us through the Word; so we should always doubt and query any supposed revelation that is not entirely consistent with the Word of God. Indeed the essence of wisdom is to reject altogether the term 'revelation' as far as we are concerned, and speak only of 'illumination'. The revelation has been given once and for all, and what we need and what by the grace of God we can have, and do have, is illumination by the Spirit to understand the Word."[29]

NOTES

Introduction: For the Sake of His Name

1. As J. C. Ryle expressed more than a century ago, "It is just as perilous to dishonor the Holy Ghost, as it is to dishonor Christ." (J. C. Ryle, "Have You the Spirit?" *Home Truths* [London: Werthem & MacIntosh, 1854], 142.)

2. Throughout this book, all three waves of the modern Pentecostal and Charismatic Movement are generally treated together—using the broad terms *charismatic* or "Charismatic Movement" as ways to refer to the entirety of the classical Pentecostal, Charismatic Renewal, and Third Wave Movements.

3. "The Charismatic Movement directly endangers the biblical understanding of mission. For there is a shift here in the central proclamation, away from Christ Crucified (1 Cor. 1:22–23; 2:2) toward the manifestations and gifts of the Holy Spirit. This leads to a certain loss of spiritual reality and balance." From the Statement of the European Convention of Confessing Fellowships at its meeting in Frankfurt, March 1990, "World Missions Following San Antonio and Manila," in *Foundations: A Journal of Evangelical Theology*, no. 26 (British Evangelical Council, Spring 1991): 16–17.

4. For example, some of the early leaders of Dallas Theological Seminary "did not hesitate to call Pentecostalism both a cult and a satanic agency, a view not uncommon among evangelicals in the 1920s" (John Hannah, *An Uncommon Union* [Grand Rapids: Zondervan, 2009], 327n61).

5. John Dart, "Charismatic and Mainline," *Christian Century*, March 7, 2006, 22–27.

6. George M. Marsden, *Reforming Fundamentalism* (Grand Rapids: Eerdmans, 1987) is a detailed account of how Fuller Seminary abandoned the principle of biblical inerrancy. Near the end of the book, Marsden reports on a course being taught in the 1980s by C. Peter Wagner (Ibid., 292–95). Marsden viewed the course, titled "Signs, Wonders, and Church Growth," as "an

anomaly" at Fuller, given the seminary's movement toward "progressive" doctrines. Marsden wrote, "The unique feature of the course was that, not only did it analyze 'signs and wonders' in Christian churches today, it also included 'practical sessions' in which signs and wonders, including actual healings, were performed in class" (Ibid., 292).

7. In much of the world, the Charismatic Movement indiscriminately absorbs the pagan ideas of local false religions into its theology. For example, in Africa, a traditional obsession with witchdoctors, demonic spirits, and ancestor worship has been largely assimilated by Pentecostal churches there. The resulting hybrid calls itself "Christian" but is actually rooted in tribal paganism. For more on this, see Conrad Mbewe, "Why Is the Charismatic Movement Thriving in Africa?" *Grace to You blog* (July 24, 2013), http://www.gty.org/Blog/B130724.

Chapter 1: Mocking the Spirit

1. Apostle Kwamena Ahinful, "Modern-Day Pentecostalism: Some Funny Oddities Which Must Be Stopped," *Modern Ghana*, September 3, 2011, http://www.modernghana.com/newsthread1/348777/1/153509; ellipses in original.

2. For example, in September 1986 a woman died of injuries sustained when someone "slain in the spirit" at a Benny Hinn rally fell on her (William M. Alnor, "News Watch," *CRI Journal*, May 10, 1994). More recently, an American woman in Illinois sued the church she was visiting when another parishioner fell backward "under the power of the Spirit" and injured her (Cf. Lyneka Little, "Evangelical Churches Catch Suits from 'Spirit' Falls," ABC News, January 27, 2012, http://abcnews.go.com/blogs/headlines /2012/01/evangelical-churches-catch-suits-from-spirit-falls/).

3. J. Lee Grady, cited by James A. Beverley, "Suzanne Hinn Files for Divorce," *Christianity Today* blog, February 19, 2010, accessed August 2102, http://blog .christianitytoday.com/ctliveblog/archives/2010/02/suzanne_hinn_fi.html.

4. "List of Scandals Involving American Evangelical Christians," *Wikipedia*, accessed May 2013, http://en.wikipedia.org/wiki/List_of_scandals_involving _evangelical_Christians. The thirty-five charismatic leaders listed at the time of this writing were: 1. Aimee Semple McPherson; 2. Lonnie Frisbee; 3. Marjoe Gortner; 4. Neville Johnson; 5. Jimmy Swaggart; 6. Marvin Gorman; 7. Jim and Tammy Bakker; 8. Peter Popoff; 9. Morris Cerullo; 10. Mike Warnke; 11. Robert Tilton; 12. Melissa Scott; 13. Jim Williams; 14. W. V. Grant; 15. Ian Bilby; 16. Frank Houston; 17. Roberts Liardon; 18. Pat Mesiti; 19. Paul Crouch; 20. Douglas Goodman; 21. Paul Cain; 22. Wayne Hughes; 23. Ted Haggard; 24. Gilbert Deya; 25. Earl Paulk; 26. Thomas Wesley Weeks, III; 27. Ira Parmenter; 28. Michael Reid; 29. Todd Bentley; 30. Michael Guglielmucci;

31. Eddie Long; 32. Marcus Lamb; 33. Stephen Green; 34. Albert Odulele; and 35. Kong Hee. The article also included an additional five who were subject to a 2007 Congressional probe for possible financial impropriety: Kenneth Copeland, Benny Hinn, Joyce Meyer, Creflo Dollar, and Paula White.

5. These videos on YouTube are well-known. Those looking for documentation can easily find these and similar examples through YouTube's search engine.

6. Benny Hinn, *Good Morning Holy Spirit* (Nashville: Thomas Nelson, 2004), 12.

7. Ché Ahn, *Spirit-Led Evangelism* (Grand Rapids: Chosen, 2006), 135.

8. Kenneth Hagin, *Understanding the Anointing* (Tulsa: Faith Library, 1983), 114–17. Rodney Howard Browne, *Flowing in the Holy Ghost*, rev. ed. (Shippensburg, PA: Destiny Image, 2000), 64. For more on the incident involving Benny Hinn, see "Elderly Woman 'Killed' by Person 'Slain in the Spirit' Falling on Her," *National & International Religion Report*, September 21, 1987, 4.

9. "Todd Bentley's Violent 'Ministry,'" accessed April 2013, http://www.youtube .com/watch?v=yN9Ay4QAtW8 (quoted excerpt starts at 5:06).

10. Thomas Lake, "Todd Bentley's Revival in Lakeland Draws 400,000 and Counting," *The Tampa Bay Times*, June 30, 2008, http://www.tampabay .com/news/religion/article651191.ece. Wagner commissioned Bentley with these words: "Your power will increase. Your authority will increase. Your favor will increase." A short time later, Wagner distanced himself from Bentley when evidence of Bentley's inappropriate relationship with a female staff member became public.

11. Benny Hinn, *Praise-a-Thon*, TBN, April 1990.

12. Suzanne Hinn at the World Outreach Center, July 1997. Her remarks were aired on Comedy Central, *The Daily Show*, "God Stuff," June 21, 1999.

13. Kenneth D. Johns, "Televangelism: A Powerful Addiction" (Bloomington, IN: Xlibris, 2006), 12.

14. Rhonda Byrne, *The Secret* (New York: Atria Books, 2006), 46. On page 59, Byrne similarly wrote, "And so the Genie of the Universe says, 'Your wish is my command!'" As George B. Davis points out, Byrne "insists that human thought, not a personal and sovereign God, rules the Universe and manipulates people, circumstances, and events in order to fulfill human desire. Ironically, this sounds like a variation of the same heresy advanced by today's prosperity preachers" (*Oprah Theology* [Bloomington, IN: Crossbooks, 2011], 74).

15. Kenneth Copeland, *Our Covenant with God* (Fort Worth, TX: KCP, 1987), 32; emphasis added.

16. *Ever Increasing Faith*, TBN broadcast, November 16, 1990.

17. Allan Anderson, *An Introduction to Pentecostalism* (Cambridge: Cambridge University Press, 2004), 221.

18. S. Michael Houdmann, ed., *God Questions?* (Enumclaw, WA: Pleasant Word, 2009), 547. Cf. Tim Stafford, *Miracles* (Grand Rapids: Baker, 2012), 162, who wrote, "In the Prosperity Gospel, wealth becomes the end, God the means to the end."

19. Like modern-day versions of Simon Magus, prosperity preachers insist the Spirit's power and blessing can be purchased with a tithe of money (cf. Acts 8:18–24).

20. Paul Crouch, "We Gave It All!" TBN newsletter, October 2011, http://www .tbn.org/about-us/newsletter?articleid=1440.

21. Paul Crouch, "Did Jesus Have Praise-a-Thons?" TBN newsletter, October 2008, http://www.tbn.org/about-us/newsletter?articleid=1218.

22. William Lobdell, "TBN's Promise: Send Money and See Riches," Part 2, *Los Angeles Times*, September 20, 2004, http://articles.latimes.com/2004 /sep/20/local/me-tbn20.

23. Crouch's Trinity Broadcasting Network is valued at well over a billion dollars. Mark I. Pinsky, "Teflon Televangelists," *Harvard Divinity Bulletin* 36, no. 1 (Winter 2008).

24. Similarly, when disappointed people at Benny Hinn's crusade are sent away without being healed, Hinn takes no responsibility. He says, "All I know is that I pray for them. What happens between them and God is between them and God" (Benny Hinn, cited in William Lobdell, "The Price of Healing," *The Los Angeles Times*, July 27, 2003, http://www.trinityfi.org /press/latimes02.html.

25. In Kenneth Hagin's booklet *How to Keep Your Healing* he tacitly acknowledged that many of his "healings" were at best temporary or at worst illusory. He blamed that fact on a lack of faith in the person seeking healing: "If you don't have enough faith in you to hold on to what you have, the devil is going to steal it away from you" (Hagin, *How to Keep Your Healing* [Tulsa: Rhema, 1989], 20–21).

26. Noting the fact that the prosperity gospel feeds on both *need* and *greed*, Paul Alexander wrote, "The world is full of suffering; that is a fact. God should care; that is a fact. The prosperity gospel combines these two facts into a preachable theology of economic hope that has the potential to take a struggling widow's last dollar. Another difficulty is that people who have plenty are taught by marketers not to be satisfied or content, so people with more than enough can still want more. Prosperity teaching exacerbates this problem when it emphasizes exorbitance by linking greed with God's blessing" (Paul Alexander, *Signs and Wonders* [San Francisco: Jossey-Bass, 2009], 69).

27. Michael Horton, *Christless Christianity* (Grand Rapids: Baker, 2008), 68.

28. For an extended discussion on the deification of human beings within Word of Faith teaching, see Hank Hanegraaff, *Christianity in Crisis: The 21st Century* (Nashville: Thomas Nelson, 2009), 129–66.

29. Paul Crouch, *Praise the Lord*, TBN, July 7, 1986. Likewise, latter rain "apostle" Earl Paulk says this: "Just as dogs have puppies and cats have kittens, so God has little gods. . . . Until we comprehend that we are little gods and we begin to act like little gods, we cannot manifest the Kingdom of God" (Earl Paulk, *Unmasking Satan* [Atlanta: K Dimension, 1984], 96–97).

30. Kenneth Copeland, "The Force of Love" (Fort Worth: Kenneth Copeland Ministries, 1987), Tape #02-0028.

31. Creflo Dollar, "Changing Your World," LeSea Broadcasting, April 17, 2002; emphasis added. On a different occasion, Dollar declared, "Now I gotta hit this thing real hard in the very beginning because I ain't got time to go through all this, but I am going to say to you right now, *you are gods*, little *g*; you are gods because you came from God and you are gods" (Creflo Dollar, "Made After His Kind," September 15, 22, 2002; emphasis added.)

32. As Allan Anderson explains, "Apart from the fact that this teaching encourages the 'American dream' of capitalism and promotes the success ethic, among its even more questionable features is the possibility that human faith is placed above the sovereignty and grace of God" (Anderson, *An Introduction to Pentecostalism*, 221).

33. Myles Munroe, *Praise the Lord*, Trinity Broadcasting Network, February 23, 2000.

34. Andrew Wommack: "The Believer's Authority," *The Gospel Truth*, April 27, 2009, http://www.awmi.net/tv/2009/week17. Cf. Andrew Wommack, *The Believer's Authority* (Tulsa, OK: Harrison House, 2009), 58–59.

35. Peter Masters, *The Healing Epidemic* (London: Wakeman Trust, 1992), 11–12.

36. John MacArthur, *Charismatic Chaos* (Grand Rapids: Zondervan, 1993).

37. In a 1991 newsletter, Jan Crouch reported, "God answered the prayers of two little twelve-year-old girls to raise our pet chicken from the dead!" ("Costa Ricans Say 'Thank You for Sending Christian Television!'" *Praise the Lord* newsletter [September 1989], 14–15). In a 2009 newsletter, her chicken story has changed. She wrote, "I *watched* Him heal my pet chicken whose eye was knocked out, *hanging* on a string, when I was 12 . . . healed in *Jesus'* name" ("Jan Crouch's Miraculous Story," TBN newsletter, June 2009, http://www.tbn.org/about/newsletter/index.php/1280.html; italics and ellipsis in original.)

38. Benny Hinn, *Praise the Lord*, TBN, October 19, 1999.

39. Cf. Thabiti Anyabwile, *The Decline of African American Theology* (Downers Grove, IL: InterVarsity, 2007), 96.

40. Benny Hinn, *This Is Your Day*, TBN, October 3, 1990.

41. "About" on Trinity Broadcasting Network's official Facebook page, accessed April 2013, https://www.facebook.com/trinitybroadcastingnetwork/info.

42. "TBN Is Reaching a Troubled World with the Hope of the Gospel," TBN announcement, April 12, 2012, http://www.tbn.org/announcements/tbn-is -reaching-a-troubled-world-with-the-hope-of-the-gospel.

43. As Candy Gunther Brown observes, "What seems most objectionable, and 'shamanistic,' to non-pentecostal Christian critics and to secular critics of American self-interested consumerism is the pentecostal concern with alleg- edly 'lower,' 'selfish,' 'this-worldly' blessings, such as healing or financial prosperity, which are often caricatured as a 'prosperity theology' or a 'health and wealth gospel' that greedy U.S. 'faith healers' have exported world- wide through their disturbingly successful use of modern communications media" (Candy Gunther Brown, introduction to *Global Pentecostal and Charismatic Healing* [Oxford: Oxford University Press, 2011], 11).

44. Paul Alexander notes the extent of this theology: "The Pentecostal prosper- ity gospel appeals to *hungry* Christians in an age of wealth and proclaims that if you have faith in God, you will be financially secure. Over 90 percent of Pentecostals and Charismatics in Nigeria, South Africa, India, and the Philippines believe that 'God will grant material prosperity to all believers who have enough faith'" (Alexander, *Signs and Wonders*, 63–64).

45. John T. Allen, *The Future Church* (New York: Doubleday, 2009), 382–83. Allen is referencing "Health and Wealth" in *Spirit and Power: A 10-Country Survey of Pentecostals*, Pew Forum on Religion and Public Life, October 2006, 30, http://www.pewforum.org/uploadedfiles/Orphan_Migrated _Content/pentecostals-08.pdf.

46. Allan Anderson wrote, "To what extent have contemporary forms of Pentecostalism become 'popular religion', in that they present only that which the masses want to hear and omit important fundamentals of the gospel of Christ? The reasons for crowds of people flocking to the new churches have to do with more than the power of the Spirit. . . . The offer of a better and more prosperous life often gives hope to people struggling in poverty and despair" (Anderson, *An Introduction to Pentecostalism*, 280).

47. Harvey Cox, speaking of the global growth of Pentecostalism, noted: "Pentecostal and Charismatic groups are well known for their emotionally explicit worship and their ecstatic utterance, which is known as 'speaking in tongues' or the 'prayer of the heart.' They are also often characterized by a related phenomenon that psychologists speak of as 'trance' or 'disso- ciative behavior.' But, as this book clearly demonstrates, the practice that initially draws most people to these groups, and the one that characterizes

them more than any other, is that they offer healing—the 'making whole' of mind, body, and spirit. Healing practices are not only integral, but they also often serve as the threshold through which new recruits pass into other dimensions of the movement" (Harvey Cox, foreword to *Global Pentecostal and Charismatic Healing* [Oxford: Oxford University Press, 2011], xviii).

48. As two scholars observe, "The fastest-growing movement within Pentecostalism has been called the Prosperity Gospel, or health-and-wealth churches. [. . . To outside observers, these churches often appear to trade in magical thinking and psychological manipulation]." (Donald E. Miller and Tetsunao Yamamori, *Global Pentecostalism* [Berkeley, CA: University of California Press, 2007], 29).

49. Vinson Synan, *An Eyewitness Remembers the Century of the Holy Spirit* (Grand Rapids: Chosen, 2010), 114–15.

50. Martin Lindhardt, *Practicing the Faith* (New York: Berghahn, 2011), 25–26.

51. "The 'Word of Faith' has been one of the most popular movements in US Pentecostalism. Not only has it been propagated in Charismatic circles, but it has influenced classical Pentecostals as well" (Anderson, *An Introduction to Pentecostalism*, 221).

52. David Jones and Russell Woodbridge, *Health, Wealth, and Happiness* (Grand Rapids: Kregel, 2011), 16.

53. "In the 1980s, this marriage was associated with hucksters and charlatans—preachers who robbed their followers, slept with prostitutes, and sobbed on camera. But in twenty-first-century America, the gospel of wealth has come of age. By linking the spread of the gospel to the habits and mores of entrepreneurial capitalism, and by explicitly baptizing the pursuit of worldly gain, prosperity theology has helped millions of believers reconcile their religious faith with their nation's seemingly unbiblical wealth and un-Christian consumer culture" (Ross Douthat, *Bad Religion* [New York: Simon & Schuster, 2012], 183).

54. Even among classic Pentecostals, the prosperity gospel has become more popular than speaking in tongues: "As *Christianity Today*'s Ted Olsen noted in 2006, only half of American Pentecostalists report having spoken in tongues—but 66 percent agreed with the premise that 'God grants believers wealth'" (Douthat, *Bad Religion*, 194).

55. Allan Anderson, introduction to *Asian and Pentecostal*, edited by Allan Anderson and Edmond Tang (Costa Mesa, CA: Rengum Books, 2005), 2. These statistics come from David B. Barrett, George T. Kurian, and Todd M. Johnson, *World Christian Encyclopedia*, 2nd ed., vol. 1. (New York: Oxford University Press, 2001). Patrick Johnstone and Jason Mandryk,

Operation World (Carlisle, UK: Paternoster, 2001), 21, 32, 34, 41, 52 have significantly lower figures. They estimate 87 million Pentecostals and charismatics in Asia, compared to 72 million in North America, 85 million in Latin America, 84 million in Africa, and 14 million in Europe.

56. Todd M. Johnson, "'It Can Be Done': The Impact of Modernity and Postmodernity on the Global Mission Plans of Churches and Agencies," *Between Past and Future*, Jonathan J. Bonk, ed. (Pasadena, CA: Evangelical Missiological Society, 2003), 10.42. Johnson notes, "In 1900 only a handful of Christians were involved in renewal movements. By A.D. 2000 over 500 million, or 25 percent of all Christians, were participants in the Pentecostal/ charismatic renewal."

57. Michael Horton is correct to note, "Celebration of the much-advertised expansion of Christianity in the two-thirds world (most notably in recent years in Philip Jenkins's *The Next Christendom*) should at least be tempered by the fact that the prosperity gospel is the most explosive version of this phenomenon" (Horton, *Christless Christianity*, 67).

58. Ted Olsen, "What Really Unites Pentecostals?" *Christianity Today*, December 5, 2006. Online at: http://www.christianitytoday.com/ct/2006 /december/16.18.html. Olsen goes on to give several specific examples: "In Nigeria, 95 percent of Pentecostals agree with that statement, and 97 percent agree that 'God will grant good health and relief from sickness to believers who have enough faith.' In the Philippines, 99 percent of Pentecostals agreed with the latter statement."

59. Jones and Woodbridge, *Health, Wealth, and Happiness*, 14–15.

60. John Ankerberg and John Weldon, writing two decades ago, warned of this blind spot in charismatic theology, "The charismatic movement as a whole has yet to integrate the great doctrinal truths of Scripture into the lives of its people. In its great emphasis upon experience with the Holy Spirit, the value of diligent study of theology is often neglected" (John Ankerberg and John Weldon, *Cult Watch* [Eugene, OR: Harvest House, 1991], viii).

61. A clear example of this is seen in Pentecostal history. The first Pentecostals initially believed they were speaking in authentic foreign languages as the apostles did in Acts 2. When it became obvious that their "tongues" actually consisted of irrational speech, it was obvious that something had to give. Regrettably, it was their interpretation of the Bible that changed, not their experience.

62. René Pache: *The Inspiration and Authority of Scripture* (Chicago: Moody, 1969), 319.

63. "There are real dangers in the 'realized eschatology' promises of instant healing, wholeness and prosperity for all. The preoccupation with these earthly concerns often comes at the expense of Christian virtues like

humility, patience and peace. The freedom of the Spirit recognized by all Pentecostals often renders them vulnerable to authoritarian leaders who may exploit their members and cause further division" (Anderson, *An Introduction to Pentecostalism*, 280).

64. In addition, as Ross Douthat points out, "Pentecostalism's entrepreneurial structure, in which every church is effectively a start-up, has always attracted ministers prone to the kind of self-aggrandizement that's more easily justified by prosperity theology than by more orthodox strands of Christian faith" (Douthat, *Bad Religion*, 194).

65. Even something as basic and straightforward as the New Testament's prohibition against female pastors (1 Tim. 2:12–14) is completely disregarded by most charismatic churches. Some of the most well-known charismatic televangelists are women, such as Joyce Meyer and Paula White.

66. Christopher J. H. Wright, *Knowing the Holy Spirit Through the Old Testament* (Downers Grove, IL: InterVarsity, 2006), 73.

Chapter 2: A New Work of the Spirit?

1. The Bible school, known as Bethel, employed a topical approach to Bible study. Historian Vinson Synan explains that the school emphasized, "the 'chain reference' idea, which was popular at the time. Major topics would be studied by following consecutive readings on the subject as they appeared in Scripture" (Vinson Synan, "The Touch Felt Around the World," *Charisma and Christian Life*, January 1991, 84). As a result, no book of the Bible was studied as a unit, and the broader context of given passages was ignored.

2. As Ralph Hood Jr. and W. Paul Williamson explain, "At his Bible school, in an all-night service, one of Parham's students, Agnes N. Ozman, received the baptism of the Holy Ghost and spoke in tongues just after midnight, January 1, 1901, thus becoming the first person ever to receive such an experience according to this new theology" (Ralph Hood Jr. and W. Paul Williamson, *Them That Believe* [Berkeley, CA: University of California Press, 2008], 18–19.

3. Charles Parham, cited in Vinson Synan, *The Holiness-Pentecostal Tradition* (Grand Rapids: Eerdmans, 1997), 44.

4. Synan, "The Touch Felt Around the World," 84.

5. As Vinson Synan explains: "The Pentecostal movement arose as a split in the holiness movement and can be viewed as the logical outcome of the holiness crusade that had vexed American Protestantism, the Methodist Church in particular, for more than forty years. The repeated calls of the holiness leadership after 1894 for a 'new Pentecost' inevitably produced the

frame of mind and the intellectual foundations for just such a 'Pentecost' to occur" (Vinson Synan, *The Holiness-Pentecostal Tradition*, 105–6).

6. As James R. Goff observes, "Parham, then, is the key to any interpretation of Pentecostal origins. He formulated the connection between Holy Spirit baptism and tongues, oversaw the initial growth and organization, and initiated the idyllic vision of xenoglossic missions. The story of his life and ministry reveals the sociological and ideological roots of Pentecostalism" (James R. Goff, *Fields White unto Harvest* [Fayetteville, AR: University of Arkansas Press, 1988], 16).

7. According to Agnes Ozman, "On January 2, some of us went down to Topeka to a mission. As we worshipped the Lord I offered prayer in English and then prayed in another language in tongues." Printed in the *Apostolic Faith*, 1951; cited from http://apostolicarchives.com/Research_Center .html. Cf. Nils Bloch-Hoell, *The Pentecostal Movement* (Oslo, Norway: Universitetforlaget, 1964), 24.

8. Cf. Jack W. Hayford and S. David Moore, *The Charismatic Century* (New York: Hachette, 2006), 38.

9. Ibid.

10. Martin E. Marty, *Modern American Religion, Volume 1: The Irony of It All: 1893–1919* (Chicago: University of Chicago Press, 1987), 240–41.

11. Joe Newman, *Race and the Assemblies of God Church* (Youngstown, NY: Cambria, 2007), 50.

12. Cf. Michael Bergunder, "Constructing Indian Pentecostalism," in *Asian and Pentecostal*, Allan Anderson and Edmond Tang, eds. (Costa Mesa, CA: Regnum Books, 2005), 181. Bergunder wrote, "In the early days, Pentecostals thought that their glossolalia was actually foreign tongues for missionary purposes. This was hitherto rather overlooked, as the Pentecostal movement quietly gave up the idea of xenoglossia later."

13. A PhD student named Charles Shumway sought in vain to prove that early Pentecostal tongues consisted of authentic foreign languages. He could not find a single person to validate the claims of the early Pentecostals (cf. Goff, *Fields White unto Harvest*, 76). In response to claims that government interpreters had validated the supposed languages, Goff states, "In his 1919 Ph.D. dissertation, Shumway censured the local *Houston Chronicle* for credulous reporting and stated that 'letters are on hand from several men who were government interpreters in or near Houston at the time [when Parham was teaching there], and they are unanimous in denying all knowledge of the alleged facts" (p. 98). The Azusa Street "tongues" were similarly recognized as non-languages by eyewitnesses who investigated them (cf. G. F. Taylor, *The Spirit and the Bride* [Falcon, NC: n.p., 1907], 52).

14. Cf. Synan, *The Holiness-Pentecostal Tradition*, 92. Vinson Synan wrote, "Parham immediately began to teach that missionaries would no longer be compelled to study foreign languages to preach in the mission fields. From henceforth, he taught, one need only receive the baptism with the Holy Ghost and he could go to the farthest corners of the world and preach to the natives in languages unknown to the speaker."

15. Charles Parham, as cited in *Topeka State Journal*, January 7, 1901.

16. Charles Parham, as cited in *Kansas City Times*, January 27, 1901.

17. "New Kind of Missionaries: Envoys to the Heathen Should Have Gift of Tongues," *Hawaiian Gazette*, May 31, 1901, 10. Online at, http://chroniclingamerica.loc.gov/lccn/sn83025121/1901-05-31/ed-1/seq-8/.

18. Hayford and Moore, *The Charismatic Century*, 42. As René Laurentin notes of Parham's view, "Repeated failures to verify the languages have discredited this functional interpretation of glossolalia" (René Laurentin, *Catholic Pentecostalism* [New York: Doubleday, 1977], 68).

19. Robert Mapes Anderson, *Vision of the Disinherited: The Making of American Pentecostalism* (New York: Oxford University Press, 1979), 90–91.

20. As Jean Gelbart notes, "On January 6, the *Topeka Daily Capital* ran a lengthy article that included a specimen of Agnes Ozman's inspired 'Chinese.' When it had been taken to a Chinese man for translation, he had responded, 'No understand. Takee to Jap.'" Jean Gelbart, "The Pentecostal Movement—A Kansas Original," *Religious Kansas: Chapters in a History*, Tim Miller, ed. (Lawrence, KS: University of Kansas, n.d), http://web.ku.edu/~ksreligion/docs/history/pentecostal_movement.pdf.

21. For an example of "writing in tongues" from the *Los Angeles Daily Times*, along with an extended explanation of the phenomenon, see Cecil M. Robeck, *The Azusa Street Mission and Revival* (Nashville: Thomas Nelson, 2006), 111–14.

22. "More Trouble," *The Times-Democrat*, [Lima, OH], September 26, 1906, 2.

23. Goff, *Fields White unto Harvest*, 5.

24. "Fanatics Admit Zion Murder," *Oakland Tribune*, September 22, 1907, 21–23. Online at http://www.newspaperarchive.com/oakland-tribune/1907-09-22/page-17.

25. Ibid.

26. Cf. Newman, *Race and the Assemblies of God Church*, 51. Newman notes, "The death of Nettie Smith [in 1904], a 9 year old, for whom her parents refused to seek medical treatment but instead sought healing through Parham's Apostolic Faith teachings, provoked an outcry against Parham that prompted him to relocate to Texas."

27. Ironically, "Parham viewed much of what he witnessed at Azusa Street as

counterfeit and discredited their experience in psychological terms" (Ann Taves, *Fits, Trances, and Visions* [Princeton, NJ: Princeton University Press, 1999], 330).

28. Newman, *Race and the Assemblies of God Church*, 53.

29. R. G. Robbins: *Pentecostalism in America* (Santa Barbara, CA: ABC-CLIO, 2010), 36.

30. Cf. Craig Borlase, *William Seymour—A Biography* (Lake Mary, FL: Charisma House, 2006), 180. Parham's proposed expedition was consistent with claims he had made earlier. As Joe Newman explains, "He claimed he would use the information he found in an old Jewish document to locate the Ark of the Covenant. According to Parham, the Ark's contents would provoke massive numbers of Jews to return to the Holy Land. Parham believed the English-speaking people were descendants of the Ten Lost Tribes of Israel that disappeared into Assyrian captivity in 722 B.C.E. Therefore, he believed Americans should support Zionism" (Newman, *Race and the Assemblies of God Church*, 51–52).

31. Goff, *Fields White unto Harvest*, 146.

32. "His views on eternal life—like his opinions on other doctrines—evolved over several years. In 1902 he issued a disjointed statement asserting that the majority of humankind would receive 'everlasting human life': 'A promised Savior for mankind: the plan was to restore the mass of the human race to what they lost in the fall of Adam, which the unsanctified and many heathens will receive—everlasting human life. Orthodoxy would cast this entire company into an eternal burning hell; but our God is a God of love and justice, and the flames will reach those only who are utterly reprobate.'" Edith Waldvogel Blumhofer, *Restoring the Faith: The Assemblies of God, Pentecostalism, and American Culture* (Champaign, IL: University of Illinois, 1998), 45.

33. Ibid., 46.

34. Ibid., 47.

35. Anglo-Israelism is aggressively promoted today by the "Christian Identity" movement, a quasi-religious white supremacist philosophy.

36. *Houston Daily Post*, August 13, 1905. Cited in Borlase, *William Seymour—A Biography*, 74–75.

37. Grant Wacker, *Heaven Below* (Cambridge, MA: Harvard University Press, 2003), 232.

38. Frederick Harris, *The Price of the Ticket* (New York: Oxford University Press, 2012), 89. Grant Wacker tempers this slightly when he notes, "In the end, Parham seemed as unsure of African Americans as they seemed of him" (Wacker, *Heaven Below*, 232).

39. Hayford and Moore, *Charismatic Century*, 46.

40. Ibid. The authors write, "Initial evidence as it would be called, though not embraced by every Pentecostal group, became the most identifying characteristic of the emerging new movement born in the first decade of the twentieth century. Parham was its architect."

41. Anthony C. Thiselton, *The Hermeneutics of Doctrine* (Grand Rapids: Eerdmans, 2007), 438. Some Pentecostals argue that, while Parham was the movement's "theological founder," Seymour deserves equal credit for popularizing the movement (cf. Hayford and Moore, *Charismatic Century*, chap. 3). It should be noted, however, that Parham was Seymour's teacher and pneumatological mentor; and it was Parham who provided the doctrinal framework for the Azusa Street revival. As Michael Bergunder notes, "Charles Parham created the threefold theological formula that was used at Azusa Street: 1) Tongues speech as the initial evidence of Holy Spirit Baptism, 2) Spirit-filled believers as the 'sealed' Bride of Christ, and 3) Xenoglossic tongues as the tool for dramatic endtime revival" (Bergunder, "Constructing Indian Pentecostalism," 181).

42. For more on the close connections between the nineteenth-century Holiness Movement and Pentecostalism, see Donald W. Dayton, "Methodism and Pentecostalism," in *The Oxford Handbook of Methodist Studies* (New York: Oxford University Press, 2009), 184–86.

43. Roger E. Olson notes, "Holiness Christians believe that any true believer in Jesus Christ can experience a complete cleansing from original sin and from the 'carnal nature' (sinful, fallen human nature) that 'wars against the Spirit.' This experience is known as 'entire sanctification,' 'eradication of the sinful nature,' and 'Christian perfection'" (Roger E. Olson, *The Westminster Handbook to Evangelical Theology* [Louisville, KY: Westminster John Knox, 2004], 79).

44. As Vinson Synan explains, "In his 1891 book, *Pentecost*, [R. C.] Horner taught that the baptism of the Holy Spirit was in reality a 'third work' of grace subsequent to salvation and sanctification which empowered the believer for service. This view was elaborated in his two volume work *Bible Doctrines* which appeared in 1909. Also prominent in Horner's meetings were such 'physical manifestations' as 'prostration,' 'ecstasy,' and 'immediate laughter,' which led to his being separated from the Methodist church. The most far-reaching effect of Horner's teaching was to separate in time and purpose the experiences of second-blessing sanctification and the 'third blessing' of 'baptism in the Holy Spirit,' a theological distinction that became crucial to the development of Pentecostalism" (Synan, *The Holiness-Pentecostal Tradition*, 50).

45. E. W. Kenyon, cited in Simon Coleman, *The Globalisation of Charismatic Christianity* (Cambridge: Cambridge University Press, 2000), 45.

46. David Jones and Russell S. Woodbridge explain the impact of this school on Kenyon's thinking: "Charles Emerson, the president of the school, was a minister of Unitarian and Universalist churches in New England and later became a practitioner of Christian Science. . . . [Also], Ralph Waldo Trine, the evangelist of New Thought, was a classmate of Kenyon at the Emerson School. While it is not clear exactly how much Kenyon observed while under Emerson's tutelage, as his later thought reveals, he clearly became familiar with the core tenets of New Thought" (Jones and Woodbridge, *Health, Wealth, and Happiness*, 51).

47. Cf. Dennis Hollinger, "Enjoying God Forever," *The Gospel and Contemporary Perspectives*, vol. 2, ed. Douglas J. Moo (Grand Rapids: Kregel, 1997), 22.

48. Ibid.

49. Coleman, *The Globalisation of Charismatic Christianity*, 45.

50. Cf. Allan Anderson, "Pentecostalism," in *Global Dictionary of Theology*, eds. William A. Dyrness and Veli-Matti Karkkainen (Downers Grove, IL: InterVarsity, 2008), 645.

51. E. W. Kenyon, *Jesus the Healer* (Seattle: Kenyon's Gospel Publishing Society, 1943), 26. Cited in Jones and Woodbridge, *Health, Wealth, and Happiness*, 52.

52. E. W. Kenyon, cited in Dale H. Simmons, *E. W. Kenyon and the Postbellum Pursuit of Peace, Power, and Plenty* (Lanham, MD: Scarecrow, 1997), 172.

53. Kenyon once stated, "It makes no difference what the symptoms may be in the body. I laugh at them and in the Name of Jesus I command the author of the disease to leave my body" (cited in Hollinger, "Enjoying God Forever," 23).

54. E. W. Kenyon, cited in Simmons, *E. W. Kenyon*, 235; emphasis added.

55. Ibid., 246.

56. Hollinger, "Enjoying God Forever," 23.

57. Cf. Anderson, "Pentecostalism," 645. Allan Anderson notes, "The development of the movement was stimulated by the teachings of healing evangelists like William Branham and Oral Roberts, contemporary popular televangelists, and the charismatic movement."

58. Cf. D. R. McConnell, *A Different Gospel* (Peabody, MA: Hendrickson, 1988), 8–12.

59. Harvey Cox, "Foreword" in *Global Pentecostal and Charismatic Healing*, by Candy Gunther Brown (Oxford: Oxford University Press, 2011), xviii.

60. Timothy C. Tennent, *Theology in the Context of World Christianity* (Grand Rapids: Zondervan, 2007), 2. Cf. Allan Anderson, who wrote of the movement in Africa: "The 'Pentecostalization' of African Christianity can be called the 'African Reformation' of the twentieth century that has

fundamentally altered the character of African Christianity, including that of the older, 'mission' churches" (*An Introduction to Pentecostalism* [Cambridge: Cambridge University Press, 2004], 104).

61. Vinson Synan, *An Eyewitness Remembers the Century of the Holy Spirit* (Grand Rapids: Chosen, 2010), 157.

62. As Robyn E. Lebron notes, "Pentecostal pioneers were hungry for authentic Christianity, and they looked to previous spiritual outpourings, such as the First Great Awakening (1730s–1740s) and Second Great Awakening (1800s–1830s), for inspiration and instruction" (Robyn E. Lebron, *Searching for Spiritual Unity* [Bloomington, IN: Crossbooks, 2012], 27).

63. Russell Sharrock wrote, "While theologically Methodism has exercised the foremost influence on the Pentecostal Movement, methodologically Revivalism (particularly American Revivalism) has been the most determining influence. The American predecessor and contemporary of Methodism, the Great Awakening, and its unique child, Frontier Revivalism, drastically changed American understanding, usage, and application of Christian faith. . . . Revivalism's distinct contribution to American religion, and thus to Pentecostalism, was the individualizing and emotionalizing of the Christian faith" (Russel Sharrock, *Spiritual Warfare* [Morrisville, NC: Lulu Enterprises, 2007], 115).

64. Justo L. Gonzalez, *The Story of Christianity*, vol. 2 (Grand Rapids: Zondervan, 2010), 289.

65. Douglas Gordon Jacobsen, introduction to *A Reader in Pentecostal Theology* (Bloomington, IN: Indiana University Press), 6.

66. Charles Chauncy, cited in Michael J. McClymond, "Theology of Revival" in *The Encyclopedia of Christianity*, vol. 5, ed. Erwin Fahlbusch (Grand Rapids: Eerdmans, 2008), 437.

67. George Marsden, *A Short Life of Jonathan Edwards* (Grand Rapids: Eerdmans, 2008), 68.

68. Ibid., 65–66.

69. Cf. Philip F. Gura, *Jonathan Edwards: America's Evangelical* (New York: Hill and Wang, 2005), 119–20.

70. Marsden, *A Short Life of Jonathan Edwards*, 70–71.

71. For example, the apostle Paul notes in 2 Corinthians 7:10 that emotions of sorrow can be either from God (leading to repentance) or from the world (leading to death).

72. Marsden, *A Short Life of Jonathan Edwards*, 71.

73. Douglas Sweeney, *Jonathan Edwards* (Downers Grove, IL: InterVarsity, 2009), 120–21. Sweeney notes that Edwards continued this theme in "a spate of publications on revival—*Distinguishing Marks of a Work of*

the Spirit of God (1741), *Some Thoughts Concerning the Present Revival of Religion in New England* (1743), *Religious Affections* (1746), and *True Grace, Distinguished from the Experience of Devils* (1753)—which, taken together, represent the most important body of literature in all of Christian history on the challenge of discerning a genuine work of the Holy Spirit."

74. Edwards similarly noted that emotional responses were not the true test of personal conversion. Rather, true revival would produce long-term fruit—a visible change in the behavior and lifestyle of those affected by the Spirit's work. In his *Religious Affections*, Edwards explained that "Christian practice is the sign of signs, in this sense that it is the great evidence, which confirms and crowns all other signs of godliness. There is no one grace of the Spirit of God, but that Christian practice is the most proper evidence of the truth of it" (Jonathan Edwards, *Religious Affections* [New Haven: Yale, 1959], 444).

75. As Douglas A. Sweeney notes, "[Edwards's] burden during the rest of his revivalistic ministry was to help others discern the Spirit's presence in their lives—to 'try the spirits,' distinguishing God's Spirit from counterfeits" (Sweeney, *Jonathan Edwards*, 120).

76. Cf. R. C. Sproul and Archie Parrish, introduction to *The Spirit of Revival: Discovering the Wisdom of Jonathan Edwards* (Wheaton, IL: Crossway, 2008).

77. Jonathan Edwards, "The Distinguishing Marks of a Work of the Spirit of God." This excerpt is from a version adapted and abridged for modern readers in Appendix 2 of John MacArthur, *Reckless Faith* (Wheaton, IL: Crossway, 1994), 219.

Chapter 3: Testing the Spirits (Part 1)

1. The incarnation—that God the Son became a real human being—is an essential part of the gospel. If Jesus Christ did not truly come in the flesh, He would have been unable to pay sin's penalty on the cross since His physical death would have been merely an illusion. He would not have been able to act as the perfect Mediator between God and man, since He Himself would have never actually experienced human existence (cf. Heb. 2:17–18).

2. Jonathan Edwards, "The Distinguishing Marks of a Work of the Spirit of God," *The Great Awakening* (New Haven: Yale, 1972), 249.

3. Ibid., 250.

4. Jack W. Hayford and S. David Moore, *The Charismatic Century* (New York: Warner Faith, 2006), chap. 1. I; emphasis in original.

5. Steven J. Lawson, *Men Who Win* (Colorado Springs: NavPress, 1992), 173.

6. Cf. Lee E. Snook, *What in the World Is God Doing?* (Minneapolis: Augsburg Fortress, 1999), 28. Snook wrote, "In practice, these churches frequently subordinate the Son, the incarnate Word of God, to the Spirit, again

implying that unless a person has received the Spirit, as these churches understand the Spirit, even faith in Christ is suspected as formalistic, insincere, and of questionable sufficiency for salvation."

7. Kenneth D. Johns, *The Pentecostal Paradigm* [Bloomington, IN: Xlibris, 2007], 23. On this point, Thomas Edgar reports the perspective of Donald W. Dayton: "Dayton says that this is more than a mere shift in terminology, since 'when "Christian perfection" becomes "baptism of the Holy Ghost" there is a major theological transformation.' A few of the changes he mentions are 'a shift from Christocentrism to an emphasis on the Holy Spirit that is really quite radical in character,' 'a new emphasis on power,' and a shift from 'emphasis on the goal and nature of the "holy" life to an event in which this takes place' " (Thomas R. Edgar, *Satisfied by the Promise of the Spirit* [Grand Rapids: Kregel, 1996], 218). According to Dayton, the shift began to take place from "a Christocentric pattern of thought and closer to a Pneumatocentric one" beginning with John Fletcher, the Methodist successor to John Wesley (Donald W. Dayton, *Theological Roots of Pentecostalism* [Peabody, MA: Hendrickson, 1987], 52). Dayton and Faupel argue further that "in Pentecostalism there was a shift from Christology to pneumatology that emphasizes the Spirit over against Christ" (Peter Althouse, *Spirit of the Last Days* [London: T&T Clark, 2003], 63). Cf. Karla O. Poewe, "Rethinking the Relationship of Anthropology to Science and Religion," in *Charismatic Christianity as a Global Culture* [Columbia, SC: University of South Carolina Press, 1994], 239, who notes that charismatic churches put the "emphasis on the 'Holy Spirit' (rather than Christ)."

8. Johns, *The Pentecostal Paradigm*, 23.

9. Frank Viola, *From Eternity to Here* (Colorado Springs: David C. Cook, 2009), 295.

10. Ronald E. Baxter, *Charismatic Gift of Tongues* (Grand Rapids: Kregel, 1981), 125–26.

11. Charismatic author Timothy Sims acknowledges, "If we, as members of the charismatic Christian community, want to return to a position of balance and credibility within the Church, we must understand one thing. We must realize that over emphasis eventually leads to error! Therefore we must begin again to place the emphasis upon the redemptive work of Christ, and the true riches available through His death, burial and resurrection. Only then can we hope to repair and restore some of the credibility we've lost, thereby bringing healing to those who have been affected by our misguided messages" (Timothy Sims, *In Defense of the Word of Faith* [Bloomington, IN: AuthorHouse, 2008], 131). J. Lee Grady, editor of *Charisma* magazine, recognizes this same problem: "The Spirit did not come to elevate Himself; He was sent to glorify Christ. In all our emphasis on the Holy Spirit's ministry and gifts and power, let's be

careful to magnify the One the Spirit came to magnify" (J. Lee Grady, *What Happened to the Fire?* [Grand Rapids: Chosen, 1994], 172).

12. Rick M. Nañez, *Full Gospel, Fractured Minds?* (Grand Rapids: Zondervan, 2005), 76. According to Nañez, Gee also criticized other aspects of the Pentecostal Movement, such as: "The manufacturing of doctrine plucked from isolated texts, interpretation of Scripture based on mere opinion, mistaking feelings for faith, and sidestepping responsibility in lieu of so-called Spirit-leadings—all were indictments that he leveled against the Full Gospel fellowships of his era."

13. J. Hampton Keathley, *ABCs for Christian Growth* (Richardson, TX: Biblical Studies Foundation, 2002), 204. Keathley wrote, "The Holy Spirit calls attention to neither Himself nor to man, but focuses all attention on the Lord Jesus Christ and what God has done in and through His Son. His purpose via all His ministries is to develop our faith, hope, love, adoration, obedience, fellowship, and *commitment to Christ*. This truth and this focus becomes a criterion by which we may judge any spiritual movement and its biblical authenticity." (Emphasis original.)

14. As Floyd H. Barackman notes, "We should be suspicious of any movement or ministry that exalts the Holy Spirit above the Lord Jesus, for it is the Holy Spirit's purpose to bear witness to Jesus and to exalt Him (John 15:26; 16:14–15)" (Floyd H. Barackman, *Practical Christian Theology* [Grand Rapids: Kregel, 2001], 212).

15. It should be noted that, in focusing on the Holy Spirit, charismatics generally emphasize only the supposed gifts and power of the Spirit. In the process, they ignore the fruit of the Spirit as well as the Spirit's work of regeneration, sanctification, illuminating, sealing, and so on. As Michael Catt observes, speaking of charismatics, "Since the early part of the twentieth century, believers have become obsessed with the gifts of the Spirit rather than the fruit of the Spirit" (Michael Catt, *The Power of Surrender* [Nashville: B&H, 2005], 188).

16. Matthew Henry, *Matthew Henry's Commentary on the New Testament*, comment on John 16:16–22.

17. Kevin DeYoung, *The Holy Spirit* (Wheaton, IL: Crossway, 2011), 17. Internal citation from J. I. Packer, *Keep in Step with the Spirit* (Grand Rapids: Baker, 2005), 57 (italics in original).

18. As Selwyn Hughes explains, "The whole purpose of the Spirit's coming was not to glorify Himself or the person who receives Him, but to glorify Jesus. . . . If He glorified Himself, then it would make Christianity Spirit-centered rather than Christ-centered. Christianity that is not linked to the Incarnation can have no fixed idea as to what God is really like. Spirit-centered Christianity would leave us going off on a tangent into all kinds

of weird areas of subjectivity" (Selwyn Hughes, *Every Day with Jesus Bible* [Nashville: Holman Bible, 2003], 745).

19. Bruce Ware, *Father, Son, and Holy Spirit* (Wheaton, IL: Crossway, 2005), 123.

20. D. Martyn Lloyd-Jones, *Great Doctrines of the Bible: God the Holy Spirit* (Wheaton, IL: Crossway, 2003), 2:20; emphasis added.

21. James Montgomery Boice, *Foundations of the Christian Faith* (Downers Grove, IL: InterVarsity, 1986), 381.

22. Charles R. Swindoll, *Growing Deep in the Christian Life* (Portland, OR: Multnomah, 1986), 188.

23. Dan Phillips, *The World-Tilting Gospel* (Grand Rapids: Kregel, 2011), 272–73.

24. Alexander MacLaren similarly taught, "Try the spirits. If anything calling itself Christian teaching comes to you and does not glorify Christ, it is self-condemned. For none can exalt Him highly enough, and no teaching can present Him too exclusively and urgently as the sole Salvation and Life of the whole earth. And if it be, as my text tells us, that the great teaching Spirit is to come, who is to 'guide us into all truth,' and therein is to glorify Christ, and to show us the things that are His, then it is also true, 'Hereby know we the Spirit of God. Every spirit that confesseth that Jesus Christ is come in the flesh is of God; and every spirit that confesseth not that Jesus Christ is come in the flesh is not of God. And this is the spirit of Antichrist'" (Alexander MacLaren, *Expositions of St. John, Chapters 15–21* [repr. Kessinger, n.d.], 81).

25. Korean pastor David (Paul) Yonggi Cho "was dying of tuberculosis [when he] was converted to Christianity. He recovered and aspired to be a medical doctor, but Jesus later appeared to him in the middle of the night dressed as a fireman, called him to preach, and filled him with the Holy Spirit" (D. J. Wilson, "Cho, David Yonggi," *The New International Dictionary of Pentecostal and Charismatic Movements*, ed. Stanley M. Burgess [Grand Rapids: Zondervan, 2002], 521).

26. "Oral Roberts tells of talking to 900-foot Jesus," *Tulsa World*, October 16, 1980, http://www.tulsaworld.com/news/article.aspx?articleid=20080326 _222_67873.

27. Linda Cannon, *Rapture* (Bloomington, IN: AuthorHouse, 2011), 16, 63, 107–8.

28. Heidi and Rolland Baker, *Always Enough* (Grand Rapids: Chosen, 2003), chap. 4.

29. Bishop Tom Brown reports that he saw Jesus "sitting in a wheelchair with a blanket over his legs" (Tom Brown, "What Does Jesus Really Look Like?" [El Paso, TX: Tom Brown Ministries, n.d.], accessed September 2012, http://www.tbm.org/whatdoes.htm.

30. Choo Thomas, *Heaven Is So Real!* (Lake Mary, FL: Charisma, 2006), 23.

31. Jeff Parks, cited in Brenda Savoca, *The Water Walkers* (Maitland, FL: Xulon, 2010), 163.

32. In the words of Creflo Dollar, "If Jesus came as God, then why did God have to anoint Him? Jesus came as a man, that's why it was legal to anoint him. God doesn't need anointing, He is anointing. Jesus came as man, and at age 30 God is now getting ready to demonstrate to us, and give us, an example of what a man, with the anointing, can do" (Creflo Dollar, "Jesus' Growth into Sonship," audio, December 8, 2002).

33. Cf. Kenneth Copeland, "Why didn't Jesus openly proclaim himself as God during his 33 years on earth? For one single reason. He hadn't come to earth as God, he'd come as man" (Kenneth Copeland, cited in Jones and Woodbridge, *Health, Wealth, & Happiness*, 70).

34. In the words of Benny Hinn: "He [Jesus] who is righteous by choice said, 'The only way I can stop sin is by me becoming it. I can't just stop it by letting it touch me; I and it must become one.' Hear this! He who is the nature of God became the nature of Satan when he became sin!" (Benny Hinn, *This Is Your Day*, TBN, December 1, 1990). Kenneth Copeland similarly taught, "The righteousness of God was made to be sin. He accepted the sin nature of Satan in His own spirit. And at the moment that He did so, He cried, 'My God, My God, why hast thou forsaken Me?' You don't know what happened at the cross. Why do you think Moses, upon instruction of God, raised the serpent upon that pole instead of a lamb? That used to bug me. I said, 'Why in the world would you want to put a snake up there; the sign of Satan? Why didn't you put a lamb on that pole?' And the Lord said, 'Because it was a sign of Satan that was hanging on the cross.' He said, 'I accepted, in my own spirit, spiritual death; and the light was turned off'" (Kenneth Copeland, "What Happened from the Cross to the Throne," 1990, audiotape #02-0017, side 2).

35. In the words of Kenneth Hagin, "Jesus tasted spiritual death for every man. And his Spirit and inner man went to hell in my place. Can't you see that? Physical death wouldn't remove your sins. He's tasted death for every man. He's talking about tasting spiritual death" (cited in Jones and Woodbridge, *Health, Wealth, & Happiness*, 70). For a full academic treatment of this teaching in Word of Faith circles, see William P. Atkinson, *The 'Spiritual Death' of Jesus* (Leiden, Netherlands: Brill, 2009).

36. Kenneth Copeland, *Believer's Voice of Victory*, TBN, April 21, 1991.

37. Dollar, "Jesus' Growth into Sonship."

38. For more on this, see chapter 1.

39. Kenneth Copeland, "Take Time to Pray," *Believer's Voice of Victory* 15, no. 2 (February 1987): 9.

40. Jeremy Morris, *The Church in the Modern Age* (New York: I. B. Tauris, 2007), 197.

41. Anderson, *An Introduction to Pentecostalism*, 152.

42. "Healing, prophesying, and speaking in tongues are common things to see at Charismatic Catholic services. . . . Charismatic Catholics are no different from other kinds of Catholic believers in terms of spiritual leadership. All look to Vatican City in Italy and to the worldwide leader of the Roman Catholic Church the Pope" (Katie Meier, "Charismatic Catholics," *Same God, Different Churches* [Nashville: Thomas Nelson, 2005], n.p. Google Books edition. Online at: books.google.com/books?isbn=1418577685.

43. The Latin phrase *ex opere operato* means "by the work worked," or (according to *The Catechism of the Catholic Church*) literally: "by the very fact of the actions being performed.'" In the Roman Catholic system, then, sacraments are not merely signs, symbols, and witnesses of divine grace toward believers; they are essential instrumental causes for the conferring of grace. Catholic doctrine treats the sacraments as meritorious works deemed necessary for salvation. The seven sacraments are baptism, confirmation, eucharist, penance, anointing of the sick, holy orders, and matrimony. Of those seven, only baptism and eucharist are proper ordinances for the church. But "the [Roman Catholic] Church affirms that for believers the [seven] sacraments of the New Covenant are necessary for salvation" (U.S. Catholic Church, *Catechism of the Catholic Church*, 2nd ed. [New York: Doubleday Religion, 2006], 319).

44. Emilio Antonio Nunez, *Crisis and Hope in Latin America* (Pasadena, CA: William Carey Library, 1996), 306. Nunez wrote, "It seems that most Catholic charismatics have not abandoned their Marian devotion. They continue to believe in their love for Mary. They venerate her as never before."

45. T. P. Thigpen, "Catholic Charismatic Renewal," *The New International Dictionary of Pentecostal and Charismatic Movements* (Grand Rapids: Zondervan, 2002), 465.

46. National and International Religion Report, *Signswatch*, Winter 1996; cited in Walter J. Veith, *Truth Matters* (Delta, BC: Amazing Discoveries, 2007), 298.

47. Along those lines, R. Andrew Chesnut explains that "Charismatic Catholicism and Pentecostalism share the common element of pneumacentrism; and one of the primary functions of the Spirit is to heal individual believers of their earthly afflictions" (R. Andrew Chesnut, "Brazilian Charism," in *Introducing World Christianity*, ed. Charles E. Farhadian [Oxford: Wiley-Blackwell, 2012], 198).

48. David K. Bernard, "The Future of Oneness Pentecostalism," in *The Future*

of Pentecostalism in the United States, eds. Eric Patterson and Edmund Rybarczyk (Lanham, MD: Lexington, 2007), 124.

49. As Peter Hocken observes, "While the Oneness churches (e.g. the white United Pentecostal Church, the black Pentecostal Assemblies of the World) have generally not been in active fellowship with Trinitarian Pentecostals, who regard their doctrine as deviant, they have always been regarded as still somehow within the Pentecostal movement" (Peter Hocken, *The Challenges of the Pentecostal, Charismatic, and Messianic Jewish Movements* [Burlington, VT: Ashgate, 2009], 23).

50. William K. Kay, *Pentecostalism* (London: SCM, 2009), 14. John Ankerberg and John Weldon similarly note, "The Pentecostal, charismatic, and Positive Confession movements in this country might be in more serious spiritual condition than they realize. Those Christians who are part of these movements need to carefully evaluate what their leaders are teaching (or failing to teach). For example, at least one-fourth of all Pentecostals, representing over 5000 churches and millions of professed Christians, are members of the United Pentecostal Church, an organization which adamantly denies the Trinity and teaches other serious errors" (John Ankerberg and John Weldon, *Cult Watch* [Eugene, OR: Harvest House, 1991], viii).

51. Gregg Allison, *Historical Theology* (Grand Rapids: Zondervan,), 235–36.

52. Interview with Joel Osteen, *Larry King Live*, CNN, aired June 20, 2005. Transcript available at http://transcripts.cnn.com/TRANSCRIPTS /0506/20/lkl.01.html.

53. Interview with Joel Osteen, *Fox News Sunday with Chris Wallace*, FOX News, aired December 23, 2007. Partial transcript available at http://www .foxnews.com/story/0,2933,318054,00.html.

54. Joseph Smith, *History of The Church of Jesus Christ of Latter-day Saints*, 7 vols., introduction and notes by B. H. Roberts (Salt Lake City: The Church of Jesus Christ of Latter-day Saints, 1932–1951), 2:428. Smith reported, "Brother George A. Smith arose and began to prophesy, when a noise was heard like the sound of a rushing mighty wind, which filled the Temple, and all the congregation simultaneously arose, being moved upon by an invisible power; many began to speak in tongues and prophesy; others saw glorious visions; and I beheld the Temple was filled with angels, which fact I declared to the congregation."

55. George A. Smith, cited in *Journal of Discourses*, 26 vols. (London: Latter-day Saints' Book Depot, 1854–1886), 11:10.

56. Benjamin Brown, "Testimony for the Truth," *Gems for the Young Folks* (Salt Lake City: Juvenile Instructor Office, 1881), 65.

57. Anderson, *An Introduction to Pentecostalism*, 24, explains that "Mormons practiced speaking in tongues in the early years, but discouraged its

practice later." Cf. Donald G. Bloesch, *The Holy Spirit* (Downers Grove, IL: InterVarsity, 2000), 180–81.

58. Cf. Edgar, *Satisfied by the Promise of the Spirit*, 218, 108.

59. Rob Datsko and Kathy Datsko, *Building Bridges Between Spirit-Filled Christians and Latter-Day Saints (Mormons)* (eBookIt, 2011), 16.

60. Cf. Grant Wacker, *Heaven Below* (Cambridge, MA: Harvard University Press, 2003), 180.

61. See the book by Fuller Seminary's president, Richard Mouw, titled *Talking with Mormons: An Invitation to Evangelicals* (Grand Rapids: Eerdmans, 2012). As the title suggests, it is an encouragement for evangelical Christians to engage in dialogue with Mormons for the purpose of greater unity.

62. John T. Allen, *The Future Church* (New York: Doubleday, 2009), 382–83. Allen explains, "Perhaps the most controversial element of the Pentecostal outlook is the so-called 'prosperity gospel,' meaning the belief that God will reward those with sufficient faith with both material prosperity and physical health. Some analysts distinguish between 'neo-Pentecostal,' which they see as focused on the prosperity gospel, and classic Pentecostalism, oriented toward the gifts of the Spirit such as healings and tongues. Yet the Pew Forum data suggests that the prosperity gospel is actually a defining feature of all Pentecostalism; majorities of Pentecostals exceeding 90 percent in most countries hold to these beliefs."

63. Anderson, *An Introduction to Pentecostalism*, 221. Anderson wrote, "Apart from the fact that this teaching encourages the 'American dream' of capitalism and promotes the success ethic, among its even more questionable features is the possibility that human faith is placed above the sovereignty and grace of God. Faith becomes a condition for God's action and the strength of faith is measured by results. Material and financial prosperity and health are sometimes seen as evidence of spirituality and the positive and necessary role of persecution and suffering is often ignored."

64. Daniel J. Bennett, *A Passion for the Fatherless* (Grand Rapids: Kregel, 2011), 86.

65. Bruce Bickel and Stan Jantz, *I'm Fine with God . . . It's Christians I Can't Stand* (Eugene, OR: Harvest House, 2008), 94.

66. Cf. John Phillips, *Exploring the Pastoral Epistles* (Grand Rapids: Kregel, 2004), 349–50. Phillips notes: "No one in Bible times preached what, in our pampered age, is called the prosperity gospel. This false gospel espouses the 'name-it-claim-it' philosophy. It says that health and wealth are the birthright of every believer. The whole concept is foreign to the New Testament, to personal experience, and to church history. The prosperity gospel is based on a total failure to distinguish between the Old Testament blessing and the New Testament blessing, between the nation of Israel and the church of God, and between God's earthly people and His heavenly people."

67. In his treatise on the *Distinguishing Marks of a Work of the Spirit of God*, Edwards also listed a number of criteria that, he believed, did not conclusively prove or disprove the Spirit's involvement. For example, Edwards contended that just because certain aspects of a movement are extraordinary or novel does not automatically disqualify it from being considered a true work of the Spirit. The fact that people respond with weeping and other physical displays of emotion does not prove anything either. Nor does the fact that the work produces strong impressions on people's imaginations— something Edwards noted was categorically different from the visions experienced by the biblical prophets. Edwards even suggested that just because some of the people involved behave in strange and imprudent ways, or even if some of them fall away into gross errors and scandalous practices, it does not necessarily prove that the work *as a whole* is not from the Spirit. (Interestingly, Edwards included the extrabiblical charismatic emphases of the radical Reformers during the Protestant Reformation as an example of erroneous practices that nevertheless did not disprove the authenticity of the Reformation.) In making these provisions, Edwards was clearly talking about unorthodox and undesirable *exceptions*, not *the rule*. His discussion of the "positive signs" found in 1 John 4:1–8 makes it clear that Edwards would never regard a movement that was *characterized* by false doctrine or scandalous behavior as being empowered by the Holy Spirit. In the same way that he denounced the ecstatic and mystical experiences of the Quakers and others like them, Edwards would undoubtedly have deplored what goes on in mainstream charismatic circles.

Chapter 4: Testing the Spirits (Part 2)

1. Jonathan Edwards, "Distinguishing Marks," 250–51. In his treatise on the *Religious Affections*, Edwards reiterated the truth that a holy life is the only sure sign of personal revival.

2. Mark J. Cartledge says of Pentecostalism: "It is largely a religion of the poor, with an estimated 87 percent of Pentecostals living below the poverty line (Barrett and Johnson 2002: 284). But it is also a tradition often associated with a gospel of health and wealth, especially in developing nations and regions" (Mark J. Cartledge, "Pentecostalism," in *The Wiley-Blackwell Companion to Practical Theology* [Chichester, West Sussex, UK: Blackwell, 2012], 587).

3. Paul Alexander, *Signs and Wonders* (San Francisco: Jossey-Bass, 2009), 63–64.

4. Steve Bruce, *God Is Dead* (Malden, MA: Blackwell, 2002), 182.

5. Philip Jenkins, *The New Faces of Christianity* (New York: Oxford University Press, 2006), 93.

6. Kevin Starr, *Material Dreams* (New York: Oxford University Press, 1991), 142–43.

7. Ibid.

8. Frisbee's secret life was well known to his friends and fellow charismatic ministers. This point is made repeatedly in the documentary film *Frisbee: The Life and Death of a Hippie Preacher*. At 39:55 in the documentary, a close friend of Frisbee's says, "At the end of the marriage, he told me that he had been staying late in some gay bars. It was a hard thing for me to understand, how he could party on Saturday night and preach on Sunday morning." Shockingly, the next spoken line, a second later, is, "And the Spirit of God moved, and there was no doubt about it."

9. Ibid., 41:19.

10. Matt Coker, "The First Jesus Freak," *OC Weekly*, March 3, 2005, http://www.ocweekly.com/2005-03-03/features/the-first-jesus-freak/.

11. Cf. Ian G. Clark, *Pentecost at the Ends of the Earth: The History of the Assemblies of God in New Zealand (1927–2003)* (Blenheim, NZ: Christian Road Ministries, 2007), 186.

12. Jonathan C. Smith, *Pseudoscience and Extraordinary Claims of the Paranormal* (Malden, MA: John Wiley & Sons, 2010), 290.

13. Hanna Rosin, "White Preachers Born Again on Black Network; TV Evangelists Seek to Resurrect Ministries," *Washington Post*, September 3, 1998.

14. Cf. "Testimonials," Peter Popoff Ministries website, accessed October 2012, http://peterpopoff.org/testimonials.

15. Smith, *Pseudoscience and Extraordinary Claims of the Paranormal*, 290.

16. Susan Wise Bauer, *The Art of the Public Grovel: Sexual Sin and Public Confession in America* (Princeton, NJ: Princeton University, 2008), 238.

17. Mark Silk, *Unsecular Media* (Champaign, IL: University of Illinois, 1998), 83.

18. David Cloud, "Recent Pentecostal Scandals," Fundamental Baptist Information Service, Way of Life Literature, December 29, 2008, http://www.wayoflife.org/database/pentecostalscandals.html. Cf. Pam Sollner, "Minister Removed After Confession of Sexual Misconduct," *Olathe News*, November 30, 1991, http://www.religionnewsblog.com/16929/minister-removed-after-confession-of-sexual-misconduct.

19. ABC News, *Primetime Live*, November 21, 1991.

20. "Clarence McClendon Cuts Ties with Foursquare after Divorce News," *Charisma*, July 31, 2000, http://www.charismamag.com/component/content/article/134-j15/peopleevents/people-events/92-clarence-mcclendon-cuts-ties-with-foursquare-after-divorce-news. Cf. Lee Grady, "Sin in the Camp," *Charisma*, February 2002, http://www.charismamag.com/site-archives/130-departments/first-word/560-sin-in-the-camp.

21. Steven Lawson, "Most Students, Church Members Defend Liardon After Confession," *Charisma,* February 28, 2002, http://www.charismamag.com /site-archives/134-peopleevents/people-events/568-most-students-church -members-defend-liardon-after-confession.

22. William Lobdell, "Televangelist Paul Crouch Attempts to Keep Accuser Quiet," *Los Angeles Times*, September 12, 2004, http://articles.latimes.com /2004/sep/12/local/me-lonnie12.

23. Paul Cain, "A Letter of Confession," retrieved February 2005, accessed October 2012, http://web.archive.org/web/20050225053035/http://www .paulcain.org/news.html.

24. CNN, *Paula Zahn Now,* January 19, 2006.

25. Kevin Roose, "The Last Temptation of Ted," *GQ,* February 2011, http:// www.gq.com/news-politics/newsmakers/201102/pastor-ted-haggard.

26. Lillian Kwon, "Ted Haggard Aims for Simplicity with New Church," *Christian Post*, July 26, 2010, http://www.christianpost.com/news/ted -haggard-aims-for-simplicity-with-new-church-46055/.

27. Cf. Audrey Barrick, "Evangelist's Husband Apologizes, Pleads Guilty to Assault," *Christian Post*, March 12, 2008, http://www.christianpost.com /news/evangelist-s-husband-apologizes-pleads-guilty-to-assault-31498/.

28. Tracy Scott, "Juanita Bynum shares 'lesbian' testimony," *S2S Magazine*, July 17, 2012, http://s2smagazine.com/18050/juanita-bynum-shares-lesbian -testimony/.

29. David Roach, "Faith Healer Todd Bentley Separates from Wife, Draws Criticism from Charismatics," Baptist Press News, August 19, 2008, http:// www.sbcbaptistpress.net/BPnews.asp?ID=28727.

30. Elissa Lawrence, "Disgraced Pastor Michael Guglielmucci a Porn Addict," *The Australian*, August 24, 2008, http://www.theaustralian.com.au/news /fraud-pastor-a-porn-addict-says-shocked-dad/story-e6frg6n6-1111117284239.

31. Cf. Laura Strickler, "Senate Panel Probes 6 Top Televangelists," CBS News, February 11, 2009, http://www.cbsnews.com/8301-500690_162-3456977.html.

32. Naimah Jabali-Nash, "Bishop Eddie Long Hit with Third Sex Lawsuit, Ga. Church Has Not Made Statement," CBS News, September 22, 2010, http:// www.cbsnews.com/8301-504083_162-20017328-504083.html.

33. Jim Gold, "Televangelist Creflo Dollar Arrested in Alleged Choking Attack on Daughter" NBC News, June 8, 2012, http://usnews.nbcnews.com/_news /2012/06/08/12126777-televangelist-creflo-dollar-arrested-in-alleged-choking -attack-on-daughter.

34. "Evangelists Hinn, White Deny Affair Allegations," CBN News, July 26, 2010, http://www.cbn.com/cbnnews/us/2010/July/Evangelists-Hinn-White -Deny-Affair-Allegations/.

35. Adrienne S. Gaines, "Benny Hinn Admits 'Friendship' with Paula White but Tells TV Audience It's Over," *Charisma*, August 10, 2010, http://www.charismamag.com/site-archives/570-news/featured-news/11683-benny-hinn-admits-friendship-with-paula-white-but-tells-tv-audience-its-over.

36. Stoyan Zaimov, "Benny Hinn Says Wife's Drug Problems Led to Divorce, Praises God's Reconciling Power," *Christian Post*, June 13, 2012, http://global.christianpost.com/news/benny-hinn-says-wifes-drug-problems-led-to-divorce-praises-gods-reconciling-power-76585/.

37. Additional examples could also be cited. For example, in 2010, televangelist Marcus Lamb, the founder of Daystar Television Network, publicly acknowledged that several years earlier he had engaged in an extramarital affair. In 2011, London-based Pentecostal pastor Albert Odulele confessed to sexually assaulting both a fourteen-year-old boy and a twenty-one-year-old young man. In 2012, Ira Parmenter—the youth pastor at Colwood Pentecostal Church—made headlines when he was arrested for having an extended affair with a sixteen-year-old girl (Sam Hodges, "Former Employee Sues Daystar Founder Marcus Lamb over His Extramarital Affair with Another Employee," *Dallas Morning News*, December 3, 2010, http://www.dallasnews.com/incoming/20101203-exclusive-former-employee-sues-daystar-founder-marcus-lamb-over-his-extramarital-affair-with-another-employee.ece; Janet Shan, "London-Based Pastor Albert Odulele Pleads Guilty to Sexual Assault of 14 Year Old Boy, Says He 'Battled' Sexuality for Years," *Hinterland Gazette*, March 11, 2011, http://hinterlandgazette.com/2011/03/london-based-pastor-albert-odulele.html; Markham Hislop, "Former BC Youth Pastor Ira Parmenter Arrested for Sexual Exploitation of Young Girl," *Calgary Beacon*, May 15, 2012, http://beaconnews.ca/calgary/2012/05/former-bc-youth-pastor-ira-parmenter-arrested-for-sexual-exploitation-of-young-girl/).

38. David Van Biema, "Are Mega-Preachers Scandal-Prone?" *Time*, September 28, 2007, http://www.time.com/time/nation/article/0,8599,1666552,00.html.

39. J. Lee Grady, *The Holy Spirit Is Not for Sale* (Grand Rapids: Baker, 2010), 87.

40. Chad Brand, as cited in Roach, "Faith Healer Todd Bentley Separates from Wife."

41. Ibid.

42. Jonathan Edwards, "The Distinguishing Marks of a Work of the Spirit of God," *The Great Awakening* (New Haven: Yale, 1972), 253.

43. Earl Radmacher, *Salvation* (Nashville: Thomas Nelson, 2000), 150. Radmacher adds, "The Word of God apart from the Spirit of God is lifeless. On the other hand, the Spirit of God without the Word of God is mute. To put it another way, focusing on the Word of God apart from the Spirit of

God leads to formalism, whereas focusing on the Spirit of God apart from the Word of God leads to fanaticism. But focusing on both—the Word of God and the Spirit of God—will lead to growth into the image of Christ."

44. Martyn Percy wrote: "A frequently repeated gibe leveled at Evangelicals was that they believed in a different Trinity to the rest of Christendom: Father, Son and Holy Scripture" ("Whose Time Is It Anyway," in *Christian Millennarianism*, ed. Stephen Hunt [Bloomington, IN: Indiana University Press, 2001], 33).

45. C. Peter Wagner, "The New Apostolic Reformation Is Not a Cult," *Charisma News*, August 24, 2011, http://www.charismanews.com/opinion /31851-the-new-apostolic-reformation-is-not-a-cult.

46. For more on the ministry of Peter Wagner, see chapter 5.

47. Jack Deere, cited in Mark Thompson, "Spiritual Warfare: What Happens When I Contradict Myself," *The Briefing* no. 45/46 (April 24, 1990): 11. This quotation was taken from a 1990 conference talk by Jack Deere.

48. Jack Deere, *The Gift of Prophecy* (Ventura, CA: Gospel Light, 2008), 141.

49. Donald G. Bloesch, *The Holy Spirit* (Downers Grove, IL: InterVarsity, 2000), 187–88.

50. As Jonathan Edwards explained, "Another rule by which to judge of spirits may be drawn . . . by observing the manner of the operation of a spirit that is at work among a people. . . . [If] it operates as a spirit of truth, leading persons to truth, convincing them of those things that are true, we may safely determine that it is a right and true spirit" (*The Works of President Edwards in Four Volumes* [New York: Robert Carter & Brothers, 1879], I:542).

51. Frederick Dale Bruner, *A Theology of the Holy Spirit: The Pentecostal Experience and the New Testament Witness* (Grand Rapids: Eerdmans, 1970), 21.

52. Jack Cottrell wrote, "In spite of all protestations to the contrary, the fact is that on a practical if not theoretical level, continuationists elevate experience above the Word of God as the final norm for faith and practice" (*The Holy Spirit* [Joplin, MO: College Press, 2007], 445).

53. See, for example, "Hi. I'm Kathy, I'm a born again, Spirit-filled, Charismatic Mormon" at Mormon.org, accessed March 2013, http://mormon.org/me/6kpv.

54. John Ankerberg and John Weldon, *Cult Watch* (Eugene, OR: Harvest House, 1991), viii.

55. William Menzies, cited in Stephen Eugene Parker, *Led by the Spirit* (Sheffield, UK: Sheffield Academic, 1996), 21.

56. John Arnott, *The Father's Blessing* (Lake Mary, FL: Charisma House, 1995), 127. On page 119, Arnott similarly wrote, "If you are afraid of shaking, laughing or falling on the floor, talk to God about it. . . . Repent and choose vulnerability. . . . You can analyze it and test it later."

57. William E. Brown, *Making Sense of Your Faith* (Wheaton, IL: Victor, 1989), 55.

58. Edwards, "The Distinguishing Marks of a Work of the Spirit of God," 256.

59. Telford C. Work, "Theological FAQ: You Describe Yourself as Pentecostal. What Is Pentecostalism About?" March 7, 2003, http://www.westmont.edu /~work/faq/pentecostal.html.

60. Cf. Gordon Fee, a charismatic commentator who contends that "Paul believed in an immediate communing with God by means of the S/spirit that sometimes bypassed the mind" (Gordon Fee, *God's Empowering Presence* [Peabody, MA: Hendrickson, 2009], 219).

61. Cf. C. J. Knieper, *I Am . . . in Charge!* (Summersville, SC: Holy Fire, 2008), 8. Tony Campolo and Mary Albert Darling similarly suggest a mind-emptying method of prayer in their book *Connecting Like Jesus* (San Francisco: Wiley, 2010), 59.

62. Annette Ware-Malone, *Life's Achievements After a Death of a Child* (Bloomington, IN: AuthorHouse, 2007), 5–6.

63. Margaret M. Poloma, *Main Street Mystics* (Oxford: AltaMira, 2003), 5.

64. Noting the way in which the Azusa Street was perceived by outsiders, one author reports, "An arresting headline in the *Los Angeles Times* of the Azusa meeting reads, 'Weird Babel of Tongues; New Sect of Fanatics Is Breaking Loose; Wild Scene Last Night on Azusa Street'" (May Ling Tan-Chow, *Pentecostal Theology for the Twenty-First Century* [Burlington, VT: Ashgate, 2007], 43).

65. Charles Parham, cited in Grant Wacker, *Heaven Below*, 125.

66. Peter Masters, "The Law of a Sound Mind," *Trinity Review* no. 272 (Nov/ Dec 2007), http://www.trinityfoundation.org/PDF/The%20Trinity%20 Review%2000246%20Review272masters.pdf.

67. In his treatise "The Mind," Jonathan Edwards made it clear that God does not bypass the mind in reaching the heart with truth. Cf. Jonathan Edwards, "The Mind," in *The Philosophy of Jonathan Edwards from His Private Notebooks*, ed. Harvey G. Townsend (Eugene: University of Oregon, 1955), 21ff.

68. Mark E. Moore, "Eyeing the Tongue," in *Fanning the Flame* (Joplin, MO: College Press, 2003), 218.

69. Raymond C. Ortlund Jr., *Proverbs* (Wheaton, IL: Crossway, 2012), 60.

70. This view is based on a misunderstanding of 1 Corinthians 14:4. As I wrote in *Charismatic Chaos*, "Paul was not commending the use of tongues for self-edification, but condemning people who were using the gift in violation of its purpose and in disregard of the principle of love. . . . The Corinthians were using tongues to build themselves up in a selfish sense. Their motives were not wholesome but egocentric. Their passion for tongues grew out of a

desire to exercise the most spectacular, showy gifts in front of other believers. Paul's point was that no one profits from such an exhibition except the person speaking in tongues—and the chief value he gets out of it is the building of his own ego" (John MacArthur, *Charismatic Chaos* [Grand Rapids: Zondervan, 1992], 279). We will discuss the gift of tongues in more detail in chapter 7.

71. William J. McRae, *The Dynamics of Spiritual Gifts* (Grand Rapids: Zondervan, 1976), 33.

72. Cf. Harry Loewen, *Luther and the Radicals* (Waterloo, ON: Wilfrid Laurier University Press, 1974), 32.

73. Edwards, "The Distinguishing Marks of a Work of the Spirit of God," 256–57.

74. For example, John Wimber, founder of the Vineyard Movement, when he first encountered visible manifestations of the Spirit's power justified them by thinking back to "events described by Jonathan Edwards, John Wesley and George Whitefield"—i.e., the Great Awakening (John White, *When the Spirit Comes with Power* [Downers Grove, IL: InterVarsity, 1988], 159).

75. That the Holy Spirit was at work in the Corinthian congregation, in spite of their wrong understanding of spiritual gifts, is seen in passages like 1 Corinthians 2:12; 3:16; 6:11,19.

Chapter 5: Apostles Among Us?

1. C. Peter Wagner, *The Changing Church* (Ventura, CA: Gospel Light, 2004), 9.

2. Ibid., 10.

3. According to Pentecostal historian Vinson Synan, "In 2004, in his book *Aftershock! How the Second Apostolic Age Is Changing the Church*, Wagner made grandiose claims about this new movement. He claimed that the charismatic movement was 'a vision unfulfilled' and that the New Apostolic Renewal Movement had taken its place as the wave of the future" (Vinson Synan, *An Eyewitness Remembers the Century of the Spirit*, repr. [Grand Rapids: Chosen Books, 2011], 185).

4. C. Peter Wagner, *The Changing Church*, 12.

5. Ibid., 10.

6. Ibid., 12.

7. C. Peter Wagner as cited in David Cannistraci, *Apostles and the Emerging Apostolic Movement* (Ventura, CA: Renew, 1996), 12.

8. C. Peter Wagner, *Wrestling with Alligators, Prophets and Theologians* (Ventura, CA: Gospel Light, 2010), 207.

9. Ibid., 208.

10. Ibid., 243.

11. "Europe Nearly Free of Mad Cow Disease," *EUbusiness*, July 16, 2010, http://www.eubusiness.com/news-eu/madcow-food-safety.5l7.

12. "History of ICA," International Coalition of Apostles website, accessed November 2012, http://www.coalitionofapostles.com/about-ica/history-of-ica/.

13. Synan, *An Eyewitness Remembers the Century of the Holy Spirit*, 183.

14. Ibid., 184.

15. "Rates," International Coalition of Apostles website, accessed November 2012, http://www.coalitionofapostles.com/membership/rates/.

16. C. Peter Wagner, *Apostles Today* (Ventura, CA: Gospel Light, 2007), 79.

17. Cf. Synan, *An Eyewitness Remembers the Century of the Holy Spirit*, 183.

18. Peter Hocken, *The Challenges of the Pentecostal, Charismatic, and Messianic Jewish Movements* (Cornwall, UK: MPG, 2009), 43.

19. C. Peter Wagner, *The Changing Church*, 15.

20. Ibid.

21. Ibid., 17.

22. Ibid., 18.

23. Ibid.

24. Ibid., 9.

25. Synan, *An Eyewitness Remembers the Century of the Holy Spirit*, 183.

26. Peter Hocken, *The Challenges of the Pentecostal, Charismatic, and Messianic Jewish Movements*, 43–44.

27. As Frederick Dale Bruner explains, "The Pentecostals frequently refer to their movement as a worthy and perhaps even superior successor to the Reformation of the sixteenth century and to the English evangelical revival of the eighteenth, and nearly always as a faithful reproduction of the apostolic movement of the first century" (Frederick Dale Bruner, *A Theology of the Holy Spirit* [Grand Rapids: Eerdmans, 1970], 27).

28. In his *Table Talk*, Martin Luther explained, "The chief cause that I fell out with the pope was this: the pope boasted that he was the head of the church, and condemned all that would not be under his power and authority. . . . Further he took upon him power, rule, and authority over the Christian church, and over the Holy Scriptures, the Word of God; [claiming that] no man must presume to expound the Scriptures, but only he, and according to his ridiculous conceits; so that he made himself lord over the church" (Martin Luther, *The Table Talk of Martin Luther*, trans. and ed. by William Hazlitt [London: Bell & Daldy, 1872], 203–4).

29. C. Peter Wagner, *The Changing Church*, 21.

30. David du Plessis, "Pentecost Outside Pentecost," pamphlet, 1960, 6.

31. Samuel Waldron, *To Be Continued?* (Amityville, NY: Calvary, 2007), 27.

32. Wayne Grudem, *Systematic Theology* (Grand Rapids: Zondervan, 1994), 911.

33. Cited in Ernest L. Vermont, *Tactics of Truth* (Maitland, FL: Xulon, 2006), 94n19.

34. In early church history, believers understood that "the doctrine of the apostles" was what was to be heeded and guarded (cf. Ignatius, *Epistle the Magnesians*, 13; *Epistle to the Antiochians*, 1). Thus, the "memoirs of the apostles" were held as canonical and authoritative within the early church (cf. Irenaeus, *Against Heresies*, 2.2.5; Justin, *First Apology*, 67; Victorinus, *Commentary on the Apocalypse*, 10.9).

35. Grudem, *Systematic Theology*, 905–6.

36. Cf. Nathan Busenitz, "Are There Still Apostles Today," *The Cripplegate*, July 21, 2011, http://thecripplegate.com/are-there-still-apostles-today/.

37. Ignatius, *Epistle to the Magnesians*; emphasis added.

38. Irenaeus, *Against Heresies*, 4.21.3.

39. Tertullian, *Against Marcion*, 21; emphasis added.

40. Lactantius, *The Divine Institutes*, 4.21.

41. *The Epistle to Diognetus*, 11; *Fragments of Papias*, 5; cf. Polycarp, *Epistle to the Philippians*, 6; Ignatius, *Against Heresies*, 1.10.

42. Clement, *First Epistle of Clement to the Corinthians*, 42.

43. Ignatius, *Epistle to the Antiochians*, 11; emphasis added.

44. Cf. Augustine, *On Christian Doctrine*, 3.36.54; *Reply to Faustus*, 32.13; *On Baptism*, 14.16; John Chrysostom, *Homily on 1 Thess. 1:8–10*; *Homily on Heb. 1:6–8*.

45. Eusebius, *Ecclesiastical History*, bk. 8, intro.

46. Basil, *On the Spirit*, 29.72.

47. Tertullian, *Against Marcion*, 21.

48. Grudem, *Systematic Theology*, 911.

49. "Finding Your Place in the Apostolic Vision," February 1999, cited in "A 'Christian Seer' Speaks Out," *Delusion and Apostasy Watch News*, accessed April 2013, http://www.cephas-library.com/apostasy/facilitators_of_change _1.html.

50. Edgar, *Satisfied by the Promise of the Spirit*, 232.

Chapter 6: The Folly of Fallible Prophets

1. Bill Hamon, *Prophets and Personal Prophecy* (Shippensburg, PA: Destiny Image, 1987), 176.

2. Jack Deere, *The Beginner's Guide to the Gift of Prophecy* (Ventura, CA: Regal, 2008), 131–32.

3. Mike Bickle and Bob Jones, "Visions and Revelations," audiotape #5. MP3 title: "4-Vision and Revelations—1988," timestamp: 10:32– 15:58, http://archive.org/details/VisionsAndRevelations-MikeBickleWithBobJones1988.

4. Pam Sollner, "Minister Removed After Confession of Sexual Misconduct," *Olathe News* (Kansas), November 30, 1991, http://www.religionnewsblog .com/16929/minister-removed-after-confession-of-sexual-misconduct.

5. For twenty-five years or longer, Jones has been issuing an annual prophecy he calls "The Shepherd's Rod." Much of it is incoherent, and the portions that are understandable are mostly wrong. The only utterances that are not manifestly wrong are either generic predictions almost anyone could make or ambiguous prognostications that are open to multiple interpretations— the kind of soothsaying horoscope writers practice. Here's a sample of how incoherent and farcical Jones's divinations typically are. The following quotation is excerpted from his 2012 "Shepherd's Rod" forecast. After deni- grating the role of the intellect in understanding divinely revealed truth, he says: "This is what he [the Holy Spirit] is beginning to deal [with]: that you would become literally love slaves, that the mind would become a love slave to the Spirit of God that's in you. Every one of you when you were born—a piece of God the Father came out at your conception. When you were con- ceived, you were conceived to live forever and you are going to live forever someplace. And you determine where you are going to live. And when that seed in you gets ready to break forth is when you begin to see Christ. You see Him first in the written Word. But it is time now that we go on and go—the Word in there—but let the Spirit of God come into us, where the Holy Spirit can reveal to our spirit the future. And then when this [points to head] becomes the love slave, it does only that what you hear here [points to abdomen]." From Bob Jones's 2012 "Shepherd's Rod" predictions, deliv- ered at Morningstar Ministries on October 2, 2011. Video online at: http:// www.youtube.com/watch?v=CYJmgmbSHP0 (excerpt starts at 4:23).

6. "Bob Jones," Morningstar Ministries website, Harvest Festival 2012, accessed December 2012, http://www.morningstarministries.org/biographies /bob-jones.

7. Benny Hinn, *This Is Your Day*, TBN, April 2, 2000.

8. Video of Rick Joyner, available at Kyle Mantyla, "Joyner: Japan Earthquake Will Unleash Demonic Nazism on America," Right Wing Watch, March 16, 2011, http://www.rightwingwatch.org/content/joyner-japan-earthquake -will-unleash-demonic-nazism-america.

9. Wayne Grudem, "Prophecy," in *The Kingdom and Power*, ed. Gary Greig (Ventura, CA: Gospel Light, 1993), 84.

10. Wayne Grudem, *The Gift of Prophecy in the New Testament and Today*, rev. ed. (Wheaton, IL: Crossway, 2000), 90; emphasis added.

11. Ibid., 100; emphasis added.

12. Wayne Grudem, "A Debate on the Continuation of Prophecy," with Ian

Hamilton, 2010 Evangelical Ministry Assembly, accessed December 2012, http://thegospelcoalition.org/blogs/justintaylor/2012/02/23/a-debate-on-the-continuation-of-prophecy/. Grudem's comments are found at 59:53.

13. Henry Blackaby, *Experiencing God* (Nashville: LifeWay, 1990), 168.

14. John MacArthur, *Charismatic Chaos* (Grand Rapids: Zondervan, 1992), 67.

15. Sarah Young, *Jesus Calling—Women's Edition* (Nashville: Thomas Nelson, 2011), xii.

16. *Westminster Confession of Faith*, 1.6; emphasis added.

17. D. Martyn Lloyd-Jones, *Christian Unity* (Grand Rapids: Baker, 1987), 189–91.

18. Waldron, *To Be Continued?*, 65.

19. For an extensive study of this issue (one that devastates the charismatic position), see David F. Farnell's multipart series, "Is the Gift of Prophecy for Today?" in *Bibliotheca Sacra*, 1992–93. Regarding the prophet Agabus, Farnell wrote, "This continuity between Old Testament and New Testament prophecy is also demonstrated by Agabus. Agabus modeled his prophetic style directly after the Old Testament prophets. . . . This can be seen in several ways. He introduced his prophecy with the formula, 'This is what the Holy Spirit says' (Acts 21:11), which closely parallels the Old Testament prophetic formula of 'thus says the Lord' so frequently proclaimed by Old Testament prophets (e.g., Isa. 7:7; Ezek. 5:5; Amos 1:3, 6, 11, 13; Obad. 1; Mic. 2:3; Nah. 1:12; Zech. 1:3–4). This same introductory phrase introduces the words of the Lord Jesus to the seven churches in the Book of Revelation (cf. Rev. 2:1, 8, 12, 18; 3:1, 7, 14). Like many Old Testament prophets, Agabus presented his prophecies through symbolic actions (Acts 21:11; cf. 1 Kings 11:29–40; 22:11; Isa. 20:1–6; Jer. 13:1–11; Ezek. 4:1–17; 5:1–17). Like the Old Testament prophets, Agabus was empowered by the Holy Spirit as the prophetic messenger (Acts 11:28; cf. Num. 11:25–29; 1 Sam. 10:6, 10; 2 Sam. 23:2; Isa. 42:1; 59:21; Zech. 7:12; Neh. 9:30). Like the Old Testament prophets, Agabus's prophecies were accurately fulfilled (Acts 11:27–28; 21:10–11; cf. 28:17)."

20. Farnell, "Is the Gift of Prophecy for Today?" in *Bibliotheca Sacra*, 1992–93. Regarding the function of New Testament prophets within the church, Farnell explains, "Prophets in the Old Testament served as the voice of Yahweh to the theocratic community of Israel. They were recipients of revelations directly from Yahweh, which revelations they proclaimed to the nation (Isa. 6:8–13; Jer. 1:5–10; Ezek. 2:1–10). Just as the Old Testament prophets served as the prophetic voice of communication and instruction from Yahweh, so New Testament prophets functioned in the same capacity. Ephesians 2:20 points out that New Testament prophets too functioned as prophetic voices for the believing community. . . . Ephesians 2:20, then,

points to the strategic, foundational role played by New Testament prophets in the formation of the church. The prophets, in association with the apostles, held the important status of helping lay the church's foundation. This would indicate the high degree of prestige enjoyed by New Testament prophets in the Christian community. Their ranking in the list of gifted persons in 1 Corinthians 12:28 places them second only to the apostles in usefulness to the body of Christ. Moreover, Paul urged his readers to desire prophecy above the other gifts (cf. 1 Cor. 14:1)."

21. Ibid.

22. Wayne Grudem, *Bible Doctrine*, ed. Jeff Purswell (Grand Rapids: Zondervan, 1999), 411.

23. Grudem, *The Gift of Prophecy in the New Testament and Today*, 80.

24. For more on Agabus, see Nathan Busenitz, "Throwing Prophecy Under the Agabus," *The Cripplegate* (blog), March 15, 2012, accessed December 2012, http://thecripplegate.com/throwing-prophecy-under-the-agabus/.

25. Robert Saucy, "An Open but Cautious Response," in *Are Miraculous Gifts for Today? Four Views*, ed. Wayne Grudem (Grand Rapids: Zondervan, 1996), 231.

26. Adapted from John MacArthur, *1 Thessalonians: MacArthur New Testament Commentary* (Chicago: Moody, 2002), 196. It is important to understand that "The apostles and their associates received, spoke, and wrote the text of the New Testament, and other spokesmen delivered supernatural utterances of practical revelation for certain temporal matters (cf. Acts 11:27–30). But prophecy also included the proclamation of God's previously revealed word. Romans 12:6 supports that contention: 'if prophecy, in proportion to our faith' (ESV). In the original, the latter phrase reads, 'according to the proportion of the faith,' which indicates that a person with the gift of prophecy had to speak in agreement with the divinely revealed body of Christian doctrine. The New Testament always considered *the faith* to be synonymous with the collection of previously revealed truth (Acts 6:7; Jude 3, 20). Thus Paul instructed the Romans that prophetic utterances must perfectly agree with 'the faith,' which is God's Word. Similarly, Revelation 19:10 concludes, 'For the testimony of Jesus is the spirit of prophecy.' Genuine prophecy reports God's own revelation of Christ and never deviates from the truth of Scripture."

27. Fred L. Volz, *Strange Fire: Confessions of a False Prophet* (Aloha, OR: TRION, 2003), 41.

28. Ibid., 43.

29. Charles Spurgeon, sermon entitled "The Paraclete," October 6, 1872, *The Metropolitan Tabernacle Pulpit: Sermons Preached and Revised*, vol. 18 (Pasadena, TX: Pilgrim Publications, 1984), 563. Italics in original.

Chapter 7: Twisting Tongues

1. Nicola Menzie, "Televangelist Juanita Bynum Raises Brows with 'Tongues' Prayer on Facebook," *Christian Post*, August 31, 2011, http://www.christianpost.com/news/televangelist-juanita-bynum-raises-brows-with-tongues-prayer-on-facebook-54779/.

2. J. Lee Grady, *The Holy Spirit Is Not for Sale* (Grand Rapids: Chosen Books, 2010), 184.

3. Dennis Bennett, *How to Pray for the Release of the Holy Spirit* (Alachua, FL: Bridge-Logos, 2008), 106.

4. Joyce Meyer, *Knowing God Intimately* (New York: Warner Faith, 2003), 147.

5. William Samarin, *Tongues of Men and Angels* (New York: Macmillan, 1972), 227–28. Cf. Felicitas D. Goodman, "Glossolalia," in *The Encyclopedia of Religion*, ed. Mircea Eliade (New York: Macmillan, 1987), 5:564. Damboriena agrees, saying, "The 'languages' I have heard consist in completely unintelligible bubblings of sound and words which not even the Pentecostals around me (and some of them had already been blessed with the gift) were able to grasp." Prudencio Damboriena, *Tongues as of Fire: Pentecostalism in Contemporary Christianity* (n.p.:Corpus Books, 1969), 105.

6. Samarin, *Tongues of Men and Angels*, 127–28.

7. Kenneth L. Nolen, "Glossolalia," in *Encyclopedia of Psychology and Religion*, eds. David A. Leeming, Kathryn Madden, and Stanton Marlan (New York, Springer: 2010), 2:349.

8. Fraser Watts, "Psychology and Theology" in *The Cambridge Companion to Science and Religion*, ed. Peter Harrison (Cambridge University Press, 2010), 201.

9. Book description for *70 Reasons for Speaking in Tongues: Your Own Built-In Spiritual Dynamo* by Bill Hamon (Tabor, SD: Parsons, 2010), books.google.com/books?isbn=160273013X.

10. John Bevere, *Drawing Near* (Nashville: Nelson, 2004), 243.

11. Larry Christenson, "Bypassing the Mind," in *The Holy Spirit in Today's Church*, ed. Erling Jornstad (Nashville: Abingdon, 1973), 87.

12. Robert Carroll, *The Skeptic's Dictionary* (Hoboken, NJ: John Wiley & Sons, 2003), 155.

13. Salvatore Cucchiari, "Between Shame and Sanctification," *American Ethnologist* 17, no. 4 (1990): 691.

14. As Kenneth L. Nolen explains, "Most Pentecostals have come to the realization that it is not God's divine purpose to bestow languages for missionary work and have had to reevaluate the biblical understanding of glossolalia" (Nolen, "Glossolalia," *Encyclopedia of Psychology and Religion*, 349).

15. Vicki Mabrey and Roxanna Sherwood, "Speaking in Tongues: Alternative

Voices in Faith," *Nightline*, ABC, March 20, 2007, http://abcnews.go.com
/Nightline/story?id=2935819&page=1.

16. Ibid.

17. Nolen, "Glossolalia," *Encyclopedia of Psychology and Religion*, 349. "Some
consider the chants of voodoo witch doctors, African animists, and the
Tibetan Buddhist Monks, the prayers of Hindu holy men, and the basic
primeval sounds produced by others in their religious settings as glossolalia.
Many of these worshipers make sounds and utterances that approxi-
mate purported languages found in the glossolalia of Pentecostal and
Charismatic worship services. . . . Glossolalia can occur in some known
psychiatric conditions such as schizophrenia and manic-depressive psycho-
sis or as the consequence of neurological disorders." Cf. Robert Gromacki,
The Modern Tongues Movement (Grand Rapids: Baker Books, 1976), 5–10.
Gromacki refers to frenzied speech (glossolalia) occurring among the
ancient Greek and early Phoenecian religions, the Greco-Roman mystery
religions, Islam, Eskimo paganism, and paganism in Tibet and China. Of
note, Gerhard F. Hasel, *Speaking in Tongues* (Berrien Springs, MI: Adventist
Theological Society, 1991), 14, 18 also includes "shamans" and "witch doctors" in the list of pagan tongue-speakers.

18. W. A. Criswell, "Facts Concerning Modern Glossolalia," in *The Holy Spirit
in Today's Church*, ed. Erling Jornstad (Nashville: Abingdon, 1973), 90–91.

19. Norman Geisler, *Signs and Wonders* (Wheaton, IL: Tyndale, 1998), 167.

20. On occasion, *glossa* can also refer to the organ of the tongue. However, it
most often refers to human languages in Scripture. For example, the word
glossa also appears some thirty times in the Septuagint (the Greek version of
the Old Testament) and always means human language.

21. Gregory of Nazianzus, *The Oration on Pentecost*, 15–17; cited in Philip Schaff,
The Nicene and Post-Nicene Fathers (NPNF), 2nd ser., vol. 7 (Christian
Classics Ethereal Library, 2009), 384–85. In this same passage, Gregory notes
that the gift of tongues undid what occurred at the Tower of Babel.

22. John Chrysostom, *Homilies on First Corinthians*, 35.1. Cited in Philip
Schaff, *The Nicene and Post-Nicene Fathers (NPNF)*, First Series, 12:209.

23. Augustine, *Homilies on the First Epistle of John*, 6.10. Cited in Augustine,
Homilies on the Gospel of John, trans. Boniface Ramsey (Hyde Park, NY:
New City, 2008), 97.

24. Geisler, *Signs and Wonders*, 167. Even when two or more different
Pentecostal interpreters listen to the same audio recording of a tongues-
speaker, their interpretations are totally different—suggesting that the
tongues themselves are not real languages that can even be translated.
(Cf. John P. Kildahl, "Six Behavioral Observations About Speaking

in Tongues," in *Gifts of the Spirit and the Body of Christ*, ed. Elmo J. Agrimoson [Minneapolis: Augsburg, 1974], 77).

25. Thomas Edgar, *Satisfied by the Promise of the Spirit* (Grand Rapids: Kregel, 1996), 147.

26. Cf. Gromacki, *The Modern Tongues Movement*, 5–10.

27. Of course, any reference to the end of Mark's gospel must be treated with care, since it is likely that Mark 16:9–21 were not part of the original text. Though not original to Mark, they nevertheless reflect the perspective of the early church and therefore are helpful in this discussion.

28. Charismatic commentator Gordon Fee acknowledges the legitimacy of the indicative view (Gordon D. Fee, *The First Epistle to the Corinthians* [Grand Rapids: Eerdmans, 1987], 624). Fee lists a number of additional scholars who take that same view.

29. Cited from Albert Barnes, *Notes on the New Testament: 1 Corinthians*, repr. (Grand Rapids: Baker, 1975), 240.

30. It is clear from the other examples Paul uses in verses 2–3 that he was using literary license to emphasize the superiority of love over even the most impressive form of spiritual giftedness imaginable. Thus, it is probably best to understand the "tongues of angels" as hyperbole.

31. As Anthony Thiselton notes in his commentary on this passage: "The one important point to make here is that few or none of the serious 'cessationist' arguments depends on a specific exegesis of 1 Cor 13:8–11. . . . These verses should not be used as a polemic for either side in this debate" (*New International Greek New Testament Commentary*, 1063–64).

32. As I have explained elsewhere regarding this passage, "for Christians the eternal state begins either at death, when they go to be with the Lord, or at the rapture, when the Lord takes His own to be with Himself. . . . In this present life, even with God's Word completed and the illumination of His Spirit, we see in a mirror dimly. In our present state we are not capable of seeing more. But when we enter into the Lord's presence, we then will see Him face to face. Now we can only know in part, but then [we] shall know fully just as [we] also have been fully known" (John MacArthur, *First Corinthians* [Chicago: Moody, 1984], 366).

33. Edgar, *Satisfied by the Promise of the Spirit*, 246.

34. Obviously, the content of the first-century revelatory gifts has been passed down throughout subsequent generations of church history in the New Testament Scripture. Thus, gifted pastors are able to proclaim the prophetic word as they faithfully preach and teach the written Word of God. In that sense, prophecy still continues today (and will continue throughout the church age), though God is no longer giving *new* prophetic revelation

to His church. One day, after the church age is over, God will again give new revelation through prophets (during the Tribulation and millennial kingdom—cf. Isa. 11:9; 29:18; Jer. 23:4; Rev. 11:3). Within the church age, however, the giving of new revelation was limited to the foundation stage of the church (Eph. 2:20).

35. Severian of Gabala, *Pauline Commentary from the Greek Church*; cited in *1–2 Corinthians*, Ancient Christian Commentary Series, 144, in reference to 1 Corinthians 14:28.

36. Though some charismatics try to force tongues into Romans 8:26 and 2 Corinthians 5:13, the context of those passages makes it clear that the gift of tongues is not in view.

Chapter 8: Fake Healings and False Hopes

1. Cathy Lynn Grossman, "Oral Roberts Brought Health-and-Wealth Gospel Mainstream," *USA Today*, December 15, 2009, http://content.usatoday.com /communities/Religion/post/2009/12/oral-roberts-health-wealth-prosperity -gospel/1.

2. John MacArthur, "Measuring Oral Roberts's Influence," *Grace to You* (blog), December 18, 2009, http://www.gty.org/Blog/B091218.

3. Granted, some of the blame also goes to Kenneth Hagin. But it should be noted, Hagin and Roberts often ministered together and affirmed one another's ministries. Furthermore, the heir to Hagin's standing as chief of the word-faith preachers is Kenneth Copeland, who went into television ministry after working as chauffeur and pilot to Oral Roberts. So even though it would not be quite accurate to portray Oral Roberts as an aggressive proponent of word-faith doctrines, he acted as more of an ally than an opponent to the movement. We might say his relationship with that movement was reminiscent of a benign grandfather who refused to correct an out-of-control grandchild.

4. David E. Harrell Jr., *Oral Roberts: An American Life* (Bloomington, IN: Indiana University, 1985), 66.

5. Ibid.

6. Vinson Synan, cited in William Lobdell, "Oral Roberts Dies at 91," *Los Angeles Times,* December 16, 2009, articles.latimes.com/2009/dec/16/local /la-me-oral-roberts16-2009dec16.

7. In addition to being influenced by Oral Roberts, Benny Hinn has acknowledged the impact of Kathryn Kuhlman—one of Oral Roberts's friends and fellow faith healers—on his life.

8. Benny Hinn, "Pastor Benny Hinn Joins Believers Worldwide in Tribute to a Great Leader and Friend," Benny Hinn Ministries website, accessed January 2013, http://www.bennyhinn.org/articles/articledesc.cfm?id=6858.

9. The *Dateline NBC* program aired December 27, 2009. Hinn broadcast a rebuttal program on December 29, 2009, which featured a video of Oral Roberts claiming, "Benny's ministry to me is characterized by the anointing of the Holy Spirit" (*Praise the Lord*, TBN, December 29, 2002).

10. Hinn resigned his position as regent of ORU in 2008. Cf. Laura Strickler, "Major Shakeup at Oral Roberts University," CBS News, January 15, 2008, http://www.cbsnews.com/8301-501263_162-3716774-501263.html.

11. "Television," Benny Hinn Ministries homepage, accessed January 2013, http://www.bennyhinn.org/television/weeklyguide.

12. Benny Hinn, *He Touched Me* (Nashville: Thomas Nelson, 1999), back cover.

13. "About," Benny Hinn Ministries homepage, accessed January 2013, http://www.bennyhinn.org/about-us.

14. Benny Hinn, *The Anointing*, 86–87.

15. Rafael D. Martinez, "Miracles Today? A Benny Hinn Layover in Cleveland, Tennessee Remembered." Spirit Watch Ministries, accessed January 2013, www.spiritwatch.org/firehinncrusade.htm. Martinez was reporting about a healing service held in October 2007.

16. Ibid.

17. William Lobdell, *Losing My Religion* (New York: HarperCollins, 2009), 183. Cf. William Lobdell, "The Price of Healing," *Los Angeles Times*, July 27, 2003, http://www.trinityfi.org/press/latimes02.html.

18. Ibid., 181.

19. Benny Hinn, *This Is Your Day for a Miracle* (Lake Mary, FL: Creation House, 1996), 21.

20. Benny Hinn, *The Anointing* (Nashville: Thomas Nelson, 1997), 49; emphasis added.

21. Hinn, *This Is Your Day*, 29.

22. Benny Hinn, *The Miracle of Healing* (Nashville: J. Countryman, 1998), 91.

23. Lobdell, *Losing My Religion*, 183–84.

24. Hinn, *The Miracle of Healing*, 89.

25. Benny Hinn, *Praise the Lord*, TBN, December 6, 1994.

26. Benny Hinn, Miracle Crusade, Birmingham, AL, March 28, 2002.

27. Hinn, *The Miracle of Healing*, 79.

28. Benny Hinn, *Rise and Be Healed* (Orlando: Celebration, 1991), 47.

29. Justin Peters, *An Examination and Critique of the Life, Ministry and Theology of Healing Evangelist Benny Hinn*, unpublished ThM thesis (Ft. Worth: Southwestern Baptist Seminary, 2002), 68. Inset quote from Stephen Strang, "Benny Hinn Speaks Out," *Charisma*, August 1993, 29.

30. Rafael Martinez, "Miracles Today?" http://www.spiritwatch.org/firehinncrusade.htm.

31. Hinn, *He Touched Me*, 177.

32. Hinn, *The Anointing*, 181.

33. Strang, "Benny Hinn Speaks Out," 29.

34. Benny Hinn, *Praise-a-Thon*, TBN, April 2, 2000.

35. Richard Fisher, *The Confusing World of Benny Hinn* (St. Louis: Personal Freedom Outreach, 1999), 146.

36. Benny Hinn, *This Is Your Day*, TBN, August 15, 1996.

37. In 2009, Hinn told ABC's *Nightline*, "I would not do this for the money. . . . What you're asking is am I using the so-called lie, that healings really happen so I can make money? Of course not." Dan Harris, "Benny Hinn: 'I Would Not Do This for Money,'" *Nightline*, ABC, October 19, 2009, http://abcnews.go.com/Nightline/benny-hinn-evangelical-leader -senate-investigation-speaks/story?id=8862027.

38. William Lobdell, "Onward Christian Soldier," *Los Angeles Times*, December 8, 2002, http://articles.latimes.com/2002/dec/08/magazine/tm-lobdell49/2.

39. Lobdell, *Losing My Religion*, 182.

40. Mike Thomas, "The Power and the Glory," *Orlando Sentinel*, November 24, 1991, http://articles.orlandosentinel.com/1991-11-24/news/9111221108 _1_benny-hinn-holy-spirit-slain. Cf. Dan Harris, who says of Hinn, "He flies in a private plane, stays in fancy hotels, wears nice clothes and jewelry" (Harris, "Benny Hinn: 'I Would Not Do This for Money'").

41. Lobdell, *Losing My Religion*, 182.

42. Thomas Edgar, *Miraculous Gifts* (Neptune, NJ: Loizeaux Brothers, 1983), 99.

43. Harris, "Benny Hinn: 'I Would Not Do This for Money.'"

44. Ibid.

45. Hinn, *The Anointing*, 179.

46. Ibid., 81.

47. Cf. Greg Locke, *Blinded by Benny* (Murfreesboro, TN: Sword of the Lord, 2005), 41. According to Locke, this incident occurred on Sunday, April 30, 2000, and was reported in the *Kenya Times*.

48. Hinn, *Rise and Be Healed*, 32.

49. William Lobdell, "The Price of Healing," *Los Angeles Times*, July 27, 2003, http://www.trinityfi.org/press/latimes02.html.

50. Harris, "Benny Hinn: 'I Would Not Do This for Money.'"

51. Benny Hinn, *Praise the Lord*, TBN, December 29, 2002.

52. Lobdell, *Losing My Religion*, 185–86.

53. Hinn, *The Anointing*, 95.

54. Mike Thomas, "The Power and the Glory," 12.

55. Hank Hanegraaff, *Christianity in Crisis* (Eugene, OR: Harvest House, 1993), 341.

56. Anthony Thomas, cited in "Do Miracles Actually Occur?" *Sunday Morning*, CNN, April 15, 2001, http://transcripts.cnn.com/TRANSCRIPTS/0104 /15/sm.13.html.

57. Robin Finn, "Want Pathos, Pain and Courage? Get Real," *New York Times*, April 15, 2001, http://www.nytimes.com/2001/04/15/tv/cover-story-want -pathos-pain-and-courage-get-real.html.

58. Hinn, *The Miracle of Healing*, 53.

59. D. R. McConnell, *A Different Gospel* (Peabody, MA: Hendrickson, 1995), 151.

60. Hinn, *The Miracle of Healing*, 69.

61. Fisher, *The Confusing World of Benny Hinn*, 222.

62. Bob McKeown, "Do You Believe in Miracles?" *The Fifth Estate* (Canadian Broadcasting Corporation), http://www.cbc.ca/fifth/main_miracles _multimedia.html.

63. Fisher, *The Confusing World of Benny Hinn*, 224.

64. Hinn, *He Touched Me*, 184.

65. Benny Hinn, Orlando Christian Center broadcast, TBN, December 9, 1990.

66. Ibid.

67. Cf. Fisher, *The Confusing World of Benny Hinn*, 7.

68. Benny Hinn, *Praise the Lord*, TBN, December 6, 1990.

69. Of course, the miracle of regeneration and salvation is a supernatural work that God still does today.

Chapter 9: The Holy Spirit and Salvation

1. A. W. Tozer, *The Knowledge of the Holy* (New York: HarperCollins, 1978), 1.

2. Charles Spurgeon, "The Paraclete," *The Metropolitan Tabernacle Pulpit*, vol. 18 (London: Passmore & Alabaster, 1872), 563.

3. In his *Systematic Theology* (Grand Rapids: Zondervan, 2000), Wayne Grudem lists "The Order of Salvation" in the following way: (1) Election (God's choice of people to be saved); (2) The gospel call (proclaiming the message of the gospel); (3) Regeneration (being born again); (4) Conversion (faith and repentance); (5) Justification (right legal standing); (6) Adoption (membership in God's family); (7) Sanctification (right conduct of life); (8) Perseverance (remaining a Christian); (9) Death (going to be with the Lord); and (10) Glorification (receiving a resurrection body). Accepting Grudem's order, we see that election occurred in eternity past. The gospel call occurs in this life, as sinners are convicted by the Word. Regeneration, conversion, justification, and adoption take place together at the moment of salvation. Progressive sanctification begins at salvation and continues over the believer's lifetime. For believers, death brings immediate entry into heaven and the end of any struggle with sin. Finally, the reception of the

believer's resurrection body comes at the rapture of the church. In each of these aspects of salvation, the Holy Spirit is at work. Our purpose in this chapter is not to provide a detailed analysis of what theologians call the *ordo salutis*. Rather, it is to highlight a number of the ways in which the Spirit specifically works with regard to the salvation of His saints.

4. Andreas J. Kostenberger, *John* in *Baker Exegetical Commentary on the New Testament* (Grand Rapids: Baker, 2004), 471.

5. Arthur W. Pink, *The Holy Spirit* (Grand Rapids: Baker, 1970), chap. 15, http://www.pbministries.org/books/pink/Holy_Spirit/spirit_15.htm.

6. One commentator explained the triune God's involvement in salvation in this way: "Our salvation involves all three Persons in the Godhead (Eph. 1:3–14; 1 Peter 1:2). You cannot be saved apart from the Father's electing grace, the Son's loving sacrifice, and the Spirit's ministry of conviction and regeneration" (Warren Wiersbe, *The Wiersbe Bible Commentary: New Testament* [Colorado Springs: David C. Cook, 2007], 460).

7. Thomas Goodwin, *The Works of Thomas Goodwin, vol. 8, The Object and Acts of Justifying Faith* (Edinburgh: James Nichol, 1864), 378–79.

Chapter 10: The Spirit and Sanctification

1. Mahesh Chavda, *Hidden Power of Speaking in Tongues* (Shippensburg, PA: Destiny Image, 2011), 44.

2. Meredith B. McGuire, *Lived Religion* (Oxford: Oxford University Press, 2008), 253n63. McGuire explains that the "Toronto Blessing" of the 1990s featured "a powerful, immediate experience of blessing by the Holy Spirit, manifested by 'gifts of the Spirit,' such as hysterical laughter, shaking, speaking in tongues, dancing, being 'slain in the Spirit,' and often accompanied by a profound sense of inner healing or transformation."

3. Sandy Davis Kirk, *The Pierced Generation* (Chambersburg, PA: eGen, 2013), 63.

4. William Elwood Davis, *Christian Worship* (Bloomington, IN: AuthorHouse, 2004), 99–100.

5. Frank Sizer, *Into His Presence* (Shippensburg, PA: Destiny Image, 2007), 102.

6. Patricia King, "Encountering the Heavenly Realm," in *Powerful Encounters* (Maricopa, AZ: XP, 2011), 116.

7. Wesley Campbell, *Welcoming a Visitation of the Holy Spirit* (Lake Mary, FL: Charisma House, 1996), 24.

8. Benny Hinn, *Good Morning, Holy Spirit* (Nashville: Thomas Nelson, 1990), 103.

9. Benny Hinn, *He Touched Me* (Nashville: Thomas Nelson, 1999), 83.

10. Kenneth Hagin, "Why Do People Fall Under the Power?" (Tulsa: Faith Library, 1983), 4–5, 9–10. Hagin reports stories of both a woman who stood like a statue for three days, and another woman who levitated off the

stage. For more on those accounts, see chapter 7 in my book *Charismatic Chaos* (Grand Rapids: Zondervan, 1992).

11. As Ron Rhodes explains, "Many who believe in this phenomenon like to cite certain passages in its support, such as Genesis 15:12–21, Numbers 24:4, 1 Samuel 19:20, and Matthew 17:6. But in every case they are reading their own meaning into the text" (Ron Rhodes, *5-Minute Apologetics for Today* [Eugene, OR: Harvest House, 2010], 222).

12. *Dictionary of Pentecostal and Charismatic Movements* (Grand Rapids: Zondervan, 1988), 790. Cited in Hank Hanegraaf, *The Bible Answer Book* (Nashville: Thomas Nelson, 2004), 82.

13. We might add that, in passages where the direction of their fall is recorded, those who fell in the presence of God's glory fell forward on their faces (Josh. 5:14; Num. 22:31; Judg. 13:20; Ezek. 1:28; 3:23; 43:3; 44:4). They did not fall backward, so that a "catcher" would need to be stationed behind them. The one exception to this might be the soldiers who arrested Jesus in John 18:6. But those were unbelievers in the process of committing a terrible crime; their experience of drawing back and falling to the ground is hardly an example for Christians to emulate.

14. Charismatics often point to some of the physical manifestations that occurred during the Great Awakening as a precedent to their modern practice. To that notion, Erwin Lutzer responds, "Are there not instances of people being 'slain in the spirit' in past revivals? Accounts that have come down to us from the days of Jonathan Edwards and John Wesley are often used to justify the present phenomena seen so often on television. Yes, there are reports of 'manifestations' of various kinds, but keep in mind that (1) many who 'fell' did so under deep conviction of sin and (2) the revivalists not only discouraged the practice, but believed that these occurrences often detracted from the gospel message itself. And (3) these manifestations did not happen because people were touched by an evangelist who gave them a jolt of spiritual power. Finally, (4) never were these manifestations put on public display to encourage others to have the same experience" (Erwin W. Lutzer, *Who Are You to Judge?* [Chicago: Moody, 2002], 101–2).

15. Hanegraaff, *The Bible Answer Book*, 83.

16. Richard J. Gehman, *African Traditional Religion in Biblical Perspective* (Nairobi, Kenya: East African Educational Publishers, 2005), 302.

17. Rob Datsko and Kathy Datsko, *Building Bridges Between Spirit-Filled Christians and Latter-Day Saints* (Sudbury, MA: eBookit!, 2011), 82.

18. Ibid., 83.

19. Rhodes, *5-Minute Apologetics for Today*, 222.

20. Michael Brown, *Whatever Happened to the Power of God?* (Shippensburg, PA: Destiny Image, 2012), 69.

21. J. Lee Grady, *The Holy Spirit Is Not for Sale* (Grand Rapids: Chosen Books, 2010), 47–48.

22. As I have explained elsewhere, "There are seven references in the New Testament to the baptism with the Spirit. It is significant that these references are all in the indicative mood. Not one of them is imperative or even exhortatory in nature. . . . The basic thing that every Christian must understand is that Paul never said, "Be baptized in the Spirit." Believers have already been baptized into the body of Christ by the Spirit, as Paul plainly stated in 1 Corinthians 12:13. There is no second work of grace. There is no added experience" (John MacArthur, *The Charismatics* [Grand Rapids: Lamplighter, 1978], 189, 191).

23. It is important to remember that biblical *narrative* is not always *normative*. Thus, the miracle accounts in the Gospels and Acts should be understood as *descriptive*, not *prescriptive*—meaning they record the unique history of what was happening in the first century, and are not intended to outline a pattern for subsequent generations of believers. (As we saw in chapter 6, the mere presence of apostles in the church was a unique feature that was limited to the first century.) The New Testament epistles, however, do instruct us to be filled with the Spirit. And in the book of Ephesians, the apostle Paul tells us exactly what that looks like in our lives.

24. Believers are to walk in newness of life (Rom. 6:3–5), purity (Rom. 13:13), contentment (1 Cor. 7:17), faith (2 Cor. 5:7), good works (Eph. 2:10), a manner worthy of the gospel (Eph. 4:1), love (Eph. 5:2), light (Eph. 5:8–9), wisdom (Eph. 5:15–16), a Christlike manner (1 John 2:6), and truth (3 John 3–4).

25. For a chronological study of the earthly ministry of the Lord Jesus Christ, see my harmony of the Gospels entitled *One Perfect Life* (Nashville: Thomas Nelson, 2013).

26. The fact that the Spirit-filled Lord Jesus never Himself experienced any of the bizarre behaviors often claimed by charismatics should alone confirm for us the fact that these supposed experiences are not from the Spirit of God.

Chapter 11: The Spirit and the Scriptures

1. Larry Stone, *The Story of the Bible* (Nashville: Thomas Nelson, 2010), 65; emphasis added.

2. For an in-depth survey of the early church fathers' commitment to the principle of *sola Scriptura*, see William Webster, *Holy Scripture*, vol. 2 (Battle Ground, WA: Christian Resources, 2001).

3. Brian A. Gerrish, *A Prince of the Church* (Philadelphia: Fortress, 1984), 25.

4. A March 8, 1968, article in *Time*, entitled "Theology: Taste for the

Infinite," http://www.time.com/time/magazine/article/0,9171,899985,00
.html, summarized Schleiermacher's approach with these words: "If God is
not dead, how can man prove that he lives? Rational proofs cannot convince the skeptic; the Bible alone is authority only to the convinced believer;
the demythologized universe no longer points to an unseen creator. One
approach to an answer that appeals more and more to modern Protestant
thinkers is the undeniable evidence of religious experience—the intuition
men have of their dependence upon God. The popularity of this insight,
in turn, leads back to the study of Friedrich Schleiermacher, the theologian
who first developed it as a basis of Christian faith."

5. For more on the supreme authority of God's Word, see John MacArthur,
   2 Timothy in *The MacArthur New Testament Commentary*, notes on 2
   Timothy 3:16.

6. Adapted from John MacArthur, *Jude* in *The MacArthur New Testament
   Commentary*, Jude 3.

7. Martin Luther, *Luther's Works*, vol. 23, ed. Jaroslav Pelikan (St. Louis:
   Concordia, 1959), 173–74.

8. Ibid., vol. 36, 144.

9. The word *also* is in the genitive case, a grammatical construction used to
   indicate source or origin.

10. Martin Luther, cited in *The Solid Declaration of the Formula of Concord*,
    2.20–22. Cited from *Triglot Concordia: The Symbolical Books of the Evangelical
    Lutheran Church: German-Latin-English* (St. Louis: Concordia, 1921).

11. Cf. Thomas Watson, in *A Puritan Golden Treasury*, comp. I. D. E. Thomas
    (Carlisle, PA: Banner of Truth, 2000), 143. Watson wrote, "The natural
    man may have excellent notions in divinity, but God must teach us to know
    the mysteries of the Gospel after a spiritual manner. A man may see the fig-
    ures upon a dial, but he cannot tell how the day goes unless the sun shines;
    so we may read many truths in the Bible, but we cannot know them sav-
    ingly, till God by His Spirit shines upon our soul. . . . He not only informs
    our mind, but inclines our will."

12. Charles Spurgeon, *Commenting and Commentaries* (London: Sheldon,
    1876), 58–59.

13. The Puritan Richard Baxter expressed that truth with this sober warning:
    "It is not the work of the Spirit to tell you the meaning of Scripture, and
    give you the knowledge of divinity, without your own study and labor, but
    to bless that study, and give you knowledge thereby. . . . To reject study
    on pretence of the sufficiency of the Spirit, is to reject the Scripture itself"
    (Richard Baxter, in *A Puritan Golden Treasury*, comp. I. D. E. Thomas
    [Carlisle, PA: Banner of Truth, 2000], 143).

14. Charles Spurgeon, "Our Omnipotent Leader," sermon no. 2465 (preached May 17, 1896), http://www.ccel.org/ccel/spurgeon/sermons42.xx.html. Elsewhere, Spurgeon added, "The power that is in the Gospel does not lie in the eloquence of the preacher, otherwise men would be the converters of souls, nor does it lie in the preacher's learning, otherwise it would consist in the wisdom of men. We might preach until our tongues rotted, till we would exhaust our lungs and die, but never a soul would be converted unless the Holy Spirit be with the Word of God to give it the power to convert the soul" (Charles Spurgeon, "Election: Its Defenses and Evidences" [1862 sermon], http://www.biblebb.com/files/spurgeon/2920.htm).

15. For more on this point, see chapter 4. It should be noted that not all who believe in the continuation of the extraordinary charismatic gifts would make such claims. For example, I am thankful for those conservative evangelical continuationists who have taken a strong stand on this issue. John Piper is absolutely right when he explains that "the Spirit inspired the Word and therefore He goes where the Word goes. The more of God's Word you know and love, the more of God's Spirit you will experience" (John Piper, *Desiring God* [Sisters, OR: Multnomah, 1996], 127). Bob Kauflin similarly wrote, "Our churches can't be Spirit-led unless they're Word-fed. A church that's dependent on the Spirit's power in its worship will be committed to the study, proclamation, and application of God's Word in its personal and congregational worship. The Word and the Spirit were never meant to be separated. In fact God's Spirit is the one who inspired God's Word . . . God's Spirit and His Word go together" (Bob Kauflin, *Worship Matters* [Wheaton, IL: Crossway, 2008], 89–90).

16. Charles Spurgeon, "Infallibility—Where to Find It and How to Use It," *The Metropolitan Tabernacle Pulpit*, vol. 20 (London: Passmore & Alabaster, 1874), 698–99, 702.

Chapter 12: An Open Letter to My Continuationist Friends

1. Bob Kauflin, *Worship Matters* (Wheaton, IL: Crossway, 2008), 86.

2. John Piper in an interview with David Sterling, "A Conversation with John Piper," *The Briefing*, October 27, 2011, http://matthiasmedia.com/briefing /2011/10/a-conversation-with-john-piper/.

3. D. A. Carson, *Showing the Spirit* (Grand Rapids: Baker Books, 1987), 85–86.

4. John Piper, "What Is Speaking in Tongues?" online video; recorded December 2012, posted by David Mathis, "Piper on Prophecy and Tongues," *Desiring God* (blog), January 17, 2013, http://www.desiringgod .org/blog/posts/piper-on-prophecy-and-tongues.

5. For more on Mark Driscoll's lurid prophecies, see Phil Johnson,

"Pornographic Divination," *Pyromaniacs* (blog), August 15, 2011, http://teampyro.blogspot.com/2011/08/pornographic-divination.html.

6. John Piper interview with David Sterling.

7. Wayne Grudem, *Systematic Theology* (Grand Rapids: Zondervan, 1994), 640.

8. Regarding Sam Storms's connection to Mike Bickle and the KCP, see Mike Bickle, *Growing in the Prophetic* (Lake Mary, FL: Charisma House, 2008), 120–21.

9. Cf. Sam Storms, "A Third Wave View," in *Four Views of the Miraculous Gifts*, ed. Wayne Grudem (Grand Rapids: Zondervan, 1996), 207–12.

10. Cf. Wayne Grudem, *The Gift of Prophecy* (Wheaton, IL: Crossway, 1988).

11. John Piper interview with David Sterling.

12. John Piper, "What Is the Gift of Prophecy in the New Covenant?" online video; recorded December 2012, posted by David Mathis, "Piper on Prophecy and Tongues," *Desiring God* (blog), January 17, 2013, http://www.desiringgod.org/blog/posts/piper-on-prophecy-and-tongues.

Appendix: Voices from Church History

1. John Chrysostom, *Homilies on 1 Corinthians*, 36.7. Chrysostom is commenting on 1 Corinthians 12:1–2 and introducing the entire chapter. Cited from Gerald Bray, ed., *1–2 Corinthians*, Ancient Christian Commentary on Scripture (Downers Grove, IL: InterVarsity, 1999), 146.

2. Augustine, *Homilies on the First Epistle of John*, 6.10. Cited from Philip Schaff, *Nicene and Post-Nicene Fathers*, 1st series (Peabody, MA: Hendrickson, 2012), 7:497–98.

3. Augustine, *On Baptism, Against the Donatists*, 3.16.21. Cited from Philip Schaff, *NPNF*, 1st series, 4:443. Also see *The Letters of Petilian, the Donatist*, 2.32.74.

4. Theodoret of Cyrus, *Commentary on the First Epistle to the Corinthians*, 240, 243; in reference to 1 Cor 12:1, 7. Cited from Bray, *1–2 Corinthians*, ACCS, 117.

5. Martin Luther, *Commentary on Galatians 4*, trans. Theodore Graebner (Grand Rapids: Zondervan, 1949), 150–72. This is from Luther's comment on Galatians 4:6.

6. Martin Luther, *Luther's Works*, vol. 23, ed. Jaroslav Pelikan (St. Louis: Concordia: 1959), 173–74.

7. Martin Luther, *Luther's Works*, vol. 36, ed. Jaroslav Pelikan (St. Louis: Concordia: 1959), 144.

8. John Calvin, *A Harmony of the Gospels Matthew, Mark, and Luke*, Calvin's Commentaries, trans. A. W. Morrison (Grand Rapids: Zondervan, 1972), III: 254. (This comment is regarding Mark 16:17.)

9. John Calvin, *Institutes of the Christian Religion*, 1536 ed., trans. Ford Lewis Battles (Grand Rapids: Zondervan, 1986), 159.

10. John Owen, *The Works of John Owen*, ed. William H. Goold (repr.; Edinburgh: Banner of Truth, 1981), 4:518.

11. Thomas Watson, *The Beatitudes* (Edinburgh: Banner of Truth, 1994), 14.

12. Matthew Henry, *Matthew Henry's Commentary on the Whole Bible* (Old Tappan, NJ: Fleming H. Revell, n.d.), 6:567. This comment is in Henry's introductory remarks on 1 Cor. 12:1–11.

13. Ibid., 4:ix. This comment is in Henry's preface to his commentary on the Old Testament prophets.

14. John Gill, *Gill's Commentary* (Grand Rapids: Baker Books, 1980), VI:237. Gill is commenting on 1 Cor. 12:29.

15. Jonathan Edwards, *Charity and Its Fruits* (New York: Robert Carver & Brothers, 1854), 447–49.

16. Ibid. 42–43.

17. James Buchanan, *The Office and Work of the Holy Spirit* (New York: Robert Carver, 1847), 67.

18. Robert L. Dabney, "Prelacy a Blunder," in *Discussions: Evangelical and Theological* (Richmond, VA: Presbyterian Committee of Publication, 1891), 2:236–37.

19. Charles Spurgeon, sermon entitled "The Paraclete," October 6, 1872, *The Metropolitan Tabernacle Pulpit* (Pasadena, TX: Pilgrim Publications, 1984), 18:563. Italics in original.

20. Charles Spurgeon, sermon entitled "Final Perseverance," April 20, 1856, *The New Park Street Pulpit* (Pasadena, TX: Pilgrim Publications, 1981), 2:171.

21. Charles Spurgeon, sermon entitled "Receiving the Holy Ghost," July 13, 1884, *The Metropolitan Tabernacle Pulpit* (Pasadena, TX: Pilgrim Publications, 1985), 30:386.

22. Charles Spurgeon, sermon entitled "The Ascension of Christ," March 26, 1871, *The Metropolitan Tabernacle Pulpit* (Pasadena, TX: Pilgrim Publications, 1984), 17:178.

23. Charles Spurgeon, "Forward!" in *An All-Around Ministry* (Carlisle, PA: Banner of Truth, 2000), 55–57.

24. George Smeaton, *The Doctrine of the Holy Spirit* (Edinburgh: T & T Clark, 1882), 51.

25. Abraham Kuyper, *The Work of the Holy Spirit*, trans. Henri De Vries (New York: Funk & Wagnalls, 1900), 182.

26. W. G. T. Shedd, *Dogmatic Theology* (New York: Charles Scribner's Sons, 1888), 2:369.

27. Benjamin B. Warfield, *Counterfeit Miracles* (New York: Charles Scribner's Sons, 1918), 6.

28. Arthur W. Pink, *Studies in the Scriptures* (Lafayette, IN: Sovereign Grace, 2005), 9:319.

29. D. Martyn Lloyd-Jones, *Christian Unity* (Grand Rapids: Baker, 1987), 189–91.

INDEX

Scripture Index

ABOUT THE AUTHOR

John MacArthur has served as the pastor-teacher of Grace Community Church in Sun Valley, California, since 1969. His ministry of expository preaching is unparalleled in its breadth and influence; in four decades of ministry from the same pulpit, he has preached verse by verse through the entire New Testament (and several key sections of the Old Testament). He is president of The Master's College and Seminary and can be heard daily on the "Grace to You" radio broadcast (carried on hundreds of radio stations worldwide). He has authored a number of best-selling books, including *The MacArthur Study Bible*, *The Gospel According to Jesus*, *Twelve Ordinary Men*, and *One Perfect Life*.

For more details about John MacArthur and his Bible-teaching resources, contact Grace to You at 800-55-GRACE or www.gty.org.